SPIRIT AND SYSTEM

RENEWALS 458-4574

WITHDRAWN
UTSA LIBRARIES

SPIRIT AND SYSTEM

Media, Intellectuals, and the Dialectic
in Modern German Culture

DOMINIC BOYER

THE UNIVERSITY OF CHICAGO PRESS

CHICAGO AND LONDON

DOMINIC BOYER is assistant professor of anthropology at Cornell University

The University of Chicago Press, Chicago 60637
The University of Chicago Press, Ltd., London
© 2005 by The University of Chicago
All rights reserved. Published 2005
Printed in the United States of America

14 13 12 11 10 09 08 07 06 05   5 4 3 2 1

ISBN (cloth): 0-226-06890-0
ISBN (paper): 0-226-06891-9

A subvention from the Hull Memorial Publication Fund of Cornell University is gratefully acknowledged.

Library of Congress Cataloging-in-Publication Data

Boyer, Dominic.
    Spirit and system : media, intellectuals, and the dialectic in modern German culture / Dominic Boyer.
        p.   cm.
    Includes bibliographical references and index.
    ISBN 0-226-06890-0 (cloth : alk. paper) — ISBN 0-226-06891-9 (alk. paper)
    1. National characteristics, German.   2. Germany—Intellectual life.
    3. Journalism—Germany.   4. Germany—Mass media.   I. Title.
    DD76.B679   2005
    943—dc22   2005012475

⊗ The paper used in this publication meets the minimum requirements of the American National Standard for Information Sciences—Permanence of Paper for Printed Library Materials, ANSI Z39.48-1992.

Library
University of Texas
at San Antonio

Für den roten Alfred

CONTENTS

Acknowledgments   *ix*

Introduction   *1*

1. Conceptualizing the Formation of Dialectical Social Knowledge   *19*

2. The *Bildungsbürgertum* and the Dialectics of Germanness
   in the Long Nineteenth Century   *46*

3. Dialectical Politics of Cultural Redemption
   in the Third Reich and the GDR   *99*

4. Self, System, and Other in Eastern Germany after 1989   *160*

5. Dialectical Knowledges of the Contemporary:
   Formal and Informal   *230*

   Conclusion   *271*

   Key Terms   *283*

   Bibliography   *287*

   Index   *309*

ACKNOWLEDGMENTS

Spirit and System saw the light of day because a few people cared about it a great deal. My first round of thanks goes to those who earned their wings on this project. Thanks to my editor, David Brent, whose intelligence and inspiring vision of the relationship between anthropology and philosophy are exceeded only by a tenacity and integrity that some might call stubbornness. I credit him with unflinching support for this project from its conceptual stages and for not cutting *Spirit and System* free at points when it no doubt would have made his life easier to do so. Likewise, I cannot begin to express my debt to Andreas Glaeser as a colleague, interlocutor, and friend for his intellectual generosity and considerable genius as we discussed many of the central arguments of this book. Much of this book remains in covert dialogue with him. I want to thank my wife, Johanna Schoss, who invested a lot of her own love, ideas, and energy into this book and who, most importantly, made it possible to write it. I want to thank my daughter, Olivia, for not noticing this book at all and thus for continuously restoring a sense of proportion to my life. Not least, I want to thank my parents, who raised me, without cynicism and largely without irony, in an environment of a genuine love of knowledge.

Second, and no less dearly, I want to thank all of my friends and colleagues who made their own important contributions to this text. These came in forms too many and too various for me to describe adequately in these few pages. If I have crafted this book correctly, they all should be able to recognize traces of their own knowledge in its pages. Special thanks go to Leslie Adelson, Arjun Appadurai, David Bathrick, Rebecca Bryant, Marcello Cherchi, Jean and John Comaroff, Owen Duncan, Jean-Louis Fabiani, Jane Fajans, Jim and Renate Fernandez, Ted Fischer, Paul Friedrich, Susan Gal, Peter Gilgen, Phil Graham, Davydd Greenwood, Bob von Hallberg,

Ulf Hannerz, Michael Herzfeld, Peter Hohendahl, David Holmberg, Doug Holmes, Don Kulick, Dominick LaCapra, Claudio Lomnitz, Kath March, William Mazzarella, Hiro Miyazaki, Viranjini Munasinghe, Francis Nyam-njoh, Moishe Postone, Jakob Rigi, Marshall Sahlins, Steve Sangren, Vilma Santiago-Irizarry, Dan Segal, Hoon Song, Hilary Strang, Terry Turner, Andrew Willford, and Jeff Williams. Thanks also to Elizabeth Branch Dyson, Claudia Rex, Olivia Hall, and Pam Bruton for excellent editorial advice and assistance.

Third, I want to acknowledge and thank the institutions that supported various phases of this research. The ethnographic and archival research was made possible by a Bundeskanzler fellowship from the Alexander von Hum-boldt Foundation in Bonn and by a Wenner-Gren Foundation Small Grant. The book was written at the University of Chicago and Cornell University. At Cornell, the Department of Anthropology has generously supported my revision efforts with research funding and leave time. A faculty fellowship from Cornell's Society for the Humanities allowed me to complete the man-uscript. A brief stint as visiting professor at the Ecole des Hautes Etudes en Sciences Sociales in Paris gave me the opportunity to expand and define my attention to the anthropology of knowledge.

Finally, I want to thank another group of friends, who helped me to understand dialectical knowledge in ways I never could have from sim-ply reading philosophy and social theory. They appear pseudonymously or anonymously in the pages that follow, so there is no way that I can fully give each of them the credit he or she deserves. Everything in this book is a product of the hours we spent together.

A people is moral, virtuous, strong when it brings forth what it wills. It defends its product against outside powers through the work of its objectification. The tension between (its potentiality and its actuality) what it is in itself, subjectively, in its inner purpose and essence, and what it really is (objectively), is thus abolished. It is with itself (actualized), it has itself objectively before itself. But then this activity of spirit is no longer necessary; it has what it wanted. The people can still do a great deal in war and peace, internally and externally. But the living, substantial soul itself is, so to speak, no longer active. The deepest, highest interest thus has gone out of life; for interest is only where there is opposition. The people lives like an individual passing from manhood to old age, enjoying himself, for he is exactly what he wanted to be and was able to achieve. Even though his imagination may have gone further, it has abandoned more far-reaching purposes; if reality did not fit them, he fits the purposes to reality. It is this life of *habit*—the watch is wound up and goes by itself—which brings about natural death. Habit is tensionless activity. Only formal duration is left to it, in which plenitude and depth of purpose need no longer to be heard. Existence has become, so to speak, external, sensuous; it is not absorbed any more in its purpose. Thus individuals die, thus peoples die a natural death. —*G. W. F. Hegel, "Vorlesungen über die Philosophie der Geschichte" (trans. R. Hartman)*

Spirit, System, and History

The night is dark, cool, and clear. Tired, a little drunk, and mesmerized by the soft, pulsing, yellow lights of Autobahn 115, Michael and I drive quickly down the remarkably empty road toward the Berlin ring. It is

April 25th, 1997 and we have just spent the past several hours at the house of a mutual friend, Joachim, a colleague of Michael's before 1989 at GDR Radio (DDR Rundfunk). It has been an evening where a relatively formal gathering gradually unwound into easy talk after several hours of drinking and joking. As Joachim and Michael, along with Joachim's wife, Tamara, and another friend, Rudi, recalled their memories of working together as radio news journalists in the German Democratic Republic (GDR), I was gradually, transitively, incorporated into their spheres of intimacy and shared memory.

In 1989–90, both Joachim and Michael sat on the democratically elected committee that had helped to guide GDR Radio through its dissolution as the centralized radio broadcaster of the East German party-state. Both now serve as news directors of different affiliates in the German public-broadcasting network, ARD, in eastern Germany. They have not seen or spoken to one another in over a year, not owing to ill will so far as I can tell but rather because of the intense demands of their new positions and the difficulty of maintaining old contacts as former colleagues have scattered to new positions and careers across eastern Germany. It is a scene that has played itself out several times during my ethnographic research with former East German journalists: the ethnographer is an excuse to reactivate old friendships and networks and to recollect relations and situations that have become hazy with disuse.

I met Michael and Joachim independently of one another after they responded to a query letter I sent to a number of eastern German media organizations seeking journalists interested in speaking to me about journalism in the GDR. Both explained that they had responded because they had recently traveled in the United States (together, as it later turned out) visiting media organizations as part of a "study abroad" program organized by the German government and aimed at exposing and acculturating younger former East German journalists to the work world of what is often termed "democratic media." They traveled to places like Washington, DC, and Phoenix, Arizona, attended seminars, observed Western journalists on the job, and, in one case, spent the night in the back of a patrol car, observing how American police work. Later, when Michael realized I know Joachim as well, he proposed that we all get together some evening to talk.

For several hours this evening, I listen and occasionally chime in as the four of them reminisce about journalistic work in the GDR and discuss other former colleagues with whom they think I should come into contact. The game, so it appears to me at any rate, is to think of the names of insiders, people who really knew what journalism in the GDR was all about, yet who were not "*zu schlecht*" (too bad), that is, who were not entirely invested in the dogma of the "party line" (see chapter 4). At times, however, the fun is also in remembering the bad ones:

MICHAEL [*to Joachim*]: What about that other guy, do you remember, the one who worked with us but who also wrote that series of books with titles like *Lenin und das Pferd* [Lenin and the Horse]? [*General laughter.*] I mean, no one bought or read it.

JOACHIM [*rubbing his forehead, searching for the name*]: Yes, yes, I seem to recall that the unions bought them all up and gave them away to people as presents.

DOMINIC: What would one find in such a book?

MICHAEL [*shrugging*]: I was too young; they were all given away by the unions by then [*chuckles*].

JOACHIM [*neatly imitating the official language of the GDR*]: We can surmise something to the effect that Lenin's relationship to the horse was substantively different from and superior to Trotsky's relationship to the horse and that Stalin's relationship to the horse was more influenced by Lenin than by Trotsky. [*General laughter.*]

DOMINIC [*picking up an earlier thread in the conversation*]: This guy sounds like he would be just as embittered now as the other [older former journalists] I was describing to you.

MICHAEL [*seriously*]: Being embittered is part of the job description. I don't think you're ever going to find anyone who isn't bitter among these people. People who worked for twenty years or thirty years in that *System* came to completely identify with it and to think it was the right thing to do—of course, when all that collapses overnight, they're going to be bitter about that.

The conversation twists and turns through the labyrinth of GDR journalism to analysis and evaluation of present working conditions in public radio. As the evening progresses, the laughter becomes louder, the analyses sharper, the occasional barbs more stinging. All of them seem to me to be ambivalent about the virtues of the postunification media despite having few fond memories about GDR Radio. They speak in somewhat lowered voices and allegorical terms about tensions with their current colleagues and management, at times referencing problematic personalities in the present by reminding one another of colleagues they shared in the GDR. A recurrent theme is the positioning and evaluation of their past professional selves. Joachim teases Michael for having been more earnest in his support of the GDR state than Joachim himself ever was ("You were always very diligent about reading what they told us to read, Michael, weren't you?"). Joachim subtly links this to Michael's decision to work at mdr, a regional broadcaster with a reputation for servicing "black" (e.g., Christian-Democratic, conservative) politics. Michael lets these comments slide, and Rudi, also at mdr, later suggests that Joachim would be happy working there as well. Joachim is adamant: "No, no. That question is closed."

Michael, in turn, ten years younger than Joachim, insists that Joachim was always an idealistic (and somewhat naïve) child of the sixties. Joachim was the true believer in socialism according to Michael, and Joachim jokes that he can neither "confirm nor deny these reports." But they can all agree that the end of the SED (Sozialistische Einheitspartei Deutschlands, Socialist Unity Party) regime's brand of state socialism was welcome. Joachim and Tamara describe how difficult it became to convince their daughter to come with them to the weekly demonstrations in Leipzig in October 1989 that many believe helped to precipitate the final collapse of the East German party-state. According to Joachim: "It reached the point where we were having conversations like 'No, not *another* demo, Mom!' 'It's not a demo tonight; it's a candlelight procession, dear. People are just going to walk around holding candles.' 'But that *is* a demo!'" Joachim pauses and, with a wry smile, admits, "The child had a point!"

Stroking his beard and looking away thoughtfully for a moment, perhaps lingering on his memories of 1989, Joachim returns to the subject of books.

JOACHIM: I'm sure that each of us in the GDR had his own private torments, but if you want to know what tormented me most of all by the end it was that you couldn't read what you wanted to read in this country. I found it truly depressing that I was forced to go tromping all over Eastern Europe to try to find the books that I wanted to read. [*Pauses.*] Still, it was something to do [*laughs*].

DOMINIC: How far away did you have to go?

JOACHIM: You could find certain books only in antiquarian shops. That's the only way you could get copies of books that the party wouldn't allow to be printed. Like those by Nietzsche or Schopenhauer or Freud. So I would go to Prague or to Budapest, where you could still find German-language books back then, although in Prague they were all very expensive. And my absolute pride and joy [*goes to his bookshelf and pulls out a slim black volume*] is this first edition of Freud. It cost me a fortune, 180 marks.

MICHAEL [*handling the book and looking at it incredulously*]: You really paid 180 marks for this?

JOACHIM: Yes, I'd have paid anything for Freud.

MICHAEL [*to Dominic*]: That would have been one-third or one-fourth of a month's wages back in the GDR.

RUDI [*to Dominic*]: But it was the only way to get hold of these kinds of books.

A little later, after dinner, the smell of homemade pizza follows us back into the living room, where we settle into two comfortable sofas to drink more wine and talk. Michael and Rudi roll their eyes and make injured noises when Joachim puts a tape by folk singer Wolf Biermann on the stereo and begins to sing along to it. The iconoclastic Biermann was a hero for many dissident Marxists in the GDR in the 1960s and 1970s and some have likened him to the Bob Dylan of the GDR. Joachim hears their displeasure behind him and shouts over his shoulder, "Stop it, you two! This man is a great poet and a great songwriter. I've always told you two you're too young to understand Biermann." Sounds of dissent continue from the sofa. "On Biermann's last birthday, I allowed myself the pleasure of watching the replay of his concert in Cologne.[1] Watching him in his prime, I was struck by what a tragic figure he's become."

RUDI: How can you call Biermann a great poet? I watched [that concert] too, and I couldn't help feeling like I was watching a Politburo guy up there talking. The whole discourse just didn't mean anything to me. And he's doing the same thing now; he hasn't changed in twenty years.

JOACHIM: I actually think the opposite; I think Biermann's changed too much. What I liked about him is that how even after he was supposedly saved by the West he would snap at the journalists and say things like "It stinks here too, I'm a communist." I liked the fact that he was equally critical of the West as he was of the GDR, but now he's backed away from all of that. I don't know why he did it. Now he says things like "I can't believe you took me seriously back then when I said I was a communist."

RUDI: All I know is that it came to the end of the concert and I thought, "This is the great concert everyone's always talking about?" I just couldn't understand it. To me, it was like watching an FDJ rally.[2]

1. Joachim is referring to Biermann's final concert in Cologne as a GDR citizen. While he was performing at this concert, the SED revoked Biermann's citizenship and never allowed him to enter the GDR again. Biermann's forced expatriation precipitated an enormous crisis in relations between the SED regime and the GDR cultural intelligentsia (Bathrick 1995: 27).

2. The Freie Deutsche Jugend (FDJ, German Socialist Youth) was a feeder organization for the SED.

We continue to dwell on the themes of creative agency versus complicity and change versus continuity for another half an hour. As in so many similar conversations that have occurred in the course of my field research, the discussion of the GDR past inevitably turns to sorting out one's subjectivity from the exterior forces of party and state that exerted so much effort to produce ideal socialist citizens. This dynamic operates like a leitmotif in many of my interviews, emerging delicately or forcefully but always turning implicitly to the question of, in the words of another journalist, "what kind of person was I in the GDR and, by extension, what kind of person am I now?" To explain this sense of historical entanglement, Joachim suggested to me on another occasion the analogy of Freud's model of neurosis, of the existence of pathogenic nuclei in the psyche that inevitably bind psychic processes like memory into orbit around them. "Then is the ethnographer something like a therapist?" I asked him. "Yes," he laughed, "but, Dominic, what you have to remember is that the real neurotic cannot be cured."

It is late when we get up to leave, and Tamara and their daughter have already long since retired to bed. We stand on Joachim's small lawn eyeing his eighteen-inch-high ornamental fence, which looks more oriented to gnomes than to people. Joachim tries to persuade all of us to stay a little longer, laughing when he sees it is a futile effort: "I don't know about everyone leaving at once. I'm not so sure about this group mentality [*Gruppenmentalität*][3] if you want to know the truth." Michael kindly offers me a ride back to eastern Berlin to save me the long S-Bahn ride across the city. As he demonstratively vaults over the miniature ornamental gate rather than opening it, Joachim shouts at him, "Hey, wait a minute, *das ist nicht in Ordnung.* You must show the proper respect!" Over his shoulder, Michael shouts back that he finds Joachim's fence "ridiculous."

As he backs the car onto the gravel road in front of Joachim's house, Michael says, "He's a good guy, Joachim." Then, thoughtfully, he adds, "It was interesting traveling in the United States with him because his English is really quite good. It turns out that before 1989 he was being considered for the position of foreign correspondent for GDR Radio in India. He trained for it, learned English and everything. But then he was eventually turned down from somewhere high up basically because . . ." There is a long pause, and I prompt him, "He wasn't *staatstreu* [loyal to the state] enough?" "Yes, something like that, which in retrospect speaks *for* his character, I think. But I'm sure he was disappointed at the time."

3. Joachim is playing on the alleged stereotypic affinity of East Germans for collective mentality and action (see chapter 4 for discussion of this discourse and its ramifications).

On the drive back to Berlin, still in a good mood, Michael begins to ask me for more details about myself and about what I will write about in my book. In response to the latter, I tell him that the book will concern the fate of East German journalists after 1989, their professional transition to life and work in the (West) German media industry of unified Germany. As I listen to myself speak, I begin to feel guilty that this rather canned description is inadequate for such a long and *gemütlich* evening. So I pause and then continue on to admit to him that in the course of this research of professional transitions and identities I have also become somewhat obsessed with understanding how East German journalists recall their work in the GDR and why they interpret their present journalistic labors in the particular language that they do.

I confess that I have become fascinated by the centrality of the term "*System*" (system) to recollection of the GDR and by how journalists so frequently rely upon it in conversation to condense the entirety of their experience with the GDR state and society in a single breath in phrases such as "that was just how it was in that *System.*" "*System*" seems to signal the certain but often anonymous forces of the party and state that enveloped journalists in the GDR and against which they struggled. Yet, in keeping with its Greek etymology, the term likewise connotes a sense of organic order—specifically, the sociopolitical order of the GDR. Many journalists admitted to me that they too had been part of the GDR *System*, whether voluntarily or not. They admitted that, despite their efforts to do "clean" (*sauber*) journalism befitting their vocation, and also because of the centrality of a Leninist model of "party journalism" to journalistic praxis in the GDR, they had become entrenched in the logic of the party and its dogmatic and inflexible understanding of socialism. Several offered me the analogy of a cog (*Rädchen*) in an elaborate, inexorable machine to describe their works and lives in the GDR.

But, more surprisingly to me, they also described post-1990 reunified German society analogously as a *System* in its operation, and the strongest salient distinction drawn between the two *Systeme* for many was that the GDR *System* was dysfunctional and eventually corrupt, whereas the West German (FRG) *System* is functional and true to its manifest principles. Both *Systeme* were depicted as equally limiting, constraining, yet in some ways enabling—like the autobahn itself, as I reflect later when I am at home writing up my field notes for the day. The autobahn was first envisioned during the Weimar Republic as an alternative (to the railroad) system of material mediation that would facilitate industry, commerce, national unity, and personal freedom. Then several years later, its plans were seized upon by Adolf

Hitler as precisely the kind of monumental network building worthy of his NSDAP's (Nationalsozialistische Deutsche Arbeiterpartei, National Socialist, or Nazi, Party) social imagination of *völkisch*-national becoming. Yet, in the end, regardless of the specific dream of pure mediation, the autobahn's enabling of rapid transport exists in ratio to the constraints on movement presented by the materialization of its network.

To my ruminations on *System*, Michael replies without missing a beat, "You mean this yearning for *System?* Yes, I see that too, and I think it's dangerous really, I think it's a bad thing, especially in the media. The GDR is a good example of a society completely that way, where order was everything."

Is it an East German longing though, I wonder to Michael, because I hear Western journalists and myself, among others, sometimes speaking in this language as well. *System* appears to me to be an apt metaphor for social totality in a variety of informal speech contexts. And, then, when I open books by Jürgen Habermas and Niklas Luhmann I find the language again, albeit in a different, more formal and elite register, in the systems-theoretical imagination of modern society. Michael is familiar with systems theory from his own post-1990 academic training and nods along thoughtfully: "Yes, you are quite right that this is not simply an East German phenomenon. But in the GDR it became an obsession, *System* became an obsession. The *System* rhetoric was everywhere. I can't tell you why but I remember that it reached absurd heights. In the 1970s, I remember that there were attempts to change words like '*Tür*' [door] into '*systemeinreisende*' and '*systemausreisende Elemente*' [system-entering and system-exiting elements]." Michael smiles wryly and lights a cigarette, squinting at the arc of road in front of us. With a sense of understatement that I subsequently always associate with him, Michael says, "It was a funny country."

We drive a little farther discussing the wild boar that live in the forest on both sides of the autobahn. After the Wall was dismantled in 1989–90, wild boar from the neighboring regions of Brandenburg repopulated the forested areas of formerly West Berlin. In the mid-1990s, a time of considerable tension and mutual suspicion between Germans of eastern and western origin, a few of my western Berliner friends made ironic associations between the rush of the wild boar and the rush of the East Germans toward the "promised land" of the West.

After a few minutes of silence, fluidly, somewhat wistfully, Michael shifts gears to the historical: "You know, Dominic, I have to tell you that I envy Americans in one respect. When I was traveling in the United States, I felt strangely more at ease than I often do at home." He takes both hands briefly from the steering wheel to gesture a wide parabola. "For you, history is not this thing, this inescapable presence that you must constantly contend with. It's hard for people in my generation, who were born after the war, to really talk about this. We weren't personally involved and yet we all share the guilt, although all I know about my own connection to what happened is that I had two grandfathers both of whom were in the army, both of whom died during the war. But that's it. But the relationship to the past is so unhealthy in Germany, and if you say something like you don't feel personally responsible, then you automatically get thrust into the corner of the radical right. I remember when I went to the Holocaust museum in Washington, DC, I was very moved by this experience and I thought that there ought to be something like that in Germany. Here of all places in the land of the perpetrators is where they need it. But of course there will never be anything like that in Germany because no one could handle it. When I was there, I was standing in front of a plaque and an older couple asked me if I could show them where Bergen-Belsen was on a map. The old man had been imprisoned there at Bergen-Belsen; he showed me the tattoo on his arm. It's hard to describe what I felt at that moment."

I nod dumbly. Since the United States promotes no sense of collective cultural accountability for any of the genocides with which it has been involved or complicit, unlike Michael I was allowed to be born into the world tabula rasa.

By the time we reach Berlin the streets are largely empty and we sail through them. When we finally near my apartment, Michael glances sideways at me and raises his eyebrows: "Well, let me know if you figure out the German longing for *System* [*die deutsche Sehnsucht nach System*]. That would be something!"

The next night, *System* is still on my mind. I go to a bar in the Prenzlauer Berg district of Berlin with my friend Stefan, a brilliant young publisher who has also recently spent time in the United States. Sitting at the long, dark-wood bar, the din of laughter and television forces us to huddle conspiratorially around our beers. I mention to Stefan Michael's characterization of the longing for *System* and ask him whether he too thinks that this is a German problem. Reflecting for a moment, Stefan leans in even more closely: "No, but I think Germans overall have been specializing in that rhetoric for decades now. The same arguments were used to justify what happened under Hitler. It's always this tendency to push the responsibility off onto the other guy, to say, 'What could I do? If I didn't do it, maybe someone else would come along and take my job and do it worse than I did.' And what's interesting to me about that position is that it is so much the absolute opposite of the American philosophy that the individual carries all responsibility for what happens to him, that there is no social responsibility, that if you're rich and successful, then that's only due to your talent or hard work. But then if you're poor though, that's also your fault for being lazy or stupid or whatever. That's the exact opposite of this German tendency to put the blame always on the next guy, and both of them I think are absurd in their own way; the truth is somewhere between them."

At this moment, I think of Hannah Arendt and her struggle to make sense of Adolf Eichmann as a moral subject. Arendt also reflected on what she called the "cog-theory" (2003: 29) that Eichmann and other Nazis offered to exculpate themselves for their actions in the Third Reich. For Arendt, the cog-theory represented an understanding of self-as-mechanism that totalitarian governments cultivated to stall "thinking and judging" in favor of an opportunistic relationship to the world or a recourse to unthinking habit (37). Arendt wrote that ironically only the legal proceduralism of determining personal accountability saves us from empathizing too strongly with Eichmann's narrative; "this whole cog-business makes no sense in its setting" (30).

This book, *Spirit and System,* is neither a trial nor an apology. It is inspired by a desire to make sense of the language and logic of *System* that so often accompanied my field research in eastern Germany. But it is also inspired by Arendt's (and others') sense of a creative moral spirit "within" that struggles to realize itself "without" against exterior forces and a propensity to habit. A work of ethnography, history, and social theory, this book seeks to call attention to, and to understand, a tension and ratio in human social knowledge between powers within and powers without. Put in other terms, my project is to engage the dialectic from an anthropological point of view: a project that requires a few preliminaries.

An Anthropology of the Dialectic

This book makes dialectical social knowledge an object of anthropological inquiry. To be clear, when I discuss "the dialectic" I am not, or not solely, referring to those modes of discourse, argument, analysis, and logic familiar to us from Greek and medieval philosophy. With "dialectical social knowledge," I mean specifically knowledges of social dynamics, relations, and forms that center on perceived ontological tensions between the temporality of potentiality and actuality and between the spatiality of interiority and exteriority. That such knowledges have a rich existence in philosophy there is little doubt, of course. Consider, for example, the epigraph to this introduction. Hegel's dialectical philosophy of history codifies the spatial and temporal tensions outlined above by interpreting human history as a process of "becoming" or "actualization" from within to without, from Spirit (*Geist*) into form, moving temporally in stages and through cycles of extension and concretization, unfolding an inner logic of purpose into ever-more-complex forms of organic realization (*System*). Temporality is powered by the ontological incommensurability Hegel posits between an inner spirit of forming and existing external forms. Meanwhile, the work of the philosophy of history is to decipher where and when the divine inner power of reason has extended itself to form humanity and where humanity has been dominated instead by appearances, forms, and "formal durations."

As endlessly fascinating as Hegelian philosophy is, my central argument in this book is that dialectical social knowledge is by no means either intrinsically abstract, technical, or the province of some inscrutable (German) philosophical "Other." What I mean by dialectical social knowledge or, more simply, "dialecticism" inheres in theory and philosophy, to be sure, but it also can be found in the ideologies of states and political movements, especially those that speak of channeling a popular spirit "within" into a more perfect social order "without." It belongs as well to the fantasies and terrors of popular culture. The recent films in *The Matrix* series provide wonderful examples. A mundane world is revealed to be the false consciousness of the most nightmarish *System* of extraction imaginable. The machines created by humanity have become a technical uncanny, now exceeding every potential of their creators in sheer force, cunning, and brutality. But even so, this terrifying system "without" contains an unassimilable human presence "within," a Neo who heroically rises again and again in the name of love to battle the forces of the out-there that would seek to extinguish Spirit once and for all.

More importantly, dialectical knowledge saturates everyday social knowledges and modes of knowing selves, others, cultures, and histories. Dialectical figurations hover around everyday distinctions and judgments concerning the differences between authentic cultural production and inauthentic imitation, between persons of genius and persons of habit, between everything that is said to cultivate desire and life and everything that is said to restrain or obstruct them. In short, dialecticism seems to be in the air around us like oxygen, nourishing social knowledge under the right circumstances. The task of this book is to pursue dialectical social knowledge across these circumstances, including a multiplicity of epistemic practices, communicative registers, historical moments, and social situations. In chapter 2, for example, I investigate the amplification of dialectical knowledge

among the educated German middle classes of Central Europe during the
nineteenth century and their efforts to define German national culture in
their own image. In chapter 4, I explore the dialectical judgments implicit
in how eastern and western German journalists evaluate one another's professionalism. In chapter 5, I describe dialectical social knowledge at play
in barroom debate and discourse in Berlin. Although I maintain that the
dialectic is not a German invention, it is perhaps fair to say, as Michael and
Stefan have testified, that it is a specialty (or an obsession) within German
intellectual culture.

   If dialecticism is something more than a Hegelian abstraction or a German cultural property, then what are we to make of it? I argue in this book
that beneath the various ontological aspirations of dialectical knowledge
lies a phenomenological tension between a sense of the extensional powers of the self and a recognition of the efficacy of external forms and relations, a tension that is often cultivated by intellectuals in the direction of
ontological dualisms such as self/world and agency/structure (see Bourdieu
1977). What I term "Spirit" and "System" represent the two poles of this
tension in the phenomenology of knowledge. If "Spirit" (*Geist*) or a similar
term tends to condense and to epitomize a sense of creative subjectivity in a
maximally pure form, then a term like "System" (or one of its metonyms or
analogues) emerges as a master trope that condenses and epitomizes external
form and mediation in its most total, organic, and abstract sense. In its barest
phenomenology, its basic humanity, "Spirit" captures the sense of the "self
within" opposed to the forms and forces of System's world "out there." In
the complex circumstances of social and historical life, the epistemic elabo-
ration of this bare phenomenology varies in its nuances and embellishments.
The phenomenological tension of Spirit and System acquires anchorage in
different language communities through different lexical terms (like *Geist*
and *System*), and these accrue socially and historically specific tendencies
of denotation and connotation (see, e.g., Dale Pesmen's exploration of the
cognate Russian terms *dusha* and *Sistema;* 2000: 3–19, 288–90).

   To simplify our task somewhat, I discuss in this book two modes of dialectical knowledge, one positive and one negative, that are intertwined in
many situations of knowledge making. I argue that, under particular circumstances, the one mode or the other may come into high relief and suppress
the other, causing wider ripples in settlements of social knowledge. By "positive dialectical" knowing (what I also describe as the language and intuitions
of *Bildung*), I refer to imagining the character of social and historical experience as the sanctifying extension of inner potentiality into external actuality. By "negative dialectical" knowing (what I also describe as the language

and intuitions of *Prägung*), I refer to imagining inner creative agency as compromised and corrupted by exterior forces and forms. The German terms *"Bildung"* and *"Prägung"* fittingly capture the distinction between positive and negative dialectical knowledges insofar as *Bildung* classically referenced spiritual-intellectual cultivation, an extension forth of inner creativity into external form, whereas *Prägung* belongs instead to the mundane world of routines and objects, denoting the process of imprinting or embossing some material with a preexistent form, from without to within.

Knowledge as a Subject of Anthropological Inquiry

This will, no doubt, seem a curious project to some, if for no other reason than that the dialectic is something (a mode of argumentation or an instrument of analysis) that we normally employ to explain something else rather than treat as an object of analysis in its own right. But the movement to treat knowledge forms and knowledge practices (including and especially those sacralized as belonging to the seemingly "transcontextual" domains of philosophy and theory) as objects of ethnographic analysis seems to me both a logical and a desirable extension of the reflexive and symmetrical interests that have oriented anthropology since the early twentieth century (see Boyer 2005b). Like other recent works in the anthropology of knowledge that have positioned our own knowledge practices as sites for critical inquiry, my project seeks to gain anthropological traction on forms of knowledge that are deeply intertwined with our academic "own" (Boyer 2001a; Brenneis 1994; Holmes 2000; Holmes and Marcus 2005; Marcus 2001; Maurer 2002; Miyazaki 2004). I do not suppose, however, that anthropological inquiry can ever fully disentangle us from the exigencies of our own knowledge practices. As I discuss more fully in the conclusion, this book is itself a phenomenon (and an autobiography of sorts) of the struggle of Spirit and System in my own place and time. My interest in writing this book has been to draw attention to dialectical social knowledge (of both others and my own) by recoupling it to its individual, social, and historical processes of formation. To do this, I propose an understanding of dialectical social knowledge that does not begin with the implicit premise (or conceit) that a book like this one, with its specialized analytic labors, could truly, theoretically, "rise above" the human experience it seeks to characterize. Rather than an emancipatory departure from dialectical knowledge, it remains very much a performance of its own object of analysis.

I pursue this inquiry in keeping with Malcolm Crick's fine observation that the anthropology of knowledge "is not a subfield but merely a reminder of what anthropology is centrally concerned with" (1982: 287). Especially if one understands the standard meaning of a term like "knowledge" to signal the sorts of habituated epistemic order produced by the human capacity for meaningful semiosis (e.g., "culture," more or less, in its postwar anthropological trajectory), one could rightly wonder how any anthropological investigation of meaningful action and experience was not also, at once, an engagement with local schemes and settlements of knowledge and modes of knowing. Such engagements have a long pedigree in anthropology. Arguments over rationality, logic, and cognition helped to codify anthropology as a discipline and discourse community in the early twentieth century via debates that critically engaged universalist paradigms of cultural and mental development (see Boyer 2005b; Stocking 1974). From early arguments over whether "primitive" peoples had the same logical capabilities as "moderns" (Lévi-Strauss 1966; Lévy-Bruhl 1996; Radin 1927) and over the relationship of mythology to science (Durkheim 1995; Malinowski 1954; Tylor 1958), through later debates over the appropriateness of emic versus etic analysis (Turner 1967; Wilson 1957), over the options of activist versus analytic engagement for ethnographers (Hymes 1969), and, most recently, over the politics and poetics of ethnographic representation (Clifford and Marcus 1986), the semiotic and epistemic interface between human individuals and communities and their social and natural environments has emerged as a central, perhaps the central, unifying polylogue of anthropology.

Likewise, this polylogue has long been both reflexive and critical. Interest in the knowledges of "others" has invited reflexive awareness of, and reflection upon, our own habits of knowing, either as subjects of Western culture or, more recently, as professional academics (Asad 1973; Bourdieu 1988; Clifford and Marcus 1986; Marcus and Fischer 1986; Radin 1927). It is in this spirit and context that current work in the anthropology of intellectuals has made vital contributions to our knowledge of epistemic practices that challenge any facile distinction between intellectual selves and others (Boyer and Lomnitz 2005; Feierman 1990; Herzfeld 1987, 1997b, 2001; Lomnitz 1992, 2001; Reed-Danahay 1997; Sahlins 1996; Taylor 1997; Verdery 1991; Warren 1998). Recent research in the anthropology of professions (notably Dornfeld 1998; Gusterson 1996; Hannerz 2003; Mazzarella 2003; Santiago-Irizarry 2001) has likewise expanded the possibility of "studying sideways" (Hannerz 1998; see also Nader 1969) other professional communities and "cultures of expertise" (Holmes and Marcus 2005) parallel to our own varieties of academic professionalism. These literatures have raised important questions about the social character of expertise and about the politics of producing authoritative social knowledge (questions incidentally first raised in anthropology as early as Paul Radin's prescient *Primitive Man as Philosopher* [1927]). Like my own effort in this book to illuminate the phenomenological, sociological, and historical conditions of dialectical theory and philosophy, these literatures have tampered with the alleged "transcontextuality" of expert knowledge, the ultimate horizon of all reflexive social science (cf. Bourdieu and Wacquant 1992; Scholte 1974; see also Sangren 2003).

If the anthropology of knowledge represents, in the end, nothing more than the honing and refining of analytical attentions that anthropology has always possessed, it is nevertheless vital, for this very reason, to pursue ethnographic research on knowledge in an attentive and vigorous way. As Michael Herzfeld has observed, "an anthropology that makes an ethnographic problem of itself offers pragmatic insight into the social worlds that it examines and to which it belongs" (1987: x). Likewise, one might add, an anthropology that identifies knowledge as its central ethnographic problem is better equipped to attend fully and frankly to the social, political, and epistemic implications of our praxis as knowledge specialists and of our epistemic relations and transactions with other human beings.

Three Studies in Dialectical Knowledge

This book, for better or for worse, has many attentions. It is precisely because of the variousness of dialectical social knowledge that my own pursuit of the dialectic exceeds a single narrational and analytical framework and instead crosses multiple genres and modes of investigation, representation, and interpretation. I move from a conceptual discussion of dialectical social knowledge (chapter 1) through historical and ethnographic case studies of the macro- and microsocial dynamics that amplify, dampen, or reify dialectical social knowledge (chapters 2–5) and finally to a set of personal reflections on my own relationship to dialectical theory and on the historicity of this book's enterprise (conclusion). In this respect, the organizational structure of the book itself both signals and unravels the dialectic. Even as I analyze the dialectical relationship of Spirit and System from front to finish, the chapters move from impersonal, abstract, and Systemic modes of interpretation and representation that epitomize professional academic writing through the analytical intimacies of history and ethnography and back to the poetic ardor of Spirit.

The point of writing from System back to Spirit is not some covert critique of theory. On the contrary, I hope that the organization of the book demonstrates how anthropology can make use of the vital heuristic and

technical insights of theoretical knowledge while simultaneously challenging (through parallel efforts of history, ethnography, and self-analysis) the
adequacy of allowing theory the appearance of a transcontextual and tran-
shistorical mode of "framing." The intent here, in short, is not to do away
with theory but rather to help specify its contribution to anthropological
knowledge as one mode of social knowledge among others.

In the spirit of historicizing and socializing dialectical knowledge across
its full range of registers, the heart of the book is organized around three case
studies drawn from modern German intellectual culture, with its rich traditions of dialectical philosophy and theory, dialectically saturated political
and social imaginations, and dialectical hermeneutics of everyday life. The
first case study focuses on the sociogenesis of positive and negative dialectical intuitions of modern society, culture, and history among German intellectuals during what historian David Blackbourn has called the "long nineteenth century" (roughly 1750–1914). I analyze these intellectuals' social
imagination of German national belonging and show how a shift between
positive and negative dialectical intuition accompanied their evolving social organization and shifting position within the social elite of the states
of German-speaking Central Europe. The second study begins where the
first ends, with the atmosphere of crisis and decline in German intellectual
culture in the late nineteenth and early twentieth centuries, with German
intellectuals' frequent negative dialectical allusions to a plague of mass culture (*Massenkultur*) sapping the inner powers of nation and knowledge, and
with their moderate and radical fantasies of redeeming social unity. Looking
carefully at the subsequent amplification and institutionalization of radical
dialectical visions within the Third Reich and the GDR, I explore the institutional cultures surrounding both states' programs of social engineering
and demonstrate how dialectical ideologies organized their efforts to control
and to harmonize mass mediation and media practices like journalism in
the name of emancipating public culture from mass culture. The third case
study begins with the collapse of the GDR and accompanies the transition of
former GDR journalists to life and work in the reunified German media system after 1990. I explore the place of positive and negative dialectical tropes
in their everyday languages and knowledges of social experience, particularly as they reflect on their professional practices, their western colleagues,
and their senses of the burden of history and of the presence of Systems
in modern life. If the first two studies explore the broader social, political,
and institutional conditions of dialectical knowledge, the third case study
accentuates the delicacy and complexity of individual intellectual lives, situations, and instances of dialectical knowledge making.

Throughout the three studies I argue that dialectical social knowledge among intellectuals (and others) can be understood in the interrelationship between social-structural forces like caste status and the division and specialization of intellectual activity (emphasized in case 1), the social and political organization of professional intellectual practice (emphasized in case 2), and the everyday intersubjective acts of knowledge making undertaken by individuals seeking to explain their social and historical environments (emphasized in case 3). Dialectical social knowledge emerges in the tension between the knowing subject and the compromising forces and conditions of epistemic context. But recognizing this phenomenological tension cannot alone account for why dialectical social knowledge becomes widely amplified in intellectual discourse in some places and times and not in others. It is, I argue, only in synthesizing a phenomenological attention to the epistemic individual with a broader "social phenomenological" analysis of the response of intellectual activity to its social environment in intellectual culture that one comes to understand dialectical social knowledge in its full complexity.

It is to a conceptual modeling of this complexity that I first turn.

Dialectical Social Knowledge

CHAPTER ONE

Conceptualizing the Formation of Dialectical Social Knowledge

It has not occurred to any one of these philosophers to inquire into the connection of German philosophy with German reality, the relation of their criticism to their own material surroundings. — *Karl Marx and Friedrich Engels, The German Ideology*

Dialectical Social Knowledge in Theory

In this chapter, I ask how we might fruitfully conceptualize dialectical social knowledge in the language of social theory. I have three objectives: to situate this project within the anthropology and sociology of knowledge, to offer a limber set of conceptual devices for apprehending dialectical social knowledge as a social phenomenon in its own right, and to work toward a theoretical schematization of the activity of intellectuals in the social formation of knowledge.

I first revisit Marx and Engels's analogy of the inverting camera obscura of ideology in order to illuminate the link between dialectical social knowledge and the division and specialization of labor in society. From Marx and Engels through Antonio Gramsci, Georg Lukács, Karl Mannheim, and the more recent works of Pierre Bourdieu and Bernhard Giesen on intellectuals and social knowledge, I trace the Marxian sociology of knowledge from its profound insights into the specific links between social-structural forces and relations and the content of knowledge produced by situated social actors to the serious functionalist limitations that recur in its various models of knowledge formation.

To circumvent this functionalist impasse, I then turn to semiologically and performatively inspired trope theory in the anthropology of knowledge (particularly the work of James W. Fernandez, Paul Friedrich, and Michael

Herzfeld), which forefronts the creative, poetic (and also, in a less abstract manner, the political) dimensions of knowledge making. I focus especially on the capacity of the theory of tropes to account for the work of terms like "*Geist*" and "*System*" in discourse, as semiotic and epistemic means of "filling the frames" of social life with meaning (Fernandez 1986: 45, 62) and for figuring the self meaningfully and indexically in context with respect to other selves. While the broader historical and social-structural conditions surrounding the formation of knowledge remain, at times, obscure in tropological models of knowledge making, the shift of emphasis to the social actor as poetic subject brings the phenomenological and communicative dimensions of social knowledge into high relief.

Through the juxtaposition of these two strains of social theory, with their respective strengths in ideological and poetic analysis, I argue that conceptualizing dialectical social knowledge in its experiential and social totality requires, if not a synthesis, then at least a recognition that they offer parallel, complementary, and equivalently important insights into the problem at hand.

In conclusion, I outline the conceptual problem of the intellectual as social actor and explain why I have chosen to make intellectuals (primarily journalists and to a lesser extent scholars, academics, bureaucrats, and philosophers) the subjects of my historical and ethnographic studies. My focus on intellectuals does not mean that I believe that dialectical social knowledge is somehow their special capacity. Rather, I argue that intellectuals are simply especially prone to dialectical social knowledge given their specialized, intensive, intimate engagement with "knowledge" itself. Moreover, it is intellectuals who have helped to objectify the phenomenological tension between creative (inner) self and compromising (external) forms and relations discussed in the introduction as dialecticism. Studying intellectuals allows us to scope the full range of dialectical social knowledge from its more reflexive, informal, intuitive dimensions to its more codified, formal, and analytical dimensions. Intellectuals may have no special claim to dialectical social knowledge but they exercise it across a wide range of registers and thus provide particularly apt subjects for research.

Revisiting Marx's Critique of Ideology

It is sometimes difficult to separate Marx's own critique of ideology entirely from the work of some of his more recent and influential interpreters, especially Louis Althusser. For Althusser, "ideology" described the system of knowledge that favored the reproduction of class domination and that manifested itself, for example, in the "know-how" taught by institutional apparatuses like schools, the church, and the army that always encouraged "subjection to the ruling ideology or the mastery of its 'practice'" (1971: 133). In general, Althusser's understanding of ideology elaborates the well-known paragraph in *The German Ideology* where Marx, writing with Engels, argues that the dominant ideas of a given epoch are the ideas of the dominant class (1978: 172–73). Althusser's whole paradigm of Ideological State Apparatuses (1971: 127–86), for all its brilliance in analyzing and specifying means of domination (cf. Foucault 1979), is built around this definition of ideology as a particular scheme of ideas functionally related to a particular class and then elaborated through institutional hegemony. One certainly should not dismiss Althusser's reading of ideology, since it indeed extends a pivotal point in Marx's theory of class domination. Yet I would argue that it recognizes only one dimension of Marx's critique of ideology. I will show that Marx's theory of ideology is not limited to the naturalization of class domination but that it also articulates Marx's sense of a more fundamental social and historical relationality of human knowledge that is due principally to the division and specialization of labor in society.

For Marx, the problem of knowledge is foremost a problem of human consciousness, consciousness that was "from the very beginning a social product" (Marx and Engels 1978: 158) and that evolved historically under different stages of material social organization. Beginning with the homogeneous "conscious instinct" of tribal humanity, social organization shapes human consciousness through the division of mental and material labor. As the division of mental labor expands, Marx argues, human consciousness becomes divorced from its immediate sensuous relationship to nature and eventually able to objectify itself as something transcendent of its material environs: "From this moment onwards consciousness *can* flatter itself that it is something other than consciousness of existing practice, that it *really* represents something without representing something real; from now on consciousness is in a position to emancipate itself from the world and to proceed to the formation of 'pure' theory, theology, philosophy, ethics, etc." (159). Yet, despite its appearance of emancipation from the world, Marx continues, mental labor actually always remains interdependent upon the practices of material labor from which it has been divided. "Pure" thinkers need to eat and to be clothed and housed, and so others positioned elsewhere in the social division of labor must offer these services on their behalf. Marx's primary criticism of the Young Hegelians, for example, was that these bourgeois philosophers had generalized the ideational privileges that their social position in capitalist society afforded them to humanity and history as a whole. They believed, like Hegel, that social evolution operated principally through ideational forces and conflicts because they themselves lived in a kind of floating world of the intellect made doubly possible by the social specialization of mental labor and by their status as members of the dominant bourgeois class.

Despite his polemics, Marx did not identify the elision of their own materiality as a matter of some shortfall of intelligence on the part of the Hegelians. Rather, he viewed their inability to recognize their "true" materiality and the true materiality of social relations in general as a phenomenon of "ideology" produced by the division of labor. For Marx, consciousness always seeks universality in the particular, and so dominant systems of ideas naturalize historical conditions through a process of inversion and representation: "If in all ideology men and their circumstances appear upside down as in a *camera obscura* this phenomenon arises just as much from their historical life-process as the inversion of objects on the retina does from their physical life-process" (Marx and Engels 1978: 154).

The tendency of human beings to project their immediate circumstantial relations as universal relations and circumstances is, I would argue, the basic phenomenological insight at the heart of Marx's theory of "ideology." Ideology is the form of consciousness that begins with the relational consciousness of parallel independent worlds of the mind and body yet is further elaborated, specialized, and transformed by the class relations of various historical eras. The common feature of every ideology that develops past the stage of "conscious instinct" is that, in each historical era, a dominant class arrogates to itself the right to articulate the ideas of the entire society. In a second section later in *The German Ideology*, Marx argues that the mental laborers of the ruling class, "its active, conceptive ideologists, who make the perfecting of the illusion of the class about itself their chief source of livelihood" (Marx and Engels 1978: 173), articulate and project key concepts that legitimate the material social order of a particular historical stage as an ordained-from-above natural reality: "we can say, for instance, that during the time that the aristocracy was dominant, the concepts honor, loyalty, etc., were dominant, during the dominance of the bourgeoisie the concepts freedom, equality, etc. The ruling class as a whole imagines this to be so" (173).

Inside the dominant ideology, as Marx expresses most fully in the section of the *Grundrisse* titled "The Method of Political Economy," conceptual convention (including theoretical and analytical conventions) expressed in the sphere of intellectual activity mirrors the evolution of the division and objectification of labor more generally. For example, only in a society where wealth-creating activity has been abstractly universalized by wage

labor does a universal category named "wealth" come into conceptual being in the minds of intellectuals like Adam Smith (Marx and Engels 1978:
240). Critical knowledge meanwhile appears only along the tension lines of
class conflict itself—Marx might have justified his own critical theory of
bourgeois society as evidence of the growing contradictions caused by the
political repression of the revolutionary class and the bourgeois hegemony
over the true economic power in capitalist society, the proletariat (173).

Already in *The German Ideology* emerge the characteristic strengths and
weaknesses of subsequent Marxian sociology of knowledge for conceptualizing dialectical social knowledge. On the one hand, Marx's critique of the
ideational dialecticism of the Young Hegelians suggests an intriguing link
between ideationalism more generally and the division and specialization
of mental activity in society. Moreover, especially in his critique of political
economy, Marx is able to correlate the manifest content of social theory both
with the exigencies of social organization in particular times and places and
with the social positionality of the intellectual (for Marx, "ideologist") as
a specialized mental laborer. In chapter 2, I develop these insights into an
analysis of the relationship of the social phenomenology of the German *Bildungsbürgertum* (the educated bourgeoisie, or cultured middle classes) to dialectical social knowledge throughout the nineteenth century. Specifically,
I ask why positive dialectical knowledge of the nation became conceptually
dominant in the centers of German intellectual culture in the first decades
of the nineteenth century and why negative dialectical knowledge of modernity had spread throughout these same centers by the end of the nineteenth
century. I argue that the dialecticism that became emblematic of languages
of German national being and national history in the nineteenth century
was ideological in Marx's sense in that it reflected intellectuals' transposition of their relational social knowledge into languages of cultural ontology
and historical teleology.

Yet, on the other hand, the place of the individual intellectual as social and historical actor remains fully obscure in Marx's analysis. Marx incorporated enough Hegelian teleology into his own dialectical paradigm of
world-historical evolution to make his theory of stages of consciousness
both functionalistic and reductive in its outlines. Although I share Marx's
sense of urgency to bring philosophy "down to earth" by emphasizing its social and historical character, I think that it matters *how* one emphasizes this
social and historical character. The reduction of idiosyncratic, "sensuous"
(in Marx's sense) labors of intellection to a generic postulate of ideology does
not produce a particularly illuminating or delicate sociology of knowledge
in this respect. Dialectical social knowledge could, under these theoretical

premises, belong to the ideational armature of only one class or another, a position that the fact of Marx's own dialectical critique of Hegelian dialecticism apparently undermines. To unravel this dilemma, I turn to later generations of Marxian theorists of knowledge and intellectual practices for inspiration as to how to make individual subjects "count," as it were, within a Marxian sociology of knowledge.

From the Critique of Ideology to the Sociology of Knowledge

Other theorists working within the outlines of Marx's critique have helped to develop and refine analytical and representational tools that I find vital for conceptualizing the social formation of knowledge. The works of Antonio Gramsci and Georg Lukács on hegemony and class consciousness, for example, serve to elaborate Marx's analysis of "mental laborers" (intellectuals) and his portrait of intellectual culture in significant ways. Gramsci introduces the variable of the intellectual as a social actor into the framework of Marx's sociology of knowledge and further distinguishes between "organic" and "traditional" intellectuals, a move that helps to account for the diverse modes of social knowledge in intellectual culture that do not conform to an orthodox class-based theory of ideology. In Gramsci's terms, Marx's class "ideologist" is a kind of "organic intellectual" whose social role in a stratum of specialized and legitimated knowledge workers is to give every group arising in the world of economic production a sense of its own "homogeneity and an awareness of its function" (1971: 5). "The capitalist entrepreneur creates alongside himself the industrial technician, the specialist in political economy, the organizers of a new culture, of a new legal system, etc." (5). Gramsci's "organic intellectuals" are often not recognizable as "intellectuals" in the traditional (Dreyfusard) sense at all: journalists, managers, technocrats, and politicians populate their ranks alongside professors and public intellectuals.

Gramsci envisages intellectual culture as a complexly articulated struggle between the organic intellectuals of any given era, who monopolize the dominant institutions of "superstructural" (e.g., cultural) production, and various factions of urban and rural "traditional intellectuals," who although once occupying the structural position of organic intellectuals themselves (like the ecclesiastics under feudal aristocracy) have corporately outlived the hegemony of the class that brought them into being and legitimated them (1971: 6–8). The social marginality of traditional intellectuals, Gramsci notes, helps to provide them with a sense of autonomous social solidarity from the dominant order and thus cultivates a sense of critical distance with regard to dominant hegemonic trends. Contra Marx, for example, Gramsci describes German idealist philosophy's social utopianism not as an organic intellectual phenomenon but rather as a traditionalist phenomenon, an "expression of that social utopia by which the intellectuals think of themselves as 'independent,' autonomous, endowed with a character of their own, etc." (8). The advantage of Gramsci's analysis is that he is able to discuss dominant institutional centers of cultural production that articulate, systematize, and reproduce the ideology of a politically dominant class at the same time that his acknowledgment of parallel traditional intellectual networks and centers helps to account for the overall heterogeneity of intellectual activity within society.

In this respect, Gramsci offers a schematic model of intellectual culture that is not unlike Lukács's more elaborate study of the historical forms of bourgeois and proletariat consciousness (1971: 110–219). Lukács too sees in the division and specialization of mental labor a foundational crippling of the intellect that replaces "true" knowledge of human interdependence with reified consciousness and that thus endows bourgeois rationalism with its contemplative intuitiveness and sense of its own epistemic inevitability (99). In the end, the predication of philosophy upon "pure thought" remains "an insuperable obstacle within the realm of thought itself," condemning even the most subtle of the philosophers to the predisposition "that the rational and formalistic mode of cognition is the only possible way of apprehending reality" (121). Lukács's insight into the "formalistic mode of cognition" is the inspiration for my own description of intellectuals' "phenomenology of expertise" below. Although Lukács sees this endemic rationalist orientation primarily as a problem of bourgeois society (cf. Horkheimer and Adorno 1994), I link it to Marx's phenomenological consideration of the relationship of the specialization of activity to the apprehension of "knowledge" in its formal dimensions.

In the end, despite a more nuanced analysis of intellectuals and intellectual culture, both Gramsci and Lukács continue to functionalize the production of knowledge in society to the dynamic of "class consciousness," a move that I consider problematic for the analysis of dialectical social knowledge for two reasons: (1) as noted above, dialectical social knowledge exceeds, in its various articulations, any single class consciousness developed on the basis of a special positionality within the organization of production in society, and (2) this sociology of knowledge predicates the legitimacy, indeed the transcendent "truth," of critical theory upon a world-historical process of class conflict. Indeed, I view critical theory as a relational knowledge. But I do not think it a relational knowledge of the world-historical variety (as

wonderful and decisive a trope of legitimation as that may be). Instead, by exploring the evolution of negative dialectical knowledge within the German
Bildungsbürgertum in my first case study, I argue that critical knowledges
of modernity saturated with tropes of spiritless formation emerged parallel
to a more utopian language of spirited national culture (*Bildung*) because of
the transformation of social relations within the German societal elite and
because of increasing specialization and capitalization of intellectual labor
among the cultural bourgeoisie itself. In this historical case, critical knowledge indexed, at an ideological level, not the class tension between the bourgeoisie and the proletariat but rather the dynamic factional tensions within
the societal elite between cultural bourgeoisie, propertied bourgeoisie, and
the industrialist aristocracy.

From Class Determinism to the Intricate
Affiliations of Intellectual Culture

To free a relational sociology of knowledge from the logic of class determinism, Karl Mannheim's model of the "free-floating intelligentsia" seems a desirable alternative. In his essay "The Problem of a Sociology of Knowledge,"
Mannheim criticizes the "method of 'vulgar' Marxism" that "consists in *directly* associating even the most esoteric and spiritual products of the mind
with the economic and power interests of a certain class" (1993: 237). Instead, Mannheim offers, as a strategy for salvaging "the element of truth in
the Marxist philosophy of history," a more fine-grained "historicism" that
breaks apart the image of a unitary class worldview (*Weltanschauung*) into
a dynamic constellation of immediate social and discursive networks that
together define particular intellectual standpoints, postulates, motivations,
and styles. Thus, for Mannheim, it is possible to make a specific historicist argument about how "modern rationalism . . . was linked to the world
postulates and intellectual aspirations of the rising bourgeoisie" (238), but
following Max Weber, Mannheim declares it impossible "to establish a historical parallelism between intellectual standpoints and social strata. . . .
Differentiation in the world of mind is much too great to permit the identification of each current, each standpoint, with a given class" (239).

Mannheim suggests instead that one conceptualize social stratification
and intellectual stratification as relatively independent features of the social
organization of intellectual production. One can define social strata in terms
of Marx's model of class, he explains, but each intellectual stratum ought to
be defined as "a group of people belonging to a certain social unit and sharing a certain 'world postulate' . . . who at a given time are 'committed' to a

certain style of economic activity and of theoretical thought" (1993: 239). A system of competing worldviews thus becomes a more decisive mediating feature of intellectual culture than positionality in the organization of material production. Not, Mannheim clarifies, that intellectuals are free of social influence, but intellectuals are fundamentally heterogeneous social strata, articulating various schemes of knowledge that may or may not fulfill the hegemonic interests of other strata (1936: 157).

This analytical move is, in fact, a quite radical departure from the mainstream Marxian sociology of knowledge since its effort to weaken class determinism threatens to sever the relationship between social and intellectual strata entirely. The "commitment" of an intellectual stratum to the economic interests of a social stratum is undetermined and always mediated by the exigencies of factional world-postulates. Therefore, it is possible to see the intelligentsia itself as free-floating (*freischwebend*) of class relations: despite the diversity of world postulates in an intellectual culture, the common educational bond of intellectuals creates a parallel sociological affinity that crosscuts the affiliations intellectuals might have to any "class" of the Marxian variety. Mannheim, to be sure, did not do away with class determinism altogether—in his major work *Ideology and Utopia* he discusses the intricate class affiliations of various intellectual strata and their historical transformation (1936: 156–64). Yet, the imperative, functional character of the intellectual as artisan of class hegemony is missing from Mannheim's analysis. The class affiliations of intellectual strata are characterized as, at least in some cases, "voluntary," stemming from the decision "to join in the political struggles of a particular class" (158). Intellectuals acquire the attributes of intention and agency in Mannheim's sociology of knowledge, a move that begins to flesh out the intellectual as a social actor in an anthropological sense.

Since, in the structure of his essay, Mannheim reflexively applies his sociology of knowledge to the sociogenesis of the problem of the sociology of knowledge, it is worth briefly discussing the historical significance of Mannheim's work as a watershed in conceptualizing the social formation of knowledge. Historian Fritz Ringer has written insightfully of the context of Mannheim's project in the midst of a heightened discourse on a "crisis of culture" and "crisis of knowledge [*Wissenschaft*]" among the orthodox majority of German academics in the Weimar period (2000: 26–27; see chapter 2 below). Ringer argues that Mannheim's outline of a historicist sociology of knowledge was, in part, an effort to replace a perceived crisis of universalist paradigms of knowledge with the synthetic certainty of a relationist vision of knowledge (29–33). It was thus not surprising that Mannheim broke not only with "vulgar Marxism" and Enlightenment rationalism but also with contemporary sociologists like Max Scheler, whose paradigms of knowledge he found predicated on either crude monocausal determinism or specious universalizing premises (see Frisby 1992; Scheler 1926).

The characteristic shift of Mannheim's sociology of knowledge is that it more fully sacrifices evaluating the validity of truth claims to evaluating the social relations that catalyze particular orientations of knowing. Mannheim himself identifies this tendency and locates it in the "oppositional tradition" of sociology that has sought to "disintegrate" ideas by paying attention not to their truth claims as such but rather to their "extra-theoretical" contexts and functions (1936: 192–93). It is telling then that Mannheim's sociologist of knowledge is less a critic of bourgeois ideology than an empirical sociologist (in this "oppositional" sense) of the historical forms and dynamics of intellectual production. "It is imperative in the present transitional period to make use of the intellectual twilight which dominates our epoch and in which all values and points of view appear in their genuine relativity. We must realize once and for all that the meanings which make up our world are simply an historically determined and continuously developing structure in which man develops, and are in no sense absolute" (1936: 85).

For Mannheim, the "problem" of a sociology of knowledge is to pursue the contexts and historicities of knowledge by producing a topography of an entire intellectual field, mapping out the various intellectual strata, deciphering their worldviews, assessing their ideological inheritances and agendas, and recording their struggles with one another. As a methodological ideal, Mannheim's problem is quite attractive for a project in the anthropology of knowledge like this one. Mannheim's sociology of knowledge demands a fine-grained empirical approach to the study of knowledge forms. Yet it also demands careful attention to the social and historical contexts of the production and circulation of particular knowledges. To these concerns (which I share), I add a commitment to understanding the phenomenological basis of social knowledge such that we, as analysts, can conceptualize why it is that we, as intellectuals, are attracted to "knowledge forms" in the first place. That is, I ask why it is that we tend to perceive "form" as the essence of knowledge and thus why we might be predisposed to think of the second part of Mannheim's method (the study of forms-in-context) to be the more trivial dimension of his venture.

On the other hand, although Mannheim's method comes perhaps closest of anything in the Marxian tradition to producing a nonfunctionalist account of the social formation of knowledge, it has two significant troubles for the study at hand. First, Mannheim's approach to genealogical and contextual work often resolves itself into a kind of historicist particularism that can deprive the sociology of knowledge of its more provocative insights into the relationality of social knowledge. In other words, Mannheim places himself at such pains to remove class determinism and phenomenological considerations (in the Schelerian sense) from the sociology of knowledge that he ignores Marx's more enlightening discussion of the phenomenological reversals of ideology through the specialization of activity. In Mannheim's sociology of knowledge, it is, as with Gramsci and Lukács, difficult to apprehend dialectical social knowledge as something more than a particular socially and historically situated scheme of knowledge.

Second, Mannheimian historicism still does not invite attention to the study of actual individual intellectual lives and practices in context. To be sure, Mannheim is deeply committed to a precise historical understanding of the emergence and circulation of particular ideas, but his focus is entirely on the already-formalized products of intellectual practice rather than on the intellectual practices that guarantee the formalization, circulation, and accreditation of ideas. His sociology therefore remains formalistic in its orientation and relatively resistant to the intimate risks and complexities of ethnographic engagement. In the first case study, my methods lie closer to Mannheim's, but the ethnographic explorations of institutional and professional life in the second and third case studies serve to deconstruct the limitations of an anthropology of knowledge that concerns itself solely with canonized ideational forms. The ratio of the complexity and idiosyncrasy of intellectual practices to the unifying motifs of social knowledge that are iterated more broadly emerges in its full historical and social specificity only with a more intense engagement with individual intellectual lives and labors.

Toward the Study of Intellectuals as Agents in the Social Formation of Knowledge

It is worth noting that recent praxis-oriented approaches to knowledge formation have given greater attention to intellectuals and intellectual practices while retaining the broader contours of a Marxian-Mannheimian sociology of knowledge. With these works, the concrete institutions and practices of intellectual life are highlighted for the first time, making it possible to refine our analytical awareness and to conceptualize the social formation of knowledge beyond the association of ideational forms. Likewise,

the competition for capital, legitimacy, and status in intellectual practice. Giesen recognizes the link between constructivism and Mannheim's sociology of knowledge and breaks apart the "free-floating intelligentsia" into a paradigm of pluricentric networks of social actors whose identity as "intellectuals" is formed by competence in particular communicative rituals and interactions. "The communication rituals specific to intellectuals facilitate reproduction of intellectuals as a sociostructural unit: bridging individual differences and combining a variety of opinions, establishing unity of internal processes and the peculiarity of the intellectual form of life" (1998: 45). Then, and from the point of view of this project this is Giesen's great leap forward, he suggests that what differentiates intellectual rituals like "academic disputations and journalistic commentaries, literary correspondence and encyclopedic classification, salon conversation and the construction of philosophical systems" from other kinds of communicative rituals is precisely that they thrive on collective identifications, on symbolic and indexical processes that negotiate epistemic order with the ambition of producing generalizable regimes of classification and knowledge.

Intellectuals thus become specialists in generalization, much as Paul Radin once argued that intellectuals (in his case, university-trained ethnologists), by virtue of their social orientation, seek and valorize the formal attributes of culture (1927: 11–18). This leaves them continuously weaving schemes of general knowledge (whether sociological or cosmological), distilling epistemic order from the contingencies and fluidity of semiotic processes. And, for Giesen, the most important forms of epistemic order that intellectuals articulate and manage are codes of generality. "By way of these rituals there arise—mostly without conscious intention, and in a manner shaped by the specific logic of the intellectual community—the ideas of the 'general,' the *Allgemeinheit*, the encompassing collectivity that lies in the other-worldly order, i.e. the very ideas that define codes of collective identity" (1998: 45).

The communicative rituals that cohere intellectual communities negotiate, as a matter of course, series of classificatory systems that reconcile individual actors to their social and physical environments. These rituals moreover have distinct and specific social logics of their own that affect the manifest content of the ideas of generality that are negotiated within them. Both Giesen and I regard, for example, the kind of sociability that developed in the voluntary associations (*Vereine*) of German-speaking Central Europe as directly related to intellectuals' cosmopolitan patriotic imagination of collective German identity in the late eighteenth century (1998: 70–75; see also

Chartier 1991). Expanding upon Benedict Anderson's classic account of the intersecting economic and technological influences upon the origin of national consciousness (1983: 37–46), Giesen's code of "the nation" originates in the ideas of social generality negotiated within the discursive channels of intellectual culture and then is spread to other social strata through public cultural institutions (the arts, mass media, education, and political discourse).

Giesen's language-oriented approach to intellectual practice is the most sympathetic of any within the Marxian-Mannheimian sociology of knowledge to the juxtaposition with trope theory that I undertake below. I find Giesen's vision of the relationship of intellectual practice, epistemic order, and the cultivation and circulation of "codes" of social belonging compelling with a few reservations. One must note, for example, that standards of intellectual competence are themselves diverse, historically dynamic, and interactive with other criteria of distinction. For example, one can be performatively and epistemically competent but with the wrong biography and identity, as we see in the case of many eastern German journalists, and still be delegitimated as an "intellectual." Such situations demand complexifying Giesen's model of ritually verifiable competence as an objective principle of legitimation. Still, even if intellectual legitimacy is not truly objectively verifiable, one can agree with Giesen that the practice of constituting and/or invalidating intellectual legitimacy may be understood as prototypically intellectual.

A second problem with Giesen's model is that he tends to focus upon the luminary voices of figures like Goethe, Schiller, and Novalis in his account, intellectuals who have already achieved post facto canonization as culture heroes of a national literary tradition. This tendency subverts the presence of other kinds of intellectual voices that were less avidly recorded or that have been ignored altogether. In the first case study, I am indeed guilty of a similar emphasis on luminary voices. But, in the book as a whole, I try to correct Giesen's emphasis on intellectual "high culture" by interpretively juxtaposing elite intellectual discourse with other, normatively lower-status, intellectual practices such as journalism, informal conversation, and even barroom arguments. Intellectual culture thus emerges in this project in a greater diversity of ritual forms, linguistic registers, and "codes."

First Synthesis

All of my critical considerations of the Marxian sociology of knowledge emphasize my discomfort with its tendency, in each new iteration, to find its

way back to functionalist and at times even teleological models of knowledge formation. At the same time, I do not want this discomfort to over-
shadow the very important insights one can gather from this strain of social
theory for the conceptualization of dialectical social knowledge. What we
learn from the Marxian sociology of knowledge is the following: (1) that it
is possible to discern a specific relationality of knowledge emerging from
the division and specialization of mental activity, (2) that this relationality
has definite ideational effects caused by its tendency to elevate relational or
positional knowledge to universal knowledge, in other words, to raise social
phenomenology into ontology, (3) that there is a tendency of mental activity
and specialized mental laborers (e.g., "intellectuals") to recognize epistemic
form as the essence and value of knowledge, (4) that the sociology (and by
extension anthropology) of knowledge must therefore counter this tendency
through the sensuous, intimate study of forms and practices of knowledge-
making-in-context, (5) that in the study of these contexts we cannot lose
sight of the refraction of *poesis* through the specialized activity, rituals, and
dispositions of intellectuals, (6) that intellectuals' own social phenomenology continuously informs their spatiotemporal categories of social belonging such as "the nation" or "modernity," and (7) that, even if we agree that
Bourdieu goes too far in his complete subjugation of *poesis* to politics, we
can never ignore the situational political dimensions of the production of
social knowledge, whose stakes are indeed the legitimate right to classify
the social world on behalf of others.

The Marxian sociology of knowledge is, in sum, crucial to the anthropology of knowledge (and, one might add, to the history of ideas) in its
insistence that ideas cannot be accurately studied sui generis, that they
must always be studied in concert with their social conditions of production, however one may choose to construe and work through those "conditions." My faith in the insights of the Marxian sociology of knowledge is
tempered principally by my concern that it does not go far enough in finding a place for individual-phenomenological and intersubjective processes of
knowledge formation within its theory. Given my understanding of dialectical social knowledge as a mode of knowing that always responds to both
individual and social phenomenology, this is a serious limitation. For this
reason, in the following sections of the chapter, I explore anthropological
variants of trope theory as a strategy for conceptualizing the individual and
intersubjective dimensions of the articulation of dialectical social knowledge about which the Marxian sociology of knowledge continues to have,
unfortunately, relatively little to say.

A Phenomenological Dilemma and the Theory of Tropes

In his sympathetic critique of Max Weber's interpretive sociology, Alfred Schutz excellently captured the central phenomenological dilemma of the sociology of knowledge (1967: 3–44). The essential problem was how the sociologist, as a self, could objectively know the subjective meaning of another person's action (let alone another's subjective relationship to his or her own psychic processes). The sociologist might well be able to attach an objective meaning to an act of another, like an utterance, for example, by placing it into an objective "meaning context" (like a language system), and he or she might even be able to read, in the combination of the other's words and bodily movements, indications (*Anzeichen*) of the other's subjective experience and intentions (Schutz 1967: 110–12). But the other's subjective experience and knowledge would remain elusive. Schutz follows Husserl in making meaning a matter of *attention,* specifically "*a certain way of directing one's gaze at an item of one's own experience*" (1967: 42; see also Husserl 1986; Merleau-Ponty 1962: 26–51). Under these conditions, the sociologist could never hope to know the meaning of another's subjective experience; at best, the sociologist could model the other's subjective experience of knowing on external indications and on his or her *own experience of knowing.* This is an imperfectly "objective" process of interpretation to be sure. But Schutz does not seem disappointed. For he has not dismissed objectivity in social science altogether but has rather only predicated it, fundamentally, upon subjective experience. What the sociologist of knowledge can be certain of based on his or her own experience of knowing is that subjective meaning exists as a domain differentiated from the many extrasubjective meaning contexts we navigate in our lives and that knowledge is formed in the interplay between subjectivity and intersubjectivity. These certainties, according to Schutz, ought to be recognized as the phenomenological foundations of any subsequent sociology of knowledge.

The limits of the self's knowledge of the subjective experience of the other is also the dilemma we face here when trying to make sense of dialectical social knowledge in phenomenological terms. This is, no doubt, in large part the reason why the Marxian phenomenological approach dwells so solidly on already-articulated epistemic forms and their relationship to abstract entities like "classes" or "class fractions." Subjective experience is discussed by Marx in his theories of alienation and fetishism (I will have more to say about these in chapter 2), but Marx appears to have very little doubt that these states of consciousness are entirely objective as well as subjective. In other words, Schutz's problem is simply not acknowledged. Hand in hand with the lack of attention to individual intellectuals and intellectual practices-in-context, this is a limitation upon the Marxian phenomenological approach imposed by an analytical method that begins with the phenomenology of class yet that never quite arrives at an adequately complex theory of the subjective experience of the Ego. If we wish to explore an opposing, yet complementary, path beginning with the phenomenology of Ego's knowledge of self and other and moving through intersubjectivity to social phenomenology, then Schutz offers a useful point of departure, one that can be seen to have influenced, directly or indirectly, other ethnographers working in the phenomenological tradition (see Behar 1996; Comaroff 1985; Csordas 1994; Daniel 1984; A. Glaeser 2000; Jackson 1989, 1996; Kapferer 1997; Pesmen 2000; Stoller 1989a, 1989b, 1997; Wacquant 2003).[2]

Schutz himself turns to communication as a key domain of action for the constitution of intersubjective relationships and understandings, and my particular phenomenological interest is in language and communicative practices. My studies do not, however, exhaustively analyze language use as a sociolinguist might. Neither are they intensively phenomenological (in a Husserlian or Schutzian sense) in method. Instead, I tack between these cardinal points of orientation, employing what anthropologists James W. Fernandez and Paul Friedrich have termed "a tropological method." That is, to explore the complex of cognition, language, and knowledge at the levels of subjective and intersubjective experience, I focus on the play of tropes in intellectual discourse, including analogical tropes like metaphor, contiguity tropes like metonymy and synecdoche, and modal tropes that link affect and language. Trope theory has already been utilized with impressive ethnographic results in the study of expressive culture (e.g., Fernandez 1982). My concern, related but contrastive, is how treating terms like *"Geist," "Kultur,"* and *"System"* as tropes can inform a study of formal and informal practices of social knowledge.

I approach trope theory here with all the familiar caveats offered by anthropologists drawing upon rhetorical theory who wish to make it clear that

2. Psychoanalytic theory would offer a path parallel to that of Schutz's phenomenology in this respect, but I do not pursue it here due to its weaker capacity, in my view, to inform a theory of semiotic and epistemic processes beyond the level of intersubjective interaction (for exceptions, see Butler 1993; Žižek 1993). This said, I think that psychoanalysis adds a great deal to a phenomenological approach to knowledge and I see tremendous opportunities for greater dialogue between phenomenological and psychoanalytic approaches in anthropology. I draw upon several psychoanalytic categories in this book, including "anxiety," "desire," and "fantasy," to fill out the individual and social subjectivity of intellectuals beyond their preferred rationalist outlines.

they do not engage tropes (particularly metaphor) in precisely the same way that philosophers of rhetoric (Burke 1969; Richards 1950; Ricoeur 1977) or cognitive scientists (Lakoff and Johnson 1980) engage them. Of the former, Terry Turner writes (including some symbolic and interpretive anthropologists like Clifford Geertz in the crosshairs of his criticism) of a tendency to treat "metaphor as a sui generis mode of giving form and identity to the otherwise inchoate experience . . . of phenomenological subjects" (1991: 126). Of the latter, Fernandez argues: "The cognitive approach to metaphor is an intellectual enterprise conducted under the sign of a more formal philosophy than anthropologists, given the thickness of the field experience and our commitment to it, could easily practice even should we wish to" (1991: 9; see also Quinn 1991). In both cases, anthropologists express concern with the methodological formalism with which tropes have been treated classically even when it comes to matters of practices of metaphorization. This concern could, of course, be extended to the semiological and structuralist poetics that constituted the proximate point of access of anthropology to tropes (particularly Jakobson 1960; Jakobson and Halle 1956; Lévi-Strauss 1966; Saussure 1966).

Andreas Glaeser cautions against the analytical reification of tropes: "Research into the *use* of tropes . . . has revealed the inherent instability of any trope in action. On the one hand, metaphors shade at their margins into metonymies by the sheer act of establishing consubstantiality in comparison. . . . On the other hand, metonymies can be transposed into metaphors. . . . The consideration of context is therefore extremely important in analyzing how a particular tropic identification functions within social interaction" (2000: 51; see also Fernandez 1986: 46). A formalist approach to tropes, in its very hypostatization of tropic forms and typologies and in its implicit characterization of tropic efficacy as a matter of tropic form, is thus in danger of missing the point (or at least an important part of the point) about what tropes are and how they work. Turner concludes that tropic figures are not sui generis forms of ideation but rather glosses and codifications of more open-ended processes of semantic and indexical figuration of self-in-context: "Metaphor, in other words, consists of the employment of the general structural principles of semantic classification (the relations of type and token, the construction of referents through the semantic contextualization of signifiers) to construct a relation of semantic identity, in a new or otherwise distinct context, between elements of semantic categories not recognized in other contexts as belonging to the same semantic domain" (1991: 128).

Paul Friedrich perhaps puts the anthropological position most elegantly when he describes tropes as "the great and little prepatterns that variously channel, influence, and determine how the speaker interrelates elements of language to each other and interrelates language itself and the rest of the world" (1991: 54–55; see also Friedrich 1996). Since "all language is always tropological" (1991: 24) according to Friedrich, the analytical language of trope theory is really a means for discerning the "entanglements" of language between human subjects and environments of objects and relations. In other words, in their continuous mediation of communication and cognition, tropes prove an ideal means for apprehending the juncture between subjective experience and intersubjective exchange in terms of conceptual, referential, and indexical processes of analogy, contiguity, formality, modality, and so on. Fernandez suggests that we consider tropes as communicative strategies of feeling and identity predication (1986: 8) that fill in the formal lexical frames of communication with rich, intersubjectively constituted webs of association. Tropes, in other words, are distillations of the complex interweaving of subjective and intersubjective expression that allow these relations to become accessible to anthropological knowledge in the study of their formal particulars.

Dialectical Tropes

Perhaps the most valuable analytical purpose of tropes for the study of dialectical social knowledge is their capacity to condense, expand, and archive the semiotic and epistemic activity of social actors. Fernandez cites the work of ethnographers such as Victor Turner (1967) and Sherry Ortner (1973) on "dominant metaphors" and "key symbols" to illustrate the anthropological recognition of how certain tropes can capture, record, or diversify semiotic settlements in communicative practices and how these settlements can then serve as key orienters to subsequent social practice. Friedrich writes of "condensation and expansion" as tropes themselves in communicative practice, tropes that alternately extract "the gist" (1991: 42) of meaning and interconnect and back-reference other tropes, both distilling and networking meanings continuously. In this respect, tropes mediate the production of the epistemic gossamer often analytically distilled as "culture." Recalling Terry Turner's criticism, we must be careful as to how we assign agency. Tropes themselves accomplish, not their own meanings, but rather the intersubjective processes of meaning formation through which social actors stake their semiotic-epistemic activity in dialogue with others, who may variously construe the intentions and significance of the tropes in question.

This is the point at which trope theory gains a great deal from phenomeno-logical insight. The "play of tropes" is, in essence, the play that can be read in the epistemic motion of intersubjective transaction.

To return to the problem at hand, one can well imagine how terms like "*Geist*" and "*System*" (and related terms) become dominant analogies within dialectical social knowledge, continuously moving from metonymy into metaphor, as the phenomenological contiguities of selfhood are raised into the conceptual analogies of identity (and alterity). "*Geist*" enters the modern era (as I will explore in more detail in the next chapter) with deep religious connotations and identifications with the "Spirit" of Lutheran vo-cation. Alongside this inheritance, the term also captured myriad subjec-tive experiences and articulations of sacred, spiritual powers "within" that bound together the individual, the community of faith, and transcendental power. Given the widespread referential capacity that "*Geist*" acquired and maintained through religious experience, it is not surprising that it (and allied terms like "*Kultur*" and "*Bildung*") would be a familiar, desirable locus of "inwardness" for new imaginations of social identity and belonging like the language of national Germanness that began to crystallize among the German middle classes in the late eighteenth and early nineteenth cen-turies. In this rich chapter of its life, "*Geist*" acquired the role of an epitomiz-ing analogy of the true inner, cultural spirit of Germanness and became what I term a "lexical totem" in the imagination of German national belonging.

One can also imagine a similar tropic trajectory for an emblem of exte-rior systematicity like "*System*." "*System*" has long referenced organically interacting elements in specialized scientific and philosophical discourse, elements whose systematicity traces the outlines of some kind of "whole" recognizable from the perspective of the subject. With the popular circu-lation of the term through religion, philosophy, and science, "*System*" ac-quires new analogical associations in application to a variety of elements perceived to stand in organic interdependency (like social systems, political systems, economic systems, etc.). Beginning with a subjective phenomenol-ogy of exteriority (and the continuous subjective search for patterns of order without), it requires no great stretch of the imagination to envision how "*System*" moved (and moves) from a token of contiguity to a routinized analogical status (see Fernandez 1986: 46).

In everyday language, "*System*" operates as a tropic condensation of so-cial and political exterior forces perceived to be ontologically separate from, and threatening to, the expressive agent within. In this respect, "*System*" is by no means a contemporary German obsession. "System" has much the same status in everyday social knowledge making in many parts of the world, certainly in the United States. It (and similar terms, such as "society") is remarkably flexible in its many figurations of exteriority-as-totality, signaling a phenomenological estrangement that often masquerades as objective judgment (in statements such as "the system wouldn't allow them to do anything else" or "that's just how the system works").

Michael Herzfeld's study of the social poetics and production of cultural intimacy (1997a) in a Cretan village offers a very apt illustration of similar tropic processes in another context (1985). Herzfeld narrates in detail the flexible and intimate idioms of fraternity and contest deployed by Glendiot men in their cultivation of self-regard, or *eghoismos* (1985: 11, 123–62), and how, among other tropic twists, the praxical contiguities of theft and thieving are continuously analogized as metaphors of the identities of locality, masculinity, friendship, and even ethnography (45–50, 163–205). The similarities between a term like *"eghoismos"* and a term like *"Geist"* speak to their common figuration of the phenomenological nexus of selfhood-in-context; their many referential differences speak likewise to the worlds apart (both linguistic and praxical) in which they evolved. The considerable advantage of trope theory for this project is its attention to this particular ratio of phenomenological unity to sociological difference, which is such a fertile basis for anthropological inquiry. My study of dialectical social knowledge thus gains comparative value in its conceptual affinity to other ethnographic studies of selfhood-in-context (the anthropological literature is, of course, enormous, but in the literature of Europeanist ethnography, see, e.g., A. Glaeser 2000; Herzfeld 1985, 1987, 1997b, 2004; Pesmen 2000; Ries 1997).

The Lingering Question of the Social

Applied anthropologically, trope theory offers a set of supple analytical instruments for studying human knowledge. It pushes past a variety of formalistic approaches to knowledge into the risks, subtleties, and idiosyncrasies of subjective and intersubjective exchanges. Yet it does not sacrifice interest in form altogether. Instead, the imperative emerging from anthropological trope theory is the need to maintain continuously the ratio and tension between the key devices of human cognition and their actual contexts of employment. This model, I have argued, is also fundamentally phenomenological. Yet its phenomenology never loses sight of subjective experience and processes of knowledge making as might a social phenomenology beginning at the level of a "class" or other large-scale social formation. In this way, trope theory is at its best sketching the relationship of the phenomenology of knowledge to everyday situations of communication and "revelatory incidents" (Fernandez 1986: ix) that may or may not contribute to broader and more persistent schemes of social knowledge. As Herzfeld writes, this approach always productively illuminates the local parameters of "importance and mereness" in human knowledge (1997a: 11).

Yet there is a lingering question of the social. Trope theory behaves magnificently in the analysis of subjective experience and intersubjective exchanges in a discrete local context. But does it operate as effectively in apprehending the knowledge making of translocal communities of discourse, in assessing the social formation of knowledge on broader scales? It is in such moments, where it is no longer possible to make connections between the subjective experience of specific social actors and the immediate meaning contexts that envelop them that the analytical usefulness of a pure trope theory begins to fade. With more "mediate" contexts at play, the very gossamer of significance that Friedrich describes becomes stretched thin. Trope theory continues to illuminate very well how the semiosis of public culture is encountered subjectively and processed in intersubjective contexts (see Shryock 2004). But trope theory does less well illuminating the complex institutional and organizational features involved in the production of "public culture" itself. This is largely a matter of scale. Given its attention to the details of subjective experience and intersubjective action, anthropological trope theory has a less well developed apparatus to account for collective formations and transactions of knowledge. I wish to emphasize that I am not arguing that one scale of attention is better than the other. If executed well, each offers something important to the anthropology of knowledge.

Second Synthesis

I will admit that I tend to see the relationship between these two strains of social theory and the phenomenologies of knowledge they outline as a relationship between the "how" and the "why" of the social formation of knowledge. Trope theory, with its fine-grained, synthetic attention to relations between human cognition and affect, between subjective experience and knowledge making, and to intersubjective communicative interaction, is, to my mind, the best theoretical armature social science has at its disposal to understand the "how" of the social formation of knowledge. But the very fundamental poetic creativity of human minds and the manifold tropic potentialities to which writers like Fernandez and Friedrich attest raise the profoundly important question as to *why*, then, some settlements of social knowledge become dominant in particular places and times and others do not. The study of *poesis* alone cannot account for the selectivity of social forms despite its valuable corrections to a Bourdieuian vision of pure semiopolitics.

In other words, let us agree that phenomenology always illuminates the social formation of knowledge. Dialecticism, for example, in its spatial and temporal figuration of inner/exterior, potential/actual tensions, is always present in some form and to some degree in human knowledge of the social. But this does not explain why dialectical social knowledge becomes so explicitly codified and dominant in German intellectual culture in the nineteenth century and produces such a rich archive of social theory and philosophy to legitimate its "epistemological" status. I am not convinced that trope theory, given the very scale of its interest, could ever persuasively address such a question. It would have to rely too heavily on theoretical synecdoche, that is, on using a limited number of cases as exemplars of a "whole" to make its case.

Rather, without losing touch with the specific insights that trope theory offers us, I would argue that we need to begin simultaneously from another point to address adequately "why" dialectical social knowledge became the intuition and indeed the passion that it did in German intellectual culture as a whole. In brief, we must also begin with German intellectuals as a social formation and seek to understand their social phenomenology as a collective phenomenon in its own right. It is, I argue in the next chapter, only at the level of the *Bildungsbürgertum* as collectivity that the "why" of dialectical social knowledge in nineteenth-century German intellectual culture begins to become clear. This is a question that demands, in some variant, a Marxian-Mannheimian approach to knowledge, proceeding as it does from exactly the opposite direction, from the sociological to the phenomenological.

Indeed, it is this very pivot between phenomenological and sociological knowledges that informs the organization of the case studies in this book and that suggests that the anthropology of knowledge compose itself of a dialogue between the two approaches. The synthesis I attempt in this book is only partial and I cannot pretend to offer a seamless metatheory at the end. For one thing, the two countercurrents of social theory tend to flow past one another even as they traverse the same middle ground (anthropology) en route to their never-quite-achieved destinations. But in the juxtaposition of the interests of individual and social phenomenology in this book I would argue that I offer a sense of greater *coverage* than were I to have simply settled myself into one current, rode it toward its destination, and consequently trivialized the other.

The cost of this expanded coverage, the reader will note, is an occasional sense of disjuncture within and between the case studies where the tension lines between the two phenomenologies of knowledge can never be entirely effaced (nor should they, in my opinion). But I am confident that the richness of the ethnography and history in the case studies will help to alleviate the rawness of these joints. The three studies together also tell a story—narrating a certain historical trajectory of dialecticism in German intellectual culture—that has an empirical integrity all its own.

Intellectuals and Knowledge

In conclusion, let me say a few words about intellectuals as the subjects of these studies. What I mean by an "intellectual" is somewhat removed from commonsensical and standard academic definitions and deserves some discussion. Intellectuals have been variously defined in a long series of literary-cultural and social-scientific debates as anything from those who must, of necessity, speak truth to power (Benda 1969; Said 1994; Zola 1998), to "men of ideas" and guardians of traditions and cultural knowledge (Coser 1965; Nettl 1969; Parsons 1969; Shils 1972), to a social stratum verging historically into a new technocratic class (Bell 1973; Djilas 1957; Gella 1976; Gouldner 1979; Konrád and Szelényi 1979), to inhabitants of spaces of ideology and legitimation (Bourdieu 1988; Verdery 1991), and to a languishing breed of public person in an era of academicization, privatization, and social compartmentalization (Jacoby 1987; Posner 2002; cf. Robbins 1993). All of these definitions seem to me to describe some of the social actors I term "intellectuals" well and others poorly. Zygmunt Bauman has written insightfully of the particular reflexive dilemma of typifying intellectuals since every effort to define "the intellectual" both purports to be definitive and remains, in the final analysis, a self-definition (1987: 8).

I define "intellectuals" as social actors who have a specialized attention to knowledge, one that I define as the *phenomenology of expertise,* an attention to the formal properties and values of semiosis, a special regard for the thinglike character of "knowledge" as a series of forms or relations that can be removed from the ongoing flow of epistemic activity and treated as distinct entities. This does not involve *imposition* of form onto epistemic activity so much as the *cultivation* of formality within epistemic activity. In any case, I view "intellectuals" as both agents and products of this process. Intellectuals are artisans of epistemic form but they also become intellectuals through the practice of their craft, through careful training in respect for and attention to "knowledge" (see also Boyer and Lomnitz 2005).

My model is clearly indebted to Marxian practice theory insofar as intellectuals' consciousness of the objective, formal character of knowledge is, in every respect, an extension of the division and specialization of labor that allows some social actors to develop a specialized relationship to epistemic form. In turn, the phenomenology of expertise is a necessary element in the ideological camera obscura at broader social levels, one that helps ideationalism to naturalize its Cartesian divorce from material-social and corporeal conditions (Boyer 2005a). But this model is likewise indebted to an appreciation of what Paul Friedrich describes as poetic "virtuosity" (1986: 46–47) as a defining feature of intellectual life. Ultimately, what I believe defines an intellectual as a social actor is less a specific inheritance or social positionality, less a functional position in a division of labor, and less a formalized set of competencies than a particular orientation to, and consciousness of, knowledge. This means that a street poet, in my definition, is no less an intellectual for his or her lack of cultural capital and credentials than a university professor. Both may well possess deep attention to knowledge and a virtuosity with respect to its making in their own networks and settings; both may well cultivate epistemic form in their own contexts.

My consideration of the relationship between intellectuals and knowledge thus returns to Gramsci's statement that all men are intellectuals even if not legitimated to function in this way in society. There is no better illustration of the truth of Gramsci's proposition than Michael Herzfeld's account of epistemically rich and savvy Glendiot men, who fully appreciate epistemic formality even if they do not possess a phenomenology of expertise as such: "Glendiots have no interest in formal taxonomies as such, but they do have an acute understanding of the ways in which formal properties can be gleaned *by actors* from *all* forms of social experience" (1985: xiv). Herzfeld elaborates the comparative dimension of his analysis more fully elsewhere (2001) when he challenges a distinction between "practical and discursive forms of consciousness" that separates intellectuals from other kinds of experts. "We can certainly say that the professionalization of social science requires us to formalize our theories, so that their discursive organization and comparative reach may be very different from those of a shepherd or a potter. To say, however, that these intellectual positions are *not* expressions of 'practical consciousness' is to deny the point that theory itself . . . is a form of social practice" (2001: 72). And, indeed, the difference is simply that theory is a kind of social practice that is oriented to the cultivation of epistemic form.

It is because of intellectuals' investment in the cultivation of epistemic form and because of their involvement in the subsequent codification, articulation, and publicization of these forms that I make them the subject of my case studies in the anthropology of knowledge. The very publicity of the intellectual activities of actors like journalists and academics makes them especially interesting from the point of view of understanding the social formation of knowledge at a full range of scales from the subjective to the multisubjective.

How and why dialectical figurations became interwoven into German intellectuals' knowledges of nation and modernity is the subject of the next chapter and the first case study. I turn now to the intuition, articulation, and play of positive and negative dialectical social knowledges across nineteenth-century German intellectual culture.

CHAPTER TWO

The *Bildungsbürgertum* and the Dialectics of Germanness in the Long Nineteenth Century

The finest characteristic of the typical German, the best-known and also the most flattering to his self-esteem, is his inwardness [*Innerlichkeit*]. It is no accident that it was the Germans who gave to the world the intellectually stimulating and very humane literary form which we call the novel of personal cultivation and development. Western Europe has its novel of social criticism, to which the Germans regard this other type as their special counterpart; it is at the same time an autobiography, a confession. The inwardness, the culture [*Bildung*] of a German implies introspectiveness; an individualistic cultural conscience; consideration for the careful tending, the shaping, deepening and perfecting of one's own personality or, in religious terms, for the salvation and justification of one's own life; subjectivism in the things of the mind, therefore, a type of culture that might be called pietistic, given to autobiographical confession and deeply personal, one in which the world of the *objective*, the political world is felt to be profane and is thrust aside with indifference, "because," as Luther says, "this external order is of no consequence." What I mean by all this is that the idea of a republic meets with resistance in Germany chiefly because the ordinary middle-class man here, if he ever thought about culture, never thought politics to be part of it, and still does not do so today. To ask him to transfer his allegiance from inwardness to the objective, to politics, to what the peoples of Europe call *freedom*, would seem to him to amount to a demand that he should do violence to his own nature, and in fact give up his sense of national identity. — *Thomas Mann, "Geist und Wesen der deutschen Republik" (trans. W. H. Bruford)*

It is characteristic of the Germans that the question, "what is German?" never dies out among them. — *Friedrich Nietzsche, Jenseits von Gute und Böse (trans. W. Kaufmann)*

The Dialectical German

Few characterizations of the "inwardness" of the "typical German" are so well known as Thomas Mann's. His entrancing portrait of the tension at the heart of "Germanness" between the demands of an inner domain of spirit, cultivation, and personality and the exterior world of the objective, the political, and the profane has itself been indexed often enough as a cultural epitome of the German nation. And, yet, the celebrated aptness of Mann's description is also a remark upon the similarity between Mann's typical German and other literary and philosophical representations of German inwardness produced throughout the eighteenth and nineteenth centuries. Mann's typical German is not far removed from the self-reflective culture hero of Goethe's *Sorrows of Young Werther* (2002) nor from the early ethnological characterizations of German loyalty, depth, soulfulness, and love of freedom penned by the likes of Kant, Schiller, Herder, and Hegel. Mann's formulation is not even compromised by Nietzsche's later characterization of the typical German as a creature of imitation and falsity, desperately searching for knowledge of its "identity." For even Nietzsche reserved a distinction between the possibility of a true and authentic Germanness rooted in an unmediated *Kultur* and the hapless lust for the external trappings of civilization and *Bildung* pursued by the mass of actually existing Germans (1980: 25–27).

"Germanness," of course, does not lack a broad range of meanings. Nor is it meaningful only in the elite registers of literary culture. Indeed, "Germanness" is an abundantly significant category of social identification among various social strata both within Europe and elsewhere (see Dieckmann 2003). One could even say that its meanings are as diverse as there are persons committed to typifying German character, although its intended and received meanings tend to cluster around certain ethnotypes like German inwardness or German austerity or German intolerance. What is particularly striking about Mann's description given the interests of this study is the way in which many of these supposed "cultural characteristics" of the typical German are woven around the core dialectical trope of a struggle between incommensurable domains, forces, and claims of inwardness and exteriority (of Spirit and System). The typical German, according to Mann and others, retreats from the world into the life of Spirit and thus seems cold and remote to those who revel in exteriority (such as, it is said, the French and the Americans). In the logic of dialectical Germanness, the normal German appears to reject instinctively what constitutes the mundane normality of many, perhaps most, other cultures—for him, to seek even "freedom" in a political sense would be an act of self-violation.

Reading Mann's distillation of German national character from the other end of the twentieth century, it is difficult not to reflect on what such a mysteriously "inward" people would be capable of. The confluence of dialectical social knowledge with the logic of ethnic nationalism in a narrative like Mann's draws dialecticism into consideration of the "contradictions" of German cultural history. One can hardly help but wonder: How did *das Volk der Dichter und Denker* (the people of poets and thinkers) come to enact the regimented terror of the Third Reich? No less brilliant and insightful a sociologist of Germany than Norbert Elias writes with a sly sense of premonition about the dialectical Germans: "In [the Germans'] wider social life, particularly their politics, the wide gap between ideal and reality, the quest for perfection, the yearning for an ideal community—the dream Reich—had its counterpart in feelings of emptiness and often of indifference, apathy or criticism; if the ideal could not be reached, it was hardly of importance what one did and how one did it" (1996: 327). Elias's portrait of Germanness reminds me of a conversation I once had with Joachim as we walked one hot day in July along the sandy banks of the Havelsee. He sighed, "It often seems to me that every German has a little Hitler in him." I asked him if he was sure it was only every German, and he smiled and replied, "You may have something there."

The Social and Phenomenological Basis of German "Inwardness"

The motivating question of this case study is how Germans became dialectical. In other words, how did dialectical social knowledge come into alignment with social knowledge of Germanness to the extent that the former often stands in for the latter? Mann leaves us a wonderful clue in his text when he begins his definition of the typical German by speaking of the German literatus who has given the world the *Bildungsroman* and ends by describing the "ordinary middle-class man" who gives the world his indifference to its exteriority. Such glosses of the intellectual and the everyman allow the social self-understanding of German intellectuals to take on the qualities of national-cultural essence, and indeed, this is the process of social knowledge formation I analyze in this chapter.

The dialectical figuration of German inwardness and world indifference is best understood by linking it to a long-term process of ideological transposition during what historian David Blackbourn (1998) has termed the "long nineteenth century" (ca. 1750–1914). In this period, the German-speaking *Bildungsbürgertum* (cultural bourgeoisie) of Central Europe translated a sense of their own collective spiritual unity and agency into social knowledge of a "world-historical" mission of national formation. In their "articulation of the nation" (Suny and Kennedy 1999), German intellectuals allowed their own deeply dialectical social phenomenology to infuse their knowledge of social belonging and social temporality. In German intellectual culture, both "Germanness" and "modernity" came to inherit traces of the dialectical self-conception of the intellectuals.

I begin to unpack this process of social knowledge formation by exploring several key categories associated with Germanness (especially *Bildung, Geist, Kultur, Volk,* and *Wissenschaft*) that operated tropically to codify and to elaborate the social imagination of the *Bildungsbürgertum*. These terms served to define both immediate and abstract social relations in spatial terms of interiority and exteriority and in temporal terms of potentiality and actuality. Then I describe how favored metonyms of intellectual identification and selfhood like *Geist* and *Kultur* were raised into key metaphors or "lexical totems" of German national identity and belonging. Studying the movement between metonyms and metaphors and between tropes and totems helps us to conceptualize how the German *Bildungsbürgertum*, through their intellectual practices and performances, helped craft, reify, and publicize dialectical knowledges of national Germanness.

But why did dialectical social knowledge acquire such a strong place in the social self-imagination of the nineteenth-century German *Bildungsbürgertum* in the first place? In the course of the chapter, I explore a number of social and historical conditions germane to understanding the dialectical social phenomenology of the *Bildungsbürgertum*. In the late eighteenth and early nineteenth centuries, the German educated bourgeoisie was a relatively translocally oriented and socially integrated caste in an otherwise highly localized and heterogeneous Central European society. They enjoyed an exceptionally elite status in German political culture in the latter half of the eighteenth century owing to their mediation of social relations between the nobility and the rest of the middle classes. Their ennoblement and entitlement relative to the other middle-class strata, along with the

relative intimacy of their networks of communication and knowledge making, helped to elicit a sense of translocal social identity and mission among
them. *Bildungsbürger* identified in their own translocal communicative
unity and in their ethic of a pure orientation to foundational knowledge
(*Wissenschaft*) a model for the German nation and for Deutschland (Germany) more broadly, a unity they ardently and continuously contrasted to
the fragmentary, vernacular character of their social milieux.

This is not to say that *Gebildeten* (educated, enlightened individuals)
possessed a collective consciousness of a Durkheimian variety. Indeed, as
we will see below, they were themselves internally diverse in terms of their
practices and knowledges. Moreover, they consistently engaged in practices
of normative distinction among themselves, opposing, for example, positive
dialectical representations of philosophical, literary, and scholarly activity
with negative dialectical figurations like the *Brotgelehrte* (the scholar for
bread) and the mercenary journalist.

Yet, in settings like that of the University of Jena in the 1790s, one
finds a convergence of voices articulating unmistakably positive dialectical knowledge of German national *Bildung,* of a process of national formation from within to without, from the cultural potential (*Kultur*) of the
Gebildeten into the actual societal forms of a cultural state (*Kulturstaat*).
By the first decades of the nineteenth century, many in the mainstream
Bildungsbürgertum (lodged primarily in universities and in state administration) were actively engaged in producing narratives of national ontology
and teleology, foretelling an inevitable actualization of the German national
spirit and its culture. The intuitiveness and resonance of these narratives
have everything to do with the *Bildungsbürgertum*'s sense of rising social
status as they came to dominate the lower ranks of German state administration and as they continued to be judged the most noble of the middle
classes by the aristocracy. *Gebildeten* fantasized that an inevitable collapse
of the estates system would place the guidance of modernizing and actualizing the German nation firmly into their hands. They now identified themselves as *Kulturträger* (literally, "culture bearers") of the process of national
Bildung. In the excitement surrounding the founding of the University of
Berlin in 1811, *Gebildeten* dreamed of a modern rational state with the university as its central institution.

The amplification of positive dialectical social knowledge among *Gebildeten* was relatively short lived, however. Beginning in the 1820s, a sense
of estrangement from the "overformalization" of modern history and sociality began to spread throughout German intellectual culture. Comparing
the Hegelian and Marxian philosophies of history, we capture the contrast

between the positive dialectical knowledge still pervading the centers of German intellectual culture and the intensification of negative dialectical knowledge on its many margins in the 1830s and 1840s. Finally, by the end of the nineteenth century, knowledges of crisis and cultural decline pervaded the academic humanist culture that had been so certain of its world-historical mission at the beginning of the century. Now, instead of sensing the imminent realization of the *Kulturstaat,* academic humanists were plagued by a sense of the dissolution of their *Wissenschaft* (science, knowledge) and the degradation of national culture.

In the second half of this chapter I will explore sociological reasons why negative dialectical knowledge began to flourish among German *Bildungsbürger* when it did. For one thing, the political gains of the middle classes stalled in the second quarter of the century, and it became evident to *Gebildeten* that the German aristocracy had no intention of ceding authority through significant political reforms. Although nonnoble *Gebildeten* continued to populate the lower ranks of state administration, the higher echelons of state power were closed to them. In the second half of the nineteenth century, the *Bildungsbürgertum* found itself further marginalized in political culture by an alliance of traditional aristocratic elites and an increasingly powerful industrial bourgeoisie (see Föllmer 2002). This alliance was accelerated by the unification of the nation-state under Prussian hegemony and consolidated by the end of the nineteenth century (Blackbourn and Eley 1984). Although some *Bildungsbürger* welcomed the unification of Deutschland as the telos of national becoming, many more decried a spiritless modernity and hollow nation governed by the exterior imperatives of industrial capitalism and bourgeois mass culture (*Massenkultur*) (Ringer 1969). *Gebildeten* were concomitantly unsettled by the growth of an industrial press and its abundance of knowledge outside their control. The escalation of mass-market publishing intersected with shifts in the social organization of knowledge making within the *Bildungsbürgertum* as well. Through the spread of professionalism in intellectual culture, *Gebildeten* had become more specialized in their epistemic activities and communicative practices and possessed a weaker sense of their collective identity and purpose as an "estate of letters." Still, especially among university professors and civil servants, a sense of the *Gebildeten* as national culture bearers remained strong. But their narratives of national becoming were less confident and more shrill, often dwelling on the threats of rampant exterior and extractive interests, like capitalism and the Jews. In academic humanist culture, shifts in the composition of the professoriate and the rising power and prestige of laboratory sciences crystallized a sense of the corruption of

Wissenschaft by materialism and positivism and a frequently voiced belief that the corruption of *Wissenschaft* signaled the cultural decline of the university and the nation into the ephemerality of mass culture.

In sum, this particular combination of internal and external social transformations during the nineteenth century gradually shifted the social phenomenology of the German *Bildungsbürgertum* from a sense of relative spiritual agency in the early decades of the nineteenth century to a sense of powerlessness and decline saturated with anxieties about the compromise of inner virtue and authentic community by shadowy exterior interests and media.

Conceptualizing the *Bildungsbürgertum* as an Intellectual Collectivity

What kind of a social formation was the *Bildungsbürgertum?* Scholars of the *Bildungsbürgertum* as distinguished as Werner Conze, Jürgen Kocka, and Reinhart Koselleck have already lamented the difficulty of answering such a question bluntly. All three have noted problems with transposing the referentiality of the categories of *Bildung* (education, self-formation, self-cultivation, distinction, culture, civilization) and *Bildungsbürgertum* (educated bourgeoisie, cultural bourgeoisie, cultural elite) into other languages (Conze and Kocka 1985: 11; Koselleck 1990: 13–14). It is as though *"Bildung,"* a term so central to early articulations of German national-cultural belonging, still retains its national semantic integrity against the sincere cosmopolitanism of its translators. That the term *"Bildungsbürgertum"* itself is a twentieth-century category only complicates matters further (Jarausch 1990: 17). Its categorical singularity easily obscures the tension lines between and within the heterogeneous networks of self-identifying *Gebildeten* (enlightened, educated individuals). These networks contained social actors as diverse as the so-called free professions of doctors, lawyers, and engineers alongside pastors, civil servants, publishers, and more marginalized figures like artists, tutors, journalists, poets, and writers. Many, but not all, of these individuals were born into families with middle-class backgrounds (with "middle class" here denoting a variety of social strata between the Central European nobility and peasantry, some elite and others less so). Many, but not all, had university training and credentials. Many, but not all, earned their livelihood from their facility with knowledge. Many, but not all, read journals and newspapers and concerned themselves with German and European literature and performances of high culture. Many, but not all, participated in the rich intellectual life offered by voluntary associations (*Vereine*) and, later, by professional associations and state cultural institutions, not to mention pursuing intellectual correspondence and opportunities for discussion, debate, and knowledge exchange in more informal environments such as those offered by coffeehouses, bars, salons, and so on (on the spread of associationalism, see Hoffmann 2000).

In the early part of the long nineteenth century, two of the most prominent institutional loci for the professional activities of *Gebildeten* were universities and state administration. Nevertheless, intellectual activity as a whole remained fundamentally heterogeneous. Indeed, it was often the case that the activities of *Gebildeten* crossed into several areas of epistemic practice that, from our present vantage point, would seem to constitute the very antithesis of disciplinary specialization and narrowness. To take a well-known, if idealized, example, Goethe was a poet, a novelist, a natural scientist, and a civil servant, and neither he nor anyone else regarded this combination of activities as dilettantism. It was, as historian Theodore Ziolkowski writes, common enough for the intellectuals of the Romantic movement to combine their literary activities with work as "university professors, librarians, civil servants, doctors, lawyers, clerics, journalists, professional scientists, and . . . a multitude of other jobs" (1990: 4). Likewise, Charles McClelland notes that professors of the period "usually functioned in a confusion of jobs and roles, holding positions outside and in addition to their professorships" (1980: 170).

This is not to imply that various intellectual activities were considered interchangeable with one another; there were, to be sure, specialized forms of training and competence at play in every setting and, moreover, a moral hierarchy of intellectual pursuits, with some, like critical philosophy in the Kantian tradition, widely heralded as a means of cultivating humanity and actualizing the nation and others, like journalism, widely construed as marginal and dangerous enterprises for any person of *Bildung.* What the heterogeneity of knowledge labors among the early *Bildungsbürgertum* actually evinces is not the absence of intellectual specialization but rather the relatively low degree of organized professionalism among the cultural elite of German society until the latter half of the nineteenth century.

Given their heterogeneous activities, social positions, and commitments, conceptualizing *Gebildeten* at either end of the nineteenth century strains most familiar categories of European social organization and stratification—among these we might include the Marxian "class" of shared social positionality in relations of production, the Weberian "status group" with their social prestige and coherence predicated upon certain monopolized competencies, as well as the juridically distinct *Stand* (estate). Virtually every researcher of the *Bildungsbürgertum* has commented on the slippery quality of retroactively defining their corporate unity since each of these classifications fit some *Bildungsbürger* well but others poorly (Conze and Kocka 1985: 10). Mannheim's "free-floating intelligentsia" would offer a desirable alternative metaphor were the *Bildungsbürgertum* not, as we will see below, so firmly anchored by their relations to other middle-class strata and to the nobility and were their central principle of social reproduction (*Bildung*) not so firmly enframed by the institutional settings of universities.

What is clear is that the positive dialectical principle of *Bildung*—encompassing a sense of individual moral refinement and cultivation, a striving for harmony and unity between the particular and the absolute, and also a more pragmatic recognition of formal education and certification—was always central to the practices of self-distinction and narratives of social identification of *Gebildeten. Gebildeten* coordinated their signs of social identity less through a specific set of activities or credentials than through the vocation of a disciplined and pure relationship to their intellectual labors and knowledge (*Wissen*), an ethic best captured by the term "*Wissenschaft.*" *Wissenschaft* denoted both "science" and "scientific knowledge" in the late eighteenth and early nineteenth centuries, but it also signaled, above all, a pure commitment of *Geist* to the formation of knowledge. *Wissenschaft* was contrasted to the "merely voluminous erudition" of scholastic knowledge; it was epitomized as an internally motivated striving for "knowledge as a totality, a unified whole" (Ziolkowski 1990: 251). "*Wissenschaft*" quickly acquired the semantic nuance and dialectical contours of a pursuit of the absolute in the immediate, a yearning to discover the primordial knowledge (*Urwissen*) at the root of all worldly circumstance.

In this sense, the principle of *Wissenschaft* recalls the phenomenology of expertise—the specialized attention and orientation to epistemic formality—discussed in chapter 1. *Wissenschaft*, of course, promised not the form or letter of knowledge but rather the spirit or internal unity of knowledge. The term nevertheless signaled a vocational commitment to universal, foundational "knowledge" for-its-own-sake that *Gebildeten*, regardless of their specific activities and identities, frequently contrasted with the narrow self-interest or mercenary orientation of the specialist. Friedrich Schelling commented, for example, on the danger that some intellectuals, "[r]ather than expend their powers struggling for insight into the living whole of knowledge, . . . confine themselves narrowly to some one specialty" (1956: 5). Johann Gottlieb Fichte, likewise, contrasted the formal degradations and exterior perversions of the literary marketplace (1873: 226) with the true vocation of the scholar: "Let him resign himself entirely to his love of his vocation and of knowledge. The peculiar nature of his occupation consists in this,—that knowledge, and especially that side of knowledge from which he conceives of the whole, shall continually burst forth from him in new and fairer forms. Let this fresh spiritual youth never grow old within him; let no form become fixed and rigid; let each sunrise bring him new love for his vocation, new joy in its exercise, and wider views of its significance" (221). Fichte juxtaposed the positive dialecticism of the true *Gebildeten*, the one who found "within him" the spirit to seek the absolute in the particular, with negative dialectical figurations of corrupt intellectuals motivated and compromised by exterior interests or necessities.

Although the term "*Wissenschaft*" was most germane to the intellectual environment of the university, the normative and ethical commitment to a pure intellectualism that the term represented was broadly recognized within the *Bildungsbürgertum* and widely articulated in the knowledge *Gebildeten* held of self and other. The man of *Bildung* was identified and recognized foremost through an inwardly focused disposition, a sense of Protestant discipline and diligence, and his vocational concern with the making of knowledge and *Kultur* (culture) above and beyond any narrow professional interest. It is precisely this shared positive dialectical conception and language of intellectual selfhood that made the *Bildungsbürgertum* sensible as a social formation and intellectual collectivity despite their diverging investments and involvements.

Key Tropes of Intellectual Selfhood: *Geist, Kultur, Bildung*

To understand how *Gebildeten* integrated dialectical figurations into their knowledge of national Germanness, some additional sense of the phenomenological and cultural nuances of the key tropes of self-identification and social belonging within the *Bildungsbürgertum* is helpful. I focus on three terms here, "*Geist*," "*Kultur*," and "*Bildung*," that were both key principles of social identification among the *Bildungsbürgertum* and key lexical anchors of dialectical social knowledge.

In the long nineteenth century, the three terms commonly and sometimes interchangeably signified an interior and harmonious creative spirit (at first universal and then, during and after the Napoleonic period, increasingly ethnic-national) actualizing itself dialectically through a process of extension from within to without. "*Geist*" (spirit, creative genius, soul) is perhaps the most elemental of these three. In the eighteenth century, the term was adapted from religious discourse and utilized by *Gebildeten* to denote the inner genius and creative capacity of the enlightened individual.

Even in secular settings, scholars have noted, the term continued to index the pietistic calling of the infinite spirit at work in the individual (Bruford 1975: 81; Ringer 1969: 83; Stecher 1914: 27–30; Weber 1958: 132–34). As the individual's center of moral virtue and creative genius, *Geist* was most often counterposed to the materiality and ephemerality of the external world, to its formal systems of power (*Macht*) and money (*Geld*), and to the materiality of the body (*Körper*). Philosopher Johann Gottlieb Fichte lectured to rapt and overflowing audiences at the University of Jena that *Geist* "as such is the ability of the productive imagination to convert feelings into representations" (1988a: 199). *Geist* was therefore defined as a capacity for creative formation (*Bildung*), which Fichte elevated over and against the state of being an "excellent business machine" (192), a spiritless creature unable to engage in the spiritual processes of representation and dialogue that moved the human race toward perfection. "*Geist* obtains its rules from within itself. It needs no law; it is a law unto itself. The person without *Geist* obtains his rules from without; he is able to do nothing but copy" (198). For Fichte, *Geist* exerts its spiritual force from within to without; it constitutes form in the external world according to its internal laws. Its antithesis is acquiescence to external order.

The vocation of *Geist*—the perfection of the inward self according to the highest ideals of humanity—permitted, as sociologist Bernhard Giesen astutely notes, the juxtaposition of agentive individuality with a strong sense of linguistic and spiritual collectivity, often signified by the term "*Kultur*" (1998: 89–90). Modeled on language, *Kultur* was commonly described as a unity at the level of spirit or consciousness that existed in contrast with external systems of political, economic, and social life (see Elias 1994: 22–23). Tropically, "*Kultur*," like "*Geist*," condensed a spatial awareness of an expansive "within." "*Kultur*" could likewise capture a sense of active cultivation. Fichte, for example, described *Kultur* like *Bildung* as the skill through which any rational, sensuous creature attained "his final goal: complete harmony with himself" (1988b: 150).

As Harold Mah notes, *Kultur* conveyed both universal moral virtue and a sense of national distinction in the philosophical writings of this period. The two senses of the term were rarely fully separable from one another.[1] For the former, Zoran Dimic argues how even Fichte's nationalism should

---

1. It is worth noting that "*Kultur*" continues to have varying nuances. Although the term is now thoroughly saturated with associations to national Germanness and "culture" in the pluralistic sense, it also continues to signify a more transnational, cosmopolitan, or universalistic sense of "high culture."

be understood as a vehicle to universal ethical action and *Bildung* and not as an end in itself (2003: 785). In the latter case, Mah shows how what he terms "tropes of cultural antithesis" (1994: 77) in philosophical and literary discourse contrasted the authentic spiritual "harmony" of virtuous inwardness with the exterior artifice that *Bildungsbürger* identified among other strata of Central European society and in other nations.

Norbert Elias writes that "*Kultur*" was articulated first as a principle of inward virtue among nonnoble German-speaking *Gebildeten* to express their social and normative opposition to Francophone and Francophile courtly culture in Prussia. It was how *Bildungsbürger* perceived the "outwardliness" of court culture that, Elias argues, accounts for the pervasive, reactive valorization of "inwardness" as the source of "true" cultural interconnectedness and value. In response to the Napoleonic occupation, the semantics of the term began to shift in the direction of signifying a national-cultural essence that differentiated the inwardness of the German from the national qualities attributed to foreign others (at first, principally the French). Over the course of the nineteenth century, "the term 'culture' was increasingly used in the sense of 'national culture' " and came to be tethered to the fortunes of the Prussian state and to its Protestant-nationalist political agenda, with a consequent weakening of the humanist and universalist connotations that "*Kultur*" had acquired in the eighteenth century (Elias 1996: 136–37; see also H. Glaeser 1993; Ringer 1969: 119; Walser-Smith 1995: 20–37, 236–37). As *Kultur* became more saturated with ethnic-national connotations, some *Gebildeten* identified themselves as *Kulturträger* (culture bearers) for the process of German national-cultural formation, asserting that the virtuous realization of German national *Kultur* (what Fichte termed a *Kulturstaat;* McClelland 1982: 50) could best be realized through the works of a spiritual and moral vanguard.

When signifying social interiority and totality, "*Kultur*" became analogous to the conception of ethnic-linguistic-territorial social belonging captured by the category of *Volk*. In this sense, the term's agrarian and temporal nuances of "cultivation of the ground" were recognized in the association of culture and soil (see Herder 2002: 282). Johann Gottfried von Herder expressed his conception of *Volk*, like *Kultur*, in terms of an invisible inner systematicity rooted in language, place, and climate that distinguished one people from another: the *Volk* "is the invisible, hidden medium that links minds through ideas, hearts through inclinations and impulses, the senses through impressions and forms, civil society through laws and institutions, generations through examples, modes of living and education" (in Sheehan 1989: 165). At the same time, Herder's conception was not pluralistic in a

semiotic tokens or emblems that *themselves* signaled a sense of social identity and belonging among speakers. In other words, the very fact that terms like *"Geist"* and *"Kultur"* were of such common parlance and of relatively predictable referentiality among *Gebildeten* was itself utilized as evidence that the kind of cultural whole the terms signaled was, in fact, a real, national collectivity (see Bauman and Briggs 2000; see also Gal and Irvine 1995 on "iconicity"; and Silverstein 2000 on "nationalist deixis").

In this way, tropes that fluidly figure self-in-context are often rationalized through communication as emblems of social identification. As I argued in chapter 1, tropes like *Geist* allow the phenomenological contiguities of selfhood to be raised into predictable conceptual analogies of identity (and alterity). *Geist's* relationship to Germanness can be schematized as follows: *"Geist"* moves (1) from lexically capturing a phenomenological sense of spiritual power and agency among *Gebildeten,* (2) to a key trope in their narratives of identification, (3) to an emblematic figuration of Germanness in discourse, and finally (4) to a widely recognized sign of the dialectical essence of German character (just as Dale Pesmen notes that the Russian cognate *dusha,* "soul," serves as a central lexical figure for articulating and ruminating upon Russianness; 2000: 14–18). By binding phenomenology to (in this case) ethnology, terms like *"Geist"* and *"Kultur"* become lexical totems of social belonging as their speech community (the *Bildungsbürgertum*) ideologically predicates its imagination of social relations in the abstract (e.g., "the nation") upon its more immediate social knowledge of selfhood and alterity.

The Translocality of the *Bildungsbürgertum* and the Dialectical Imagination of National Germanness

The preceding sections give insight into how dialectical tropes came to suffuse knowledge of national Germanness, but we have yet to explore *why* this was so. Historians of modern Germany have often noted a special relationship between the educated estates (*gebildeten Stände*) and the articulation and circulation of knowledge of national Germanness. James Sheehan argues for the efflorescence of ideas of translocal Germanness beginning in the late seventeenth and early eighteenth centuries within "a literary culture, composed of readers and writers who were joined through an expanding network of publishers, periodicals, lending libraries and reading societies" (1981: 8). Fritz Ringer (1969) and Ernest Bramsted (1964) have detailed the idealist agendas of national cultivation that were expressed through academic work and literature of this and later periods. Bramsted writes that the educated middle class of the nineteenth century "fought indeed for the same ends as the capitalist middle-class, namely, for a constitutional state based on property and culture" (129), but they did so in the name of national *Bildung* rather than in the names of productivity and profit. Bernhard Giesen concludes that the *Bildungsbürgertum* was "the carrier of the modernization process in the German states" (1998: 64) and "the carrier of the moral codification of national identity" (78), in contrast to the English, Dutch, and French cases, where, he argues, the traditional feudal bourgeoisies and urban merchants and guildsmen occupied these vanguard roles in the modernization process. As Sheehan and Giesen point out, unlike other European cultural elites (particularly French and British), the German *Bildungsbürgertum* elaborated its knowledges of national belonging free of centralized state apparatuses, of systematized translocal institutional and professional frameworks, and also of a strongly socially integrated commercial bourgeoisie (Blackbourn 1991: 4).

According to these histories, it was the very vernacularity and locality of German-speaking Central Europe that allowed *Gebildeten* to imagine themselves as uniquely gifted to guide national unification on a moral, cultural, and political basis. Sheehan paints a bleak portrait of actual Germanness in the eighteenth century in the period when *Gebildeten* first began to identify themselves as the "culture bearers" of the German nation. His characterization is worth quoting at length:

> Central Europe's political fragmentation in the early modern period is well known. Small states, free cities, ecclesiastical territories, and semi-autonomous estates were scattered across the political landscape in bewildering profusion. And even this array of political units is a good deal less cohesive than it might seem if we think of political sovereignty in our own terms. Many of these "states" were themselves cut up by a number of internal civil, judicial, and fiscal boundaries; some were not made up of contiguous pieces, but were joined only by the ruler's personal sovereignty; others had to endure enclaves of independence or conflicting sovereignty within their borders. Looked at from a broad perspective, therefore, "German politics" appears as a hopelessly complicated web of conflicting jurisdictions, uncertain sovereignties, and deep local divisions. Looked at from the perspective of most contemporaries, on the other hand, there was no such thing as a "German politics." Like most other Europeans, an individual's political world was a small and personal one, limited to the village, town, or estate in which he lived. . . .

   Political fragmentation reflected, and was in turn reinforced by, economic conditions in eighteenth-century central Europe. The communications network was poor. Roads were almost always primitive, hard
to use at best, impassable when the weather was bad. River traffic was
impeded by natural hazards and by a frustrating profusion of tolls and
restrictions. Economic activity, therefore, tended to be locked in separate islands, which were then linked by intermediaries to a regional
system of markets. Quite distinct from these local economies were the
rather small number of enterprises which engaged in commerce across
national and linguistic frontiers. These firms, usually to be found only
in commercial centers such as Frankfurt and Hamburg, were part of an
international system of exchange. For our purposes, it is important to
emphasize that there was nothing particularly *German* about either the
local or the international economies. Farmers and craftsmen had little
contact with their counterparts in other regions, and none of them had
much in common with the bankers and merchants who moved upon a
European stage. There was no common currency or legislation, no communications network or national market center which joined all of them
together. And so, when their various goods moved from place to place,
they were taxed like any others. To the tax official or toll collector, there
were no "German goods"; everything beyond the boundaries of their own
localities was equally foreign. (1981: 6–7)

Although "Germanness" existed as a principle of ethnic and linguistic
identification in a plurality of local and regional variations across Central
Europe, it was an identification continuously compromised by much more
immediately significant identifications and institutions of local community (*Heimat*), feudal corporation, estate, and religion (see Applegate 1990;
Confino 1997; Sabean 1984; Walker 1971). There was, at any rate, little
interest in or conversation over translocal Germanness on the part of the
vast majority of the Central European population. Sheehan concludes that
"there is not much we can call *German* in either the local cultures of the
masses or the European cultures of the elites" (1981: 8). The middle classes
were themselves highly localized, as David Blackbourn notes: "the bourgeois presence in the patchwork of German states that existed at the turn
of the eighteenth and nineteenth centuries was less than imposing. Weak
and fragmented, like 'Germany' itself, the various bourgeois groupings were
frequently tied to the small German courts either as suppliers or as employees, the so-called 'servants of princes' (*Fürstendiener*); and they were over-
shadowed by an aristocracy that enjoyed legal privileges in the corporate

or estates-based society (*ständische Gesellschaft*) and viewed the modest middle-classes with disdain" (1991: 4).

It is perhaps unsurprising that national Germanness was imagined most actively within the narrow stratum of Central European society that historian Mack Walker has termed the "movers and doers" (1971: 119).[2] The movers and doers, according to Walker, consisted of an assortment of translocally oriented migrant populations, including "bureaucrats, peddlers, professors, merchants, wage laborers and dispossessed peasants," whose mobility and social horizons exceeded those valued by the citizens (*Bürger*) of German towns. *Gebildeten* belonged to this translocal population as much by necessity as by inclination. Central European students often traveled far from home to attend university and sometimes had attended several universities in different cities by the time they completed their studies. Many returned home to work after receiving their credentials, but others continued to move, working as tutors for wealthy families or as journalists while searching for more stable careers (Bruford 1962, 1965; Walker 1971: 128–33). Underemployment or unemployment was a frequent companion of intellectual life in Central Europe, as universities routinely produced more graduates than local universities or bureaucracies (the most lucrative, stable employers) could employ. For this reason, the migrant intellectual was a widely identified social category in Central Europe and one that was often classified by local *Bürger* as simply another kind of vagrant *Störer* (disturber) of the virtuous rhythm and parameters of town life (Walker 1971: 120). Feelings of social anxiety and tension were reciprocated by the intellectuals, who routinely referred to locally invested *Bürger* as philistines (*Spiessbürger*) so immersed in their own sorry home (*Heimat*) that they were unaware of the richness of the Deutschland around them.

Through their travels and professional engagements, *Bildungsbürger* tended, for both intellectual and pragmatic reasons, to develop translocal relationships and correspondences. Despite the translocal scale of these

2. Historians agree that, demographically, the *Bildungsbürgertum* belonged to the elite stratum of Central European society and that they clustered in urban areas. In 1850 only 13 percent of the population of German-speaking Central Europe belonged to the middle classes. And only 5 percent of the population belonged to what might be identified as the nonnoble elite, including *Bildungsbürger* and relatively wealthy *Besitzbürger* (propertied bourgeois) (Kocka 1988: 12). The nobility composed a mere 0.5 percent of the population (Wehler 1987: 159). Wehler (1995: 127) further estimates that as of 1870 the number of Prussian-German academics, self-employed writers, journalists, professional writers, Protestant ministers, and others who could be included in the "social formation" of the *Bildungsbürgertum* amounted to only approximately 180,000 individuals, children included (only 0.75 percent of the population of Prussia, which at that time was 24.57 million).

relationships, records of epistolary correspondence demonstrate that they could be remarkably intimate given the strong institutional nexus of the university and the relatively small size of the artistic, religious, and professional networks that linked to it (see Giesen 1998; Ziolkowski 1990).

The translocal communicative intimacy that *Gebildeten* experienced conditioned their imagination of translocal social intimacy centered on Germanness and Deutschland (Giesen 1998: 67–70; see also B. Anderson 1983). Their ideal Deutschland was, however, future oriented and conditional on their own historical agency. *Gebildeten* construed themselves as representing a unifying sublating spirit of Germanness in sharp dialectical contrast to the fragmented actuality of German-speaking Central Europe. *Gebildeten* thus modeled both the qualities of national Germanness and the inner spirit of Deutschland foremost upon themselves. Language, the tissue of translocal communication, became essential to their models of nationhood (see Herder 2002: 65–164). The spiritual energy, universal orientation, and inner systematicity signaled by terms like *"Geist," "Kultur,"* and *"Bildung"* became qualities they valorized in Germanness more generally. At the same time that *Gebildeten* disparaged other *Bürger* for their local conceits, they identified themselves as culture bearers whose spiritual purity and ethics of *Wissenschaft* could guide the process of national *Bildung*.

My argument is that the central tensions expressed by dialectical social knowledge—unity versus particularity, interiority versus exteriority, and potentiality versus actuality—saturated the social imagination of the *Bildungsbürgertum* in the late eighteenth and nineteenth centuries. Ideologically, in Marx's sense, they transposed their social phenomenology as national ontology. Our next task is to explore in more detail why the ratio of positive dialectical to negative dialectical knowledge in their social phenomenology, and thus their sense of the health of the nation, shifted over the course of the long nineteenth century.

The Ennoblement of the *Bildungsbürgertum* and Positive Dialectical Knowledge of National *Bildung*

Let me begin this exploration by sketching the relations between *Gebildeten* and other strata of the Central European social elite on the eve of the long nineteenth century. On the one hand, we have noted the estrangement from other segments of the middle classes reported by *Gebildeten*. Yet this oppositionality is easily overstated. Although *Gebildeten* differentiated themselves actively and vocally from the philistinic locality and exteriority of the "industrial burgher" (Schelling 1956: 39), they frequently shared kin relations and intermarried with the artisanal, commercial, and industrial middle classes. Furthermore, the *Gebildeten* lifestyle was in many respects indistinguishable from that of their more locally invested relatives.

> It is in fact here, in the realm of cultural and social identity in the broadest sense, that the *Besitz-* and *Bildungsbürgertum* was probably most united. This bourgeois identity included a widely shared belief in hard work, competition, achievement (*Leistung*), and the rewards and recognitions that should flow from these; in rationality and the rule of law, in the taming of nature, and in the importance of living life by rules. Correct table manners, sartorial codes, the emphasis placed on cleanliness and hygiene, and the importance attached to timetables (whether in the school or on the railway) all provide instances of the way in which these bourgeois values operated at the level of everyday life. (Blackbourn 1991: 9; see also Kocka 1988: 26–29; and Frykman and Löfgren 1987)

On the other hand, the relationship of *Gebildeten* to the Central European nobility was riven by the vagaries of uneven reciprocity. Like other middle-class groups in the eighteenth century, *Gebildeten* had little institutional self-sufficiency and depended upon their relationship to aristocratic networks, aristocratically dominated state administrations, and occasionally courtly culture for both social legitimacy and economic support. Yet, in the minds of the literati at any rate, aristocratic patronage of *Gebildeten* was far from ideal. W. H. Bruford writes: "Patrons were few and far between, there was as yet a much smaller reading public and, most important of all, there were no effective copyright laws" (1965: 272). The relatively small size of the literate audience (15 percent of the population in 1764 and only 25 percent by the end of the eighteenth century, according to Schenda [1970]), combined with widespread practices of state censorship and unauthorized republication (see also Johns 1998), meant that writers in Germany earned a fraction of what, for example, their British contemporaries did. Bruford describes how even the exceptionally widely read and esteemed Goethe earned only the equivalent of 22,500 British pounds in royalties over his lifetime, considerably less than what Sir Walter Scott earned in three years from his novels alone (1965: 279). At the same time, while there were examples of genuine conviviality between some middle-class *Gebildeten* and nobility in courtly circles, aristocratic rules of etiquette strongly differentiated nobility from nonnobility, which had the effect of sealing off the most intimate spheres of aristocratic sociability from even the most illustrious nonnoble *Gebildeten* like Goethe and Schiller (see Bruford 1965: 74).

Beginning in the mid–eighteenth century, however, the reciprocities between *Gebildeten* and nobility began to deepen both inside courtly culture
and outside it in the institutional domains of universities, administration,
and civil service. *Gebildeten* found their social status significantly elevated
as nobility came to recognize the distinction of *Bildung* (in the sense of educational and moral refinement) as a kind of ennoblement of spirit that justified sporadic estates conversion and integration into the elaborate ceremony
and hierarchy of courtly culture. Rather than a new practice, this is better
seen as an acceleration of an older aristocratic strategy for managing relations with the middle classes by ennobling a few at the expense of the many.
Still, the frequency of bourgeois ennoblement increased in the first half of
the nineteenth century even as some hereditary nobility strongly impugned
the practice (Wehler 1989: 153).

The reasons for the accelerated ennoblement of bourgeois in the nineteenth century are complex. Sheehan describes how, by the end of the eighteenth century, the old aristocracy's dominance (*Herrschaft*) over German
society was becoming threatened by an expanding and heterogeneous population of "non-noble élites" who "based their own claims to power and
prestige on different grounds: wealth, political competence, educational
accomplishment, moral superiority" (1989: 132). There were also, as Blackbourn and Eley describe (1984: 125), pragmatic political and economic interests at stake in many parts of Central Europe that encouraged an increased
coordination and alignment of noble and nonnoble elite interests. The shift
from agrarian to commercial and industrial economies throughout Central
Europe, for example, began to erode the economic dominance of the landed
aristocracy while concomitantly increasing the wealth and social influence
of certain sectors of the middle classes.

At the same time, universities, the central site of social reproduction of
the *Bildungsbürgertum,* increasingly mediated traditional aristocratic control over state administration. From the mid–eighteenth century onward,
university education became a rite of passage to significant administrative
positions for young aristocrats (McClelland 1980: 52–53). Historian Charles
McClelland has calculated that from 1714–36 to 1737–60, the average percentage of government officials in Hanover who had attended university
jumped from 56 to 82 percent, and among nonnobles (who made up only
12 percent of officials overall during this period) the average percentage increased from 71 to 89 percent (1980: 46–52). As McClelland concludes, *Bildung,* at least in its sense as an index of university education, progressively
represented an honorific sign of ennoblement among the nobility. But it was

a principle of distinction that also allowed for expanded nonnoble access to the aristocratic sphere of state administration via university education.

Indeed, it was the case that in the first half of the nineteenth century, the lower ranks of officialdom (*Beamtentum*) were increasingly drawn from the ranks of the university-educated nonnoble elite, usually those who had studied law. This group of civil servants (*Beamten*) came to form a companion center of gravity to university culture within the *Bildungsbürgertum* throughout the nineteenth century (Fehrenbach 1994: 14; Kocka 1988: 70). Historian Thomas Nipperdey estimates that, by 1848, 68 percent of civil servants were of middle-class heritage, whereas only 32 percent were nobility, the inverse of the eighteenth-century pattern (1983: 325). Although the higher echelons of state bureaucracies continued to be dominated by the nobility (see Wuthnow 1989: 393), the *Bildungsbürgertum* acquired a significant share of influence in state administration by virtue of the social distinction and "ennobling spirit" of *Bildung*. This influence, it must be emphasized, was denied the majority of the German bourgeoisie throughout most of the nineteenth century. *Bildungsbürger* accordingly gained relatively lofty social status, social power, and quasi estate privileges that raised their social distinction, not least in their own minds, considerably above that of the propertied bourgeoisie, the *Besitzbürgertum* (Nipperdey 1983: 260).

This sense of social elevation was strengthened by the patterns of interelite conviviality that developed after the mid–eighteenth century. Networks of voluntary associations proliferated in Central Europe after the mid–eighteenth century, and scholars have often remarked on the centrality of associational life (*Vereinswesen*) to the crystallization of middle-class publics and to their models of nationhood. The institutional networks of reading societies (*Lesegesellschaften*), language societies (*Sprachgesellschaften*), patriotic societies, and Masonic lodges that spread across Central Europe and elsewhere are often interpreted as institutional crucibles for modes of discourse and informational exchange that integrated bourgeois virtues of egalitarianism and individuality into a new "public culture" (*Öffentlichkeit*) that opposed itself to the hierarchical social order of the estates system (Giesen 1998; Habermas 1991; see also Chartier 1987, 1991; Hoffmann 2000, 2003; Zammito 2002). Indeed, *Gebildeten* operating through these associations did much to coordinate the communicative basis of the cultural elite and to codify Herder's and Schleiermacher's proposition of the linguistic unity of the nation (see Bauman and Briggs 2000) in the form of a standard "High German" register based upon a literary canon (see Blackall 1978; Hohendahl 1989).

Although it is undoubtedly true that voluntary associations were central to middle-class cultural and political life, it is mistaken to understand them as a strictly nonnoble sphere of interaction and intimacy. These societies were relatively open to the nobility as well (Sobania 1996: 180). In her study of bourgeois-aristocratic relations before 1848, Elisabeth Fehrenbach estimates that in some cases polite societies drew as many as a third of their regular members from the nobility (1994: 24). This was also true of early language societies committed to programs of linguistic cultivation (*Sprachpflege*) and standardization (*Spracharbeit*), whose memberships were often significantly mixed or even dominated by nobility (von Polenz 1994: 112–17). By the mid–nineteenth century, bourgeois social clubs with names like "Harmony" and "Concordia" were financed largely by propertied bourgeois, operated by *Gebildeten*, and frequented by a mixture of nobility, *Bildungsbürger*, and respectable *Besitzbürger* (see Sobania 1996). The clubs' activities were centered neither on politics nor on informational exchange in any pragmatic sense but rather on the presentation, appreciation, and discussion of expressions of high *Kultur* (art, literature, music, and theater), whose proper consumption could occur only within a sufficiently cultivated audience.

The voluntary associations were not simply institutions of bourgeois class development therefore but rather institutional spaces in which aristocratic and nonnoble, and *Bildungsbürger* and *Besitzbürger*, networks became knotted. *Kultur*, in its sense of "high culture" and a sumptuary economy of distinctive knowledges, values, tastes, and practices (see Bourdieu 1984), became something of a social binding force among the German social elite that counterbalanced structures of intraelite distinction like endogamous marriage preferences (Bramsted 1964: 17; Fehrenbach 1994: 6; Kaelble 1988: 122). By hosting rituals of cultivated consumption, the *Gebildeten* in turn attained a certain kind of liminality, a "structural invisibility, ambiguity and neutrality" (V. Turner 1967: 99) within the social elite. This liminality allowed what had hitherto been their own principles of distinction like *Bildung* and *Kultur* to circulate more widely among the social elite as a whole and to become, over the course of the nineteenth century, recognized as distinctions of "German" culture and character.

The ability of *Bildungsbürger* to manage elite conviviality in the early nineteenth century amplified their sense of occupying a leading role in the modernization of German society. This impression, in historical retrospect, seems somewhat fantastic given that programs of "modern" social and economic reforms were in fact spearheaded by *gebildete* nobles and self-identifying modernizers like King Friedrich Wilhelm III's ministers Baron

Heinrich von Stein and Prince Karl von Hardenburg, who pursued a "double thrust towards releasing social energies and reducing corporate distinctions" (Blackbourn 1998: 83). In the first decades of the nineteenth century, their reforms accelerated both the erosion of the estates system and the process of centralized and rationalized state building. Although such reform programs gradually "emancipated" the middle classes and the peasantry from some of the worst restrictions they had faced in the eighteenth century, the centrality of state administration to the modernization process had the significant and not unintended effect of shielding traditional aristocratic authority and privileges through the rational mechanisms of a modern state bureaucracy (Blackbourn 1991: 4–5; Breuilly 1992: 10; Sheehan 1992: 51–52).

As Nipperdey notes, administrative and judiciary powers were gradually transferred from the aristocracy to the state from 1815 to 1848 (1983: 256) just as the nobility solidified their control over the higher ranks of state administration. German statecraft in the nineteenth century allowed the German aristocracy to exercise control over German society through modern technologies of administration, militarization, and standardization (Wehler 1989: 148). While the uninterrupted and unadulterated character of this control is open to question (see Blackbourn and Eley 1984), it is certainly fair to say that, via the ranks of officialdom, aristocratic families occupied a decisive presence within the political elite of German society until the First World War (Kaelble 1988: 111). The institutionalization of *Bildung* after the Prussian General Code of 1794 (including the *Gymnasium* system of secondary schools and reformed universities) assured state control over the economy of spiritual distinction that otherwise could have constituted a threat to aristocratic supervision over processes of elite social reproduction (see Ringer 1969: 23; Ziolkowski 1990).

Still, from the point of view of *Gebildeten* in the early nineteenth century, at a time of rising social status, cultural influence, and expanding presence in state administration, it is not difficult to imagine how their cultivation as an ennobled caste among the middle classes would contribute to a general sense of agency and mission with regard to national *Bildung*. *Gebildeten* did not, in fact, consider themselves subordinates in the process of state formation during this period. Many philosophers and literati writing from the 1790s to the 1810s clearly imagined themselves to be the spiritual vanguard of a process of social modernization. Likewise, as Nipperdey writes, nonnoble civil servants experienced themselves with a kind of world-historical agency: "The civil servants felt as though they were a new aristocracy of intellect, expertise and achievement—above all in opposition to the old feudal order, but also in opposition to the commercial, industrial bourgeoisie and to 'demagogic' and popular movements: with respect to the *Volk*, the civil servants stylized themselves with a well-meaning paternalism" (1983: 322).

The image of the man of *Bildung* as paternal culture bearer for the nation epitomizes the positive dialectical knowledge of national Germanness that *Gebildeten* articulated during this period. Germanness was often depicted as *in statu nascendi*, as coming into a being that exterior circumstance had long denied it (see Giesen 1998; Ziolkowski 1990). As the *Bildungsbürgertum* attained a level of social coherence, status, and influence previously unknown to them, their social imagination of Germanness symmetrically flourished with dialectical under- and overtones of becoming and harmonious actualization.

Nowhere else in nineteenth-century Europe did an intellectual cultural elite acquire both as strong a sense of their corporate identity and as certain a knowledge of their mission in the process of national formation as the *Bildungsbürgertum* did (1) through their cultivation as an ennobled caste fusing *Wissenschaft* to the practice of administration and (2) through their mediating presence between the aristocracy and other middle-class strata. These are social-structural conditions that help to explain the intuitiveness of the culture-bearer narrative and the amplification of positive dialectical social knowledge as features of the social phenomenology of the *Bildungsbürgertum*. In turn, one might note, *Gebildeten*'s codification and expression of their social phenomenology as dialectical ontology are what allow scholars like Kocka and Giesen to retrospectively declare the *Bildungsbürgertum* the "carrier group" of bourgeois modernization in Central Europe, as though what the *Gebildeten* phenomenologically encountered as inevitable at the turn of the nineteenth century was actually teleological.

The University of *Wissenschaft*
Imagined as the Nursery of the Nation

We gain a more precise sense of the dialectical character of the *Gebildeten* "mission" when we look at their programs of social reform in more detail. One of the most important of these programs in the early nineteenth century (from their point of view) was university reform and the constitution of a modern national university. The university became a powerful locus of critical attention for *Gebildeten* in the late eighteenth century as they promoted the ethics of enlightened *Wissenschaft* (science, knowledge). They depicted these ethics in opposition to the majority of German universities, which still upheld the late-medieval tradition of *universitas* as an ecclesiastical institution dominated by scholastic methodology and a theological faculty. An earlier wave of university reform in German-speaking Central Europe had already taken place over a hundred years earlier with the founding of new universities with more pragmatically oriented curricula at Halle (1694) and Göttingen (1737). Overall, however, this first reform "movement" constituted, from an institutional perspective, less a coordinated program than a series of idiosyncratic experiments that had little impact on the educational practices of the majority of universities in Central Europe. As Ziolkowski writes, "By the end of the last decade of the [eighteenth] century many serious reformers were calling for the abolishment of universities, which were regarded as relics of past monastic life and utterly unsuited for present realities, while the very title of 'professor' had become a cue for ridicule" (1990: 227).

In 1807, in view of the Napoleonic occupation of Germany and spurred by a delegation of professors from the suspended University of Halle, King Friedrich Wilhelm III commissioned plans for a new central university in Berlin. Even before the reluctant Wilhelm von Humboldt was enjoined to administer the new university's formation, a great deal of excitement spread throughout intellectual networks both inside and outside Prussia that the true spirit and culture of the nation would be brought to fruition with the first truly modern and enlightened university in and for Deutschland. Proposals for the university were solicited from influential scholars like Fichte and the philologist Friedrich August Wolf, while others, like Friedrich Schleiermacher (1956), published unsolicited treatises on the subject of universities that were widely read and discussed among *Gebildeten.* These proposals differed substantially in their particular visions of how to constitute a university that was both "modern" and "German," yet all conceptualized the reformed university as a key threshold in national *Bildung* owing to its fusion of the ethics of *Wissenschaft* with the power of the state (Ziolkowski 1990: 286–308; McClelland 1980).

The reformers who turned their attention to the University of Berlin argued for the maintenance and reform of the university *specifically as an institution of nation building.* Universities were imagined to be capable of serving both as an example for the nation (in their epistemic orientation to the universal and absolute) and as a vehicle for the production and harmonization of the nation through the pedagogy of citizens.

Schleiermacher proposed, as did most of the self-identifying philosophers among the reformers, that the philosophical faculty should constitute the center of the new university and therefore of the nation: "In it alone the whole natural organization of knowledge is contained—philosophy in its purely transcendental aspect as well as in its scientific and historical aspects" (1956: 259; Ziolkowski 1990: 289). Philosophy (in its literal sense of "the love of wisdom") was identified as the soul of *Bildung*. Any true person of *Wissenschaft* would be by definition a philosopher in the manner of his or her orientation to the pursuit of knowledge. Following Kant's *Der Streit der Fakultäten* (1798), reformers imagined a new role for the philosophical faculty, which had traditionally been a lower faculty offering basic and even remedial education to students before they moved on to one of the higher faculties of theology, law, or medicine. Schelling, for example, defined the proper activity of the philosopher as the search for primordial knowledge (*Urwissen*), by which he meant the fundamental unity of knowledge often obscured by the capacious erudition of actual knowledge (*reale Wissen*). The other faculties (medicine, law, theology) were said to be compromised by their orientation to external, worldly necessities rather than to the inner, philosophical imperative of *Wissenschaft*.

With the fusion of the university to state administration, reformers imagined that the entire German *Volk* (people) could be schooled in the ethics and vocation of *Wissenschaft*. This is the essence of Fichte's proposal for the University of Berlin, "Deduzierter Plan einer in Berlin zu errichtenden höheren Lehranstalt" (1956), that he submitted to the king's cabinet chief Karl Friedrich Beyme in 1807. Ziolkowski writes that Fichte's plan "was too radical in its expectations to provide the basis for administrative action," but in its radicality, Fichte's proposal articulates the social vision of the culture bearer in a particularly vivid way.

Fichte begins by contrasting *Wissenschaft* itself, as a creative and progressive mode of knowledge formation characterized by the use of reason (*Verstand*), with the "simple repetition" characteristic of earlier academicism (1956: 128) and of mechanical learning (*mechanischen Erlernen*) (130). Fichte repeatedly describes the adherent of *Wissenschaft* as an artist (*Künstler*) of learning, and he envisages the new higher educational institution as "*eine Schule der Kunst des wissenschaftlichen Verstandesgebrauche*" (a school of the art of the *wissenschaftlich* use of the intellect) (131). Such artists are not abundant among the "common mass of the *Bürgertum*" (139), who instead train their children to approach their lives and education equally as *Broterwerb* (as a means of supporting themselves), viewing knowledge (*Wissen*) as a luxury rather than as an essential element of their being. This is because the ennobled spirits (*veredelten Geiste*) required to transcend this immersion in and service to the profane dimension of life can be fostered only "through a life of *Wissenschaft*" (140). Yet Fichte counsels that the true scholar should not therefore disdain the normal *Bürger;* rather, he should adopt a paternal and pedagogical relationship toward him (141). For it is the *geistiges Zusammenleben* (spiritual life-together) that this new institution of higher education will make possible that will create a new class of scholars, who will in turn provide "the first general school of the *Volk* . . . and for the nation" (143).

It is incumbent upon the educated estate of society, according to Fichte, to orient itself to the historical mission of transmitting the totality and systematicity of *Wissenschaft* to the noneducated estate (the *Volk*), thus cultivating a nation in its image. In order to produce a cultivated national totality, however, Fichte reasons, the reformed university will have to be organized as a "*sorgfältig gepflegte Baumschule*" (a carefully cultivated nursery) (1956: 166) where future educators of the people (*Volkslehrer*) can be culled from the "wild" forest of their profane brethren, ordered as a brotherhood (*Korps*), and supported by the state free from the profane distractions like managing money and provisioning their own bodily nourishment. In turn, once sanctified as doctors of philosophy, these students must have first claim on all administrative positions, for the state, in Fichte's vision, requires the spiritual orientation of philosophically endowed scholars in order to ennoble the scope and practice of administration itself. Fichte derides provinciality as an impediment to both knowledge and administration—thankfully, the ennobled graduates will not see themselves as Prussians or Bavarians or Saxons but rather recognize themselves in their national totality and act accordingly in the translocal interests of the fatherland. Once securely in possession of the state, the *Volkslehrer* can complete the process, upon which Fichte does not comment in any specificity, of forming the *Volk* as *Nation* (217).

Although self-consciously revolutionary in its proposal for the organization of the university as a nursery for the nation, the central elements of Fichte's vision resonate in the more moderate, pragmatic, and ultimately administratively influential writings of Schleiermacher and Wilhelm von Humboldt as well. The status of *Wissenschaft* as a practice with potentially revolutionary consequences for German state and society is, for example, echoed in von Humboldt's assertion that supporting *Wissenschaft* was of vital significance for the state "so that no action of the state is simply mechanical" (1956: 379). Von Humboldt reasoned that a central commitment to *Wissenschaft* would sanctify the state as an institution dedicated to the "intellectual national character of the Germans" (379). For the same reason, Humboldt disdained the higher educational model of the (French) academy of sciences as lacking the essential connection to society that the *wissenschaftliche* orientation to knowledge brought into being through its fusion of research and pedagogy.

Schleiermacher argued, albeit more equivocally than Fichte, that the university had a deep reciprocal relationship to the fatherland: *Wissenschaft* could not flourish in its natural totality without sponsorship by the state, but the state likewise required *Wissenschaft* because it represented the unity of knowledge within a single language (*Sprache*). Schleiermacher, like Fichte, derides German vernacularity and asserts instead the fundamental unity of a German language-nation-territory under the rubric of the German fatherland (*deutsches Vaterland*). He then contrasts this "natural" relationship of a single state to a single language area with the "unnatural" contemporary German situation of numerous, jealously competing states fighting for sovereignty (1956: 227). Although these petty political entities scorn *Wissenschaft* for its idealistic orientation, Schleiermacher intimates that, in fact, their true jealousy is toward its natural unity. The process of national *Bildung* will require state administration to imitate the systematicity and totality of *Wissenschaft* itself. Ziolkowski writes that Schleiermacher's pamphlet was responsible for publicizing to a wide audience a model of the university that had first been outlined by Schiller and Schelling in the 1790s at the University of Jena. Ziolkowski argues that the pamphlet was responsible for shifting elite public opinion away from long-standing rationalist prejudices against universities and toward "the belief in the university as an institution combining all the faculties and unified by a central faculty of philosophy professing an 'encyclopedic' approach to knowledge" (1990: 290).

Yet it was Fichte's more radical vision of the university that resonated among a younger generation of *Gebildeten* politicized as patriots and "nationalists" in the context of the Napoleonic Wars. They embraced the idea of the university of *Wissenschaft* less in the sense of *Wissenschaft* as a self-fulfilling vocation than in its capacity for assisting the state in the *Bildung* of the nation. In the second number of the *Berliner Abendblätter* in October 1810, Adam Müller wrote that the university was "not being founded as a mere feast for the scientific *gourmands* of Europe" but rather in service to the fatherland and that the university's immediate purpose was the *Bildung* of a class of civil servants who would be useful to the state (in Ziolkowski 1990: 299–300). Fichte was appointed the first rector of the University of Berlin by von Humboldt and in 1811 lectured passionately in his first public address that the university was "the visible representation of the immortality of our race in that it permits nothing truly essential to perish" (Ziolkowski 1990: 304). Fichte saw no essential contradiction between the culture of the university and that of the rational, enlightened Prussian state;

rather, he saw the real threat to academic freedom coming from those "wild" students who were incapable of embracing their true vocation and the true mission of the university and who instead spent their time drinking and dueling (Ziolkowski 1990: 305). Fichte resigned as rector only four months after his address, in protest of a case of anti-Semitic student dueling tolerated by the faculty senate (which included Schleiermacher among its members).

Indeed, the ideal University of Berlin was viewed by many, in true dialectical fashion, to be "in ruins" from its moment of actualization (see Readings 1996), entangled in profane politics by the same forces of scholarly specialization and political intrigue against which Fichte and others had written with such fury. The faculties were in tension with one another over the distribution of power and resources from even before the inauguration of the university, driving von Humboldt to write in desperation to his wife in 1810 that scholars were the "most unruly and least-easily satisfied class of mortals" (in Ziolkowski 1990: 302). The professoriate as a whole remained in tension with students, who, behaving much as they always had, proved unwilling or incapable of embracing the revolutionary role of *Volkslehrer* that Fichte imagined for them. And exterior political life intruded with a vengeance in the form of the War of Liberation in 1813, drawing students and professors away to patriotic causes. As students and professors returned after Napoleon's defeat, Romantic discourse on the revolutionary potential of the university was less common and more muted.

Still, in 1818, during his own inaugural address at the University of Berlin, Hegel both recognized the setbacks to the reformers' plans for the university and reaffirmed his own faith that philosophy remained emblematic of the intellectual and national character of the Germans (Ziolkowski 1990: 308; Hegel 1997: 47). Hegel referred to a "spirit of youth" in describing a philosophical Deutschland entering into its phase of national *Bildung*, "for this is the beautiful time of life that has not yet been caught in the *System* of the narrow purposes of need and which is still capable of the freedom of disinterested *wissenschaftliche* activity" (1997: 48).

From Hegel to Marx: Shifting
Dialectical Philosophies of History

In the philosophical activity of academic culture during this period one finds some of the most apt and lasting formulations of the dialectical social knowledge of *Gebildeten*. Hegel himself, for example, contributed greatly to codifying the social imagination of his caste as dialectical ontology, a contribution that was duly recognized in the broad resonance of Hegelian philosophy in German academic culture in the 1820s and 1830s (Toews 1980: 71–94).

In Hegel's own words, philosophy is always a child of its time (1991: 21–22) and his conceptualization of the dialectic is no exception. Hegel argued that the dialectic was something more than what Greek philosophers had made of it: "The moving principle of the concept, which not only dissolves the particularizations of the universal but also produces them, is what I call *dialectic.*" "This dialectic, then, is not an *external* activity of subjective thought, but the *very soul* of the content which puts forth its branches and fruit organically" (1991: 59–60). Hegel emphasized that the dialectic was not solely a conceptual device or method; rather, it represented an ontohistorical, divine principle of extension and actualization that unfolded, in part, through conceptual devices and methods.

Hegel's entire philosophy of history indeed hinges on a sense of positive dialectical formation from internal potentiality into external actuality. The divine Idea explores its potentiality and realizes itself in the world through the medium of its world-spirit. The activity of the world-spirit in turn produces form in ever-more-complex systems of organic actuality. This process of organic becoming is shot through with tension at every turn, as the forming spirit confronts already-existing forms-in-the-world, cancels or incorporates them, and evolves new, higher manifestations. Hegel explained that organic actualities, or *Gestalten* (forms, manifestations), encompassing everything from natural to cultural to political order, enjoy a duration in the world while gradually losing the sanctifying presence of spirit until they enter into a state of tensionless formality that Hegel termed *Gewohnheit* (habit) (1986: 100). Yet the apparent endpoint of spiritless formality was always the moment of rebirth for Hegel, the moment at which *Geist* began to extend itself once again. If, as Hegel noted, we are sometimes given to "mourn the passing of once vigorous and flourishing life," then we must also recall that "ruin is at the same time emergence of a new life" and that "the Spirit, devouring its worldly envelope . . . , emerges from [it] exalted, transfigured, a purer Spirit" (1953: 88–89).

Hegel's philosophy of history provided a seductive dialectics of the contemporary for German intellectuals in the 1820s and 1830s. For example, he positioned *die Germanen*[3] as exemplifying the highest realization yet of

3. "*Die Germanen*" might best be translated in this context as "the Christian, Germanic peoples of Northern Europe." *Die Deutschen* (the Germans) were a subset of *die Germanen*. This is an important clarification for assessing Hegel's sense of Germanness in his philosophy of history. His argument concerning *die Germanen* was therefore less an ethnic-nationalistic characterization of Deutschland than a distinction between Anglo-Saxon and Latinate peoples, as Hegel construed the French.

the concept of freedom in history (1986: 539–40) and projected the modern rational state as the vehicle for the highest reconciliation of individual and collectivity. Although Hegel's rational state was not the existing Prussian state (as is sometimes accused), Hegel's state bore many similarities to the reformed Prussian state envisioned but never fully realized by reformers like Hardenburg, Stein, and von Humboldt. It was, to be sure, consonant with the ideal of the *Kulturstaat* that Fichte and others argued was emerging on-tohistorically from the inner spiritual unity of *Kultur.* As Hegel wrote in his lectures on the *Philosophy of Right,* it was inevitable that the ethical substance of a *Volk* (in other words, its *Kultur* in the post-Napoleonic sense) would develop dialectically toward formalization as a state (§349; 1991: 375). Hegel articulated *Gebildeten* social phenomenology in a transcendental id-iom, removing human agency and politics from the process of modern state formation (and, of course, from the process of articulating philosophy and teleology). Instead, Hegel's philosophy of history theorized and theologized the evolution of the nation-state as a phenomenon of the divine and rational Idea of freedom realizing its potentiality in the world.

The realization of the Idea was, of course, no simple process. It unfolded in stages of *Geist* and *Gewohnheit,* at every phase rich in ontohistorical tension between forces of creation and duration. Where negativity entered Hegel's model of history (see, e.g., his discussion of "negative freedom"; 1991: 37–40), however, it always entered as a phase of cancellation en route to a higher, positive synthesis. A negative dialectical power that worked from without to within to pervert or counteract the creative, rational power of *Geist* extending from within to without would have been the antithesis of Hegel's entire philosophy of history. And, in a sense, it was.

At the height of its resonance in Prussian intellectual culture, Hegelian philosophy confirmed the positive dialectical temporality and cultural agency that *Bildungsbürger* sensed pervading their lives and labors. Yet, as times and fortunes began to change for the *Bildungsbürgertum,* the dialec-tical disposition of its philosophers became, if no less teleological in their certainty of the relentlessness of historical formation, more pessimistic in their evaluation of the relationship between spirit and form. By the 1830s and 1840s, what was understood as Hegel's underestimation of (or apologet-ics for) the negative dialectical agency of actually existing social and political order became a key point of departure and contention for the post-Hegelian critics of German modernization, who mushroomed on the margins of the mainstream *Bildungsbürgertum* (see Breckman 1999).

For these intellectuals, *Gestaltung* (formation) constituted not the punc-tuation of the positive dialectic of historical becoming but rather what I have described in the introduction as a negative companion principle to *Bildung*, or *Prägung* (formation from without to within). Post-Hegelian critics often described a progressive corruption of *Geist* by external form, a negative dialectics that could be identified in processes like the spread and intensification of industry and in administrative overformalization. Most importantly, forms-in-the-world were no longer conceived to be the inert *Mittel* (means) that Hegel had depicted. *Gebildeten* critics of capitalism's translocal organization of commerce and production and of the state's apparatus of bureaucratic *Macht* (power) understood these *Systeme* not as pure media of sublation but rather as counterfeit exterior orders with powers of their own that tended to deform and to constrain human spiritual power.

One of the most talented and ultimately influential of Hegel's critics was Karl Marx. Marx's reformulation of the Hegelian dialectic of history provides a wonderful glimpse of the shifting ratio of positive dialectical to negative dialectical intuition and knowledge among the *Bildungsbürgertum* in the mid–nineteenth century.[4] Marx's distinction of a positive dialectical process of "objectification" (*Vergegenständlichung*) from a negative dialectical process of "alienation" (*Entfremdung*) proved his crucial correction to Hegel's philosophy of history (1971: 561). Like Hegel, Marx saw the production of objective forms as the central dynamic of both ontology and epistemology. But Marx located the agency of objectification in human practice (*Arbeit, Tätigkeit*) rather than in the unfolding of a transcendental Idea. Remaining within a Hegelian framework of world-historical becoming, Marx theorized that man would eventually become the "result of his own work" (1967a: 321). Through his historical *Arbeit* (activity, work, practice, labor) man would achieve his ideal form, and natural social being, as the unmediated extension of his vital inner energy. This is the process of "objectification" contrasted in the *Economic and Philosophic Manuscripts of 1844* to "estranged labor" (Marx and Engels 1978: 71; see also Marx 1971). Marx contrasted the potential, self-fulfilling character of human activity as *Bildung* to the externally imposed and directed character of activity under contemporary conditions of private property and wage labor,

4. As a law student at the University of Berlin in the 1830s, the young Marx absorbed the Hegelianism that was so much a part of Prussian university culture and intellectual culture as a whole (Berlin 1963; Mah 1986). But he confronted the limits of Hegelian idealism in the institutionalized anti-Semitism that prevented him from either an academic or a civil service career and in the increasing state suppression of radical Hegelians more generally (Breckman 1999: 272). Moving into radical politics and journalism, Marx came to contrast his humanistic historical materialism to Hegelian idealism and the mechanistic authoritarianism of the Prussian state, which he increasingly regarded as two sides of the same coin.

[Under free human production] my labor would be a *free manifestation of life* and an *enjoyment* of *life*. Under the presupposition of private property it is an *externalization of life* because I work *in order to live* and provide for myself the *means* of living. Working *is not* living.

Furthermore, in my labor the *particularity* of my individuality would be affirmed because my *individual* life is affirmed. Labor then would be *true, active property*. Under the presupposition of private property my individuality is externalized to the point where I *hate* this *activity* and where it is a *torment* to me. Rather it is then only the *semblance* of an activity, only a *forced* activity, imposed upon me only by *external* and accidental necessity and *not* by an *internal* and *determined* necessity.

My labor can appear in my object only according to its nature; it cannot appear as something *different* from itself. My labor, therefore, is manifested as the objective, sensuous, perceptible, and indubitable expression of my *self-loss* and my *powerlessness*. (1967b: 281–82)

Marx argued that private property and the generalization of wage labor permitted abstract, exterior imperatives (like the accumulation of capital) to dominate natural, "free" human production, making this production only the "semblance of an activity" in terms of its contribution to human self-realization. "Capital" was Marx's core trope for this negative dialectical condition of contemporary human activity, representing human labor power congealed into seemingly autonomous forms that could then be extracted away from their creators by a *System* of social production. Capitalism, in Marx's analysis, was a social order defined by the abstraction and accumulation of human labor power through the institution of wage labor, an institution that radically narrowed the heterogeneous nature of human activity in order to make it more formally productive and responsive to the demands of the *System* of production as a whole. The systemic dynamic of capitalism, according to Marx, demanded ever-increasing surpluses of formalized human labor power (see Postone 1996). This meant the increasing recruitment of human beings to wage labor and the increasing exploitation of those already under its power. In its dialectical essence, Marx's capitalism was a social dynamic that propelled formalization for-its-own-sake, making human beings slaves to their own natural propensity for objectification through *Arbeit*.

Humanity's historical solution to the slavery of capitalism could only come, theorized Marx, through the collective recognition of the wage-laboring class (the proletariat) of their own unity and agency to seize political, economic, and cultural hegemony away from the class of capitalists and to thus complete humanity's evolution into a self-aware, global, classless society. This final historical phase of communism—which Marx famously described in such little detail—would maintain the apparatus of production that capitalism had built yet would reorient it to the satisfaction of human needs, including principally the need to replace wage labor with opportunities for creative self-realizing activity (along the lines of the famous "hunt in the morning, fish in the afternoon" parable from *The German Ideology*).

On the one hand, Marx's model of history seems thoroughly negative dialectical in its critique of the enslavement of human spirit and activity by the formalizing, externalizing *System* of capital. On the other, the place of communism in Marx's philosophy suggests a horizon of positive dialectical knowledge. Under communism, Marx promised, *all* human beings would, for the first time in human history, be able to recover their polymorphous productivity, to realize themselves fully as objects of their own labor, and to recognize themselves in their common species being as "humanity." By transcending alienation, the *Prägung* of capital would be dispelled and *Bildung* restored to history. In this way, the negative dialectical character of capitalism can be read as belonging to a deeper positive dialectic of world history insofar as capitalism produces, *inevitably* according to Marx, the requisite social conditions for human self-realization under communism by bringing all humanity together for the first time in human history into a single productive apparatus. Unlike the writings of later social theorists like Max Weber, for whom a negative dialectic of rationalization was the dominant logic of world history, Marx's writings in the 1840s surge with an exuberant sense of the possibility of seizing history away from the powers that were deforming it. Within the fierceness of their criticism of capitalism, early socialists ultimately held forth a vision of capitalism's transience, of the possibility of restoring a positive dialectic to history through collective revolutionary intervention (see chapter 3).

The Social Transformation of the *Bildungsbürgertum* and the Amplification of Negative Dialectical Knowledge

If we take the spread of criticism of capitalism and the state as a sign of a broader dampening of positive dialectical social knowledge in German intellectual culture, how might we account for this shift? I will discuss three factors that help explain, first, the proliferation of negative dialectical knowledge on the margins of German intellectual culture and, later, by the end of the long nineteenth century, the increasing saturation of the centers of intellectual culture (especially academic culture) with negative dialectical knowledge of Germanness and modernity. The first factor is the stalling of middle-class political influence in the wake of the end of the political reform movement of the first decades of the nineteenth century, upon which the great hope of the *Kulturstaat* had been predicated. A second factor is the internal shift in the social organization of the *Bildungsbürgertum* from a relatively undifferentiated "estate of letters" with a shared ideal of *Wissenschaft* to an intellectual culture whose discourse communities were often isolated from one another by professional institutions and specialized languages. The third factor is the rise in social status and political influence of the *Besitzbürgertum* as a result of the explosive second stage of industrialization in Germany in the last quarter of the nineteenth century, which culminated in an alliance of *Besitzbürger* and aristocratic interests that Blackbourn and Eley describe as defining the political culture of Wilhelmine Germany (1984).

In the first two decades of the nineteenth century, nonnoble *Gebildeten* enjoyed a social phenomenology of rising social and political influence that was in no small part indebted to the presence of the political reform movement to deconstruct certain elements of the estates system and to "modernize" state administration. As we saw above, for example, the political decision taken by the modernizers in 1807 to found a new University of Berlin inspired great excitement and expectation among *Gebildeten.* Both moderates and radicals fantasized a central place for the university in the state and predicted that an enlightened administrative caste trained in the *Wissenschaft* of the university would define and realize the future of Deutschland. It was quite plausible to imagine at this moment that the state would become an instrument for the realization of universal freedom and national *Bildung* via the mediation of *Gebildeten.* After all, this is precisely what political philosophers like Fichte and Hegel asserted was the fate of Germany in the unfolding logic of world history. The final defeat of France in 1815 boded well, seeming to remove the most serious exterior threat to the realization of Deutschland.

After 1819, however, the horizon began to cloud. Prussian reformers were swept from office, and their successors became increasingly concerned with suppressing political radicalism in university culture, which, although it had proved valuable for the anti-Napoleonic cause, seemed a danger to the aristocratic authoritarian state in the reconstruction period. Metternich's Karlsbad Decrees of 1819 extended regulative and repressive state control over university culture, focusing particularly upon censoring and limiting student radicalism and liberalism. The decrees signaled the codification of state control over modernized German universities, and it slowly dawned upon *Gebildeten* that the state would not become an extension of the university but rather that the university would become a functional element within the state. Finally, the decrees made explicit the fragility of the ideal of "academic freedom" that had been heralded with such certainty only a decade before and "introduced an element of intimidation into the universities that conflicted with the hopes of the neo-humanists for complete liberty" (McClelland 1980: 147).

Although by no means a decisive act in themselves for the stalling of middle-class social elevation and political influence, the Karlsbad Decrees signaled the retardation of further social and political reforms that were essential to the social imagination and realization of the *Kulturstaat*. It is unsurprising therefore that a more widespread intuition of and discourse on the compromise of the true values and purpose of *Kultur* by the state began to develop among *Gebildeten*, particularly among those on the margins of intellectual culture, that is, outside the primary networks of university culture and the civil service, where faith in the Hegelian vision of the rational state remained stronger.

In the 1830s and 1840s, more ambivalent signs emerged for the *Bildungsbürgertum* about their future. On the positive side, the expansion of state administrations throughout Central Europe guaranteed some constituencies in the *Bildungsbürgertum* a significant, if subaltern, presence in the political elite via officialdom. Likewise, the interstratal conviviality and *Kultur* orientation of voluntary associations continued to ensure the liminal significance of *Gebildeten* and their arts to languages and knowledges of Germanness circulating among the social elite. On the negative side, the ranks within and social specialization of *Gebildeten* were increasing, and the numbers of underemployed, low-status intellectuals operating on the margins of the state increased proportionally. University enrollments tripled between 1805–10 and 1830, and although state funding for universities increased, so did state regulation and intervention (McClelland 1980: 148–49). Still, as late as 1848, it was quite possible for nonnoble *Gebildeten*, both moderate and radical, to imagine themselves poised on the verge of seizing decisive political influence away from the aristocracy. As Fritz Ringer writes, "Among the 830 deputies at the Frankfurt Assembly of 1848, at least 550 were graduates of universities. Almost 20 percent of the representatives were professors, scholars, or secondary teachers; another 35 percent were administrative or judicial officials; nearly 17 percent were lawyers; 13 percent were theologians and clergymen, municipal officials, doctors, military officers, and writers" (1969: 44). The *Bildungsbürgertum* were dominant in the assembly by comparison to commercial and industrial middle-class strata, who furnished less than 7 percent of the deputies.

But, in the end, the much-anticipated "revolution" of 1848 was deeply disappointing since the aristocracy proved it had no intention of ceding administrative control through significant parliamentary reforms. Although even after 1848 civil servants continued to understand themselves as a sanctifying spirit within the power structures of the bureaucratic state (see von Harnack 1942), their subaltern status was increasingly institutionalized via the continued dominance of the lower aristocracy in leadership positions. "In Prussia, the aristocracy dominated all levels of government, accounting for 62 percent of the provincial governors, 73 percent of the district superintendents, and 62 percent of the county commissioners in 1888–1891" (Wuthnow 1989: 393). In the state-affiliated *Bildungsbürgertum,* self-consciousness of their social and political importance did remain relatively high, precisely because of the state's monopoly over higher education and professional reproduction (Blackbourn 1998: 209–10). But this sense of self-importance was increasingly wedded to conservative fears about a further expansion of social democratic institutions and equality before the law (fears of suffrage law reform that would democratically enfranchise local or regional elections, women's rights, and so on). Fritz Ringer describes the "mandarin" mentality of the professoriate at the end of the nineteenth century as typified by their sense of social entitlement and privilege and by their conservatism and strong disaffection for social and cultural modernization (1969: 253–69).

The political culture of German-speaking Central Europe developed in a direction after 1848 that never again allowed the *Bildungsbürgertum* to recapture the sense of agency and euphoria in national *Bildung* that they had sensed before 1819. The bourgeois-liberal political parties that became more active in their opposition to Prussian oligarchy in concert with the first moderate phase of industrial expansion in German-speaking Central Europe in the 1850s and 1860s (Sheehan 1989: 731–47) found themselves consistently opposed and undermined by aristocratic interests in state administrations (Wuthnow 1989: 398–99). Gordon Craig writes that the "basic purpose" of the constitution of the first unified German nation-state, composed by Otto von Bismarck in 1871, "was to create the institutions for a national state that would be able to compete effectively with the most powerful of its neighbours, without sacrificing, or even limiting, the aristocratic-monarchical order of the pre-national period" (1978: 39). Nonnoble political interests were structurally restricted by Bismarck's constitution since the

parliamentary body, the Reichstag, had few powers of initiative of its own
and mostly reacted to the program of the chancellor, who was appointed directly by the king (Craig 1978: 44–47). As Margaret Anderson has aptly put
it, Germany had a weak government but a strong state (2000: 413). Although
some *Gebildeten* participated in electoral politics, particularly in the Progressive and National-Liberal parties (Sperber 1997), many of the most privileged *Bildungsbürger* regarded the political arena as a morass of selfish and
unenlightened interests categorically distinct from the inner flames of *Geist*
and *Kultur*. In this light, Thomas Mann's epigraphic "typical German" looks
more and more the quintessential member of the scholarly mandarinate,
voicing his soulful inwardness (*Innerlichkeit*) against the exterior presence
of modern politics and society deemed both pernicious and ephemeral.

Meanwhile, the *Bildungsbürgertum* experienced significant changes in
the social organization of knowledge making during the latter half of the
nineteenth century. As noted above, the networks of *Gebildeten* expanded,
diversified, and specialized in the second half of the nineteenth century. One
of the most important conditions of diversification and specialization was
the development of professional networks into associations that began to
gradually establish themselves as institutions that were semiautonomous
of state control. Professions like law and medicine, which had long been
regulated by German states to cultivate them as functional elements of
civil administration (John 1991; Weindling 1991), began to win rights of autonomous determination after 1871 (Jarausch 1990: 8–22; Wehler 1987: 226–
38). The professionalization of the *Bildungsbürgertum* was by no means
teleological but rather incremental, uneven, and itself a matter of contemporary essentialization. For journalists, it took well into the first decade of
the twentieth century for their mode of specialized intellectual practice to
develop the institutional features of "a profession," and even then it was
not recognized as a legitimate "vocation" by most *Bildungsbürger*. Yet it
was true that the social imagination of the *Bildungsbürgertum* as a relatively undifferentiated "estate of letters" bound together by a common epistemic foundation and ethics of *Wissenschaft* was more difficult to sustain
in the face of increasingly salient professional identities, domains of expertise, and social networks and institutions. The "estate of letters" continued
to be held forth as a normative ideal, but the experiential reality of more
specialized intellectual practices and discourse challenged it at every turn.
Professionalism also transformed older forms of associationalism over the
last third of the nineteenth century as professional associations and their
cultures of expertise became powerful forces in intellectual life (Jarausch
1982: 259). Formerly generalist social clubs increasingly became forums for

the exchange of technical professional knowledge, as high-cultural activities were now more often the province of state-funded institutions supporting the arts (Sobania 1996: 189).

The professionalization and specialization of knowledge making were most acutely felt within university culture. Ringer describes how German academic culture of the late nineteenth century was saturated with pessimistic assessments of the decline of *Wissenschaft* into a hive of seemingly incommensurable expert knowledges: "They spoke of a decline in the vitality of their intellectual traditions, a loss of meaning and relevance. . . . They began to suspect that universities had been neglecting their proper function of spiritual leadership, that mandarin culture had been forsaken by its guardians as well as by the rest of German society" (Ringer 1969: 253). In the academics' social imagination, the fate of *Wissenschaft* and the fate of the nation were so entirely interwoven that signs of crisis in the former were often taken to reflect crises of the latter. Ringer cites the popular philosopher Rudolf Eucken lamenting "a sinking of life into the profane, the secular, the vulgar. And all that amidst remarkable progress at the periphery of life, amidst an amazing virtuosity in technical achievements. . . . We find ourselves involved in a serious intellectual and spiritual crisis, which we are unable to master" (254). Eucken's designation of failed "mastery" as the locus of crisis is telling. "In a curious way," Ringer concludes, "the whole theory of cultural decadence was a projection of the intellectual's personal fears and doubts upon the rest of society" (267). Ringer describes the anxieties of academic humanists that their influence upon the nation was waning at the end of the long nineteenth century, that modernity was slipping beyond their control. Likewise, he details the many initiatives, both radical and moderate, they proposed for restoring the university and the scholar to what was now viewed as their traditional, proper role as culture bearers of the nation (269–304).

One of the reasons that German academics sensed themselves victim to exterior pressures and powers was the heterogeneous abundance of knowledge production in German public culture that accompanied the development of a mass publishing industry oriented toward an expanded and differentiated literate audience. They defined the category "mass culture" (*Massenkultur*) precisely in opposition to their own sensibilities of artisanal intellectual productivity and audience (see McClelland 1980: 180 on the guildlike character of academic knowledge making).[5]

---

5. It is striking that foreign visitors, such as the young American student James Morgan Hart, who attended several universities in Germany in the 1860s and 1870s, often combined glowing

Mass culture signaled an inversion of the harmonious unity of *Wissenschaft:* its very diversity, expansiveness, and seemingly predatory character as a "culture industry" (to use Horkheimer and Adorno's phrase) was what revolted academics. Mass culture lacked depth and "groundedness" (*Gründlichkeit*) they insisted; it was wholly devoted to the formality of sales and the superficiality of entertainment. Heinrich von Treitschke, the noted historian and Prussian nationalist, expressed these fears pointedly in an address at the University of Berlin in 1895:

> the wider culture spreads, the more shallow it becomes: the thoughtfulness of the ancient world is despised; only that which serves the aims of the immediate future seems still important. When everyone gives his opinion about everything, according to the newspaper and the encyclopedia, there original mental power becomes rare, and with the fine courage of ignorance, which marks an independent mind. *Wissenschaft,* which, once descending too deep, sought to fathom the inscrutable, loses itself in expansion, and only isolated pines of original thought tower above the low undergrowth of collections of memoranda. (1915: 222)

In narrating themselves as isolated guardians of true *Kultur* towering over the abundant undergrowth of mass culture, academics like Treitschke exemplified the phenomenological estrangement of artisanal knowledge makers from the increasingly mediated production and circulation of knowledge represented by new epistemic industries like advertising, mass-market publishing, and partisan political culture.

But there were also signs of crisis for humanistic academics closer to home in the transforming social production of knowledge within the university itself. The guildlike organization of knowledge production within research universities was strained by a second period of rapidly expanding student enrollments beginning in the 1870s: average university enrollments rose from about 600 in 1870 to close to 3,000 in the prewar years (Jarausch 1982: 31). Yet, concomitantly, the proportion of high-status *ordinarius* professors (the social core of the academic professoriate) declined

---

praise of both the deep vocational character of German academic life and its level of professionalization. Unlike Hart's experience of American intellectual life, it was unthinkable that a German professor would have practiced any other profession during his lifetime: "I was made to feel that a German university, however humble, is a world in and for itself; that its aim is not to turn out clever, pushing, ambitious graduates, but to engender culture" (1874: 257). In other words, the university's primary orientation was to (re)produce itself.

relative to more marginalized, *extraordinarius* professors and *Privatdozenten*. Whereas in 1864, *ordinarius* professorships still accounted for 49 percent of all academic teaching positions, by 1910 their proportion had dwin-
dled to 32 percent (Busch 1959: 75–76). More significantly for the humanists,
the evolution of modern departmental structures was hastened by the imperial state's interest in promoting research in the chemical, physical, and
military sciences and in engineering. The addition of new faculties and research commitments changed the distribution of status within the university. Whereas philosophy had become the dominant university faculty in the
first decades of the nineteenth century (inheriting this distinction from the
theological faculty), by the end of the nineteenth century the philosophical
faculty was being rapidly supplanted by what the historian Theodor Mommsen named *Großwissenschaft* (big science) (Jarausch 1982: 24). The capital-
intensive character of equipping laboratory research in many of these fields,
alongside their technological achievements, siphoned resources and attention away from the other faculties and offered another focal point for a sense
of experiential crisis and decline among humanists. In response, humanists
complained of a crisis in *Wissenschaft* generally. They spoke disparagingly
of knowledge practices and practitioners that had become more positivisti-
cally and pragmatically oriented and effectively subservient in their scholarly work to shadowy forces outside the domain of the university. According
to one contemporary, "Present-day *Wissenschaft* stands under the decisive
influence of an almost anarchistic positivism that borders on an exploitation
of science and which no longer concerns itself with the whole of knowledge"
(in Busch 1959: 81).

The polemical character of these judgments is underscored by the fact
that the academic caste remained an exclusive and socially high-status
group throughout this period since the proportion of students per 100,000
of the population rose from 32.4 in 1870–71 to only 93.7 in 1914 (Jarausch
1982: 31). Yet, for many, even a modest expansion of the academic caste was
considered to be more evidence of the "watering down" of academic standards and of the pragmatic compromise of the ideals of pure *Wissenschaft*
in the era of mass culture. The former view was mirrored in the discourse
of the imperial political elite, who saw the "overproduction" of scholars
beyond the needs of state administration and university research as a guarantee of the creation of an "academic proletariat" (69) who would be prone
to political radicalization and instability (52–54). Jarausch concludes that
few unemployed academic graduates actually did become political radicals
(69), in part because of the continuous expansion of the civil service during

this period (74; the total number of officials in the empire almost quadrupled between 1871 and 1907, reaching over two million individuals, or 6 percent of the adult male population; Wuthnow 1989: 394) and in part because the Bismarckian state did all it could to marginalize socialists institutionally, thus cultivating a professoriate with typically moderate to conservative political leanings. But fantasies of radicalization, of impending crises, and of the need for radical solutions remained abundant within the mainstream *Bildungsbürgertum* throughout the latter half of the Second Empire, leading to widespread tacit support for a variety of "integrationalist" (Holmes 2000) political programs.

A third factor contributing to the amplification of negative dialectical social knowledge in German intellectual culture was the rise in relative social status and influence of the *Besitzbürgertum* within the middle classes during the Second Empire and the concomitant decline in relative prestige and power of the *Bildungsbürgertum*. German industrialization was rapid, beginning with coal, iron, steel, textiles, and engineering in the 1850s and 1860s and followed by a "second industrial revolution" in chemicals, optics, and electrics in the 1890s. Industrialization vastly increased the relative political power and social prestige of the *Besitzbürgertum* (Blackbourn 1991: 6–7). Moreover, the agency and imagination of the *Besitzbürgertum* were, by now, both translocal and national. Indeed, industrial expansion was also predicated upon the creation of translocal infrastructural media such as railroads, shipping, and roads. In 1879 railroads alone accounted for 62 percent of all capital stock in industry and commerce in Germany (Wuthnow 1989: 379). The formerly localized industrial and commercial strata of the middle classes thrived within the mediating systems of the imperial nation-state and exponentially consolidated their economic and political power.

A fantastically wealthy entrepreneurial and industrial *Großbürgertum* (haute bourgeoisie) emerged in Germany that became the center of networks of elite sociability among the middle classes (Augustine 1991; Kaelble 1988). Although courtly circles remained closed off to all but a select handful of nonnoble industrialists like the Krupp family, both aristocrats and *Gebildeten* participated actively (if often only decoratively) in *Großbürger* social networks. *Bildungsbürger* did continue to play a role in these networks, as historian Dolores Augustine suggests, helping, as they long had, to "mediate between the very disparate value systems and conventions of the bourgeois and noble guests" (1991: 62). But it was clearly a reduced and subaltern role, oriented to facilitating the harmonization of *Großbürger*-noble relations and leaving little room for the advancement of corporate

Bildungsbürger interests, were they even able to conceive such interests in these terms any longer. The culture bearers had been reduced to an amusing diversion in elite networks of sociability.

The more salient social dynamic was the conciliation of *Großbürger* and aristocratic relations. Augustine notes, for example, that the extent of sociable interaction between the traditional Prussian aristocracy and the (largely Jewish) nouveau riche of Berlin was remarkable given historic anti-Semitism and allowed "the Jewish elite of Berlin . . . [to] cultivate connections which could be mobilized to further its economic and political interests" (1991: 58). As the *Großbürgertum* removed themselves from urban pollution to suburban or landed environments, they re-created luxuriant imitations of bygone aristocratic wealth and privilege, purchasing castles and even ennoblements, which brought them into greater conviviality and filiality with the "more impecunious nobility" (Blackbourn and Eley 1984: 229; see also Blackbourn 1998: 365). Yet, as historian Helmut Kaelble argues, haute bourgeois and aristocratic industrialists remained, on the whole, largely endogamous in marriage practices (1988: 119), suggesting that some principles and practices of noble/nonnoble distinction remained robust (see also Kaudelka-Hanisch 1993).

The social alliances of *Großbürger* and aristocrats were cemented by aristocratic investiture into the industrial economy as a strategy for safeguarding their social status. This phenomenon created a pragmatic harmony of interests between the political elite and the new economic elite, allowing the two strata to negotiate the rapid economic and technological transformation of Germany to their common advantage outside a democratic-parliamentarian model. In fact, as Geoff Eley argues, the "industrial-agrarian alliance in Wilhelmine politics" did not signify the retardation of *Großbürger* political power so much as it signified a "rational calculation of political interest" to forestall socialist challenges to the state (in Blackbourn and Eley 1984: 125). Indeed, socialist and other modes of radical political activism developed as a primary route through which more marginalized members of the *Bildungsbürgertum* (outside university culture and the civil service) sought to challenge the economic and political alliance between *Großbürger* and the nobility.

Yet, as Ringer's study of the conservative and pessimistic social imagination of German academics suggests, it was not only among socially marginalized *Gebildeten* that negative dialectical knowledge amplified. Sensing their status on the decline within the social elite, the discourse of both the centers and the margins of German intellectual culture was saturated with negative dialectical tropes that opposed the perduring principles of *Geist* and

Kultur to the exteriorities of bureaucratic and capitalist *Systeme* and their deformations of culture, knowledge, and history.

The Surfeit of History

Negative dialecticism acquired many forms and crossed many registers of expression in German intellectual culture of the late nineteenth century. Philosophy and theory, as always, gave dialectical knowledge its most highly ontologized representation. If the sober teleological certainty of Hegel and the critical passion and revolutionary vision of the early Marx epitomized the ratio of positive dialecticism to negative dialecticism of their moments and positions in intellectual culture, then philosophical and theoretical activity of the late nineteenth century also tended to codify a contemporary *Gebildeten* social phenomenology (outlined above) of accelerating social and cultural overformalization and decline.

Although an ambivalent dialectician himself, Max Weber's analogy of the "iron cage" of rationalization remains one of the most vivid articulations of his contemporaries' sense of the domination of external form over inner spirit: "No one knows who will live in this cage in the future, or whether at the end of this tremendous development entirely new prophets will arise, or there will be a great rebirth of old ideas and ideals, or, if neither, mechanized petrification, embellished with a sort of convulsive self-importance. For of the last stage of cultural development, it might well be truly said: 'Specialists without spirit, sensualists without heart . . .'" (1958: 182). What is particularly striking in Weber's diagnosis of contemporary society is the absence of a clear horizon of historical *Bildung,* such as, for example, communism offered Marx. Weber does not rule out the possibility of a rebirth of Spirit, but his historical imagination centers on the horizon of an endless rule of *System.* Modernization, for Weber, was typified by the apparently limitless penetration of instrumental rationality into spheres of social organization and action (cf. Simmel 1900). The cultural possibilities of history were thus increasingly steered by the progressive rationalistic organization of society. Under these conditions, Weber lamented, the lingering premodern community (*Gemeinschaft*) of language and culture became increasingly difficult to recognize and to sustain, let alone to retrieve in the era of rational administration (see also Tönnies 1887).

A sense of the excess of form in the modern era also defines the more radical and polemical voice of Friedrich Nietzsche.

The surfeit of history of an age seems to me hostile and dangerous to life in five respects: through such an excess the contrast of inside and outside, discussed above, is generated and the personality weakened thereby; through this excess an age comes to imagine that it possesses the rarest virtue, justice, to a higher degree than any other age; through this excess the instincts of a people are impaired and the maturing of the individual no less than of the whole is prevented; through this excess the belief, harmful at any time, in the old age of mankind is implanted, the belief of being a latecomer and epigone; through this excess an age acquires the dangerous disposition of irony with regard to itself, and from this the still more dangerous one of cynicism: in this, however, it ripens even more into clever egoistic practice through which the vital strength is paralyzed and finally destroyed. (1980: 28)

By a "surfeit of history," Nietzsche meant the flood of spiritless modern formation and especially the excess of luxuriant, technical, but ultimately "enfeebling" (7) modern knowledge. He held the excess of modern formation responsible for weakening and artificially individualizing modern man. Ridiculing the claim of Germans to "inwardness," Nietzsche described "us Germans of the present" as a people sleepwalking through a life of (poorly) imitated forms (26). If the Germans perhaps did contain the content of some potent inner unity, it would be hard to detect "since all those beautiful fibres are not entwined into a strong knot: so that the visible deed is not the deed of the whole and a self-manifestation of this inner being, but only a feeble and rude attempt of some fibre or other wanting for the sake of appearance to count as the whole" (26). In his critique of history Nietzsche set himself the task of striving for the *"unity of the German spirit and life after the annihilation of the opposition of form and content, of inwardness and convention"* (27). In other words, Nietzsche sought to transcend a dialectics of history that he envisioned as ruthlessly negative and exterior to the spirit and life of humanity. Unlike Weber, Nietzsche did dream of a revolutionary disjuncture that would abolish the dominant logic of modern history. But he did not put his faith in a positive dialectical reawakening. Nietzsche offered instead the decidedly nondialectical antidotes of the "unhistorical" and the "superhistorical," that is, "closed being" (art) and "eternal becoming" (religion) (62), which he contrasted to the surfeit of history in his age.

Locating Mass Culture in the "Mediatic Journalist"

It is important to emphasize that negative dialectical social knowledge of the *Systeme* of modern sociality had less technical and more informal representations as well. Negative dialecticism was intimately integrated, for example, into common strategies and intuitions of social identification and alterization in German intellectual and political culture. Certain persons and certain classes of persons were typically, metonymically, figured as anthropomorphic embodiments of *System*. Given the interest of future chapters of the book in the rhetorics of selfhood and alterity among journalists, it is worth considering briefly how and why journalists were one of the most routinely designated anthropomorphs of *System* in German intellectual culture of the long nineteenth century.

If the enlightened civil servant and especially the scholar were continuously depicted as the normative ideal of intellectual selfhood because of their embodiment of the principles and ethics of *Wissenschaft* and *Kultur*, then negative dialectical foils always accompanied these positive dialectical figurations. The marginal, itinerant *Brotgelehrte* (scholar for bread) was a frequent trope of alterization, to be sure, but there was likely no category of *Gebildeten* who were more despised than journalists. Rolf Engelsing writes that the "majority of journalists at the end of the nineteenth century were socially ostracized. They were outcasts without corporation" (1966: 42). Intellectuals with more status, like civil servants and academics, commonly aligned the work of journalism with the prostitution of *Geist* to political and material interests (even as not a few of them supplemented their own incomes from the state by writing pseudonymously or anonymously for newspapers).

Discourse on the spiritlessness of journalists and journalism had certain established narratives that clustered along three axes: (1) journalists wrote anonymously or were forced to change their ideas often, (2) journalists were lazy, penurious people who had failed at their "real" vocations because of a lack of character and conviction (*Gesinnung*), and (3) journalists' creative labors were essentially mercenary and they would readily sell themselves and their writing skills to the highest bidder. Gustav Freytag's play *The Journalists*, first performed in 1852, represents a kind of inventory of the negative stereotypes that accompanied the nineteenth-century German journalist. At one point, Schmock, epitomizing the convictionless journalist, states proudly that he has "learned to write in all directions. I have written left and again right. I can write in all directions" (Freytag 1897: 54). In the play, as in mainstream intellectual culture more broadly, knowledge of the increasingly abundant, heterogeneous, and politicized print media culture of the late nineteenth century was condensed and distilled in the caricature of its practitioners. "The journalist" became a vagabond intellectual who lacked any true spiritual vocation or regular means of subsistence; he presented a figure at once pathetically marginal and potentially threatening to the positive *Bildung* of the nation. He belonged, as Weber famously wrote, "to a sort of pariah caste that is always estimated by 'society' according to its ethically lowest representative" (1926).

Yet, ironically perhaps, most journalists conceived themselves to be *Gebildeten* of good standing and firmly committed themselves to the caste ideals of a *wissenschaftliche* approach to knowledge and to the elevation of national culture. While it is true that some journalists (*Journalisten*) led marginal existences piecing together a living from a variety of freelance writing contracts and other work, a caste of salaried editors (*Redakteure*)[6] had already emerged in the late eighteenth century, the majority of whom were evidently *Gebildeten* of (at least prior) good standing.[7] Kurt Brunöhler's sociological study of ninety German editors and publisher-editors (*Verleger-Redakteure*) in the first half of the nineteenth century suggests that the majority of German professional journalists were employed as teachers, professors, or civil servants before occupying their posts and that approximately half of them resigned their editorial positions within ten years (1933: 52–57; see also Zöller 1925: 31–33). As Engelsing writes, "By the beginning of the twentieth century, the core of the professional ranks had a definite professional ethos [*Berufsethos*]. Whether public opinion wanted to believe it or not, the journalistic profession also obeyed a professional honor [*Berufsehre*] and a sense of professional coherence [*Berufsvollkommenheit*]" (1966: 274).

The vocational ethos and professional praxis of the nineteenth-century editors was oriented to the cultivation and formation of "public" knowledge of social life, especially knowledge of political culture and its effects upon other spheres of social life. Very much in the spirit of the unifying practice of *Wissenschaft*, the editor's vocation was to integrate the seemingly unrelated details of the *Nachrichten* (news, information) by carefully bringing

---

6. The distinction between *Redakteur* and *Journalist* remains largely a contractual distinction based on long-term salaried employment versus short-term or freelance journalism.

7. Fully 81 percent of all German *Redakteure* between 1800 and 1900 had some form of university training, and 55 percent had training in philosophy (Requate 1995: 143, 162). Moreover, German editors came overwhelmingly from elite nonnoble families. Requate estimates that after 1870, 57.5 percent of German editors came from the families of *Bildungsbürger* and civil servants, while a further 18 percent were children of merchants and entrepreneurs (1995: 139). By comparison, Requate estimates that only 15.5 percent of the *Redakteure* came from farmer or laborer backgrounds and only 3 percent came from backgrounds where the father was a military officer, a profession largely limited to the aristocracy in this period (Geyer 1990; see also Deák 1992). The majority of professional journalists thus probably had respectable backgrounds in the elite strata of society, contrary to popular imagery of a half-starved intellectual rabble of *Brotschriftsteller* (literally, "writers for bread") who were ready to write anything for anyone providing they received payment (Wehler 1987: 533; McClelland 1991: 34).

a harmony of hermeneutic order to them that revealed the broader significance of otherwise particularistic events. The vocation of the editor was captured lexically in the normative ideal of the *Meinungsbildner*, an "educator" or "formalizer" of public opinions. Journalism was experienced by editors not simply as professional writing but rather as an extension of the ethic of *Wissenschaft* they had encountered in the university. They interpreted their work as contributing to the formation of an educated "public," who could, as Fichte had envisaged for his *Volkslehrer*, guide the masses to nationhood. As Karl Philipp Moritz, editor of the *Vossische Zeitung*, wrote in 1784, a newspaper was "perhaps the best vehicle through which useful truths could be circulated among the *Volk*" (1784: 3).

But, as Engelsing notes, journalists' claims to be contributing to national *Bildung* were rarely acknowledged by contemporaries; instead, journalists were relentlessly represented as antinational in their character and activities. The bookseller Leo Wörl wrote in 1881 that "journalism is counted among those dishonorable trades that move outside the social organism, like shepherds, tinkers, dentists, gypsies, and actors" (in Engelsing 1966: 42; Retallack 1993: 189). This odd assortment of antisocial trades is logically connected by their common identification as transgressors (either physically or symbolically or both) of the boundaries of the national "body."

In this sense, Wörl might well have associated journalism with Jews, who were frequently made, across Central Europe (and elsewhere; see Postone 1980), to epitomize and embody the imagination of antinational and transnational forces of exchange and value. Indeed, in the Second Empire, journalism became increasingly associated with Jewish agency in the nation-state and with anxieties about the polluting spread of Jewishness in German national culture. Both popular print media and the Jews were accused of being agents of national degeneration by the leaders of the state-centered intellectual culture, even as (indeed, because) the presence and influence of the press in German political culture increased (M. Anderson 2000: 368–73). In 1862, future Prussian chancellor Otto von Bismarck described the liberal opposition press as being "in the hands of Jews and other dissatisfied types who have failed at their real vocations, and who confuse ideas and seek to make suspect the best intentions of the government" (Schulze 1931: 154; also Keyserlingk 1977). Despite the demographic reality that the Berlin press in 1900 had only 18 percent Jewish press workers, in comparison to 68 percent Protestants and 11 percent Catholics (Requate 1995: 141),[8] the

---

8. Requate goes on to note, however, that conservative and government-related newspapers employed many fewer Jewish German journalists (10 percent) than liberal and social democratic

so-called *Pressjuden* (press Jews) and *jüdische Pressbengeln* (Jewish press rascals) were a standard feature of Bismarck's diatribes against the critical press (Schulze 1931: 174–76). Bismarck's public reference on another occasion to a "Jewish Clique" in the liberal press that included "Bach, Hock, and other Jewish journalists, although Bach is not a Jew" (Schulze 1931: 174), demonstrates the fluidity of Jewishness as a trope in political rhetoric.

The liberal "Jewish" press was seen not only to epitomize the heterogeneity of political culture in the Second Empire but also to constitute a powerful vehicle of that heterogeneity. In this respect, much of what Moishe Postone says of the phenomenological origin of European anti-Semitism in the search to produce meaningful local knowledge of opaque translocal relations can be extended to the negative image of journalism as well:

> [A] careful examination of the modern anti-Semitic worldview reveals that it is a form of thought in which the rapid development of industrial capitalism, with all its social ramifications, is personified and identified as the Jew. It is not merely that the Jews were considered to be the owners of money, as in traditional anti-Semitism, but that they were held responsible for economic crises and identified with the range of social restructuring and dislocation resulting from rapid industrialization: explosive urbanization, the decline of traditional social classes and strata, the emergence of a large, increasingly organized industrial proletariat, and so on. In other words, the abstract domination of capital, which—particularly with rapid industrialization—caught people up in a web of dynamic forces they could not understand, became perceived as the domination of International Jewry. (1980: 306)

As the "embodiment of the negative principle" (Horkheimer and Adorno 1994: 168), anti-Semitic tropes operated efficaciously in political discourse to establish a dangerous frontier of alterity "within" that could be indexed to generate popular fear and to inflame nationalist identification in the service of the state. James Siegel writes in another context of the Indonesian imagination of the Jew as a "mediatic" menace who "acts out of nowhere" (2001: 302; also Arendt 2004: 83; Gilman 2003) and who thus must be feared everywhere. In contrast to the figuration of the Jew, however, the German journalist's heterogeneous political affiliations spared his caricature the role of

---

papers did (28 percent) (1995: 141). Many elite Jews in Germany entered journalism because, as one of the few unregulated professions, it was a possible career path to those blocked entrance to the professoriate or to other educated professions on ethnic-religious grounds.

serving as the essential trope of antisociality in German public culture. Even the most virulent critics of the liberal press were able to identify wholesome and patriotic journalists in the much smaller conservative press, which lessened the journalist's embodiment of *Prägung*. Bismarck himself started his political career as a journalist in the conservative press, read newspapers voraciously throughout his life, and wrote avidly for the governmental organ, the *Norddeutsche Allgemeine Zeitung*.

If the Jew "became a negative anthropomorphism of generalized exchange in all its alienating dimensions" (Newborn 1994: 48–49; cf. Dundes 1984: 119–30) in German public culture of the late nineteenth century, then the German journalist became something else, I would argue: *an anthropomorphism of epistemic mediation itself*. In other words, the figure of the journalist was typically made to embody the excessive, mediating, particularistic menace of mass culture and modern knowledge. As Treitschke testified on behalf of his caste, there was now too much knowledge and it was spread too thinly. Emile Durkheim once diagnosed this anxiety as recognition of the "contagiousness of the sacred" (1995: 224, 325–29), of the intrinsically fluid and indeterminate character of semiosis, which stimulates social ritual. In their efforts to locate and assuage anxieties about the contagiousness of mass culture, *Gebildeten* made the excoriation of the journalist into a ritual practice that had the effect of signaling the proper margins and boundaries of "authentic" *Wissenschaft*.

Dialectical Radicalism in Late Imperial and Weimar Political Culture

Another symptom of the blurring margins of *Gebildeten* social experience at the end of the long nineteenth century was the dissipation of political energy and agency from the traditional centers of the *Bildungsbürgertum:* universities and officialdom. At the same time, German political culture was gradually radicalized by a plurality of counterpublics that emerged around dissenting mass political movements, their print media, and their associational life. These theaters of political and intellectual activity held only tenuous connections to the networks of the mainstream *Bildungsbürgertum*, who remained institutionally ensconced within the imperial state. And yet, in the years leading up to the First World War, they became spectacular presences in German public culture in ways that profoundly challenged, as we have seen, the social self-imagination of academic and bureaucratic cultures.

In the second case study (chapter 3) I will explore the contours of negative and positive dialectical knowledge within two kinds of political movements that gathered political momentum in the last decades of the nineteenth century and that emerged as strong players in German political culture during the economic and social turbulence of the Weimar era: the neo-conservative or ultranationalistic movements that fed into popular support for the Nationalsozialistische Deutsche Arbeiterpartei (NSDAP) and the Nazi regime and the socialist movements, whose tradition the Sozialistische Einheitspartei Deutschlands (SED) communist party-state (the German Democratic Republic) claimed in 1949. Both movements shared a common object of animosity—bourgeois mass culture—despite the vast differences in their political ideologies and programs. More precisely, the common enemy against which the plurality of radical socialist and radical nationalist political movements in Germany arrayed themselves was the totalized and totalizing *System* of modern mass society and its perceived alienating effect upon humanity and human culture (see Gay 1968: 70–101; Jarausch 1982: 345–66; Schorske 1955: 177–88; Stark 1981: 4–9).

Significantly, on both extremes of the political spectrum, radical movements articulated a positive dialectical mission to reestablish the power of true *Kultur* in society in order to transcend or to reverse the negative dialectic of bourgeois modernization. Socialist and communist movements positioned their intellectuals and political organizations as a scientific vanguard and medium for the self-realization of the proletariat, or "the people" (*Volk*), as a new collective force of modernization (see Konrád and Szelényi 1979; Szelényi 1982; chapter 3). Neoconservative and nationalist movements typically called for a revolutionary *völkisch* reintegration of *Kultur* around traditional "German values" and traditional social institutions like the family, for the assimilation or exclusion of foreigners, for the complete synthesis of state and public culture, and so on (see Mosse 1964; Jarausch 1982: 345–66; Stark 1981; chapter 3).

Both kinds of political movement oriented themselves to mobilizing broad audiences among the politically disengaged, presenting rhetorics of radical change to the many who were unsettled by the deepening social and economic crisis of the Weimar Republic and, Arendt would argue, by modernity itself (Arendt 2004: 610–16). The seeming inability of the democratic state to stabilize the republic in the early 1930s only further fed popular fantasies of all manner of extractive menaces sapping the strength of Deutschland from inside and out. In the last desperate years of Weimar, it was not only radicals for whom a transformation in the course of modernity seemed at once imperative and desirable. Indeed, many, not least many German academics and civil servants, were initially pleased when the NSDAP seized power with promises of revolutionary cultural integration buttressed by familiar narratives of cultural decline and redemption. But it was less the mainstream *Bildungsbürgertum* than other, formerly marginalized *Gebildeten* who played central and decisive roles in both ultranationalist and communist movements, as they sought to realize their ideological ambitions within and beyond the framework of the state. In a way that Fichte would have undoubtedly found perverse, the political organizations of the NSDAP and SED states imitated the *Gebildeten* ideal of the *Kulturstaat* by fusing a network of intellectuals to the apparatus of state administration. Each movement promised a sanctification of the state from "within." This political model promised to obliterate the specter of bourgeois mass culture once and for all and to replace it with a harmonized economy of public *Kultur* befitting the unity and spirit of the *Volk*. In the next chapter I will explore dialectical social knowledge in the political and cultural ideologies of national socialism and communist-socialism in Germany and analyze the institutional life of dialectical knowledge among those professional intellectuals responsible for redeeming public *Kultur* from mass culture.

CHAPTER THREE

Dialectical Politics of Cultural Redemption in the Third Reich and the GDR

Today aesthetic barbarity completes what has threatened the creations of the spirit since they were gathered together as culture and neutralized. To speak of culture was always contrary to culture. Culture as a common denominator already contains in embryo that schematization and process of cataloging and classification which bring culture within the sphere of administration. And it is precisely the industrialized, the consequent, subsumption which entirely accords with this notion of culture. By subordinating in the same way and to the same ends all areas of intellectual creation, by occupying men's senses from the time they leave the factory in the evening to the time they clock in again the next morning with matter that bears the impress of a labor process they themselves have to sustain throughout the day, this subsumption mockingly satisfies the concept of a unified culture which the philosophers of personality contrasted with mass culture.

All the violence done to words is so vile that one can hardly bear to hear them any longer. — *Max Horkheimer and Theodor Adorno, Dialektik der Aufklärung (trans. J. Cumming)*

If Hegelian philosophy captured the sense of national *Bildung* among *Gebildeten* in the first decades of the nineteenth century and if the Nietzschean critique of the "surfeit of history" was one of many epitomes of growing anxieties among *Gebildeten* concerning the relentless "progress" of modern society in the second half of the nineteenth century, then the excoriation of overformalized mass culture by *Gebildeten* in the late nineteenth and early twentieth centuries found one its most subtle, elaborate, and enduring articulations in Max Horkheimer and Theodor Adorno's *Dialectic of Enlightenment*. This text, a conversation between two émigrés from the Third Reich, is a magnificent composition of negative dialectical knowledge in its portrait of a progressive "disenchantment of the world" by reason beginning with mythology and culminating in the mass culture of bourgeois society and fascism (1994: 3). The dialogue exhibits its dialecticism in its constant interpretation of form as the antithesis of *Kultur* ("To speak of culture was always contrary to culture . . ."). With deeply Marxian and Nietzschean textures, Horkheimer and Adorno present a chilling narrative of the hypostatization of reason in human culture and of the incremental "neutralization" of the human intellect's inner *poesis* by reason's "distancing" and "abstracting" rationality (11, 13).

Interestingly, Horkheimer and Adorno identify the dialectic itself as the modality of Enlightenment (*Aufklärung*) chiefly responsible for neutralizing authentic *poesis*. They argue that the dialectic is the elemental mode of distancing rationality, creating abstract distinctions between subjects and subjects and between subjects and objects, since in "dialectical thinking . . . everything is always that which it is, only because it becomes that which it is not" (1994: 15). Historically, this dialectical process of differentiation and identification matures into the formalism and "universal interchangeability" of mathematical and scientific reasoning (12) and culminates, in conjunction with capitalism, in the exposure of all society to the solvent technical logic of rationality (13). All objects, all the creative powers and delicate capacities of humanity, are, for Horkheimer and Adorno, "liquidated" by the "triumph of repressive equality" in modern bourgeois society. Individuality is dissolved into collectivity, reduced to common denominators, and thus neutralized.

Yet, even in this setting of despair, a positive dialectics of intellectual agency lingers on (see also chapter 5), for it is only in the "aesthetic barbarity" and spiritless forms of modern mass culture that the deceiving, liquidating character of Enlightenment becomes truly recognizable to a spirited few as the negative dialectical logic of history. Horkheimer and Adorno pursue a strategy of critical engagement with reason and rationality that Adorno describes elsewhere as "negative dialectics," "insight into the constitutive character of the nonconceptual in the concept" (2003: 12). Adorno's negative dialectics seeks to challenge Enlightenment by recovering all those nonconceptual dimensions of reality that have been disenchanted by idealistic rationality (11). In *Dialectic of Enlightenment*, this practice takes shape as a seemingly endless polemic against the corruption of spirit by form. It is a practice that has an effect similar to that of Mann's world-rejecting Germanness, an assertion of inwardness through the excoriation of the counterfeit exteriorities and appearances of the world. Adorno's "negative dialectics" are, in my language of analysis, positive dialectical, and this may help to explain some of the utopianism that has been associated with the Frankfurt School and its critical theory ever since.

From the first case study we have some sense of the plurality of forces and dispositions that convene in Horkheimer and Adorno's account. We turn now to the social consequences of the amplification of negative dialectical knowledge in German intellectual culture and political culture in the twentieth century. On the eve of the First World War, a cynic might argue that much of the negative dialectical knowledge described in chapter 2 amounted to little more than the ineffectual grousing of alienated academics and other marginalized intellectuals. It was only after the First World War and then again toward the end of the Weimar era that radical political movements whose ideologies were saturated with negative dialectical social knowledge of modernity and with utopian, positive dialectical visions of cultural redemption made serious bids to seize control of the German state. And it was only with the seizure of power by the Nationalsozialistische Deutsche Arbeiterpartei (NSDAP) in 1933 that dialectical social knowledge truly became centered, however unevenly, in the logics of state administration and policy and allowed to organize programs of social reform and cultural renewal.

Of course, neither Horkheimer nor Adorno would willingly have identified themselves with these programs. Appeals to the collective properties and powers of the *Volk* were valorizing precisely the kind of reified and generic collective "culture" they denounced with such venom. Redeeming *Kultur* was not a project they would have imagined possible through collective political mobilization—the "mass-ness" of bourgeois and fascist society was indeed the problem itself. To the extent that Horkheimer and Adorno imagined possible interventions into mass culture, these were all of an avant-garde, artistic character. At most, one could say that the Frankfurt School's critical theory responds to the same social phenomenology of intellectual culture that inspired the socialist and fascist movements of German political culture and thus shares similar attentions and concerns with the historical *Prägung* of spirit by form.

The Political and Cultural Imaginations of the NSDAP and SED Parties

My central concerns in this study are how dialectical social knowledge influenced the political and cultural imagination of the leadership of the NSDAP and the SED and how dialecticism, both negative and positive, pervaded the institutional culture of mass media production in the Third Reich and the GDR. The reader will note a shift in scope from the first case study, where we engaged intellectuals as a social formation in German-speaking Central Europe during the last half of the eighteenth through the nineteenth century. This case study, by contrast, has a more limited temporal and social scope. I will primarily analyze German political culture and the institutional culture of mass media production in the periods 1933–45 and 1949–89. It is clear that, with respect to both foci, other choices could have been made. I could, for example, have undertaken an intensive study of university cultures in the NSDAP and SED states or a comparative study of journalistic cultures in the Cold War FRG and GDR. Why then choose to study media and journalism? And why in the two German party-states?

In responding to these questions I would make four points. First, the decision to focus on media and journalism largely develops out of the normative consideration of mediation that emerged in the concluding sections of chapter 2. If epistemic mediation itself was a key source of anxiety for *Gebildeten* and a stimulus for their excoriation of mass culture, then where better to look for the tension and play between negative and positive dialectical social knowledges of cultural decadence and redemption than within institutional cultures of media production themselves? Second, both the NSDAP and SED leaderships gave immediate and significant attention to monopolizing control over mass media production and positioned mass media reform as a central pillar of their social revolutions, since they viewed the heterogeneity of mass culture itself as a proximate cause of cultural decline. Moreover, the leadership of both parties imagined that the coordination of media representation would harmonize and unify *Volk* consciousness. So, in this sense, by choosing to focus on media, we are following the movements' own distribution of emphasis in their programs of social revolution. Third, the comparative focus on the Third Reich and the GDR prompts us to look beyond the considerable ideological differences between the two regimes and to discern a link between the phenomenological problem of mediation and the amplification of negative dialectical knowledge. This link reciprocally illuminates the phenomenological dimension of political radicalism in Germany and, indeed, why revolutionary programs of cultural redemption adopted the particular discourses they did. Finally, though the institutional culture of media is a particularly apt case for assessing dialectical social knowledge, I would contend that features and findings of this analysis could be applied more broadly (see Boyer 2003a), certainly to other regimes and to other dimensions of institutional culture in the Third Reich and the GDR.

The problem of mediation was central to the political ideologies and cultural reform programs of both the NSDAP and the SED. The two parties viewed their interventions against bourgeois society as critical for arresting the overformalization of modern society and for unifying the dissolute heterogeneity of representational forms that they believed typical of bourgeois mass culture. In turn, both parties envisioned themselves as mediums of the collective *Kultur*al awareness and power of the *Volk* and as proxies of the collective will of the people.[1] Since the leadership of both parties identified mass culture as having had a decisive negative influence on the *Volk*, reforming mass culture was predicted to rebalance the relations of interiority and exteriority in society in favor of a positive dialectical release of authentic cultural vitality and creativity into social formation (comparatively, see Arendt 2004: 533–34). I have argued elsewhere (2003a) that these dialectical visions link the "party-state" as a historically specific social-political formation to discourse on the dangers of mediation that circulated in the complex and thriving intellectual culture of the late nineteenth century and to the positive dialectical visions of national *Bildung* that circulated in German intellectual culture in the early decades of the nineteenth century.

As a cautionary note, this study's gestures of comparison are quite limited: I note a general convergence in the dialectical social knowledges of bourgeois mass culture held by the NSDAP and SED and more specific similarities in their visions of journalism and public-cultural redemption and in their strategies and techniques of media control. I do not argue, however, that there were broad similarities between the two party-states' internal political organizations or between their official ideologies, policies, or agendas (see Kershaw 2000: 36–40). At a strictly organizational level, the NSDAP regime did not develop the same kind of administrative apparatus that one found in the GDR; the relationship between party and state in the Third Reich was neither constitutionalized nor systematized and it operated, for the most part, through more informal channels (Arendt 2004: 514; Broszat 1981: 193–234; Kershaw 2000: 69–92).

In terms of party ideology, Nazi discourse was also less centrally and bureaucratically negotiated than in the GDR. And the idioms in which NSDAP and SED dialectical knowledges were articulated always diverged significantly. The Nazis favored primordialist-tribalist and biological-racialist

1. This is particularly clear with the SED in their adoption of a Leninist language of a political and intellectual "vanguard" status for the Communist Party. For the NSDAP, as for other nationalist movements, the vanguard status of the nationalist party is more implicit in the public discourse of party leaders because essential ethnic or racial ties are emphasized as the basis for political mobilization.

idioms that rejected modernity *tout court* in favor of the release of nonmodern bonds and powers. The SED embraced the teleology of modernization, decrying how bourgeois society resisted and stalled the process of social *Bildung*. Their favored idioms were praxeological (focusing on the energy and activity of the *Volk*) and scientific-modernist (focusing on the emancipatory *Wissenschaft* of the party).

Finally, I wish to be clear that my comparative analysis neither seeks to neutralize the horrors of the NSDAP genocide nor to replicate a popular West German narrative that collapses the Third Reich and the GDR into an undifferentiated and uninterrupted German "authoritarian tradition" (see chapters 4 and 5). My concern with investigating dialectical social knowledges in the two German party-states issues rather from an attempt to understand political radicalism in Germany in the twentieth century as a response to the sense of estrangement from modern society felt deeply and widely in German intellectual culture and elsewhere in the late nineteenth century. This both does and does not illuminate the specificities of the Nazi rise to power and its consequences. I entirely reject Norbert Elias's intimation (see chapter 2) of a cultural teleology leading from German Romanticism to Auschwitz. What my analysis shows instead is that, in the decades leading up to the Nazi seizure of power, negative dialectical knowledge of modernity had amplified in intellectual and political discourse to the extent that social knowledges of cultural decline were widely familiar throughout German society. If one wishes to understand popular sympathy and even enthusiasm for Nazi political rhetoric in the 1930s, it is important to note that there was a sense in which Nazi discourse on modern *Prägung* was strikingly mundane despite the intensity and perversity of its racialist, ultranationalist idioms. My analysis may help to explain how both the NSDAP and SED regimes were able to tap into a phenomenological sense of estrangement from exterior social forms and "modernity" and into contemporary dialectical knowledges of cultural decline in order to recruit support and legitimacy for their specific ideologies.

Premonitions of a Party-State

It is well known that when Adolf Hitler and the NSDAP came to power in Germany in 1933, they articulated a revolutionary social mission to restore the power and dignity of the German *Volk*, to promote the interests of the national community (*Volksgemeinschaft*) and the fatherland (*Vaterland*) above all else, and to transform radically the course of Germany's collective destiny.[2] Historians have not ignored the fact that this mission had no fixed charter but was rather constantly negotiated and revised in the early years of the Reich as the regime lurched from crisis to crisis. Martin Broszat (1966, 1981) and Norbert Frei (1993) have analyzed Hitler's rise to power and the organization of the NSDAP state in detail and have seriously undermined the "führer myth" of Hitler's total authority and unity of political purpose by emphasizing the complexity and sometimes chaos of the organization of state power in Germany between 1933 and 1945. Such works caution us against teleological readings of the Nazi rise to power. Hitler would not have come to power were it not for the misplayed brokerage and containment strategies of his conservative allies in 1933 (Broszat 1981: 57–92; Frei 1993: 3–27); nor would he have consolidated his power without violently repressing the more revolutionarily minded factions of his own movement in 1934 (principally, the Sturm-Abteilung [SA] brownshirts; Frei 1993: 31–69). Moreover, although Hitler's authority in the NSDAP never faced serious challenge, the central leadership of the NSDAP was loosely integrated and organized by personal relationships and networks rather than by bureaucratic procedures (Broszat 1981: 44; Kershaw 2000: 69–92). The central leadership had to negotiate its authority continuously with respect to the central government, the Reichswehr (the German armed forces), the regional party organizations operated by more or less ambitious and influential area commanders (*Gauleiter*), and the Schutz-Staffel (SS) and SA. After 1934 there were no oppositional political organizations within Germany (making the Third Reich de facto a single-party-state), and most positions of influence were held by party members (*Parteigenossen*) within the government. Yet the relationship of party to state was also uneven at different levels of administration and in different parts of the country. At times, the relationship was haphazard, with powerful party officials holding sway while lacking any recognized governmental position (Kershaw 2000: 69–92).

2. Hannah Arendt's *Origins of Totalitarianism* (2004) remains, to my mind, one of the most brilliant and insightful analyses of the Nazi movement ever written. Although I find myself at variance with her stress upon a fundamental disjuncture between Nazi racialist nationalism and earlier modes of national and racialist ideology in Germany and Europe, Arendt makes a compelling case that NSDAP leaders viewed their propagandistic emphasis upon the *Volksgemein-schaft* during the Reich as simply the first phase of a larger project of social *Bildung* that would also eventually involve the "purification" of the German *Volk* of "unworthy life": "The Nazis did not think that the Germans were a master race, to whom the world belonged, but that they should be led by a master race, as should all other nations, and that this race was only on the point of being born. Not the Germans were the dawn of the master race, but the SS. The 'Germanic world empire,' as Himmler said, or the 'Aryan' world empire, as Hitler would have put it, was in any event still centuries off" (2004: 533).

All this paralleled the lack of centralizing institutions in the party organization itself (e.g., the NSDAP never constituted a Politburo) despite or perhaps because of Hitler's great centralization of authority in his person. Writing on the never-resolved relationship of party and state in the Third Reich, Broszat argues that the Nazi regime had a fundamentally triangular power structure, "a Party-state-Führer absolutism" (1981: 195), which "alternated between revolution and authoritarian brake on revolution and mixed the two together." In her analysis of Nazism, Hannah Arendt emphasizes "that a movement—if the word is to be taken as seriously and as literally as the Nazis meant it—can only have a direction, and that any form of legal or governmental structure can be only a handicap to a movement which is being propelled with increasing speed in a certain direction" (2004: 517–18). Nazism was indeed pervaded by a sense of urgency to propel the process of social becoming forward at an ever-accelerating rate. Arendt captures how the Nazis' almost hyperdialectical ideology of becoming shaped the "peculiar onion-like structure of the movement, in which every layer was the front of the next more militant formation" (2004: 534).

For these reasons, the Nazi "party-state," such as it was, was at best a kind of premonition of the political organization of the mature SED party-state, a self-unraveling cohabitation of a single party and state administration that nonetheless projected itself ideologically through its propaganda apparatus as a *Kulturstaat*-like fusion of spiritual power and administrative structure channeling the will of the people. To be sure, the reason that the regime's unity of purpose in its public representation of itself always exceeded its actual unity of purpose had something to do with the early organization of the Hitler movement as a charismatic cult, with the constant desire of the regime for broad mobilization, which required concessions to traditional sentiments and practices, and with Hitler's own widely acknowledged preference not to be troubled with administrative matters that he considered beneath his station as the leader of the Nazi revolution. Hitler, himself a poet, painter, and nationalist, exposed his own intellectual preferences by interesting himself more in the imagination of the future of the master race and with securing and maintaining his own position of dominance as führer than in the profane business of micromanaging the everyday administration of the Reich.

Hitler, the "Genuine Artist"

It seems unthinkable, according to any of the common definitions of the term I outlined at the end of chapter 1, to describe Adolf Hitler as "an intellectual." And yet, sociologically speaking, in the years leading up to the First World War, he shared a life similar to that of many marginal *Gebildeten*. Known as a dandy and aspiring artist in his provincial town of Linz, he traveled to Vienna to train at the Viennese Fine Arts Academy. Rejected in his application to the academy, and ignoring the advice of family members to seek employment instead in the civil service, Hitler circulated for several years on the outskirts of mainstream intellectual culture and political culture in Vienna, often living on the edge of hunger. He was passionate about high *Kultur* (especially opera), fascinated and revolted by Viennese politics, and spent many days and nights stalking the city, sponging up popular pseudoscientific theories of racial and cultural decline, and feverishly drafting a variety of plans for, among other things, monumental public architecture (a fascination that never left him) and systems of mass transit (Jones 2002: 35–55).

Hitler's NSDAP began as a charismatic movement and developed a solidly lower-middle-class electoral base in the late 1920s and early 1930s before its seizure of power; the NSDAP was less an industrial "worker's party" than a petit bourgeois party supported by an amalgam of skilled artisans and unskilled workers, low-level officials, merchants, and so on (Hofmann 1993: 184–87). Yet the NSDAP also had a solid core of *Bildungsbürger* in its leadership ranks, many of whom had had at least some university training and had been influenced by the social knowledges of cultural crisis and decline circulating in academic culture in the first decades of the twentieth century. This core of *Gebildeten* was responsible for managing much of the social imagination of Nazism, from relatively mundane matters of domestic policy (e.g., building the autobahn system) to the ideological and administrative work of the Final Solution. Of the fifteen participants at the Wannsee Conference in 1942, eight held doctorates. Conference convener Reinhard Heydrich's father had been a composer and director of a conservatory in Halle.

Despite Hitler's legendary detestation of the class of bourgeois he termed "intellectuals," it is perhaps not surprising that he left a place in his social imagination for the work of "genuine artists" like himself. In September 1933, for example, Hitler wrote an essay entitled "The Renewal of Theater," published in *Die Deutsche Bühne:*

> Theater will naturally also have to renew itself. But the renewal must proceed from within to without. And to those people who believe that they can ignore this and do things just as before under a new mask, they are powerfully mistaken. They will have to be reeducated from the ground up. Those who do not wish to reeducate themselves will be

destroying themselves without us having to lift a finger. . . . The genuine artist will come to us of his own accord because we are the builders. Every real art is a kind of building and to that end the artist will recover his lost energy only when he joins us. (In Wulf 1966: 145)

Alongside the imperiousness and menace of his rhetoric, Hitler's speeches on the arts are saturated with dialectical figurations of a course of intellectual and cultural renewal "from within to without." Every "genuine artist" is further promised a return of "lost energy" once he reeducates himself in accordance with the Nazi mission.

The NSDAP reciprocally declared Hitler the great architect of Germany. The führer alone was said to have the intellectual power to call forth "the future German being," as the Nazi poet Hermann Burte put it:

A book was written, not poetry in a low common sense, and yet a poem, a view of a new people in a new state! The man who wrote it is called Adolf Hitler! . . . Yes, the books live and not only the books—living men emerge and charge them with life! Here is the primordial and model image of the future German being! The spirit journeys forth before the deed as the morning wind goes before the sun! Before he embarks upon his work, the great statesman of the Germans is a kind of poet and thinker, his mind clarifies for itself how things ought to be in the world of things! A prose comes into being with a surging quality uniquely its own, a march-like step . . . (In Mosse 1966: 142–43)

Burte floods his text with a mode of emphatic and primordialist dialecticism that exemplifies the works of many Nazi writers. The theme of German spirits and perfect bodies exerting their energy over the world was quite common. Burte's text additionally outlines the mission(s) of the intellectual in the Nazi movement. Hitler, leader in intellectual life as in all domains of social life according to Nazism, is depicted as the architect and orchestrator of the "new people in a new state." Yet lesser artists were still promised an important role in helping to direct the surging becoming of "the future German being."

The *Gleichschaltung* of Political and Public Culture

Two of Hitler's earliest and most effective campaigns (in 1933 and 1934) were to secure Nazi control over political culture and the mass media. He and his conservative allies accomplished the domination of political culture through de facto bans on the left-wing parties, the Kommunistische Partei Deutschlands (KPD) and the Sozialdemokratische Partei Deutschlands (SPD), and through the dissolution or incorporation of the other middle-class parties. The Law against the Establishment of Political Parties (July 1933) and the forced coordination of the regional governments with the Nazi central government helped to cement the Nazi monopoly in political culture.

To manage mass media in the Third Reich, Hitler established Josef Goebbels as head of a new Reich Ministry for Propaganda and Popular Enlightenment in March 1933 and allowed him to work to coordinate all public-cultural production through his ministry. In October 1933, the Law on Editors released journalists from the control of their publishers and made them instead beholden to the state (Frei 1993: 64). The fact that these moves preceded what seemed both then and now like far more pressing political and social reforms demonstrates the attention and significance that Hitler and fellow leaders in the party accorded to mass mediation as danger to and instrument for their movement. An effective use of mediation and publicity was deemed necessary for mass mobilization behind the Nazi cause in the 1930s, just as the NSDAP recognized its debt to the Hugenberg press for much free publicity in the 1920s, which helped to create a public profile and legitimacy for what began as a much more marginal movement. As Frei writes, "A marked tendency to stage itself as if Germany were a vast theatre lent the Third Reich certain theocratic traits. Marches, colour-parades and torch-light processions, in which brown shirts and swastikas formed the unmistakable distinguishing surface characteristics, had already given the 'movement' a unique identity during the Weimar period" (1993: 83–84).

The Nazi emphasis on mass, coordinated movement can be understood as a performance designed to simulate the ideal, harmonized *Volkskultur* of which Germans were felt to have been robbed by the exteriorizing, individuating tendencies of bourgeois-Semitic mass culture. Likewise, the Nazi strategy of asserting a coordinated political control (*Gleichschaltung*) over public culture can be understood as a strategy for forcibly integrating and harmonizing the decadence and confusion Nazis attributed to the modern culture industry. Hitler had already partly theorized this strategy in *Mein Kampf* when he wrote that to turn back the deleterious "modernization" of national culture, cultural activity could no longer proceed in the decentered unorganized way that served Jewish and capitalistic interests. Rather, for Hitler, Nazism had to focus single-mindedly on the necessity of cultivating an integrated *Volk* consciousness among the masses. Its technique was the polemic:

The nationalization of the great masses can never take place by way of
half measures, by a weak emphasis upon a so-called objective viewpoint,
but by a ruthless and fanatically one-sided orientation as to the goal to be
aimed at. That means, therefore, one cannot make a people "national" in
the meaning of our present "bourgeoisie," that is, with so and so many
restrictions, but only nationalistic with the entire vehemence which is
harbored in the extreme. (In Mosse 1966: 8)

Hitler's social vision was dialectical in the sense that national and racial
Bildung were essential leitmotifs of the Nazi cause (despite the fact that
Nazis often articulated this cause as a "recovery" of a timeless unity of
which shadowy "historical" forces like Jewry were said to have drained
Germans). Likewise, the *Prägung* of mass culture was a standard theme of
his public performances. Hitler was obsessed with excoriating heterogeneity (from the biological to the semiotic) and with subjugating every manner
of mediation to an essential cultural unity. The Nazi *Gleichschaltung* engaged a variety of cultural institutions with the same fundamental aim of
harmonizing the production of public culture around the führer and party. It
was said that every genuine artist committed to the Nazi revolution would
be rewarded with an unmediated connection to the powers of the *Volk*. For
example, a Nazi reformer in the university system, Gerhard Krüger, characterized Nazism as an opportunity to recapture the harmonious *Gebildeten*
subject of the early nineteenth century that had, in a Nietzschean idiom,
degenerated through "one-sided" specialization:

> During the nineteenth century, the ideal of the harmonious man as clas-
> sic liberalism viewed it, gradually degenerated into the one-sidedness of
> specialists who no longer had any true connection with the community.
> Specialized education and the overrating of the intellect bred that "spir-
> itualized" human whom nobody has characterized as trenchantly and
> as ironically as Nietzsche, who countered him with the demand for a
> sound, healthy lust for life. The university bred the "brain man," the
> "instructor." The university itself, and with it its teachers and partly
> even its students, lost all relationship to the people and the state. (In
> Mosse 1966: 305; see also Hahn 1998: 74)

The *Führerprinzip* as Antidote to Mediation

Hitler's views on mass media in the context of the NSDAP cause were not
fundamentally dissimilar to those held by Bismarck and other conservative

figures in mainstream political culture in the Wilhelmine period: the press was useful, even vital, when employed by the state as an extension of its political culture. Otherwise, mass media tended to cultivate disharmony between public culture and political culture and therefore constituted a dangerous and potentially degenerative influence on the nation. Hitler shared Bismarck's disdain of the mass press for its convictionless pursuit of "objectivity," of the liberal press for its critical and ultimately reformist position on state power and for its cacophonous discourse on the nation, and of the socialist press for its incitement of the working classes—the pliant, potent, yet ignorant and dangerous "masses"—against the ruling order. The "mediatic journalists" (see chapter 2) of the mass press were abundant in Hitler's social imagination and always suspected for their Jewishness. Hitler often condensed Jewish and journalistic specters of mediation together in speeches against the "Jewish sidewalk-press" and the "Jewish newspaper-vipers," who poured "poison into the hearts of their readers" (Frei and Schmitz 1989: 39; see also Koszyk 1972: 349). Hitler also held that a Jewish newspaper cartel was responsible for undercutting Germany's war effort in 1918 and that this cartel had then reveled in the degenerate state of the German *Volk* during the Weimar period.

Breaking this spectral cartel required the nationalization of the mass media through the monopolization of its productive apparatus by the state. By reorganizing the social organization of media production, the heterogeneity of media messaging typical of the extant mass media would be replaced by a "ruthless and fanatically one-sided orientation," a monosemy, which Hitler saw as essential to awakening the spirit of the *Volk* to its destiny. Hitler and Goebbels sought, more energetically and systematically than in other domains of Nazi policy, (1) to suppress polysemy and plurality in public culture by arrogating control over mass media production to the state or to party loyalists and (2) to institutionalize a series of techniques of media surveillance and control via the propaganda ministry that it was believed would help refine and harmonize mediation into alignment with the *Gedankengut* (literally, "trove of ideas") of the führer.

By coordinating mass mediation around the intellectual productivity of the führer, it was believed that monosemous messaging could be achieved on a mass basis. Not unlike the "party line" (*Parteilinie*) that centralized epistemic authority in the person of the general secretary of the SED, the application of the Nazi *Führerprinzip* (leadership principle) to media production was explicitly conceived as an antidote to the heterogeneity and barbarity of mass culture. The führer was alone held capable of awakening the masses to the power of the movement. For this reason, the Nazis preferred radio technology to print technology since radio allowed the führer's voice to enter, "unmediated" as it were, into domestic spaces so it could infuse and align them with his spirit.

Leading Nazi intellectuals tirelessly promoted the coordination of the press as an event of world-historical disjuncture. Through rebirth as instruments of the party, journalism and media technology would cease to exhibit the Semitic, antinational influences for which they long had been feared and reviled. The executive director of the Nazi Press Chamber, Ildephons Richter, while justifying the liquidation of the Catholic press in 1935, set out the NSDAP's broader goals for its mass media: "Based on the will of the *Führer* it can only be an instrument in his hand through which he can educate and lead every fellow-German as a member of the national community. . . . The positive task of every single newspaper can only be that of bringing the fund of ideas of National Socialism to the reader, to clarify for him the National Socialist *Weltanschauung* [vision of the world], and all to the single end of educating him to National Socialism" (in Hale 1964: 172).

Techniques of Media Control

Despite their pretense to a teleological national mission, the NSDAP's effort to purify mass media of polysemy faced certain obstacles. Problems with party and state control over media production were mostly resolved in the first years of the Reich. Radio was already a state-monopolized technology in the Weimar period, and the transition to Nazi leadership proceeded relatively smoothly by contrast to the highly privatized and diversified print media. In many cases, the NSDAP invoked national interest to seize the property of Jewish and liberal press magnates and to place these institutions instead into the hands of party loyalists or, as in the case of the Ullstein and Mosse publishing empires, into the hands of party holding companies (Frei 1993: 130). The Nazis also organized lightning-quick purges of newspaper staffs in the early years of the Third Reich to secure a press free of outspoken critical voices (Hale 1964: 76–101). After the war began in 1939, the party instituted a regime of military censorship that allowed it to remove or to intimidate wayward publishers and journalists.

In practice, exercising the *Führerprinzip* in media became most often a bureaucratic affair. Under the rules of Goebbels's ministry, every newspaper in Germany was required to send the ministry a copy of each printed edition, which was carefully scrutinized and evaluated for ideological errors (Hale 1964: 41). The ministry developed two other primary techniques for maintaining blanket influence over the press: the centralized distribution of all news reports through the Deutsche Nachrichtenbüro (DNB), the party-controlled German newswire agency, and daily press advisories (*Pressean-weisungen*) that refined party argumentation on specific issues (Frei and Schmitz 1989: 30–34; Koszyk 1972: 370–79). By filtering flows of news reports through the DNB, Goebbels limited the access of German newspapers to information that might contradict the party leadership's interpretation of events both nationally and internationally. The press advisories meanwhile ranged from reminders to reprint Goebbels's speeches in their entirety to warnings to avoid particular topics or words altogether. One message to the press on 26 January 1937 stated, "A western German newspaper has engaged itself polemically against Thomas Mann. Such articles are absolutely undesirable. Thomas Mann should be extinguished from the memory of every German because he is not worthy of bearing the title 'German'" (Frei and Schmitz 1989: 31). Another advisory, from 28 February 1939, instructed: "A newspaper printed a report entitled 'Give the Jews Madagascar!' and affixed the subtitle 'Our Standpoint.' Our standpoint, however, is only that the Jews leave Germany. We are relatively indifferent to where they actually go" (Frei and Schmitz 1989: 31; see Bohrmann 1984 for other examples).

This daily calibration of media messaging, along with the propaganda ministry's authority to involve itself more surgically in ridding particular papers of offensive employees or of their printing licenses, helped to solidify a press by the mid-1930s that produced texts more or less in keeping with the official party rhetoric crafted by Hitler and a handful of other leading Nazis. However, there were many cases when Hitler chose to exercise his right of intellectual leadership in a more immediate fashion. As the war wore on, Hitler's decisions regarding the press became increasingly mercurial as his tolerance for anything he found personally offensive in the media waned. He ordered the closure of Germany's last remaining paper of any international reputation, the *Frankfurter Zeitung*, in 1943 against Goebbels's advice, justifying the decision, according to one witness, "I don't like the name; it must be closed down" (Hale 1964: 289).

Scissors in the Head and Writing between the Lines

In general, the seizure of the means of media production was a relatively simple task next to the disciplining of professional journalists, trained in the Wilhelmine and Weimar eras, to participate enthusiastically and creatively in the publicization of NSDAP ideology. The fact that the Third Reich was never able to train a generation of journalists in keeping with Hitler's model of the "genuine artist" meant that the party could count upon only a relatively small percentage of journalists as energetic *gleichgesinnten* (of shared conviction) Nazis (Frei and Schmitz 1989: 122). Media administration and censorship therefore became all important, a circumstance that Goebbels himself often lamented as encouraging ineffective mechanistic propaganda rather than genuine creative collaboration in the spirit of the movement (Frei 1993: 91). Goebbels privately confided a fellow intellectual's sympathy for the fate of German journalists to his aide, Rudolf Semmler, saying that he "would find it intolerable, and for any person with intellectual power undignified, to attend daily at the official press conference [and] to have ten commandments, all beginning with 'Thou shalt not,' handed out" (in Hale 1964: 251–52). In the ideal Reich, there would be no need for media control since journalists would share the inner convictions (*Gesinnungen*) of the führer and would enthusiastically and creatively extend these forth into public culture. But, in the actual Reich, many journalists and other professional intellectuals were highly ambivalent about, if nonetheless tolerant of, Nazi orthodoxy.

Norbert Frei suggests that the "poverty of Nazi cultural production" more generally was a major reason for its weak impact among *Gebildeten* and other social strata (1993: 91). Frei argues that in education, literature, art, architecture, music, theater, and film, Nazi efforts to coordinate intellectual activity through the *Führerprinzip* produced limited results and certainly failed to produce the kind of coordinated public *Kultur* of which Nazi leaders had dreamed in the first years of the Reich. Efforts to win popular support for Teutonic cult events like the open-air *Thingspiel* performances were not widely successful. Audience tastes continued to be diverse and solidly traditional; although the works of Jewish, communist, and avant-garde intellectuals were strenuously forbidden, jazz music, for example, although reviled by Hitler and other leading Nazis as "nigger music," was tolerated throughout the Nazi period as a concession to middle-class tastes (91–99).

The propagandistic content of the Reich press likewise found far less public resonance, less still in the final years of the war, than the Nazi leadership either desired or imagined. Journalists, other than diehard Nazi sympathizers, characterized themselves in negative dialectical terms as indentured servants of a "propaganda machine." The testimony of Joachim Schieferdecker, a former editor at the Nazi paper *Völkischer Beobachter,* gives some sense of how journalists perceived and articulated the ratio of Spirit to System in the Nazi press:

> Twice daily the so-called press conference was held in the propaganda
> ministry at which the "Tagesparole" [daily slogan] of the Reich Press

Chief was released with endless commentaries. Taken down stenograph-
ically and placed on our desks for guidance, the material amounted daily
to ten or twelve closely typed pages, containing many prohibitions and
few permissions. It prescribed the treatment of the specified themes with
regard to space, tone, headlines and placement down to the last detail. If
it were a recurring theme the directive might be valid for a month during
which time it had to be carefully observed. The initiative of the editorial
staff was mainly exercised, at least occasionally, in attempting to evade
the prescriptions. During the war, when the V-B described Roosevelt as
a "gangster," "criminal," or "madman," and Churchill as a "drunkard"
or "idiot," these expressions did not come from the vocabularies of the
editors but were officially prescribed; and if repelled by these rude characterizations we dared to use other expressions, we were reprimanded or
warned. From 1933 onward editors became more and more simply rubber
stamps for officially stated views, placing their mark on the daily copy to
indicate that they had worked the material, and nothing more. The DNB
reports, almost fifty per cent of which the press was required to publish
in their exact wording, served as directives to be strictly followed by
the editors. As independent journalism the work of professional editors
from 1933 to 1945 did not deserve even the name, because the essen-
tials of access to unbiased information, the open door to sources, and
the necessary respect of official and private persons for the profession of
journalism simply did not exist.

During the war these conditions steadily worsened. The military
censorship kept the press on even shorter leading strings, and one had
to be constantly on guard lest one touch some fancied military secret or
violate some similar regulation. It is no joke, for example, that the word
"Russian" was prohibited and had to be replaced by "Bolshevik," so that
the censor made out of a "Russian winter" a "Bolshevik winter." To the
journalist was left hardly more freedom of action than to lend his good
name to this anonymous official nonsense, and by every unguarded word
he might use he ran the risk of being called sharply into account. (In Hale
1964: 246–47; see also Martens 1972; Sänger 1978)

In response to the feeling of being made to service the spiritless mass
production of "anonymous official nonsense," Nazi journalists reported
developing two primary defensive mechanisms to protect their sense of
vocational spirit from its daily compromise with state supervision of and
intervention in their intellectual activity: (1) journalists tended to rigorously self-censor their own media labors in order to avoid drawing exterior

attention from the media control bureaucracy, thereby drawing censorial power "within" their own intellects; and (2) journalists sought, by continuously reflecting upon the coding practices of the propaganda ministry, to produce small acts of written heroism that resisted the monosemous pretensions of propaganda. The former practice was known colloquially as the *Schere im Kopf* (scissors in the head), while the latter was described as writing and reading *zwischen den Zeilen* (between the lines) (Frei and Schmitz 1989: 121–22). In the case of the "scissors in the head," the analogical relocation of the censorial force inside the journalist's mind salvaged some sense of intellectual agency by construing censorship as a kind of game, where the journalist sought to outwit the spiritless bureaucratic logic of power (*Macht*). Walter Dirks, remembering his journalistic experiences in the 1930s, wrote: "We were certainly for the most part calm and level-headed types who thought about the risks. . . . Should I risk this sentence, or would it be better to cross it out? And that kind of thing naturally has its own charm, no? Times of censorship lend the pen a certain power" (in Frei and Schmitz 1989: 126). Another Nazi journalist, Karl Silex, remarked that censorship in those days was experienced as part of one's professional challenge, "like a game where both sides have hidden cards, after a while it even becomes fun" (126).

The reality of party journalism in the Third Reich, as it was also in the GDR, was a complex calculus (in de Certeau's sense, 1984: xix) between censorship and circumvention, duty and fear, willing participation and half-hearted resignation, belief in the potential of the party-state to strengthen the nation and depression at the reality of the violence and intolerance (both physical and semiotic) that accompanied the actualization of party dogma. Yet, as we will see below for the GDR case as well, Nazi journalists' remembrance of their professional experience often centers dialectically on the times when their creative powers of *Geist* were able to defeat party *Macht*, if only temporarily, by "writing between the lines," coding esoteric criticisms or critical allegories of the regime without being called to account. Although, by any measure, these efforts did little to divert or disturb the flow of party ideology, the critical creative potential of journalistic subterfuge looms large in memory as a positive dialectical redemption of Spirit from the pervasive climate of System. Erving Goffman terms such minor acts of mischief in institutional contexts "secondary adjustments" that provide "almost a kind of lodgment for the self" (1961: 54–55). Unable to publish intellectual activity that in any way departed from the hermeneutic settlements of the party leadership, for all but the most convinced party members the whispered discussions they had in the hallways, the ideas for stories they locked in a desk drawer, or the moment when they slipped a subtle word-play into an article were the foundations for journalists' continued sense of self as *Gebildeten.*

The Formation of the SED State

In 1949, the SED inherited a very different Deutschland than the NSDAP had in 1933—a nation of refugees living in a ruined landscape governed by four different occupying armies, each of which endeavored to create a German state according to its own interpretation of "democracy." In the Soviet Occupation Zone, the deteriorating relationship with the western allies prompted the Soviet Military Administration to engineer a fusion of the SPD and KPD in April 1946 into a single state socialist party, the Sozialistische Einheitspartei Deutschlands (SED) (Richert 1958). Buoyed by Soviet support for the establishment of an eastern German communist republic, the SED immediately proclaimed their own historical caesura and promised the first genuine people's republic on German soil. Despite the geopolitical exigencies of the bifurcation of the German nation-state and the Soviet Military Administration's hand in placing the GDR under their control, the SED depicted their rise to power as a people's revolution and their platform as an extension of principles promoted by the German social democratic and communistic movements of the nineteenth and early twentieth centuries. The GDR was, according to the SED, a marvelous opportunity to realize at last the *Kulturstaat* long denied the *Volk* by industrial capitalism, of which, the SED determined, Nazism was simply the most radical and deformed variant, proving Lenin's general rule that all capitalism tended toward monopolism and thence toward institutionalized barbarism.

As with the Third Reich, the GDR was from its inception a state governed by a single political party. The government was nominally legitimized as a multiparty democracy through the existence of a plurality of political parties (Christlich-Demokratische Union Deutschlands, Liberal-Demokratische Partei Deutschlands, National-Demokratische Partei Deutschlands, Demokratische Bauernpartei Deutschlands). Yet these parties were principally political entities for show weakened by rigged elections and by SED moles infiltrating their highest ranks. Their leadership characteristically endorsed the hegemony of the SED on any matter of significance. The party presses of these so-called *befreundete Parteien* (befriended parties) were subject, moreover, to the same media control apparatus that handled the much larger media institutions of the SED and the state-controlled electronic media (radio and later television). The GDR state, to a much greater extent than the Third Reich, operated as an extension of the SED party organization; the true power center in the GDR government was the SED Politburo, and the nominal supraparty (*überparteiliche*) political institutions like the *Volkskammer* (parliament) all functioned as rubber stamps for policies developed by the Politburo and, in particular, by the general secretary of the SED himself. The SED party-state justified its right to govern by immediately claiming the mandate of the *Volk*. The preamble to the GDR state constitution reads, "As a fulfillment of their will, the German *Volk* has empowered this constitution to guarantee the freedom and rights of persons, to formalize communal and economic life according to principles of social justice, to serve societal progress, to support friendship with all other *Völker*, and to secure peace" (*Verfassung* 1950).

Socialist *Kultur* and Cultural Policy

Although the SED and NSDAP utilized many of the same communitarian tropes—tropes inherited in turn from the nineteenth-century *Bildungsbürgertum*—as totems of social belonging in their political culture and public discourse, the nuances of meaning that terms like "*Volk*" and "*Kultur*" acquired in each party's discourse were quite different. Unlike the Nazi uses of "*Kultur*" to signify a timeless national-cultural essence or racial power, for example, the SED used "*Kultur*" to signal a praxeological understanding of human activity undergoing dialectical, historical development. In a GDR textbook on the theory and practice of socialist journalism, "*Kultur*" is defined as "the totality of the ends and means of human activity," in short, as the nexus of human praxis that Marx situated at the center of the production of society and history. Under capitalism and "*Volk*-hostile imperialistic mass culture" (Poerschke et al. 1983: 231), however, *Kultur* was said to have become overformalized and estranged from the true soul of human activity, thus permitting both the reification of *Kultur* into commodity forms and the accumulation of the finest human cultural products by a few at the expense of the majority.

Realigning human praxis and *Kultur* became a central theme of SED cultural policy and was normally articulated in positive dialectical terms as restoring to the *Volk* their true relationship to their *Kultur*al productivity:

> The incontrovertible first maxim of the socialist cultural program states that all *Kultur* belongs to the *Volk*. The *Volk* are the creator of *Kultur* and therefore all values of *Kultur* must flow back to them. Under socialism, we abolish the artificial division of *Kultur* inherited from antagonistic

social relations, where there is a *high* culture for the benefit of a "spiritual elite" and a *low* culture for the "great mass" of the *Volk*. By eliminating the isolation of workers from the considerable achievements of humanity, *Kultur* is realized for the first time as an inalienable human right. (Poerschke et al. 1983: 230)

The SED declared that the historical caesura of the GDR would reverse the cultural deformation of the elite culture/mass culture split and provide all members of the *Volk* equal and unalienable access to the totality of *Kultur*al production. This represented their own idiosyncratic vision of the *Kulturstaat*—a state that mediated and monitored the organic flow of creative energy to and from the *Volk* collective so that the formalizing, exteriorizing properties of bourgeois mass culture were avoided. In principle, the *Volk* could thus become the unmediated master of its own dialectical progression.

To give SED cultural policy due credit, the GDR did invest significant resources in making "high-cultural" activities more broadly available to nonelite strata through, for example, a network of community cultural centers that sponsored local music, art, and theater projects. What texts survived the elaborate state control mechanisms in print media were distributed widely and cheaply; poetry and literature were published in (by western standards) huge print runs with little thought to profit or even to recouping costs; opera and theater tickets were discounted, thus making high-cultural performances affordable to a broader spectrum of citizens than in the West; and so on. On my first trip to eastern Germany, in 1993, I roomed in Leipzig with a couple (he a construction foreman and she a laboratory assistant) who, although they identified themselves as "normal working-class people," were able to talk at great length and in great detail about, for example, the acoustic differences between concert halls in Leipzig and Dresden. They told me that the GDR's sponsorship of *Kultur* was something they remembered fondly and something they felt the West Germans always seemed to forget in their criticism of the SED regime.

On the other hand, even if one believes that the SED's cultural policies were well intentioned, there is little doubt that, in terms of its institutional practices, the SED party-state regulated its cultural institutions in an even more invasive fashion than the Nazis had (Bathrick 1995; von Hallberg 1996). Actual cultural expressions were continuously, obsessively scrutinized by party functionaries for evidence of "progressive" or "reactionary" tendencies on the part of the producer, who would then be either lauded or criticized accordingly. Despite attributing the source of all *Kultur* to the *Volk*'s inner creative powers, the SED determined that the proper course of historical formalization could not be undertaken by actually existing masses without supervision and guidance. The masses were said to have only a sensuous understanding of social processes, not a scientific understanding of them: "the multivariate phenomena, events, and processes which the masses confront in their daily life and daily struggle are not investigated scientifically by them. Instead, the masses simply encounter, experience, feel, and sense them" (Poerschke et al. 1983: 84).[3] Lacking a "scientific" orientation to their praxis, the masses could never develop a revolutionary collective awareness of their own cultural power. To acquire *Wissenschaft,* the masses had to rely on the party, which would provide intellectual guidance and assistance on their behalf.

Mouthpieces of the *Volk*

In short, the party determined that those who composed the *Volk* needed to be constantly educated in their own world-historical character and mission under socialism. Hence, the state, in the memories of many East Germans, behaved toward its citizens like an *Oberlehrer* (head instructor). Like the NSDAP, the SED described its pedagogical orientation and practice as "propagandistic." Unlike the NSDAP, the SED conceived the *Wissenschaft* of Marxism-Leninism as the essential force and primary medium of its pedagogy of the masses, not the oratorical inflaming of nationalist passions or the sensual power of mass spectacle. In stark contrast to mainstream intellectual views about journalists in the late nineteenth century, the SED considered journalists to be among the party's most important *Volkslehrer* (educators of the people) since media work put them into daily and intimate contact with the *Volk*'s knowledge and praxis of cultural expression. The ideal of socialist journalism epitomized the relationship of party-state to *Volk* more widely. The journalist was defined as a kind of tutor of the *Volk* in matters of social theory and a medium of the *Volk*'s expression of their inchoate social knowledge.

The *Handbook of GDR Journalism* defines the work of the socialist journalist in explicitly world-historical terms: "To be a herald of the party, a

---

3. Patronizing images of the honest yet unsophisticated worker abound, for example, in SED publications on the media. "The newspaper teaches and educates. It does so with the singular goal of not only explaining the world but also of empowering people to change it. Yet learning can be strenuous and not everyone does it gladly. Especially when each and every article's form and content speaks to the reader like a schoolchild. Newspaper making is therefore not least about making reading and perusing a pleasurable experience, in order to make revolutionary learning joyful" (Röhr 1968: 153).

standard-bearer of the republic and the nation, a mouthpiece of the *Volk*, a messenger and a zealous sponsor of socialism, peace, and freedom—that is the mission of journalism in the GDR. If performed masterfully, the journalist becomes two things: the educator of people and the co-former of history [*Erfüllt er sie mit Meisterschaft, dann wird er beides: Bildner des Menschen und Mitgestalter der Geschichte*]" (*Journalistisches Handbuch* 1960: 20). As GDR media theorist Hermann Budzislawski put it, echoing the language of the Nazi journalist's relationship to the *Gedankengut* of the führer: "The journalistic personality in a revolutionary class is the executor of its trove of ideas, its voice, and its organizer" (1966: 18). Besides serving as the "mouthpiece of the *Volk*," the journalist was expected to be a loyal party soldier (*Parteisoldat*), mediating the will and science of the party without question. In the ideology of the party, where the party was already no more than the medium and proxy of the people's will, these two expectations for mediation were in no way contrary to one another. And yet, reconciling the knowledge of GDR citizens with the knowledge of the party proved to be the defining problem of socialist journalism for the entire duration of the GDR.

The Press of a New Type

The SED's model of socialist journalism, which was termed the "Press of a New Type," was first unveiled at the party's first press conference on 9 and 10 February 1950 and then institutionalized incrementally over the course of the next decade. Although the SED leadership had determined from even before the GDR's inception that their mass media should follow the Soviet model as its best example (Blaum 1985: 24; Richert, Stern, and Dietrich 1958), there was significant resistance to this model among many professional journalists who sought, after repression in the Third Reich, to recover the Weimar-era liberal press rather than a new monopolized party press. Some of these journalists founded the Verein der Deutschen Presse (VDP), a journalist's union, in 1946 to provide an autonomous regulatory body for professional practice. With the GDR's founding, however, the VDP was quickly integrated into the state's trade union umbrella organization (the Freier Deutscher Gewerkschaftsbund), and by the late 1950s it had ceased to function effectively as an advocate for professional autonomy from the state (Blaum 1985: 40–47).

The SED leadership initially sought to win skeptical journalists to its cause by publicly challenging what they portrayed in negative dialectical terms as "bourgeois *Nur-journalismus*" (journalism for its own sake). SED media theorist Hermann Budzislawski clarifies what distinguishes a "socialist journalist":

> The socialist journalist does not, as the bourgeois literatus does, consider it a degradation or an unbearable sacrifice of originality to follow the party line and to fulfill his especially complicated and singular function as a "cog and screw" of the unified party mechanism. Since the goals of the party, to which the journalistic revolutionary is committed with body and soul, correspond to the laws of historical necessity, there is in principle no contradiction between assuming a personal responsibility for the journalistic guidance of the masses and a complete assimilation [*Einordnung*] into the party apparatus. (1966: 18)

The reference to the function of the journalist as a " 'cog and screw' of the unified party mechanism" is culled from Lenin's writings on the press (1962: 45). Here, we encounter the image of System framed in positive dialectical terms, emphasizing the importance of individual sacrifice to the collective mission and organization of the party-state. In Lenin's theory of socialism, the positive systematicity of the party mechanism is consistently distinguished from the negative, extractive systematicity of bourgeois mass society.

The influence of Soviet press ideology on the SED "Press of a New Type" should not be underestimated, but there is also little evidence to suggest that the Soviets directly forced the SED to adopt a Leninist press. Instead, it appears that the SED elite quickly recognized their own political interests and cultural agenda in Lenin's classic formulation:

> The role of a newspaper, however, is not limited solely to the dissemination of ideas, to political education, and to the enlistment of political allies. A newspaper is not only a collective propagandist and a collective agitator, it is also a collective organiser. In this last respect it may be likened to the scaffolding round a building under construction, which marks the contours of the structure and facilitates communication between the builders, enabling them to distribute the work and to view the common results achieved by their organised labour. (1961: 22)

The flagship SED newspaper, *Neues Deutschland*, was indeed organized explicitly according to Lenin's model and served as the crucible for the calibration and dissemination of the "party line" on any matter of social import. Within the SED party organization the central party newspapers further functioned as proving grounds for cultivating and testing the loyalty and leadership capabilities of ambitious young party members.

In 1954, the SED cemented its control over the training of journalists by founding a School of Journalism at Karl-Marx University in Leipzig, the party's new central university for the GDR (Klump 1978). Increasingly, the SED demanded that anyone who was to hold a prominent position in the GDR media had to have successfully completed training at Leipzig. By 1958, even the VDP publicly relented: "Those who wish to educate must themselves be educated. That means that our journalists must be penetrated [*durchdrungen*] by the correctness of the most advanced form of *Wissenschaft* and stand on the firm foundation of the power of the workers and farmers" (in Blaum 1985: 43). This "most advanced form of *Wissenschaft*" was Marxism-Leninism, and the site where journalists would be educated in the future was the School of Journalism at Karl-Marx University. By the 1960s, almost all GDR journalists were trained through the Leipzig program (with the exception of the infrequent cases of so-called *Quereinsteiger*, journalists who entered the profession later in life after having pursued another career). Although SED membership was not explicitly required to enroll, it was clear to all who studied there that the SED's vision of party journalism was the only legitimate model for professional practice (Klump 1978; Osang 1996).

Five Principles of Socialist Journalism

The program at the School of Journalism emphasized five essential principles of socialist journalism: *Parteilichkeit* (politicality), *Wahrheitstreue* (loyalty to the truth), *Wissenschaftlichkeit* (scientific rationality), *Massenverbundenheit* (connection to the masses), and *Kritik* (criticism) (see Blaum 1985: 100–101; Boyle 1992: 154–55). *Parteilichkeit* recalled the tradition of "politicality" and shared political conviction associated with nineteenth-century party presses (see Requate 1995). The Leipzig program taught that "the principle of *Parteilichkeit* consists in the conscious and willing selection of party affiliation in the interests and goals of the working class and for social progress according to the fundamental ideas of Marxism-Leninism" (Poerschke et al. 1983: 103). "Conscious and willing selection of party affiliation" was a particularly important normative ideal since the SED was adamant that its journalists were not cajoled functionaries but rather that, *voluntarily* and *enthusiastically*, they had come to the same interpretive judgments as the party elite had.

Since the SED could not imagine itself transmitting anything less than purely truthful messages to the masses, the second principle, loyalty to the truth, encouraged journalists to remember that the cultivation of mass consciousness was also an actualization of the "true" and virtuous course of collective *Bildung*. "The socialist journalists' loyalty to the truth, that is, the necessary striving for true recognition in the interest of the working class, demands that what the journalist maintains in his published statements correspond to the facts of the case" (Poerschke et al. 1983: 114). Of all the principles of socialist journalism, the disjuncture between the ideal and the reality of the principle of loyalty to the truth was perhaps the greatest from the point of view of GDR journalists and the source for much irony, sarcasm, and negative dialectical wisdom among them, even for those who were sympathetic to the party. GDR journalist Günter Simon quotes one of his senior colleagues to this effect, who beautifully summarizes countless similar statements I heard in the course of my own field research: "It's a lousy feeling to be made to write about the sun streaming down from the blue firmament every single day, when outside there's actually thunder and lightning" (1990: 14).

The reason for this disjuncture was that, according to SED media policy, any critical representation of the GDR in its own media was seen to stimulate the counterrevolutionary threat of the West. The stakes of negative representation were cast in a language of treason against the *Volk* and against their state. Could whatever minor virtue there was in criticizing the SED's housing policy, for example, outweigh the far more injurious effect that giving the western class enemy (*Klassenfeind*) fodder for their media smear campaigns (*Hetzkampagnen*) would have? Erich Honecker, the SED general secretary from 1971 until 1989, is reputed to have made the remarkable declaration at a Politburo meeting, "In *our* country, it is *we* who will determine whether the truth is being told or not!" (Simon 1990: 89). Meanwhile, truth was placed on an installment plan, with the final payoff only to occur with the full realization of socialism on a global basis.

The third journalistic principle, scientific rationality, invokes and echoes the intellectual self-conception of nineteenth-century *Gebildeten*. *Wissenschaft* was understood by the SED as a sublating spiritual-intellectual orientation that would—much as in Fichte's idiom—guide, coordinate, and unite the masses in the *Bildung* of a more perfect society. The perceived rigor and systematicity of that "most advanced" mode of *Wissenschaft*, Marxist-Leninist philosophy, was identified as the source of and model for the desired unity of the *Volk*. The SED leadership and its *Volkslehrer* were the bearers of *Wissenschaft* who educated the masses in the socialist vision of the world and who supervised and guided their historical evolution as a fully self-aware *Volk*.

The fourth principle of socialist journalism, connection to the masses, elaborated this Fichtean logic. Since the spiritual creative energy of *Kultur* was defined as belonging, ultimately, to the people, journalists were urged to work in close connection to the masses at all times. The *Handbook of GDR Journalism* describes the principle as follows: "[Journalists] are the flesh of the people's flesh and will always write and speak their language, because the journalist's heart is the heart of the people, he is their servant, no more and no less" (*Journalistisches Handbuch* 1960: 16). Obliterating Marx's distinction between mental and material activity in the social division of labor, the SED often used tropes of organic-biological interconnection to substantiate the ideal of the party's "connection to the masses." In other journalistic training materials, the journalist is analogized as the head and ideational powers of the social body as distinct from the sensory powers, muscular energies, and skeletal structure of the masses. The SED often depicted itself as the central nervous system of the *Volk*, allowing the masses to rise above the animal intelligence that bourgeois society was all too happy to maintain in them.

One of the Leipzig textbooks captures the dialectical character of tropes of the masses precisely: "When we speak of the 'masses' in connection with the principle of connection to the masses [*Massenverbundenheit*], we absolutely do not mean by that a certain amount, in the sense of a numerical quantity, of people, but rather we mean a certain quality of people, that is, the *Volksmassen* [mass of the *Volk*]" (Poerschke et al. 1983: 118). The distinction of *Volk* as an inner quality as opposed to a quantity helped the SED to differentiate the mass culture of the party-state from the bourgeois mass culture it condemned. The party, by means of its journalists, meant to nurture and refine this inner quality into a perfected external expression in public culture.

In her evaluation of reader letters to the GDR press, Ellen Bos notes that, in practice, the principle of connection to the masses fell far short of its positive dialectical intention. She writes of the formulaic repetitive responses to these letters that "one gets the impression that the concept of connection to the masses came to assume, at least partly, the character of an 'empty phrase' without referential significance that was employed, so to speak, in a ritual function" (1993: 70). The formulaic character of this principle in practice had a great deal to do with the fact that the issues that readers typically submitted to journalists to be addressed in the media tended to be too pertinent to or critical of the party's interpretation of its success (e.g., commodity supply problems and interminable waiting lists for desired goods like automobiles) for party journalists to publicize them. Indeed, journalists sometimes had to author reader letters themselves to guarantee a sufficient number of suitable queries and comments.

The final principle of socialist journalism, criticism, is the most elusive. A fundamental tenet of SED ideology was that its scientific analysis of the world was capable of illuminating existing (dialectical) contradictions in society and of resolving them through relentless criticism. SED public discourse was, true to this tenet, interlaced with criticism of socialist underachievers and apologetics for the difficulty of realizing an ideal socialist society given the perduring threat of exterior intervention from a world not wholly aligned to the socialist cause. In practice, the *Kritik* principle was tangled with dialectical uncertainties. On the one hand, some criticism of the failure of material systems and forms could be tolerated insofar as it only strengthened the SED's political imagination of itself as the uncompromising vanguard of perfect societal *Bildung*. On the other, criticism of the *Wissenschaft* and planning of the SED and its leadership could not be tolerated. Criticism of minor SED officials was acceptable in some cases, but normally only post facto, after the party had decided that this or that official had fallen out of favor. As with so many axioms of GDR journalism, the journalist was caught between the party's transcendent vision of its world-historical purpose and its tenacious defense of its political and moral legitimacy to govern. In journalistic practice, the latter constraints made the fulfillment of the former nearly impossible to realize.

In the end, the *Kritik* principle was fulfilled almost entirely by concentrated criticism of West Germany, the West German media, and, more generally, bourgeois imperialism. FRG media scholar Wilfried Scharf described the composite image of life in West Germany offered by the East German media:

> The Federal Republic of Germany appears exclusively as a state whose government is striving for arms buildup, that is in a permanent condition of economic crisis, that is trying to dismantle its welfare system, that protects Nazis and Neo-Nazis, and that, in a revanchist way, seeks the expansion of German territorial boundaries. Irrationality and superstition prevail in the FRG because West German citizens are afraid of seeing the awful reality of their situation. (1985: 255)

Through such critical practice, the *Handbook of GDR Journalism* ordained the socialist journalist an agent of the education of "a new German man" and the savior of the *Volk* and its "national idea" from the martyrdom of the "antinational," irrational tendencies of western capitalism (*Journalistisches Handbuch* 1960: 17).

By upholding the five principles of socialist journalism, the *Handbook* further assured the socialist journalist that she or he would never suffer the immoral fate of the West German journalist:

> Under the spell of imperialism generally, and in West Germany particularly, the kind of journalist who garners the greatest accolades is he who conceals his inner depravity within a toga of virtues worn merely for show. This intellectual Cain works toward the fratricide of Germans by spreading calumnies about life under socialism, especially socialism in the GDR, which consist of distorted and contorted reports and ill-willed, hateful inventions. By contrast, journalists win respect and affection in the GDR by utilizing newspapers, radio, and television to contribute intelligent advice for how to raise our social standards [*Niveau*]. It is incumbent upon them to use all of their ability, knowledge, and extraordinary powers of influence to affect immediately the racing events of our time and to achieve new victories in the name of socialism. (1960: 19)

SED discourse on mediation outside the GDR is replete with negative dialectical tropes of the false images and inner depravities plaguing the *Volk*. The SED scarcely needed to invoke the specter of Jewish mediation since the West German "class enemy" consistently doubled in its place.[4]

The *Lenkungssystem:* Objectives and Institutions of Media Control in the GDR

Beyond training socialist journalists, the monopolization of media culture by the SED after the 1960s involved the development of a complex series of structural and ritual controls on media practice, a so-called *Lenkungssystem* (guidance or control system) that was as extensive and present in the everyday life of socialist journalism as it was absent from the theoretical and pedagogical outlines of socialist journalism.

---

4. This is not to say, however, that anti-Semitic rhetoric had no place in the GDR. Historian Jeffrey Herf offers an excellent discussion, for example, of the SED's effort to purge itself of the specter of Jewish "cosmopolitanism" in the 1950s (1997: 106–61). The political persecutions of Jews that followed in the GDR testify to resonances between the NSDAP's and the SED's political self-imagination as the spiritual stewards of a German *Volk* under assault by the exteriorities of modernization and by mediation's human agents.

The fundamental objectives of media control for the SED were, as they were for the NSDAP, (1) transcending the abundantly heterogeneous mediation associated with bourgeois mass culture and (2) replacing it with an integrated, monopolized, and monosemous public culture consonant with the harmonious collectivity associated with the *Volk* and its *Kultur*. These objectives organized the logic of the *Lenkungssystem* at every level of its institutional organization. At an infrastructural level, media monopolization began with the restructuring of the media networks in the GDR during the 1950s and 1960s to guarantee a centralized organization for the dissemination of news from centers in Berlin to regional peripheries (Boyle 1992: 129–37). New production centers for radio and television production were constructed in Berlin and its suburbs. Meanwhile, the print media were organized into a district (*Bezirk*) system that channeled party supervision from Berlin to each district-level SED office and to its regional newspaper (*Bezirkszeitung*), some of which had as many as twenty local editions with total circulations ranging from 150,000 to 600,000 (the SED flagship paper, *Neues Deutschland*, by comparison published over a million copies a day for the country's population of roughly 16 million).

Although the SED prohibition on the distribution of any information from a non-GDR source created a theoretically closed economy of news, the penetration of West German radio and television into all but the northeastern and southeastern corners of the GDR presented constant evidence of mediation beyond the SED's control. West German television in particular made the SED elite profoundly anxious, leading to calls for a "round-the-clock ideological engagement in the ether with bourgeois ideology" from General Secretary Erich Honecker in 1976 (Holzweissig 1983: 13–14). One weekly GDR television program, *Der Schwarze Kanal* (The Black Channel), focused on the refutation of western media reports and offered frequent ad hominem assaults against western society.

To further limit the threat of excessive western influence, the SED set up a central news information service, the Allgemeine Deutsche Nachrichtendienst (ADN), and a central news photo service (see Boyle 1992: 138–40; Minholz and Stirnberg 1995: 203–14) to channel flows of "legitimate" information within the mass media. ADN became an official state institution in 1953 and provided almost all the foreign correspondents for the electronic and print media, established a vast local-correspondent network throughout the GDR, was the only legitimate access to western press and wire service reports, and controlled all publishable photos. ADN thus exercised critical selective influence over what information could be publicized in the GDR media, especially in terms of foreign affairs. Radio and press coverage would often simply reproduce ADN reports verbatim, since every journalist knew the serious professional danger of inaccurately rewriting an ADN report. By restructuring institutional channels of mediation, the party could and did guarantee a great deal of homogeneity in media forms simply as a result of limiting message flows.

The Party Line

The SED was aware that controlling the infrastructure of mass mediation did not alone guarantee the harmonization of mass mediation. So the party developed a complex set of practices for coordinating the *Wissenschaft* of the party with the media production of individual media organizations. All these practices centered upon the constitution, distribution, and incorporation of the party line, the party leadership's hermeneutic settlement for a given object of representation in the world. The SED believed that the institutionalization of the party line, like the Nazi *Führerprinzip*, would control and sublate mass mediation and thereby stimulate the development of *Volk* consciousness among the masses.

A diagram of the distribution network of the party line would be pyramid shaped. At the tip was the general secretary of the SED, a figure who, like the Nazi führer, embodied a fusion of intellectual power and administrative power that radiated downward and outward. The supreme arbiter of the *Volk*'s will, the general secretary's judgments as to how the exterior world must be interpreted and represented (a principle I have termed elsewhere "hermeneutic power"; Boyer 2003a) were held sacrosanct at all inferior levels of party hierarchy (see Holzweissig 1997: 33–34 and Boyle 1992: 167 for outlines of these relations). Below the general secretary, within his "cabinet"—the Politburo of the SED (numbering about twenty individuals)—the various ministerial secretaries played an important daily role in transposing the party line into actual policies and programs in each of their governmental jurisdictions. In keeping with the logic of party vassalage, the secretaries' own opinions were sacrosanct at every level below that of the general secretary. In strict observation of bureaucratic stratification, any sign of discord with the party line in the lower hierarchical ranks of the party was greeted with immediate public censure, party disciplinary action, and, in the worst cases, also with being "sent into the desert" (*in die Wüste geschickt*), as party parlance described being cast out of the fertile cultural Eden of the SED.[5]

---

5. Between 1981 and 1988, GDR state records indicate there were 163,285 political investigations (*Parteiverfahren*) undertaken in the GDR to determine whether certain SED members or

Unlike Hitler's inconsistent application of the *Führerprinzip* to Goebbels's propaganda ministry, the depth of personal involvement in the everyday business of media production on the part of the general secretaries was, to quote media historian Gunter Holzweissig, "unimaginable" (1997: 60). Like his predecessor, Walter Ulbricht (1950–71), General Secretary Erich Honecker (1971–89) dutifully and daily proofread the first few pages of the party central organ, *Neues Deutschland* (which contained the most precise formulation of the party line with regard to foreign and domestic news, coverage of party events, and political commentaries), made corrections down to the level of punctuation and diction, read a plethora of West German papers, scribed acrimonious and sometimes cryptic responses to them, and handed these on to the Politburo's secretary of Agitation for general circulation.

At the 1990 trial of Secretary of Agitation Joachim Herrmann, a former chief editor of *Neues Deutschland* documented Honecker's media work in his testimony:

Former general secretary Honecker had reserved for himself the right to personally supervise the media, in particular the central organ of the SED, *Neues Deutschland*. It was my job to make sure that ND functioned smoothly and in keeping with the directives of the general secretary as well as with party declarations. Every day we had to supply the general secretary, via [Agitation Secretary] Herrmann, with a sketch of the following day's ND. That meant pages 1 and 2 had to be provided in detail as well as the major articles from all other pages. There was little leeway for the journalists on page 2 because it was overloaded with protocolary news reports, or on page 3, where as a rule letters and formal greetings to the general secretary had to be printed, or on the foreign news page, which was predominantly determined in advance and where we were obliged to print the news reports delivered to us by ADN. Honecker

---

candidate members "had to be distanced from the party because they stood against the general line of the party, because they denied the successes of our socialist state, or through un-party-like behavior or continuous grumbling and grousing damaged or betrayed the GDR" (in Modrow 1994: 262). There were three possible outcomes of such proceedings: warning (*Rüge*), serious warning (*strenge Rüge*), or expulsion (*Ausschuss*). During the same period, some 62,124 (or 38 percent) of the political investigations resulted in expulsion (262–65). For expelled journalists, this also meant a *Berufsverbot* (professional ban), meaning one was no longer licensed to practice journalism in the GDR. One expelled journalist I interviewed nevertheless was allowed to teach classes on journalism at a secondary school.

and Herrmann themselves determined even how the articles should be placed on the pages. (AZ: 111-1-90-3: 6)[6]

Honecker also routinely wrote news bulletins to be circulated by ADN, which became (like *Neues Deutschland*) an effective and efficient institutional medium through which the general secretary could channel his hermeneutic power. Honecker worked closely with Secretary of Agitation Herrmann to ensure that his articulation of the party line would be circulated without emendation or corruption. Rolf Schablinski, the assistant director of ADN from 1979 to 1989, testified as follows at the 1990 trial of Herrmann:

> There was a comprehensive system in place for the coordination of information [*Informationen*] and news reports of national and international characters. All reports that were considered important had to be sent through the so-called "supply system" either by telephone or in writing to Herrmann's office. The decision whether the report in question could appear as is or whether it had to be rewritten or whether Agitation would rewrite it themselves was made there. ADN was obliged to publish the reports in question exactly as they were returned to us by Herrmann's office. Herrmann himself had to confer with Honecker and the two of them reserved for themselves the final decision-making power about whether a particular report might be published or not.
>
> Herrmann gave all of the reports to Honecker, who personally edited them and released them. Herrmann then took these rewritten reports to be sacred. Nothing could be changed or altered or added to them, even if they were factually incorrect or if the report was written in such a way as to be unintelligible. (AZ: 111-1-90-3: 8)

I have confirmed with several former ADN journalists the fact that Honecker's prose was always taboo to further editorial intervention (see also Boyle 1992: 171; Arnold and Arnold 1994: 103–4). These journalists reported that no one dared to challenge the general secretary's epistemic privilege even in cases of sophomoric grammatical errors and blatant misspellings. In an institutional media culture where no journalist or editor with whom I spoke described a feeling of professional autonomy over his or her daily

---

6. A copy of this document, possibly originally from the Stiftung Archiv der Parteien und Massenorganisationen der DDR (SAPMO) in the Bundesarchiv-Berlin, is now in my possession.

practice, only the general secretary was allowed the unmediated expression of Spirit.

With this privilege, in the political imagination of the SED, came the general secretary's responsibility for exerting his hermeneutic power to unify the potential chaos of knowledge in public culture. This accounts for the otherwise-perplexing issue of why a head of state would spend so much of his time writing newspaper commentaries and scrutinizing television broadcasts, even to the point of making layout decisions. That the general secretaries of the SED devoted so much of their time to, in essence, practicing journalism is perhaps the best evidence we have of the dialectical importance of emancipating the *Kultural* productivity of the *Volk* from mass culture for the SED state. Honecker, for one, appears to have applied an obsessive, artisanal care to his negotiation of epistemic and semiotic order through the media. It is rumored that he, on occasion, even personally matched newsreaders' ties with the background sets of *Aktuelle Kamera*, the GDR nightly news program.

Agitation and Propaganda

In concert with the general secretary's deep personal involvement in media production at ADN and *Neues Deutschland*, responsibility for comprehensively managing mass media in the GDR fell to the Agitation Division of the Central Committee (for the SED press), to the GDR state Press Office (for the non-SED press), and to the State Committees on Radio and Television (for the electronic mass media). The "state" autonomy of the latter two state regulatory offices was largely illusory, however, since the Press Office and both state committees received daily instructions and feedback from the Agitation Division, were directed by loyal SED elites, and referred all major decisions directly to the secretary of the Agitation Division, who was appointed as a member of the Politburo (Holzweissig 1997; Boyle 1992). The Agitation Division therefore possessed nearly complete authority to monitor the entire GDR mass media, to make any changes in personnel and content they deemed necessary, and to give journalists hourly, daily, and weekly updates of minute adjustments to the party line, handed down to them in turn from the Politburo. To be clear, there was no formal censor's office in the GDR nor even official "censors" in the media control apparatus. In the first place, such an office would have violated the GDR constitution, which until 1968 explicitly claimed freedom for the press (see Holzweissig 1997: 13); but, more importantly, it would have violated the SED's own claim to legitimacy as a proxy for the *Volk*. If indeed the SED had the power of *Wissenschaft* it claimed and if it had correctly interpreted and expressed the will of the *Volk*, then what need would there be for censorship?

Instead, the work of the Agitation Division was officially "advisory" rather than interdictory as it issued a continuous stream of supplemental advisories on changes in the party line to the heads of the GDR media (Arnold and Arnold 1994: 98). The primary ritual for disseminating these advisories was the infamous (among journalists) Thursday "argumentation session" also known colloquially as the "*Argu*" (Bürger 1990; see also Büro Schabowski DY 30/IV 2/2.040/6 and consecutive files),[7] to which the heads of the major GDR media organizations were "invited." These were formal meetings held in the Central Committee building and supervised by the director of the Agitation Division, who was a direct subordinate of the secretary of Agitation. Their purpose was threefold: (1) to articulate the party line for the upcoming week along with detailed instructions about which events were of particular ideological significance, (2) to circulate a list of tabooed themes and words, which were not to be circulated in the GDR media, and (3) to mete out specific criticism or praise for individual organizations who had or had not fulfilled the expectations of the party elite over the past week. Although these argumentation sessions were supposedly dialogues between the Agitation experts and leading journalists about how best to fulfill the injunctions of socialist journalism, most participants recall them in negative dialectical terms as didactic monologues intended to discipline leaders of the GDR media into acknowledging the absolute authority of the party line.

Hans-Dieter Schütt, then chief editor of the SED Youth League daily, *Junge Welt*, describes the Wednesday meetings of the Agitation Commission that preceded and prepared the material for the larger Thursday gatherings as follows:

> As a rule we waited there for more than an hour for [Agitation Secretary] Herrmann, who always arrived out of breath from a meeting with Honecker. Then he held a three- or four-hour monologue about current events and that was that. It was basically just like receiving orders in the army, but at a more elite level. I still have in memory the mental image of a group of intimidated, nodding, feverishly note-taking, but, above all, silent media leaders, myself included. In the most extreme cases, they might throw significant glances at one another, but then certainly with the feeling that they had probably gone too far. Resistance with one's eyebrows! (In Holzweissig 1997: 26–27)

7. All the documents I cite can be found in the SAPMO collection in Berlin (but see n. 5).

Although Schütt described the *Argu* to me as a ritualized genuflection to the power of the party line, others who attended explained that the meetings actually delivered other kinds of information as well: ministers, directors of state firms, and other experts were invited to speak on a wide range of topics, often quite frankly. What was absolutely clear to those listening, however, was that any information that chafed against the party leadership's vision of its own success was to be held strictly in the confidence of an intellectual elite (who the party believed were intellectually mature enough to cope with the contradiction between official narrative and perceptual reality) and under no circumstances was to be made public (see Zimmermann and Schütt 1992).

Holzweissig offers a sample list of taboos and rationales taken from the notes of Dieter Langguth, an assistant director in the Agitation Division from 1984 to 1989 (1997: 38). A few of the more striking interdictions follow:

> Don't use the term, "State Circus." (It could make the state seem ridiculous. Out of spite, one newspaper then used "GDR Circus." This was promptly forbidden as well.)
> Nothing about formaldehyde. (People could become afraid of getting cancer.)
> Nothing about putting, lawn bowling, villas, or boulevards. (They awake desires which we are not capable of satisfying.)
> Don't photograph the fruit on the tables at official receptions. (Otherwise the people will become envious.)
> Nothing about bratwurst kiosks. (People are already eating enough meat.)
> Nothing about homemade gliders. (People may think to escape.)
> Nothing about Formula 1 racing. (We can't afford it.)"

As Langguth's list shows, the taboo system was largely oriented toward economic issues, specifically to failures of the SED planned economy to achieve sufficient productivity to satisfy popular demand. Many of the taboos were aimed at blocking consumer desire by removing potentially disharmonious lexical stimuli from popular awareness. The taboo system was a pedagogical technique coupled to a particular "language ideology" (see Gal 1998; Irvine 1992; Kroskrity 2000; Schieffelin, Woolard, and Kroskrity 1998; Silverstein 1976, 1979, 1985; Woolard 1998) that assumed that without the public representation of a sign or of a lexical construction such as "Formula 1 racing," neither public consciousness of its referentiality nor the actual object of reference would be significant: literally, "out of mind, out of sight."

The weekly ritual of the *Argu* was augmented by frequent phone calls from the Agitation Division to various individual media organizations with post facto (most often negative) reactions to specific articles or broadcasts (Arnold and Arnold 1994: 107). It is difficult to gauge the scale of this feature of the *Lenkungssystem* because the majority of advisories were apparently delivered orally and without record (Holzweissig 1997: 37). One chief editor I interviewed calculated that he received calls from Agitation functionaries on average perhaps twice a week, but that high-ranking functionaries from other ministries felt free to call him as well if, for example, they wished to express personal outrage for what they saw as a less-than-glowing representation of some operation under their jurisdiction.

Political Errors

Several former chief editors of GDR media organizations I interviewed agreed that, contrary to the party leadership's conceptualization of the party line as a harmonizing force in media production, the abundance of advisories, warnings, and censures often arrived on their desks in a haphazard way, with the weekly, daily, and hourly updates from the Agitation Division sometimes contradicting one another and with the threat of personal intervention by Honecker or Herrmann always on the horizon. Against the backdrop of the, in experience, many-headed hydra of the "party line," chief editors had the unenviable task of assessing every actual line of text produced within their institutions for "political errors" (*politische Fehler*) in the reportage. "Political error" was a term used broadly to denote any perceived dissonance between a given media representation and the party line.

According to the testimony of former employees, some chief editors felt comfortable towing the party line and in exercising disciplinary authority within the *Lenkungssystem*. Others, however, seemed concerned by the arbitrariness of the taboo system and attempted to protect their journalists from its most severe affects. Although there are few written records documenting party disciplinary actions against journalists, my interviews with several journalists who were given *Berufsverbote* (professional bans) in the GDR suggest that reasons varied from repeated failure to exhibit an appropriate respect for the party line to unintentional political errors that were magnified in the Agitation Division's opinion by subsequent rebroadcasting of them in the western media.[8] Holzweissig contends that, by the 1980s, the

8. Holzweissig has collected a few other cases of disciplinary actions (1997: 135–52), and rumors and stories abound among journalists. The archival evidence is thin in the remaining files

severity of punishments had lessened (1997: 148) owing to increasing uncertainty within the upper echelons of the SED about the continued solvency of the GDR; imprisonment for political errors became less common.

Chief editors, at any rate, appear to have had some authority to insulate their journalists from the Agitation Division, especially if they had good personal *Beziehungen* (connections) in the Central Committee and were willing to "take some heat" for articles that were deemed to contain serious errors. One journalist explained to me:

> My chief editor did that [disseminated the taboos] with noticeable reserve; he couldn't actually say it in words; if he had, he'd have lost his job. But somehow he denied the whole process. He let us know without saying it directly that the people who were giving him these directions *von oben* [from above] were people who didn't think about what they were doing, who had no idea about making newspapers. He used to keep a board up in his office with everything that he'd been told was taboo to write about, that we weren't permitted to write about, and it was clear to everyone that this board symbolized his opinion that the people who were giving him these orders were idiots because if you couldn't write about all of these things, well, then there would be nothing left to write about.

In an interview in 1997, a former chief editor of a GDR newspaper explained to me that, in his experience, the taboos were differentially binding: "What you have to understand was that it was a character issue. If you wanted to see strict orders [*Befehle*] in these advisories, it was entirely possible to do so. But you could also see them as guidelines." Journalists even at the most carefully supervised institutions such as *Neues Deutschland* described to me a newsroom atmosphere where journalists could discuss even politically sensitive issues among trusted colleagues relatively openly. It was also understood, however, that to publicize the results of any of these debates and dialogues would constitute a political error of the greatest magnitude.[9]

---

of the Agitation Division and the GDR Press Office. Relatively little work has been done to date in the Stasi (state security) archives on disciplinary actions taken against journalists, although it appears as though there were few cases of official Stasi operations (so-called *Operative Vorgänge*) against individual journalists. The common wisdom among specialists on the Stasi files is that journalists, as opposed to writers, for example, were simply too politically reliable and loyal on the whole to constitute an area of special interest for the Stasi.

9. By way of comparison, it is important to note that most western media professionals also segment information into categories of "private" and "public" circulation (see Buchsteiner 1997; Tuchman 1978).

Crafting Words, Clarifying Meanings

I once asked a GDR-era chief editor to explain the logic of the taboo system to me and, in particular, why it was that the party went to such lengths to establish mastery over words. He replied:

> The printed word was so important because everything was predetermined. In the opinion of the leaders, nothing was supposed to happen that they hadn't planned in advance. There was no spontaneity. It wasn't permitted. So [for journalism] the most important dogma was "it had to *look* good." Therefore the headlines had to be right and the political line had to be right. . . . The leadership lived through the printed word and the spoken word on television. . . . It's a crazy case of wishful thinking. It's voluntarism, no? It's like saying, "I want something to be true," and then when I see it the next day in the newspaper, I can say to myself, "See, the newspaper says it's true too!" *Wunderbar!*

According to my interlocutor, the SED found in the apparent "fixity" of the printed word a mimetic sign of their authority and *Wissenschaft* to call forth a more perfect social world. Indeed, a perfectly crafted word—monosemous, stable, and orthodox—was considered the best proof of the party's redemption of *Kultur* from mass culture. The successful engineering of meaning on a collective basis would symbolize a positive dialectical redemption of epistemic form itself from the barbarous polysemy and empty formality characteristic of mass culture. According to Michael Holquist, "the monologic terror of indeterminacy" is "the essence of all censorship" (1994: 21). In this respect, management of the printed word and its meanings became the basis for the cultivation of a *Volk* awareness and self-consciousness.

It is for this reason that the censorial processes of the SED focused so closely on the exacting calibration of the referential properties of language, especially in print media (rather than, for example, radio, where Agitation surveillance and discipline, while continuous and at times intensive, were generally pursed less rigorously; see Klein 1993). It is worth noting that the SED's belief in their agency to engineer meaning on a collective scale is only a somewhat extreme variant of an understanding of language that anthropological linguist Kathryn Woolard describes as typically European in that it "reveal[s] a tendency to see reference or propositionality as the essence of language, to confuse or at least to merge the indexical functions of language with the referential function, and to assume that the divisions and structures of language should—and in the best circumstances do—transparently fit the structures of the 'real world'" (1998: 13). Woolard argues that there is a tendency in European-language communities to interpret meaning as the essence of language. This understanding of how language works, while partial, nevertheless invites projects of engineering meaning in order to control communication and the formation of knowledge.

The SED leadership were greatly concerned, however, that their ability to control meaning in the GDR was compromised by the ethereal presence of bourgeois media in the GDR. For this reason, the SED invested an exceptional amount of time and energy in the language of the GDR media itself in order to provide the greatest possible insulation of the GDR public from the mediation of the western class enemy. For language to be any good for socialism, as Maxim Gorky once proclaimed, it had to be rid of the "pernicious toxin" of the inherited meanings of bourgeois philistinism (Gorky 1934: 64; see also Zima 1975: 90).

Discourse on language produced within GDR universities often thematized a tension between the semantic abundance of language and the desired goal of linguistic "clarity." Vagueness and ambiguity in public language, hallmarks of the epistemic heterogeneity and polysemy of mass culture, had to be minimized at all costs. As GDR media scholar Karl-Heinz Röhr counseled journalists:

> One must write about unclear topics in as clear a way as possible. One must explain why they are "unclear." One must remove a lack of clarity wherever possible especially when this is a result of the vagueness of statements or of their ambiguous nature. One must write attractively and interestingly even when one is dealing with special and difficult questions. And one must do all of this because the masses are truly waiting for the responses to these questions and problematics. (1968: 156–57)

Media historian Rolf Geserick notes that most academic work produced within the GDR on media language focused on the problem of how to wring greater "linguistic effectivity" (*sprachliche Wirksamkeit*) from media representation and, to this end, advised that journalists utilize "clear structures of argument, logical consistency, easily recognizable sentence constructions, a high proportion of verbs, avoidance of abstract formulations, novel constructions, moderate closeness to common speech, concreteness, beneficial redundancies, originality and entertainment value" (1989: 297–98). The motivating question was how to increase the "receptivity" of citizens to GDR media messages and thus to the rightful epistemic order, the *Wissenschaft,* determined by the SED party elite.

The journalist's relationship to language was a central problem in theoretical and practical considerations of socialist journalism. The *Handbook of GDR Journalism* offered a comparative discussion of the different languages of representation available to the journalist for depicting everyday life in the GDR:

> Our life, which ought to be reflected in journalistic language, is filled with contradictions and with struggle and motion. The journalist stands in the middle of the fray, takes sides, and fights on the front lines. For this, he needs a polemical, powerful, and accurate language. . . .
>
> So-called functionaries' German [*Funktionärsdeutsch*], the dry, scarcely concrete kind of German influenced by abstract expressive constructions of scientific discourse, nevertheless is capable of unambiguous descriptions of important issues. It is therefore ten times better than the nebulous flattery behind which many scribes of the imperialist bourgeoisie attempt to conceal reality. Still, the vanguard of the working class cannot isolate themselves through their language. We are undertaking the greatest revolution in German history. We must therefore find a language that dignifies such an epoch and that is worthy of the entire nation. (*Journalistisches Handbuch* 1960: 187)

The ranking of possible journalistic languages in this passage is revealing. Worst of all is the "nebulous flattery" of bourgeois journalism, which sweetens and conceals "reality" through its ornateness of representation. Better, but still not perfect, is the functionaries' German; it alienates the *Volk* through its abstraction, but at least it is honest and dictates a correct and earnest order over the contradictions and motion of everyday life. The best form of language is the "polemical, powerful, and accurate language" of SED imagining. The SED believed that only a relentless, collective effort could develop linguistic forms strung taut with poetic spirit and yet capable of absolute referential precision; likewise, they believed that only such precise language would be worthy of the inner spirit of the nation (see also Zima 1975: 86–88).

Of course, precision and accuracy in matters of language were largely in the eye of the beholder. The East German writer Stefan Heym once attempted, as an experiment, to inform himself solely through watching *Aktuelle Kamera* on GDR television (1993). His conclusions provide insight

into the language of GDR media and into the equally intimate and estranging effects of this language on those positioned outside, in Heym's case just
outside, the networks of its creation.

The language is High-GDR, well-groomed bureaucratese, full of high-
sounding substantives trimmed with matching adjectives. The sentences
demand deep breaths from their readers and deep concentration from
their listeners. Comprehension is made easier though by certain clichés,
which are generously scattered through the texts. These are code words
that immediately provoke specific associations in the minds of a public well trained by newspaper lectures, collective meetings, and school
courses. If you had inadvertently switched on this channel, you'd identify
the station instantly: no one talks this way except on GDR television.

I offer below a by-no-means-complete list of what I picked up during
this month. Think of it as a psychological test.

	is/are always	
change		far-reaching
realization	" "	single-minded
exchanges of ideas	" "	comprehensive
atmosphere	" "	creative
requests	" "	prioritized
advice	" "	in-depth
decisions	" "	far-sighted
foundations	" "	unshakable
relationships of trust	" "	indestructible
declarations	" "	impressive
realization	" "	complete
strengthening	" "	universal
requirements	" "	fundamental
recognition	" "	international
growth	" "	dynamic
approval	" "	shared by millions

You see, it's all about incantations: the fuller one's mouth is with
them, the greater the effect. It is reminiscent, like so many things about
Aktuelle Kamera, of relaxation through self-hypnosis—your heart beats
calmly, your solar plexus radiates warmth—and the process is completed
by further phrases in this lofty language. . . . At some point it attains
a poetic quality. Thus, on the 10th of October we learn in connection
with the awarding of the Karl-Marx medal to the GDR Academy of the
Sciences that scientific-technical progress is *an inexhaustible and ever*

more strongly flowing spring from which human life, material as well
as spiritual, may be comprehensively enriched. (1993: 94–95)

Heym recognizes the careful intellectual labor encased in the language
of GDR television. He admits the somatic effects ("relaxation through self-
hypnosis") of its routines, to whose amniotic warmth, after hours of denying
its epistemic validity, he was finally forced to succumb. What is so strange
about "this lofty language" for Heym is that its primary mediating function no longer appears to be representation but rather incantation—the language not only signals state power but also seeks to conjure a certain kind of
consciousness through the hypnotic repetitiveness of its formulas. As SED
Politburo member Günter Schabowski once wrote, one had to believe in
socialism for it to work (1991: 119–20). The public language of GDR media
was designed precisely to incant a genuine *Volkskultur.*

The Institutionalization of Satire

It haunted the SED no end that, despite the care and energy that the party
devoted to cultivating *Volkskultur,* its labors were not widely appreciated.
Indeed, it is fair to argue that the majority of GDR citizens found the language of GDR media less than seductive and many appeared to tune out
its *Wissenschaft* entirely. The SED developed a number of strategies for
addressing this problem, including market oversaturation (printing in runs
well above any demonstrated demand), ideological repetitiveness (since the
masses did not appear to be "getting the message"), and policing families'
reception of western television and radio. One of their more creative, but
less well known, strategies deserves brief mention: the party-state granted
a monopoly over the satirical representation of life in the GDR to the magazine *Eulenspiegel.* On the face of it, sponsoring a satire magazine might
appear to run starkly against the grain of SED public-cultural policy, which
sought to relentlessly purify the mediated image of the GDR.

Nevertheless, the SED was well aware that satires on the party, state,
and socialism were pervasive and popular among GDR citizens.[10] SED leaders hoped that a state monopoly on satire could channel satire toward a

10. Comparatively, see Achille Mbembe's brilliant exploration of the "intimate tyranny" that
links the *commandement* and its targets in authoritarian states (1992: 22). Although missing some
of the vulgarity and obscenity of the Cameroonian case, parodies of state power were common in
the GDR. The general secretary's intellectual powers were often loci of satires that suggested that
he was really quite stupid or that his ideas were really stolen from other functionaries or from the
West. For a sample of GDR-era jokes, see Wagner 1994, 1996.

progressive end and that *Eulenspiegel* would serve to integrate moderate self-criticism into the party's hermeneutics of everyday life in keeping with the socialist principle of *Kritik* (Klötzer 1996: 33). Beginning in the 1950s, the SED granted *Eulenspiegel* an exclusive legal right to represent social problems in a satirical form, and true to prediction, it quickly became one of the most popular GDR publications.

As one might expect, *Eulenspiegel*'s popularity was a source of both pride and concern for the party-state, and the magazine attracted a great deal of attention from the Agitation Division. The chief editor of *Eulenspiegel* operated in continuous negotiation with Agitation functionaries and with the Politburo over the boundaries of permissible social satire such that the magazine did not "deliver any ammunition to the class enemy" (Klötzer 1996: 31). The general rules for *Eulenspiegel,* as former journalists explained to me, were that moderate social satire was tolerable providing (1) the object of satire was life in the GDR and *not* the SED itself and (2) the satire portrayed its object as being a singular pathological case and not an example of systemic failure. The SED and its *Wissenschaft* thus maintained their sacralized character, down to the level of wordplay, as one former *Eulenspiegel* journalist recalled for me:

> There was [an] article I wrote about a club owner who was slipping booze to kids, you know putting rum into their cola, and the punch line of the article was "I guess that's why they call it the Free German Youth [FDJ] and not the *Alcohol*-Free German Youth." And again I had to discuss everything with the chief editor. He basically said the piece was good but he thought we'd have to take that last line out. Because, you see, you couldn't parody anything having to do with the SED. For two hours we discussed this point. I wanted to see if he would give up, but he was determined to let me know that it was wrong for me to write that. . . . You couldn't do word-plays that had to do with the SED. That's why he wanted me to take that pun out.

I asked him whether the editor's point was that one was not allowed to parody the SED, and he replied: "You see, this work wasn't precise like mathematics for example. He didn't know what would happen to him if he ran it. He didn't know if there was someone higher up who would take offense to it and make trouble for him."

Yet, my interlocutor continued, the low-ranking party-state functionary was fair game, assuming that the two basic principles of legitimate satire were otherwise maintained:

I guess there were perhaps times when we disturbed the otherwise comfortable lives of the functionaries. . . . People were always asking me suspiciously, "How is it that you heard about me actually?" When *Eulenspiegel* wrote about someone, it was like losing a point for them in general. By contrast, if *Neues Deutschland* wrote about someone, it was like scoring a point. Because they would ask those typical *Neues Deutschland* questions like "By how many percentage points have you exceeded this year's plan?" and those kinds of questions were obviously not part of our praxis at all.

The relationship to Agitation was often strained. *Eulenspiegel* was instructed to obey special taboos and at one point earned itself a full-time censor for several months, who proofread the galleys for the entire magazine before it was allowed to go to press (Klötzer 1996: 31). At other times, criticism would come directly from the general secretary or from Politburo members like Gunter Mittag (the GDR planned-economy czar) who were personally offended by something they had read in the magazine. As another *Eulenspiegel* journalist related to me, the magazine, like *Neues Deutschland*, received a great deal of direct attention from the Politburo:

> There were sometimes special taboos for *Eulenspiegel*. For example, construction was a favorite theme of ours because there was always so much that went wrong. And there were cases when the chief editor and the author of a particular piece would be called down to Agitation to give an account of their behavior. And, well, you can forget [Director of Agitation] Geggel, you couldn't get anywhere with him, but there were a few guys at Agitation who were sympathetic to us. They would say, "We really appreciate what you're doing in *Eulenspiegel* but you see that Mittag called up today really angry and he says he's got a criminal indictment all ready to go for you guys. Now don't worry about that, it won't come to that, but for three months nothing more about construction, OK?" And so, for three months we didn't write anything about construction. Even the people in Agitation, in the Central Committee, everyone who read [our parody], knew that it was true, but it wasn't *permitted* to be true. Then came the *Eiertanz* [dance on eggs].

The Comfort and Cunning of System

The metaphor of the "dance on eggs" evokes the frustration of working as a journalist in a System that set ideological conditions for reality and then persecuted those whose senses and intuitions were at variance with these conditions. But the "dance" also captures the intimacy and occasional conviviality of censorial relations in GDR media culture. Journalists, not only at *Eulenspiegel*, interpreted the "sympathy" of Agitation as a kind of collegiality, and their guidance as tantamount to an informal fraternal sense of competitiveness. At times, such moments of engagement with Agitation were recounted in terms not unlike the Nazi journalists' feeling that censorship was a game, and one that could even be enjoyed.

Yet, more often, journalists noted this possibility of finding comfort or even pleasure in System as its very cunning. As one of my interlocutors explained to me, the spiritual consequences of accommodating the System through self-censorship and convivial relations with Agitation made him and his colleagues wish at times for a more unequivocally agonistic relationship to "a real censor":

> We often said to one another that if we'd had a real censor, it would have been much better for us. Of course. You know, to have a censor where you write something out and then he draws a line through it. Then you write against him, then you can try to outwit him. Our Polish colleagues did that. They had a censor and it was the greatest fun for them to try to slip something through on him. And the next day, when it was printed, they could say, "What are you looking at us for? The censor okayed it!" We were our own censors, each of us had to act as a censor, and that is naturally not good. For the soul.

My friend Karl offered me perhaps the most poignant narrative I ever heard of the relationship of Spirit to *Lenkungssystem* in the GDR media. His tale, told to me late one night after many glasses of beer, was of the gradual perversion of his socialist ideals and good intentions by the exigencies of party journalism, catalyzing an eventual intellectual and emotional retreat from his work as a high-ranking ADN journalist into nonjournalistic projects like writing rock lyrics and fiction writing:

> I always wanted to help people. From the very beginning when I was at a factory newspaper, I wanted to do something for the workers—that was my passion. If you came up through the ranks in journalism, if you were from a working-class family and didn't have any background, like me, then when you were working for a factory newspaper you really were doing it for the workers, to try to help them in some way. To do something

for the workers, you know? That was what I always tried to do back then; that's why I would try new things out for them. That's why I would have people come on my local TV show and do these talk shows with them. Even before talk shows were invented yet! I invented them! I invented them because I thought this was a way to bring the issues alive for people, and I would record the conversations and transcribe the tapes myself. I was always trying to think of ways to do something for the workers. You know to help the lads [*Kumpel*] out, yes, to do something for the lads. But then, however, as you went up in the hierarchy, you began to say, hey what's all this? You saw that no one had any idea what was going on outside. As you got higher, you realized that the people weren't the same anymore. That you were surrounded by the rulers instead of the workers and that the rulers were completely cut off from what was going on below them. Then you were corrupt. You were up there with the leaders and you were corrupt. That's how it always happened. But that's something you learned slowly, and after a point you realized it was hopeless and you withdrew into your own work. But that's not how it was at the beginning at all. When you started out in a factory newspaper, your attitude was, hey, let's do something for the lads, let's help the workers out. Only later, when you were already deep into the System, did you become corrupt. That's how the System was designed. It was very clever.

As he spoke, Karl sometimes shouted at me, at other times whispered. By the end of his narrative, his eyes were moist and averted as he spoke into the funnel of his beer glass. Karl's narration of the dialectic of his professional development is identical in its plot to Hegel's portrait of the dialectical process of *Gestaltung* (the extension of Spirit in the world, the moment of severance from the sanctifying agency "within," and the consignment to the world of formal duration and formal mechanisms "without"). Karl's dialecticism, however, was neither sober nor abstract but came from personal memory and was shot through with powerful emotion.

To further unravel the intellectual and emotional entanglements of Spirit and System in GDR media culture, in the final three sections of this chapter I will focus on the play of positive and negative dialectical knowledge in the accounts of three kinds of persons most directly engaged with GDR media: the functionaries in the apparatus of media control, the GDR "public" itself, and the journalists whose dialectical knowledges of self and other we will follow, in the third case study, into the post-GDR world of media in eastern Germany.

Censorship as a Vocation

It is unfortunate that I was never able to convince a former Agitation employee to speak with me about work in the GDR (see Boyer 2003a). Yet reading through the archived correspondence of the GDR Press Office and the SED's Agitation Division (comparatively, see Drescher 1991), one gains some insight into the daily labors and self-conception of the party functionaries responsible for managing information flows and for refining the language of the media. Besides monitoring daily media production, these individuals spent a great deal of time proactively refining the language of the media itself, honing their argumentation, counteracting the argumentation of the class enemy (most often in the form of media messages from West Germany), and rigorously integrating the most recent pronouncement of the general secretary into the flow of media messages.

The archival records give their reader a sense of the intellectual energy that the functionaries invested into conceiving ways to increase the "effectivity" of journalism and the "receptivity" of the masses to media representations. The daily litany at Agitation, for example, was to "increase the level [*Niveau*] of journalistic activity" (e.g., DC-9/20, DC-9/8). A language of modernist *Bildung* was omnipresent, as internal discourse continuously referenced the "progress" and "development" of both journalists and audience. Every evaluation of a text was explicitly oriented to how the actuality of media work in general could be further perfected. This meant combating perceived laziness and inattention among journalists, selecting themes that would cast the GDR in a positive light, and, overall, calibrating media representations to fit the party's *Wissenschaft*. Dr. Kurt Blecha, head of the GDR Press Office, explained during one internal pep talk: "Sure, we emphasize success-oriented propaganda, but only because we are successful and not perhaps because we are interested in glossing things over. Still, we don't nail up our remaining inadequacies on bulletin boards; rather, we work single-mindedly to bring into order what is not yet in order" (DC-9/1022). Even citizens' letters that had circulated to Agitation were answered, privately, with a great deal of care, sometimes generating two single-spaced typed pages of apology for empty store shelves or interminable waiting lists framed by careful (but rarely formulaic) explanations of the difficulties of maintaining a socialist economy in a capitalist world-system (DR-6/151 and consecutive files; DC-9/111 and DC-9/112).

The degree of textual and linguistic detail the functionaries occupied themselves with evinces their artisanal relationship to language. As one policy document stated: "there are no details that are not worth debate"

(DC-9/1022). An upcoming television program might warrant several single-spaced typed pages of commentary, ranging from an evaluation of the political message of the program to commentary on the costumes and talent of the actors (see Agitation 35680). Consideration was given down to the level of word choice as to how best to popularize party ideology. For example, one subject of debate was which slogan would have a better effect: "Down with the imperialistic arms' race!" or "Down with the imperialistic arms' buildup!" (DY30/IV 2/2.040/6). How should the amount of crude oil deliveries from the Soviet Union be expressed, as "over 17 million tons" or "17.08 million tons" or "in value of 2.7 billion rubles" (Agitation 33918)? Of course, the pyramidal organization of the distribution network of the party line remained intact at the level of these textual encounters, so answers to even such apparently minor questions of signification were routinely referred upward to the secretary of Agitation for final determination.

For the most part, the archives record the optimism of the functionaries in their work and their confidence in the world-historical significance of their labors to the further *Bildung* of journalism and public culture in the GDR. On the other hand, moments of whispered self-doubt have been related to me by chief editors who routinely had to deal with Agitation employees. According to this testimony, the functionaries were not oblivious to the limited success of their cultural labors to influence collective opinion and cultivate collective consciousness. Somehow, the quest for pure language always seemed to conclude in *Funktionärsdeutsch*. Their careful labors to cultivate a harmonious and progressive public culture never successfully rid it of polysemy and particularity except when they created a linguistic order so specialized and esoteric that only a select few understood what it meant. No matter how precise their operations upon language were, there was always the lurking danger of a double entendre such as "State Circus" or of an empirical percept of productive failure that would necessitate further taboos and recalibration. The environment of actually existing socialism seemed stubbornly unwilling to conform to the ideological conditions set for it, and so the functionaries remained sensitized to the limits of their intellectual agency.

The Public Culture from Another Planet

Whereas, in the admittedly limited insight we have into Agitation functionaries' self-awareness, we glimpse negative dialectical knowledge dispersed into a professional routine characterized by an institutionalized sense of positive dialectical mission, one can fairly say that negative dialectical knowledge entirely saturated the accounts of GDR media I gathered from former GDR citizens. I found it quite difficult to discuss the GDR media at length with any of them—most would cut me off with a shrug or a scowl or a "that shitty propaganda machine!" I often sensed a level of discomfort in these conversations as though the very existence of the GDR media was an embarrassment best forgotten. It was certainly one of the least fondly remembered elements of the party-state (trailing only perhaps the Stasi, the Wall, and the endemic commodity shortages). Those who did discuss the media with me in more detail recalled the party-state's public culture as distancing, "like listening to reports from another planet" as one woman put it. One young man reported to me that his family and friends had nick-named their local SED paper, the *Lausitzer Rundschau,* the *Lügenrudi* (lying Tom) and commented that its reportage was a daily object of derision in the household. For those who had no place or role in the production of public culture in the GDR, the party-state seemed to offer an always didactic, often estranging, and sometimes bizarre series of media representations that seemed, despite their continuous reference to *Volk* and *Kultur,* to have little interest in their alleged public or their local knowledges.

There were a few notable exceptions to cold memories of the GDR media. The decision in 1991 to shut down the only GDR-era rock music station, DT 64, catalyzed an unprecedented public outcry for what many said was one of their most beloved media sources before 1989 (Ulrich and Wagner 1993). Others expressed warm memories to me of family-oriented GDR print media publications like *Die Wochenpost, Das Magazin,* and *Eulenspiegel.* On the other hand, SED daily newspapers were generally remembered with disdain and not a little hostility. "They [the party] actually thought we would believe all that crap they told us! We had eyes, no?" The informal dialectics of many of my interlocutors contrasted their intelligence and acuity to the jargon, disingenuousness, lies, or simply "shit" broadcast by the party through their media. These judgments became differentiated in longer discussions. I gathered there that the political and economic coverage drew the greatest ridicule and that the press was mostly read for local news, sports reports, and literary reviews. Radio was listened to for music and cultural reports, and GDR television was watched for crime dramas, movies, children's programs, and other entertainment programming.

Among active SED members, engagement with the party's *Wissenschaft* through the media was more sustained. Reading the local party newspaper was often a household ritual, and those clued into the constant intrigues transpiring within the SED Politburo reported to me that one could read "between the lines" to learn, for example, which Politburo member had fallen out of favor with the general secretary based on how they were positioned relative to one another in photographs. By seeking and finding the "hidden codes" in media representation, more engaged members of the audience of GDR media were able to reclaim a sense of interpretive agency over a domain of knowledge that all too often seemed monolithically exterior and opaque to their intellectual powers.

My friend Marianne, who was training to be a journalist in the late 1980s, wrote me recently to explain that the more ideologically charged domains of GDR news coverage such as domestic politics and economic news were identified as biased or even simply false and were read critically or ironically even by loyal party members: "People read the newspaper from the back forward, first local news, then sports, arts, *Vermischtes* [potpourri], and then the news reports from around the world. Domestic political coverage was only read occasionally, and the economic news never." She continued:

> My parents were also loyal SED members; they certainly read *Neues Deutschland* more seriously than I did. But they also didn't find it entertaining, I think. They "studied" it so to speak. And my father usually fell asleep when he read it on the couch on the weekends. My parents didn't continuously "agitate" us but they were rather true to the party line. As we became older, we regularly confronted them with what was going on in everyday life. As you can imagine, things became quite turbulent at home. [We told them] What people were saying in the train, in the bus, in the pubs. What was happening in the workplace. What jokes were being told about the Politburo. *Es gab ja wirklich eine Wunsch-DDR in den Medien und eine echte DDR im Alltag* [There really was a dream-GDR in the media and a real GDR in everyday life].

The "dream-GDR" of GDR media, so it seems, had little purchase outside the immediate spheres of its production. In a country where everyday knowledge was saturated with tropes of distancing (irony), the irony of the gulf between media representation and the "everyday reality" of life in the GDR merited special attention. It was a constant source of jokes and everyday satire (see Wagner 1994, 1996). In their effort to redeem public culture from the dissolute heterogeneity of bourgeois mass culture, the SED managed instead to accelerate and to reinforce the enclosure and retreat of East German communicative practices from the state-sponsored public sphere, a phenomenon that is well captured by Günter Gaus's description of the GDR as a *Nischengesellschaft* (society of niches; 1983). The referential feature of language upon which the SED had balanced their grand hope of a unified

Volk consciousness was precisely the aspect of language they could not systematize. The public culture of the SED seemed so neurotically obsessed with manipulating reference from the "top down" that it finally evolved into an esoteric caricature of its intention to redeem *Kultur* on the *Volk*'s behalf.

Between Ideals and System: Memories of Journalism in the GDR

Compared to the functionaries and to the audience of GDR media, its practitioners, GDR editors and journalists, offered the greatest complexity of positive and negative dialectical knowledge in their narratives of GDR media. In all, I interviewed over a hundred former East German journalists in 1996, 1997, and 2002 and developed closer relationships with about twenty individuals.[11] In the interviews that focused on their memories of journalism in the GDR, I asked my interlocutors to comment on what had drawn them to the profession in the first place, what their experiences had been (when applicable) in the training program at Leipzig, and whether they could reconstruct for me the everyday work world of party journalism and their experience of the *Lenkungssystem*.

Most interviews began with autobiography: in what kind of a family they had been raised, where they went to school, how they arrived at university, what journalistic positions they had held before and after graduating from Leipzig, and so forth. My interviewees tended to discharge these questions rapidly, invoking a "typical GDR career" beginning with an *Abitur*,[12] mandatory army service, a successful application for a one-year *Volontariat* (internship) at a media organization, followed by their paper or station sending them to the *Rotes Kloster* (red cloister), the colloquial name for the School of Journalism in Leipzig, for the four years of required training in socialist journalism. It was clear from several of the biographical narratives that, especially among younger journalists who were educated in the 1970s and 1980s, they were to some extent preselected for journalistic careers based on a demonstrated competence in party ideology from a young age. Kin and class relations also played an important role, although one less openly

---

11. All of my interviewees were guaranteed pseudonymity, less for an American audience than in the event that some of my research might eventually appear in German-language translation. In Germany, the issue of complicity with the SED regime and criticism of the FRG media system are still issues sensitive enough to impact careers. Therefore, unless I am citing an already-published interview, all the names I offer in this book (but not biographical details) are invented.

12. The *Abitur* is a secondary school degree earned upon graduation from a *Gymnasium*. In both Germanys, an *Abitur* typically allowed a student to attend university.

discussed: children of high-ranking party members, including media elites, were preferred for journalistic training because they had an established socialist pedigree. Likewise, I met several journalists with rural or working-class backgrounds who felt they were cultivated for this job by the party because they fit the normative ideal of a "working-class intellectual," intelligent but not cosmopolitan and thus naïve about the ways of the world and willing to absorb and to commit themselves to the party's hermeneutics of everyday life. During the *Volontariat* period, screening decisions were made within the hierarchies of individual media organizations as to which interns had the necessary blend of party discipline and intellectual talent to proceed to Leipzig.

Journalists' evaluations of their experiences at the School of Journalism varied widely. Some shuddered as they recalled it and dismissed it as a complete waste of time, nightmarish and full of endless ideological droning and precious few opportunities to learn how to write well. Others differentiated between what they described as oppressive ideological indoctrination and a solid training in trade skills (*Handwerk*) that has served them well in the unified German media. Thomas K. (b. 1966), a newspaper journalist in Chemnitz before and after 1989, answered my question about what, in retrospect, he felt he had learned about journalism at Leipzig: "Everything about the mechanics of journalism, the education in the trade, was very solid. Of course, that had a political function too. One thing that proves the quality is that one of our methodology books was used in Dortmund [in West Germany] even before 1989. I only learned that fact after the Wall came down and I went west to visit Dortmund."

Despite the absence of training in independent research skills at Leipzig, several individuals told me that a good background in stylistics and the mechanics of journalistic writing (e.g., how to construct a proper news bulletin) has given them an edge when competing for jobs with western Germans.[13] Others emphasized that they learned *theoretically* how to produce good journalism from the Leipzig program even if the SED media control apparatus did not then permit them to utilize this knowledge. Still others told me that the political significance of the printed word in the GDR rendered them

13. In the FRG, journalism retained its traditional status as a marginal *Gebildeten* profession and thus some of the mediatic image of nineteenth-century journalism. There are now a few professional schools for journalism in western Germany on the model of the Institut für Journalistik founded at the University of Dortmund in 1984. Yet the majority of western German journalists I encountered had had no specific professional training in journalism. Most had academic backgrounds of one kind or another and had moved by way of internship positions from the university directly into editorial positions.

much more attuned to issues of style and connotation than their western counterparts, and thus capable of more nuanced prose styles as well. This impression of the superior literary skills of some eastern journalists was a view corroborated by a few of the western German managers with whom I spoke as well. Jochen S. (b. 1941), the assistant chief editor of a major Berlin daily, spoke approvingly of their East German hires: "There were some initial problems with certain people, and some of them are also no longer here now. But mainly we're quite happy with them and think that they are some of our best. One thing they learned at the *Rotes Kloster* or wherever in their training—I think they were very highly trained—was how to write well, and so they are definitely some of our best writers."

I also tried to ascertain journalistic motivations. I asked my interlocutors what had allowed them to struggle through the Leipzig program. Was it a belief in the vocation of socialist journalism as *Volkslehrer* or a sense of party discipline and honor? Some journalists were quite frank in replying that they enjoyed being journalists less because of the work itself and more because of the social status it awarded them in the eyes of the state and because of the considerable perks journalists enjoyed that were denied to the majority of the GDR population (like travel opportunities and a priority on waiting lists for desirable goods like phones). But, then, there were also journalists like Heinz S. (b. 1958), who told me in no uncertain terms that they were unequivocally committed from the beginning to the party's vision of journalism and that they approached their work with great enthusiasm as a means of contributing to the socialist cause:

> My premise was, naturally, to defend this state as an alternative to the Federal Republic of Germany. And one of the reasons I was so attached to this System was the absence of any other alternative as I saw it. The FRG was absolutely not an alternative as far as I was concerned, and GDR socialism had achieved a certain position and I saw my people as deeply rooted in socialism. So naturally I came to see that my role as a journalist was to help socialism forward via the daily life of a newspaper. To take this ideology and to convey it to the readers. To deal with things going on in the real world, and certainly, you looked around yourself and saw that things weren't functioning, that there was this gap between desire and reality, but you didn't let that hinder you from doing what you thought was the right thing to do.

For most of my interlocutors, I would say that the emotional contours of their recollection of journalism in the GDR moved between a sense of

vocational commitment to socialism, a sense of pragmatic interest and justification, a sense of frustration with the daily exigencies of party journalism,
a sense of guilt at the gulf between media representation and "real life" in
the GDR, and a sense of depression at the fear and dislike most GDR citizens
felt for journalists and the media. Peter W. (b. 1945), for example, articulated
a complexity of vocational and political motivations ranging from simply a
desire to write to a commitment to the ideals and mission of socialism:

> For me it was certainly in the first place a desire to write. Like I told you,
> I started by writing for a small factory newspaper [*Betriebszeitung*] and
> gained an interest that way in journalism as a profession and in writing
> itself. And really I just grew into it from there. And we wouldn't be telling
> the truth if we were to say that there wasn't also a certain political mo-
> tivation there as well. But that's how we were raised and that's what we
> grew into. We also naturally attempted under these conditions to make
> the best of it that we could. But in retrospect I think it was really a purely
> vocational [*berufliche*] motivation. Also for the technical side of the job.
> I mean, when one has the opportunity to write and to express oneself and
> to read one's texts the next day in the paper, and to know that possibly
> someone's interested in it and that you would get certain responses, that
> is naturally interesting. That's what spurred me on.

The dialectical analogy of "growing into" party journalism was quite
common. It allowed my interlocutors to define the gap between their initial
vocational commitment to journalism and their subsequent "habituation"
to the realities and expectations of party journalism. In it, one hears echoes
of Karl's and Hegel's dialectics of *Gestaltung,* of the path between the first
blush of Spirit and the mature mechanisms of System. In my first interview
with him, my friend Albert offered a particularly moving narrative of his
life as a GDR journalist from an initial desire to reach out to the world, to
a recognition that he was being treated as an instrument of the party, to
a realization that there was no way to break the dogma of the party and a
feeling that one thus had to resign oneself to a life of cosmetic resistance
and tactics for survival:

> My first point of access to journalism was a desire to talk to the world.
> To be honest, it had nothing to do with the party back then. Then later of
> course through the training came the self-understanding and feeling that
> you were the arm of the party, a piece of the party. And, indeed, that's
> how they saw us too; we were treated as a tool [*Werkzeug*], in the sense

of with a great deal of attention [*Achtung*] but also with a great deal of respect. And that's important to note, there was *no* ambivalence toward us as one encounters in the West, but then again no one really listens to you in the West either. With us, it was clear from the start—we *had* to obey and we *did* obey without a doubt. What you hear often nowadays though is that, in principle, there was basically no other path for us to have followed than the one we did. Don't believe that if someone tells you that; it's nonsense. We had endless debates in the editorial collective [*Redaktion*] about the form of our program, about what was being asked of us, if it was right or wrong. . . . You have to understand that the *ideal* of journalism in the GDR seemed completely reasonable. Journalism was supposed to show life as it really is [*lebensnah sein*]. That's a good thing, isn't it? Journalism was supposed to be cosmopolitan [*weltoffen*], also a good thing, no? Journalism was supposed to unlock the intellectual inheritance of the working class, and why not? It all *sounded* good. The problem was that you ran into the worst problems you could possibly imagine if you ever tried to put any of these ideals into practice. Because the reality was that "to show life as it really is" meant photographing Honecker forty times at a rally. . . . But [*sighing*] in the end we couldn't break with the dogma of the party, that's true of course. . . . I remember when I was first starting out that my older colleagues—older colleagues, mind you, who'd been doing this job much longer—said to me, "Listen, you just have to find little ways to make the job more bearable; you have to find some way to sprinkle chocolate on the shit we do here." And people did that, they found little things they could do that no one called them to task for, so even if in the end all the changes were only cosmetic changes, which they were without question, you need to recognize that there were efforts to try to do some things better.

Albert stressed a point that many of my interlocutors were determined I understand: that GDR journalists were, for the most part, neither fools nor party hacks. They truly believed in the ideals and promise of socialist journalism but were perpetually haunted by the incommensurability between these ideals and the institutional and professional realities of journalism in the GDR. The everyday experience of party journalism, many said, was deeply dehumanizing, a matter of finding minor ways to sweeten "the shit" of the work. But through a combination of faith and habit they persisted. "In the GDR," another journalist explained, "you talked yourself into things, bit by bit." More than once, I was told that, if I wanted to understand how journalists felt about their GDR past, I should "go read Osang," who had the talent with language to articulate their feelings better than they could themselves.

Alexander Osang, now a foreign correspondent for *Der Spiegel*, has won several major journalism prizes in Germany and has a kind of celebrity status among many journalists, both eastern and western. He has written a moving short essay about his three years as an editor at a SED newspaper in the late 1980s. The essay, "Somehow I Keep Going," is a narrative of the "bit by bit" incrementalism of party journalism referred to above. It begins:

> It was hardly a courageous question. As I punched it into my old rasping typewriter, people were marching by below on Karl-Liebknecht Strasse screaming "Freedom of the Press!" up at the windows of our newspaper office, where we had fortified ourselves. Freedom of the press? It was October 7th, 1989, and I was supposed to write an article about an FDJ torchlight procession. No simple matter this. At the procession I had watched thousands of happy young people marching down Unter den Linden and how, as they passed Erich Honecker and Mikhail Gorbachev, they burst out into cheers of "GDR, our Fatherland!" I had heard the anoraks of the state security people there to supervise the event rustling behind every bush. And then, at home, on West-TV, my former countrymen were waiting for me in some West German train station or another. They were yelling "Great," "Amazing"; they wore stonewashed jackets and tears of joy. Meanwhile, I was packing all of my confusion into a single rhetorical question, "Are torchlight processions in keeping with the times?" Like I said, not a courageous question, given that thousands of people in this country suddenly had other, far-wider-reaching questions. Beyond that, I hadn't even written "This country doesn't need torchlight processions anymore," although that is exactly what I had been thinking.
>
> Not a courageous question, but at that point still an unusual one. When I opened my newspaper the next day, I read my opening question, "Are torchlight processions in keeping with the times?" and, following it, a hefty "YES." Then an exclamation point.
>
> I nearly fell where I stood. I ran to the assistant chief editor, the one who had written the "YES!" Too busy, he said, but scribbled me a note later to the effect that he had gotten "cold feet." Then I ran to the second assistant chief editor and demanded my copyright rights. "You don't even know what a copyright is, young lad," the man said to me. He was right about that. I left his office, thought about quitting, but before I did

anything else, I wrote a report about VEB Bergmann Borsig and how they had exceeded the planned production of turbine impellers by a couple of units.

That's how it always had been. The first thing you did was to keep going. And after fifteen similar humiliations, you became numb or a drinker or a cynic. And after a hundred of these humiliations, you were ready to start humiliating other people. I was well on my way there. I was no longer capable of defending myself. Somehow I kept going. I stuck it out.

I didn't even remember how it had all started. Maybe during my first interview for an internship position. The very first question which the old hiring editor of the *Berliner Verlag* posed to me was, "Are you already a member of our party?" *Our* party? I wanted to be a sports reporter. What in God's name did that have to do with the party? And how was it that *his* party was suddenly *our* party? What was being taken for granted here? Perhaps what I should have done at that moment was to get up, go away, and never have come back. But I started to talk myself into it. They couldn't all possibly be like this old sack here, right? So I answered him, "Not yet."

Maybe this first "not yet" was what broke my backbone. Maybe I simply hadn't any left by then. Who knows? At any rate, I knew from then on what the priorities of this profession were. And I surrendered to them. I knew that party membership counted more than talent. It wasn't about authenticity, it was about *Parteilichkeit.* And if I didn't know it then, I suspected it. And everything that followed afterward only made me more certain. (1996: 107–8; see also Steul 1996)

At the end of the essay, Osang depicts himself sitting in front of a dossier of his GDR work:

And so I am sitting helplessly in front of this stack of dusty files that our archivist fetched out of the cellar of the building. The files contain articles from a time that is really not so long ago. Stilted lead articles about saving coal and holiday gatherings of the FDJ. Sweet little local reports about the swimming pool in Pankow and the restaurant up in the Berlin television tower. Pages-long, incomprehensible descriptions of new technical developments like the "automatic coupling device for non-short-circuit-protected feeding elements."

Softball questions to FDJ functionaries like, "How has your host city been preparing for your holiday festival?"

> The texts are completely alien to me. But at the bottom of each I see
> my name. (1996: 110–11)

Osang's text conveys beautifully the sense my other interlocutors shared
that one grew into party journalism one humiliation at a time. Also resonant
is Osang's sense of estrangement from the past objects of his professional
labor and from the person who, sharing his name, gradually acculturated
himself to the routines of party journalism. His fear at what he might have
become had not 1989 occurred was a sentiment echoed by other journalists
as well. Many, especially younger journalists, told me that they feared what
the System would have done to them over time. They wondered whether
they would now be like *die alten Kollegen* (the older colleagues) who had
been physically, emotionally, and intellectually devastated by the *Wende*
(turn, change) of 1989. Echoing Michael's commentary in the introduction,
one journalist explained that, in her experience, "the older colleagues were
zu tief [too deep] in the old System to change." They had, in other words,
already become creatures of form, spiritless creatures of habit.

Given the centrality of System to many of my interlocutors' reflections
on the GDR media, I found it striking that it was often difficult to prompt
journalists to differentiate their memories of media control, to describe specific techniques or rituals, for example. System often simply was, in memory, a twisted mass of editorial adjustments, taboos, disciplinary actions,
anxieties, and thwarted hopes. The word "System" managed Herculean
labors of tropic condensation, bringing together under a single lexical head-
ing the entire exteriority of the GDR media apparatus, of everything that
compromised the Spirit of self. Recalling the details of System seemed to
have a genuine psychic cost. In response to a series of questions along these
lines, Michael S. (b. 1951) spoke openly of his self-loathing, of how the burdens and enclosure of the System produced anxious, guilty journalists:

> In terms of the model of our profession we had very little latitude. But we
> often didn't even realize that we didn't have it. There was no censor, but
> there was the *Schere im Kopf.* Our chief editor was thoroughly anxious.
> His business was to determine exactly how far we'd be permitted to go.
> That was the primary function of the chief editor. It was a closed System.
> The people we interviewed knew what we wanted to hear, so we never
> felt that we weren't permitted to describe what was actually happening.
> You see, it was doubly warped. There was no reason to do anything else.
> We knew more than we could write about obviously, that there was a bad
> situation in the economy, limited media freedoms, and so on. And there

was increasingly a bad feeling among us, and our consciences became
rather burdened by the end. Journalists had an ever lousier image in society. I didn't even tell anyone I was a journalist. It made me feel uneasy.
I always carried that feeling around with me. Everyone was dissatisfied
but no one ever did anything; we were too completely bound into the
structures and too frightened for our own existences. That would have
brought the whole System into doubt, and no one ever thought to question the System fundamentally. *No one* raised those kinds of issues!

Albert, too, once confided in me that his alcoholism was a direct result of
the compromises he had to make with his own social democratic ideals in
order to survive as a SED party journalist. Other journalists explained to
me that they saw the writing on the wall early on and developed parallel
creative outlets to anchor a positive sense of intellectual selfhood outside
their professional praxis.

In my conversations with former GDR journalists, the identification of
Spirit was indeed always intertwined with the recognition and rejection of
System. In truly dialectical fashion, the one made little sense without the
other. The recognition and rejection of System was an assertion of Spirit;
the extension of Spirit always encountered its antitotem in System. As a
journalist from Dresden explained to me, "For myself, I worked hard before
1989 to try to make this a good newspaper by finding any small way I could
to improve things. Others maybe were satisfied, or they had given up already,
I don't know. I was no dissident. I *wanted* the GDR, but I often felt hemmed
in. You couldn't write something because you heard that Berlin didn't want
that, and they were so sensitive up there; they imagined the class enemy
everywhere in everything. I tried to do my profession well, but the room
one had was small."

Other interlocutors ended their interviews with me on a somber note of
the missed opportunities (*verpaßte Chancen*) of socialist journalism. For all
its chronic failures, they said, socialist journalism was still oriented toward
a nobler ideal, the *Bildung* of the *Volk,* than western journalism, which had
simply sacrificed itself to international capitalism and its mass culture. As
Albert noted, at least journalism had *Achtung* (attention, respect) and a special purpose in the SED party-state. Even with its profound restrictions, one
still had hope for the intellectual agency of socialist journalism. One man
lamented that after 1989, media work lacked any sense of integrated social
purpose: "In the GDR, we were always striving for something. Here, you can
do anything but it never goes anywhere." A great many others noted similarities between the Systems of the GDR and of unified Germany in terms

of the constraints they placed upon journalism. It was not so much that they judged the two institutional cultures of media production to be the same as that they viewed them as being equivalently Systemic in their mechanistic organization and hostility to creative individual expression. For this reason, memories of the GDR and judgments about contemporary Germany became interwoven with surprising ease.

In the next chapter, I will explore journalists' everyday knowledges of Spirit and System in more extensive and personal detail. I will begin with an ethnographic foray into the ruins of the GDR media, a foray that connects dialectical memories of East German journalism to dialectical knowledges of the contemporary in eastern Germany.

CHAPTER FOUR

Self, System, and Other in
Eastern Germany after 1989

The social sciences should receive due credit that they have mounted success upon success in researching the East German. How could the country possibly *zusammenwachsen* [grow together] if we were not aware that the East German does his gardening comparably more often than the Wessi[1] [University of Leipzig], is more satisfied with the condition of the environment [government study], and, possibly for this very reason, suffers less often from hay fever [Robert Koch Institute, Berlin]. Moreover, we have learned that the East German is a better lover [Sigmund Freud Institute, Giessen] but nevertheless is more successful at lovemaking without consequences [Federal Office of Statistics]. The East German still speaks more rarely [Free University of Berlin], yet his silence is explained somewhat by the fact that he watches cable TV more often and in longer stretches than the Wessi does [Society for Consumer Research, Nürnberg].

Yet, suddenly, the problem of all *Wissenschaft* arises, namely that each new finding generates more questions. And the solution to the basic problem—what the East German is anyway—is pushed, in view of this wealth of facts, ever further into the distance.

But the Potsdam Institute for Nutritional Research has recently delivered us a new direction for our investigation: according to their most recent research, the East German does not prefer to eat in canteens. Although the selection of foodstuffs has clearly improved since the *Wende*, the price and the taste of the offerings continue to cause offense, so says a survey of workers and various firms. Notable exception: hospital canteens.

1. "Wessi" is a slang term for "West German," the Westie.

It seems that not only does the East German love better than the West German but he eats better as well. Not so fast. The East German also eats more meat and fat [German Agrarian Society], which is not particularly healthy.

But wait! Can't we find in this apparent contradiction the key to understanding the East German? You just have to put the facts together and then you have the solution: the East German is a libertine. Like some easy-rider of the '90s, he races his Japanese car in the left-hand lane [personal inquiry] while listening to the Puhdys on the radio and drinking a can of the local beer [Society for Market Research]. He and his wife stop for a romp in the forest [Sigmund Freud Institute in connection with the Federal Office of Statistics] until his happy trip concludes at the closest hospital, where he buys a steak at the expense of his insurance company and bites heartily into it. Remember, he has the healthier teeth [Information Office of German Dentists]. Later, he makes himself comfortable in his bed, whines about what he'd rather be doing, whines a bit more about the Wessis [Institute for Market Research, Leipzig], and then drifts happily off to sleep. — *Werner Kohlhoff, "Der Ossi, das bekannte Wesen"*

Being, were it not apprehensible as a relationship, would be equivalent to nothingness. — *Claude Lévi-Strauss, The Naked Man*

Nalepastraße, Berlin: 6 July 2002

We agreed to meet at the old water tower near the exit of the Ostkreuz S-Bahn station in part because Albert tells me this is where he used to wait for the bus every morning on his way to work at the central production complex of GDR Radio at Nalepastraße and in part because Albert wants a big landmark he knows I will not miss. The last two times we have met he has found me loitering in the vicinity of the *Treffpunkt* (meeting place), and once even walking in the wrong direction, so his confidence in my knowledge of eastern Berlin has been somewhat shaken. Also, landmarks are loci for stories about the GDR for Albert, and Albert takes special pleasure in narrating the GDR to me. Our destination on this warm, sunny Sunday morning is the Nalepastraße radio production complex, a place that Albert has already described to me in some detail over the years we have known one another. Albert has told me that Nalepastraße was once almost a village unto itself along the Spree River, with thousands of journalists and technical and nontechnical support staff working within its walls and with its own shops, bank, hairdresser, sports center (complete with sauna), restaurants, and pubs.

Even for some time after the *Wende* (turn, change) of 1989, Nalepastraße continued to be well populated as debates raged over whether eastern Germany should retain some kind of regional radio and television broadcasting that would be oriented to the needs and expectations of the eastern German public. Nalepastraße still had possible futures in this scenario even though the German Unification Treaty had already federalized public broadcasting in eastern Germany by placing it under control of individual state (*Länder*) governments. Ultimately, however, the plan of Helmut Kohl's hand-picked Bavarian czar of eastern German public broadcasting, Rudolf Mühlfenzl, prevailed (Boyle 1992: 325–70; Spielhagen 1993).

Mühlfenzl opined that to maintain an eastern German radio station for an eastern public would be to keep alive a pathogenic "GDR identity," which would be harmful to the process of integrating and normalizing East Germans as citizens of the Federal Republic (Boyle 1992: 365–67). Mühlfenzl instead favored dismantling any programs aimed at all of eastern Germany in favor of full regionalization of broadcasting. Public broadcasting in eastern Germany was henceforth divided among four affiliate stations (NDR, mdr, SFB, and ORB)[2] in the West German ARD public-broadcasting network, and Nalepastraße was reclaimed by the sandy Prussian prairie.

For several years now, Nalepastraße has lain mostly fallow, and every once in a while Albert has wondered to me, when we discuss journalism in the GDR, what has become of it. A few weeks previously, I proposed to him that we take a trip to see the place. Albert was immediately intrigued by the idea, but when I mentioned our plan to Joachim and Michael, both former employees of Nalepastraße, to ask if they wanted to accompany us, both reacted quickly, almost shuddering, "Oh no, no thank you."

Albert arrives at the water tower a few minutes after I do, walking quickly and holding in his left hand two cloth bags, one a vivid yellow bag with the Pynchonesque icon of Deutsche Post on it and the other with a blue symbol of the European Union and the slogan "*Der Euro kommt*" (The euro is coming) printed beneath. I ask him if this is not old news since the new currency is already here. Albert shrugs and says that he picked it up at "some euro-themed event" the night before and quickly recounts his latest adventures in Berlin's new political nightlife. Since the German government

---

2. ARD voted in March 2003 to fuse ORB and SFB into a new affiliate that would serve both Berlin and Brandenburg (Radio Berlin Brandenburg, or RBB).

relocated from Bonn to Berlin, Albert has explained to me, "every night there is some party thrown by one of the *Landesvertretungen* [state embassies to the federal government] or by some foundation. And once you get your name onto the invitation list for these kinds of events, you can basically live off them. I have a friend, honestly, who never eats at home. He just spends every evening touring from one of them to another." The previous week, Albert and I and this friend had attended "Caribbean Night" at the newly built glass and steel Mecklenburg-Vorpommischer embassy near Potsdamer Platz, where we mingled with seven-foot-tall inflatable rum bottles and the political elite of eastern Germany decked out in complimentary straw hats and enjoying complimentary Dutch cigars and Mojitos.

At the sumptuous tropical buffet, Albert played the Ossi (Eastie) a little bit, oohing and aahing over all the exotic fruit he had never seen in the GDR and asking women nearby to advise him on how best to open and eat them. Then, once he had their attention, Albert regaled them with stories of his culinary deprivations in the GDR or with the story of sighting former Chancellor Helmut Kohl at a similar function a few months previously and how he had eaten from the buffet with both hands "like an animal." Outside, as we waited for his friend to pull up his silver Mercedes and drive us on to "German-Turkish Friendship Night" at the Konrad Adenauer Foundation, we watched the new Government Quarter being built around us, carved out of what had formerly been the no-man's-land where the Wall ran between the two Berlins. The razor-edged edifices of Potsdamer Platz twinkled in the twilight to the west and south. Not fifty meters from where we stood, near Voßstrasse by my best guess, Hitler's *Führerbunker* still lay, unacknowledged and gorged with concrete, beneath the yellow sand.

We do not wait long at the water tower before Albert's friend Karl-Hans arrives in his car to drive us down the Köpenickerstrasse to the radio city. In his "GDR life," as Albert calls it, Albert was for many years a radio journalist specializing in politics and current affairs. Eventually, despite his well-known and -discussed drinking and womanizing, he became the chief editor of a radio news program, and in the *Wendezeit* (*Wende* period) he even became the chief editor of GDR Radio, shortly before its dissolution. Albert is one of the very few former East German journalists I know who has enjoyed true professional success in both the GDR and the FRG media systems. After the dissolution of GDR Radio, Albert was able to rebuild his career by moderating a widely respected weekly current-affairs program that allows him to travel across Germany hosting roundtable discussions on resonant public-cultural issues. Now he receives more inquiries than he can handle to moderate other kinds of events. As our mutual friend, Marianne, tells me, however, she feels that Albert's recent success has not really changed him:

> [Albert] still has his sense of humor but he also strikes me as somehow older and wiser now, you know? He really is right about a lot of things, you know that? He really is very often correct in his interpretations of what happens around him. That's one of the things I like about Albert— even though he now has a long-term position and even now that he is known about town and people find his program very fine—he still main- tains his old way of life. He still lives in the same apartment, still shops at the same stores and eats at the same places. It's as though he doesn't entirely believe what has happened to him, and I really appreciate that about him. You know that he can be a bit of a cynic, but that's because he sees what a false world journalism can be and that is how he main- tains his distance from that. I, too, feel that it's extremely important to be able to remind oneself that there's a world outside journalism that's important too.

Others who know Albert personally or by reputation are more critical. Another friend, Gregor, a magazine reporter in his midthirties from Bavaria who has lived and worked in eastern Berlin and eastern Germany since 1989, once startled me with his reaction when Albert's name arose in conversation (see chapter 5).

GREGOR: Oh, he [Albert] is another one of these guys [*shaking his head and making a low growling sound in the back of his throat*] where you are always thinking [*growls*]—
DOMINIC: I know Albert and he's fine, he's a good journalist—
GREGOR [*still growling*]: He was the last chief editor of GDR Radio, wasn't he?
DOMINIC [*annoyed*]: I don't know what your point is. *Er ist schon zweimal gegauckt worden* [He's already been through Gauck twice].[3] He's clean.
GREGOR: Wwweeelll, I don't know about that either. [*Sharply.*] Listen, that's not the point anyway. What is he, maybe fifty-five or sixty years old? So he spent

3. The verb *gaucken* is a neologism of the 1990s. It is utilized as a slang term among eastern German journalists to describe the process of having had one's name run through the federal agency responsible for managing the files of the former GDR state security apparatus (the Stasi) to check whether one had served as an informer for the security apparatus. Joachim Gauck was the first director of this agency, and his name has come to tropically condense the entire investigative apparatus and its procedures.

thirty years stuck in the middle of the GDR Radio propaganda broadcaster. So what business does he have being a journalist now? My point is that these old guys who were deep in the middle of the GDR System have no business working as journalists anymore. They shouldn't be allowed into the *Öffentlichkeit* [public sphere]; they should find something else to do with themselves. They should give up their positions to younger people, preferably from the east, you know, people who don't have their *Vergangenheitsbelastung* [burden of history/the past].

DOMINIC: But if he's [a good journalist]—

GREGOR: Listen, I'm not saying these guys are all bad journalists. Not at all. Some of them are great, they do great research, they write up a good story, have interesting conversations with people. It's not even a question that they are somehow working in the media and plotting to bring back the GDR or to spread communist politics or whatever. What I am saying is that no matter what these guys do, they will always have this dark side to their past to contend with, and it's in here [*grabbing his forehead with both hands*], it's in here that they can't escape. Because they carry that *Vergangenheitsbelastung* around with them constantly, they are always thinking about it, they can't escape it. So they can't engage this history in a critical way as they should. They can't see the GDR past objectively.

I hear intimations and accusations of journalistic Spirit weighed down by a "surfeit of history" quite often in conversations with both eastern and western German journalists about particular eastern German colleagues. Interestingly, however, Albert has admitted as much to me in several conversations we have had about the fate of former East German journalists in the unified German media system. In our very first conversation, some eight years ago, he related something a friend had said to him which he thought made a great deal of sense: "The East German journalist is not yet free." At the time, Albert was in contractual limbo, waiting to see whether his labor contract (*Arbeitsvertrag*) at SFB would be made permanent or not, and he was very anxious about his future. I attributed his somewhat estranged relationship to "freedom" to this situation, especially in light of other comments he had made that it was difficult to feel emancipated when one constantly had to worry about being let go from one's job. This summer though, waiting with him on the S-Bahn platform at Hackescher Markt, I brought the theme up again since Albert had finally received the equivalent of tenure as a journalist at SFB. But it seems that Albert actually had had in mind something more along the lines of Gregor's analysis.

DOMINIC: So, Albert, tell me truly, is the East German journalist finally free?

ALBERT [*perplexed*]: Which East German journalist?

DOMINIC: You told me once that "the East German journalist is not yet free."
I think you meant journalists in general and I was wondering whether you
still felt that way.

ALBERT [*laughs*]: Aha, yes, what I meant by that was something that my friend
Konrad Franke . . . once said to me. He said to me some time ago that the
eastern journalist [*Ostjournalist*] would never really be free, I mean in the
sense that everyone talks about "freedom" now. Someone who spent, I don't
know, two decades working in conditions like those in the GDR would never
be fully free of them. Somewhere in the back of one's mind would always
be hovering things like "*die bessere Welt*" [the better world] or "*Respekt
vor Obrigkeit*" [respect one's superiors] no matter how long one worked
under these [present] conditions. It would be nothing overt but rather a
creeping sense of entanglement. There would also be the character issues,
the caution and modesty [*mimes this by drooping his head and bending
his body forward as though to curl into a ball*], which would never go
away.

DOMINIC: I see, but is this really true, for example, in your case?

ALBERT [*quickly*]: Yes, I definitely see this in myself as well. I have seen this
at various stages in my career as well. I can often fool the West Germans,
though. They often are very surprised to find out I am an East German, that
they are speaking with someone who was actually there, because, at some
event in a place like Hamburg, I'm sure that an East German never takes
the stage.

Despite Albert's professed "creeping sense of entanglement" with the
GDR, I have found that he has also developed a stronger critical and "objective" (in the sense of distanced and thoughtful) relationship to the GDR past
than most eastern and western Germans whom I have met have. Gregor's
standards for historical "objectivity" aside, I am certain that Albert does not
repress his emotional and intellectual struggles to come to terms with his
GDR past. I have always thought that Albert was able to make his professional transition as successfully as he did because he is as close to a trickster
figure as GDR Radio ever produced. He is himself an exceptionally sharp observer of people and a fine ethnologist who not only insightfully deciphers
the social dynamics and logics around him but also restlessly publicizes
the results of his interpretive labors. One of his specialties is dialectical social knowledge of "easternness," and he happily plays the Ossi, the hapless

easterner stultified in his moral *Bildung* by the social System of a *Verbrecherstaat* (criminal regime), embodying these stereotypes in a way that allows him to perform and explore their caricatures, to recognize himself in some, and to confront his audience (especially West Germans) with the absurdity of others. In other contexts, he likes to "fool the West Germans" about his origin, to surprise them with an easternness that does not fit stereotypical expectations.

In turn, however, this strategy of deconstructing his easternness has cost Albert something in his relationships with former colleagues from GDR Radio. He only keeps in close contact with a few, although a larger group of thirty or forty assembles every October to go out for an evening. Albert describes how some of them give him trouble and whisper behind his back about his newfound "westernness," about what kind of person he *must have become* to work at SFB, a broadcaster long associated with FRG propaganda in the GDR. Of one, formerly close friend, he says:

> I saw him again recently at a May Day gathering and he was shocked "How is it that you are here?" He really couldn't believe that a journalist from SFB could possibly attend a May Day rally. Then he said to me somewhat sheepishly, "Well, you know I'm not really listening to that much radio anymore." Then there was a pause for a couple of breaths and he said, "Actually, I'm not really listening to your station much anymore." And I said to him, "Rudi, if you're trying to say that you don't listen to my program anymore then that's OK." Another long pause. Then he said, "You know what, Ali, a couple of old communists like you and me don't have anything to feel guilty about. We shouldn't condemn ourselves." "What are you talking about?" I asked him. "You and I shouldn't condemn ourselves, because the ideal which we pursued was impossible to realize. That's the truth, our ideals were simply ones that were impossible to realize [*unmöglich zu verwirklichen*]." [*Turning to me:*] Can you believe that? He basically wrote off everything he did in his life just so he wouldn't have to feel guilty. My god, I just don't know . . . [*shaking his head*]

Albert's willingness to say things that no one else will say and his capacity to objectify social dynamics in a humorous, often self-effacing way have served him equally well in both GDR and FRG journalism. As Albert has said to me on more than one occasion, journalists in the West are much the same kinds of people as journalists in the East, and once one has learned the personality types and how to handle them, one should be equally successful in either System.

⋄

We are now driving down the Köpenickerstrasse toward the radio complex. I produce and open a bag of fresh pretzels, which fill the car with the aroma of baked bread. I reach over to offer them to Karl-Hans and Albert, commenting to Karl-Hans that since Albert is now alone in his apartment (his wife having left him a few years before and his youngest daughter having just moved into her own apartment) we need to make sure that he has enough to eat. Albert catches my point of reference. About a week beforehand, at the reception following a program he had moderated, Albert leaned in conspiratorially to show me the pretzel he had just stashed in his jacket pocket. "This is a habit from the old days. You see, in the GDR, the first thing you did was to put something away for later," he said more loudly, overemphasizing the gesture of looking around to see if anyone had noticed. Karl-Hans chuckles with a mouthful of pretzel but Albert shouts from the backseat that he should take no notice of the "fantasies of this American that I survive only through public assistance." Karl-Hans and Albert worked together for over twenty-five years at GDR Radio; Karl-Hans served as assistant chief editor at Radio Aktuell while Albert was chief editor, and Karl-Hans later became chief editor himself. Later, Albert tells me that Karl-Hans is the closest thing he has to a biographer since he remembers events and relationships in Albert's life that Albert has long since forgotten. As the complex comes into view, Albert and Karl-Hans begin to discuss with more excitement the layout of the complex, how it was constructed around an old furniture factory in the 1950s, but as the number of employees increased, new buildings and dozens of cheap, low-lying barracks were built to house them.

The entire complex is sealed to agents of the class enemy by a sturdy red brick wall and at the gatehouse we are stopped by two not-entirely-enthusiastic security guards, who shake their heads somberly that it is impossible under any circumstances to visit the complex unannounced but especially on a Sunday. Albert quickly brandishes his SFB identification card and talks to them with frequent gestures in my direction. Two former employees of GDR Radio are accompanying an American social scientist who absolutely *must* tour the premises as a part of his research. Albert quickly determines that the guards are also former GDR citizens and softens his tone, speaking to them fraternally about the need to support independent research of "our" past. With this, Albert is able to convince them to call their supervisor, whom Albert then talks into giving us a special pass. The

Entrance to Nalepastraße, the central production complex of GDR Radio

guards shake their heads as we are leaving, warning us that the place is in bad shape. Once inside the complex, Albert picks up his pace, walking ahead of us and then stopping to point out to me one building or another and to explain their former functions. To Karl-Hans, he turns more frequently, grabbing his shoulder and pointing to one place or another, especially those associated with former colleagues and their drinking adventures.

A few days after our trip to Nalepastraße, Albert sends out an email report to the group of GDR Radio colleagues with whom he stays in regular contact. He narrates a space much more semiotically abundant and emotionally resonant than my more superficial narration can capture. The complex, for Albert, contains twenty-seven years of events, routines, and relationships. The report begins:

> The massive stony trashcan at the entrance to GDR Radio where Hermann Börner used to sit and wait for a taxi has disappeared, gone. The crabapple tree behind the guardhouse has gone barren. The Lamberzweg is ruined; the barracks where Dr. Udo Krause and radio pastor Ernst Goltzsch used to have a drink has been torn down. Across the way, the low stone building in which, for decades, GDR sports reporters used to play skat and make their foreign currency calculations still exists. Dark gray. Disappearing behind thick shrubbery (schnaps bottles could

be tossed, unseen, out of the windows) are the remains of the quarters
which once housed the best minds and voices of the music department.
The giant tree behind Block E is full and beautiful. It could be sold to Hol-
lywood. The corner barracks where once the sociologists and listener-
mail researchers (spies) once worked is open, empty, and clean. Here and
there are calendars and posters from HALLO [Voice of the GDR]. The
glass doors to Block E are locked but the glass is gone. One can enter the
building. But the notices in the event of fires and civil emergencies are
missing from the walls. . . .

We wander the complex for three hours, at first with much excitement
and interest, laughing at people and adventures recollected from their days
in the GDR. Later, we more often walk quietly with a certain sense of reverence. The grounds have gone wild since the complex was vacated. Some
of the buildings are locked, others are so overgrown with shrubbery that
the entrances have become impassable, some doors stand wide open. One of
the open buildings is, ironically, as Albert observes, the old security building, and herein we find bookshelves still stacked with protocolary manuals,
files and office supplies scattered everywhere, and a small gated area where
Karl-Hans and Albert joke to me that class enemies and political prisoners
used to be held. They make me stand inside it. Chairs are stacked up in one
room; a smashed television squats in another. Documents, packing materials, and carpet remnants are strewn everywhere. In every room, the linoleum
is patchy, cracked, and curling; the remaining GDR-era curtains are dirty
and woeful. A stench of mildew hangs in the air in every room. Water damage is evident on the ceilings and walls; the ceilings have crumbled and a
thin layer of chipped paint covers the floors. Kitschy stickers and posters
still cover some of the office doors, the last detritus of everyday professional
irony and iconography. The wall clocks have long ceased to function.
    Albert rummages here and there for souvenirs of the trip while Karl-
Hans scoops documents off the floor to show to me. He tries to explain in
more detail the functions of the various offices and the procedures that the
security office regulated. Albert's most significant find is a ring of capsular
aluminum keys that were used to gain access to the broadcast studios. "We
nicknamed them *Bomben* [bombs] because of their shape and you were in
for it if you lost yours; remember, Karl-Hans?" In the canteen, silverware
and dishes still stand on the shelves covered with dust, giving the room
a postapocalyptic feel. Albert points out a half-eaten sandwich still on its
plate. Someone has smashed the urinals and the sinks in the men's room
next door. "What was the point of that?" Albert wonders aloud. "These were

View toward the sauna, Nalepastraße

all new fixtures put in after the *Wende.*" In the women's room, there are
unopened bags of sanitary napkins on the shelves. Albert finds a small blue
plastic hand mirror that he says is what the women of GDR Radio once used
to make themselves beautiful for the likes of Karl-Hans and him.

Albert leads us to Block E, which is where he and Karl-Hans worked, and
fortunately the glass door has been shattered so we can step right through.
We climb the wide stairwell to his old office, which is still filled with strewn
papers from his tenure. I find a sheaf of news bulletins from ADN dated
1981. Albert begins to sort through these, reading passages aloud, occasionally handing me things to put in his bag. He finds a stack of purple information brochures from February 1991 wherein a younger, more earnest looking
Albert promises in his "From the desk of the editor" introduction that

> [t]his station, presently receivable within all five new federal states and
> far beyond, wants to accompany the process of the *Zusammenwachsen*
> [growing together] of the German states and wants to help clarify how
> unified Germany can move into a European future. We at Radio Aktuell
> understand that our role in this process will be a small one. But the ap-
> proximately 140 journalists, music editors, production managers, and
> technicians here are working as hard as possible to contribute to the re-
> alization of the hopes for unified Germany.

Canteen in security building, Nalepastraße

Albert hands one of these brochures to me and takes a few others for his bag. Then he pushes the dozens of others into a neat pile by the wall. Albert asks me to take a photo of him standing right where his desk used to be. As I am fumbling with the focus button, Albert turns to Karl-Hans and says seriously but softly, "To think, I spent twenty-seven years of my life here." Karl-Hans nods and looks out the window. Looking at the photo again as I write this, Albert has a confident smile and a twinkle in his eye. He made it out.

Albert and Karl-Hans want to look into the editing rooms and broadcast studios in the basement of Block E but these have been shut to protect whatever equipment still lies within. Nearby, there is what looks to have been some kind of a buzzer system with the name "Manfred Klein" handwritten below it. Klein was the general director (*Generalintendant*) of GDR Radio

Gated area, security building, Nalepastraße

for the year after the *Wende* and formerly the chief editor of the news division of GDR Radio for almost two decades (see Klein 1993). Karl-Hans says to me, "Klein is another one who had a reputation as a drinker. He also had a reputation for firing women who didn't respond to his advances while he was drunk. Of course, *das ging nicht* [that didn't play] in the GDR, just as it isn't allowed today either. But of course nobody said anything about it. And I'm sure none of the women made too much trouble about it either." Water drips everywhere in the basement and some rooms have close to an inch of standing water in them. We hurry through these hoping that there is not a live wire somewhere.

Albert and Karl-Hans want to walk over to the bank of the Spree to see if they can find a bench where they used to sit and drink and watch the boats come down the river. Albert is leading the way as Karl-Hans and I

Hallway, Block E, Nalepastraße

lag behind. Karl-Hans is shaking his head at the ruins around him: "It's a shame that all of these buildings are just left here wasted. What they should do is to refurbish them a bit and let homeless people live here." Or maybe offer them to immigrants, I add. "No, no, the immigrants deserve something better. If they come to this country and are placed at the bottom of the ladder like this, then things will never get any better for them." The spot by the river is quite beautiful and serene and Karl-Hans points across toward the Plänterwald in Treptow to show me where he used to catch a ferry to work. He then reminds Albert of the old joke about the drunken journalist who decided to swim across the river to the West not realizing that the western bank of the Spree was still in the GDR. "He climbs up on to the bank, saying 'Thank God, I'm in the land of freedom!' And the guy on the other shore says to him, 'Welcome comrade, you *are* in the land of freedom, the GDR."

On the way back to the entrance we pass through an area of prefab barracks-style buildings. Albert points one out to me where the GDR Radio "anti-Solidarity" group worked in the 1980s.[4] Albert turns to Karl-Hans and says, "If they had only released the names of *those* people earlier. I'm sure that fully 95 percent of them worked with the Stasi, not as normal *IM* like you and me and Dominic,[5] you understand, but the really bad ones." In front of another building, Albert stops cold and says to us, "I don't know why, but I have distinctly bad memories of this building." Karl-Hans laughs and says, "That's because we were both fired there, first you, then me, and the woman who was in charge then said to Albert, 'You probably should be in charge here instead of me so I'm going to recommend to the advisory board that they not extend your contract.'" We find nearby that Block B, one of the few buildings in the complex still actively occupied because its two concert halls are under landmark protection, still has a café in service. Slumped in black leather chairs to rest, Karl-Hans beats me in a game of chess in about ten minutes. Albert meanwhile stalks around the café, urgently attempting to get one of his old coworkers and girlfriends on the phone to tell her where he is. Karl-Hans whispers to me, "With Albert, it's hard with all the women, the girlfriends, the companions, to keep them all straight." After leaving a couple of cryptic messages on her voicemail, Albert gives up.

Our last stop is the administration building, Block A, where Albert notices that his former barber still has an office and leaves him a note. We test the elevator but Karl-Hans is not taking any chances ("Not that I don't have the utmost faith in GDR engineering," he jokes) so he makes Albert turn on his cell phone again to see that it has power before we get in. On the top floors we find the locked offices of the old chiefs of GDR Radio, which have now, appropriately enough, been taken over by the agency responsible for liquidating the property of the GDR state broadcasters. "Liquidator" is typed on the nameplates of several doors. Downstairs, Karl-Hans shows me where the supermarket was.

As we exit this last building, Karl-Hans sighs deeply and says with a slight tremor in his voice, "It's hard to imagine that we spent twenty-six or twenty-seven years of our life coming to work here every day. Even if it was

---

4. The SED was deeply concerned about the influence of the Polish Solidarity movement in the GDR in the 1980s. Agitation developed a special "anti-Solidarity" initiative in GDR media to combat and contain what was perceived as the work of the class enemy.

5. Albert is toying with the way in which he and many other employees of the GDR state are lumped in with the *inoffizielle Mitarbeiter* (unofficial employees, informants) of GDR state security (the Stasi). Albert classifies me as an *IM* as well in part because he notes similarities between my investigative procedures and my note-taking on informal interactions and the work practices of Stasi informers.

View of Nalepastraße from Block A

supposedly criminal what we were doing." He pauses. "It's hard for me to explain what I feel right now." Albert's eyes gleam as he gestures around him saying to me, "You can't imagine what pictures are in my mind right now. I'm remembering when I first saw this place in 1965, saw that big building over there [Block A] and I was just a kid from the country [*Dorf*] then and then I was taken on a tour and saw all the unimaginable things here, like *Cutterinnen* [female tape editors]. I can't begin to explain it."

On the ride home, we drop Albert back at his apartment in Lichtenberg, but since Karl-Hans is driving west to Charlottenburg to visit his wife, he gives me a ride west to my sublet in Moabit. As we near Alexanderplatz, I ask Karl-Hans if Albert is the same now as he remembers him in the GDR.

KARL-HANS: Oh, we're the same, not identical, but the same [*Ach, wir sind die selben geblieben, nicht die gleichen, aber die selben*]. Albert was kind of a hero back then. He always seemed to be able to do things that no one else could get away with. He'd drive to West Berlin, for instance, to interview members of the western Communist Party who had *Berufsverbote* in the West. You know, there was a time when there really was a genuine *Berufsverbot* in the West for certain people. [*Laughs.*] There were only five or six of them, of course, and we knew them all by name. . . . [or] he would telephone West Berlin or telephone, my God, JAPAN. Talking on the telephone to Japan! That caused him trouble! He telephoned Japan to talk with Kurt Masur, and I heard that was even discussed in the party meetings, where some of our colleagues stood up and complained, "If he's talking to GDR people, why on earth is he calling them in Japan instead of talking to them here?"

DOMINIC: So people thought of Albert as a kind of maverick back then?

KARL-HANS: No, listen, it's difficult to explain to someone who didn't know him. It wasn't for nothing that he was named head of the politics department at GDR Radio. People clearly respected his intelligence and his abilities. And the director himself, although he was seventeen or eighteen years older than us and a man who was true to the party and to the party line, he supported Albert strongly. I remember that the party leadership constantly wanted to sit Albert down to talk with him about his drinking. And they contacted the director and tried to convince him to have this conversation with Albert, but he always stalled them every time they tried to make an appointment, either he wasn't there or Albert wasn't there, or someone wasn't there. . . . It went on this way for a long time such that the conversation never took place. Or with me, for example, there was one time I went over to ADN, because I was due to go to the Caucasus with a photographer to do a story in connection with the GDR culture magazine *Freie Welt,* in which of course Soviet culture featured prominently. So we went over to their office on Alexanderplatz, and when we got there, I showed them my professional identification but they wanted to see my personal identification instead. Otherwise, I couldn't go in. Well, fortunately, I just happened to have my personal identification with me, but I muttered something about "this shitty bureaucracy" and I must not have noticed that there was somebody standing there in the corner. Because by the time I got back to the office, the boss was looking for me asking what the hell had happened over there. Someone had called and said I had "compromised the security" over there. And he asked me, "What, were you drunk?" And I said, "Look at me, I just came from there! How could I have been drunk?" "That's a load of crap!" he yelled back. Then he must have talked with the director about it. Later, the director called me in and was speaking to me in Saxon, in a thick Saxon accent, saying [*imitating it in high pitch and sharpness*], "*Bist Du reuisch?*" [*Laughs.*] He meant "*Hast Du Reue?*" [Do you have remorse?] But that's a Saxonism so he kept asking me *Bist Du reuisch? Bist Du reuisch?* And I said, "*Na, klar*" [Well, sure] and he replied, "OK then you can consider yourself to have been rebuked professionally and by the party leadership as well!" Because he was also a ranking party member. Then he said, "What you have to do is to write up one or two pages explaining exactly what happened and how you are repentant." So basically nothing happened to me. My punishment was to write up these two pages

on how everything happened and he just signed his name to it. [*Laughs.*] So
that's how it was, but I never got into any real trouble because of it.

DOMINIC: So he was a decent man then, this director?

KARL-HANS: Yeah, absolutely, and anyone who tells you differently is a liar.
[*Pauses.*] But, anyway, with Albert, you know, a lot of people wondered, myself included, how he managed to stay at a place like SFB. And I always asked
him, "Ali, what is it like over there?" and he would answer, "Just the same as
it was with us in the GDR." Because, you know, people are more or less the
same everywhere, so it's not that surprising that you find similar situations
and personalities to those in the GDR.

⌀

At the end of the last chapter, I discussed the ratio of Spirit to System in
former GDR journalists' memories of their past professional life. In Albert
and Karl-Hans's tour through Nalepastraße, we glimpse the intricacy and
delicacy of dialectical knowledge in actual situations of knowledge making.
I have spent a good deal of time in the past two case studies arguing how various social conditions of intellectual life dampen or amplify different modes
of dialectical social knowledge. But, at Nalepastraße, one recognizes the analytical limitations and ethnographic dilemmas of relying too strongly on
a functionalist argument that dialectical social knowledge predictably results from just this or that combination of proximate sociological causes.
If dialectical social knowledge is certainly conditioned by the broader social relations and dynamics of intellectual life, it is also a matter of particular attentions, engagements, and juxtapositions in the course of everyday
experience.

At Nalepastraße, one hears the idiosyncrasy and embeddedness of dialectical knowledge, how dialectical knowing is always significantly immediate in its concerns and reference. Statements like Karl-Hans's "Even if it
was supposedly criminal what we were doing," Gregor's "They shouldn't
be allowed into the public sphere," or Albert's claim that FRG journalists
and GDR journalists were not such different kinds of people after all do, to
some extent, reflect the contours of common settlements of social knowledge in postunification Germany. Perhaps, at some level, they could even
be viewed as what Bourdieu termed social "dispositions," particularly in
how these individual statements can be associated with a distribution of familiar knowledges of self and other between eastern and western Germans.
Yet these are also statements *about* familiar social knowledges, involving
individual processes of departure either to challenge them through the production of counterknowledges or to verify and to elaborate them.

Therefore, studying common settlements and trends of dialectical social knowledge as I have done, while entirely necessary for this project, is
not sufficient. Instead of simply confirming the sociological conditions implicit in dialectical knowledge, the preceding vignette *augments and challenges* our knowledge of these conditions by returning our attention to the
equivalently powerful phenomenological dimension of dialecticism. As Albert, Karl-Hans, and I navigated Nalepastraße, one sees how dialecticism
emerges in fits and starts from the subtle, ongoing process of construing
selfhood across a series of individual attentions and environmental frames.
The process is at once subjective and intersubjective, both introspective and
communicative. They each had their private memories, associations, and
oblivions with respect to the shifting landscape of our tour. We all shared a
certain sense of wonder, but mine, unlike theirs, was predicated on my lack
of prior experiential knowledge of the place. At many points, they conferred
with one another to coordinate memories and knowledge of events and relations. At other times, they addressed me from a stance of authority, seeking
to narrate either specific events or a more general sense of what it was like
working at the complex.

The tour, like life more generally I would add, was uneven in its semiotic
and epistemic qualities. Some signs of the past would stimulate torrents
of recollections for Albert and Karl-Hans, whereas, elsewhere, they had to
struggle to make associations they knew or suspected they once had had.
In some cases, as with Karl-Hans's unsuccessful attempt to condense his
twenty-six years of life at Nalepastraße into some kind of pithy reflection,
the bounty of emotion simply exceeded efforts of epistemic containment or
communication.

I would certainly say that there was a good deal of dialectical social
knowledge produced on our trip, a great many reflections on the relationship of the self as creative agent to the exterior forces of the media control
System and to the System of the party-state more generally. But the connection of dialecticism to specific communicative situations and encounters,
its interweaving with other dimensions of knowledge making, the ratio between false starts and fully developed ideas, and the subtleties of silences
and vague allusions all suggest how complex the intersubjective dynamics
of dialectical knowledge ultimately are. It is my hope that in our shift from
the second to the third case study, from history to ethnography, I can re-
center *our* attention on the intimacies, individualities, and loose ends of
dialectical social knowledge.

In the next four sections, I briefly discuss common dialectical stereotypes of East German and West German cultural character in postunification

Germany: the Ossi as a creature of spiritless habit perverted by the authoritarian System of the GDR and the Wessi as a superficial creature of spiritless arrogance and self-interest enacting the dehumanizing principles of
the capitalist System. I link these stereotypes to strategies of construing social identity and alterity that developed in both Germanys during the Cold
War. The partition of Germany as a "price" for the Third Reich helped to
create a durable "ethnologization" of Nazism and the Holocaust. For this
and other reasons, Germans lived (and live) with anxiety and guilt over the
apparent "Germanness" of the Third Reich. But the partition also allowed
each Germany and its citizens to imagine the "more German Germans" on
the other side of the Wall and gave them ample opportunities to explore
incipient postnational identifications.

I suggest that the dialectical apparitions of Ossis and Wessis in unified
Germany reflect the residue of Cold War strategies of social identification
that have been mapped over a new set of social distinctions between western Germans as "nationals" and eastern Germans as "regionals." To study
this recent shift in patterns of dialectical knowledge more concretely, I look
in more detail at the institutional and professional politics surrounding the
fusion of the former GDR and FRG media systems after 1990. In media organizations in eastern Germany one discovers how the social distinction of
"longitude" (East/West) has come to saturate institutional culture ranging
from everyday conversations to journalistic assignments to labor politics.
Eastern journalists are treated, generally, as journalists with a more limited range of expertise than western journalists. Higher-status journalistic
methods (like investigative reporting) and higher-status knowledge of national and international issues are implicitly gendered "western" and are
thus treated as beyond the purview of the eastern German journalist. I query
why eastern journalists appear to embrace this regional subjectivity as virtue
and necessity despite the fact that this identity appears to deny them national subjectivity and equivalent professional status as journalists.

To answer this question, I move into deeper ethnographic engagement
with the dialectical social knowledges of self, other, and system of individual eastern and western German journalists. I explore how two of my
friends, Brigitte and Marianne, naturalized their eastern and western identities with regard to longitudinal others. A further discussion of eastern journalists' narratives of the *Wende* of 1989 and its fleeting space and time of
non-Systemic positive dialectical becoming reveals a powerful conceptual
equivalence between System and normal life. The contrast of the fragile,
unspeakable character of pure Spirit with the banality of System suggests
the extent of negative dialectical social knowledge in the poetics and politics

of establishing selfhood and belonging in postunification Germany. Finally, returning to my friends Joachim and Michael, I narrate one path of personal *Bildung*, one self-conscious exercise of Spirit against System, in Joachim's decision to leave journalism altogether and to pursue instead a career as a writer.

Ossis and Wessis

I have written at greater length elsewhere of the schismogenetic properties of "longitude" (East/West relations) in everyday and expert social knowledges circulating in postunification Germany (2000; see also Berdahl 1999; A. Glaeser 2000). I will not rehearse these arguments and descriptions at length here. Rather, I simply note that, especially in eastern Germany, longitude is a key principle of social distinction and identification whose associations, while abundant in their variety, tend also to cluster around certain routine figurations. On the one hand, we have the Ossis, the "Easties," who are portrayed as lagging behind western society and civilization (A. Glaeser 2000: 143–85), a bit slower, a bit clumsier, just out of sync enough to be recognized by their clothing, their gait, their language, or their posture. Albert once took me to a *Bockwurst* (sausage) stand near the Alexanderplatz that he calls "the soup kitchen of former functionaries" to show me some "real Ossis," former GDR state employees who had never been able to "arrive in the West." We stood near the entrance while Albert speculated on each exiting patron's former job in the party-state's bureaucracy. I asked him what he looks for in spotting an Ossi, and he replied, gesturing toward a man in a crisp blue shirt and slacks with his head inclined slightly forward, "principally, this sense of resignation that they exude, as though a burden was on them." He immediately contrasted the downtroddenness of the Ossi to the former Stasi officers he knows who live in his neighborhood, who also have little to do but sit around and complain about the West constantly: "But you can see by their demeanor, by the way they carry themselves and by their sense of self-righteousness that these were people who once commanded others. And *that* they haven't lost."

The Ossi, by contrast, belonged and belongs to the ranks of the commanded, the perpetual *Mittel* (means) of history. For Albert, the genuine Ossi is someone who in the GDR was made step-by-step into a functional mechanism of the System and who now continues to live out a formal existence in the new System with little function or agency, like an old railway line around which traffic has been diverted but which is worth no one's trouble to remove. In all of its many representations, the Ossi is a creature and sign of habit, of formal duration. Among some western Germans and younger eastern Germans, the Ossi is an amusing or annoying caricature, portrayed at times as a kind of country bumpkin in a polyester suit and at others as a kind of inveterate ingrate, the *Jammerossi* (whiny Eastie), who exists precisely to blame the West and capitalism for all his or her miseries. For eastern Germans of Albert's generation, however, the Ossi is no laughing matter: "I feel real empathy for these poor dogs," he says to me quietly as we walk away from the *Bockwurst* stand.

The Wessi, on the other hand, inverts the resigned inwardness of the Ossi. The Wessi is nothing if not self-assertive, a bit loud, a bit flashy and aggressive, and, in the more extreme instances of *Besserwessis* (know-it-all Westies), prone to profess to knowing everything better. If the Ossi, stultified and numbed to the outside world by the GDR System, looks to the Wessi in a kind of awed estrangement, then the Wessi is said to feel nothing but disdain for everything eastern. Wessis have no time and patience for the *Gründlichkeit* (thoroughness, groundedness) of the East German. They are frenetically, frantically active. As inveterate careerists and opportunists, they are incapable of managing and maintaining real social and emotional relationships with other human beings. One hears nothing of a Wessi's family life or domestic sphere because they are so often portrayed as creatures of external form and motion. In their relentless competitiveness and self-promotion, they show no signs of empathy (see Boyer 2001c).

One journalist offered me an extremely careful and thoughtful description of *Westdeutschen* (West Germans) that captures the language and logic of more offhanded derogations of Wessis as well:

> They [West Germans] are more formal, they wear masks, in general all of them do, among individuals there are some exceptions. I've known several West Germans who didn't wear masks at all. But there are a great many of them who have these poker faces. And a terrible quality of West Germans—no capacity for self-doubt. West Germans are not open [*offen*], they're more difficult [*schwerer*], they're not alive [*lebendig*] at all. But this is what this life has done to them. After living here for a while, you come to understand why. This will certainly be our fate as well if this society keeps progressing in the direction it's going. Not for me or for my daughter but farther along. They [the West Germans] would never say, "No, I'm not so good at that, I doubt that I could manage that, someone else could do that better." But self-doubt, I think, is a precondition of creativity. And easterners have certainly developed far too much self-doubt, but to completely get rid of it, or to completely deny its outward

expression, even though they naturally possess it as human beings, I don't know . . .

If the Ossi often seems to be state socialism incarnate, the generic human "ready-made" of a totalitarian System, then the Wessi often comes across as an anthropomorphism of the classical marginal-utilitarian market, with its competitive individuality, zero sums, and lack of imagination of social relations beyond those of competition and supply and demand. Perhaps the most important point to make is that Ossis and Wessis are equivalently deemed products of their respective Systems, qualitatively different and, yet, essentially similar as creatures constituted by the *Prägung* of System. Regardless of the intensity and oppositionality poured into their stereotypes, the Wessi, like the Ossi, is a person of form, constituted from without to within, and unable to recover the openness and liveliness of a Spirit unclaimed by System and history.

Vergangenheitsbelastung: The Ethnology and Inescapability of the Other Germany

With the Ossi and the Wessi, we have the essential dyad of contemporary dialectical social knowledge of easternness and westernness in eastern Germany. Below, I explore the tropic elaborations and conceptual clarifications of this dyad in more ethnographic detail. This exploration requires, however, some further historical framing. As we saw with the negative dialectical imagination of bourgeois journalism in the preceding case study, the confluence of longitudinal distinction and dialectical knowledge was a central feature of the narratives of citizenship and belonging sculpted by the governments of the Cold War Germanys. This is not to say that easternness and westernness have not existed as broader valences of translocal social imagination both in Germany and elsewhere in Europe for a long time. As Larry Wolff has argued, the social imagination of eastern Europe originated at least with the Enlightenment in western Europe and secured, in part, the West's sense of historical progressiveness and civilization by narrating the cultural stasis or even backwardness of its immediate East (1994: 4; see also Gal 1991; Herzfeld 1987). Within contemporary Germany, one can still hear the residue of these timeworn modes of social identification when one is in the Rhineland and asks, for example, about Berlin and hears a litany of complaints about the "culture of the steppes."

Yet, whatever the long run of knowledges of East/West difference in Central Europe, longitudinalism acquired distinctive valences of reference in the aftermath of the Third Reich and in the formation of the two Germanys. John Borneman has written extensively of the narrational strategies that the two German states utilized after 1949 to "define, regularize, institutionalize, and normalize the domestic practices of the self" (1992: 75). Borneman notes the curiously reciprocal character of the two states' understandings of their mandates, as each staked a parallel claim to be providing the better model for the dissolved nation-state:

> In this process of mirror-imaging, the two states fabricated themselves as moieties in a dual organization. The catchphrase in the West was "integration into the West"; leaders pointed the finger at the "totalitarian East Zone," and simultaneously embraced many formal aspects of the liberal-democratic model of their occupation forces, above all free-market capitalism and parliamentary democracy. In the East, policy was initially directed toward negation of what the Germans in the Third Reich had been; leaders depicted themselves first and foremost as anti-fascist and anti-war. Very soon, however, they began to represent themselves in positive terms—as democratic and socialist—and began to take on concrete and enduring characteristics, often borrowed from the Stalinist model of the Soviets. In this battle of state-building, the concrete practices of past Nazism quickly dropped out of contention as the mirror-image against which the present was viewed. (17)

I have argued at greater length elsewhere (2000, 2001b) that the Cold War "process of mirror-imaging" that Borneman describes never did fully escape reference to Nazism and to the Holocaust, although, as Borneman rightly notes, the "concrete practices" of Nazism per se were less often utilized as foils for state legitimation.

The partition of the nation-state as a consequence of Nazism and the Second World War inevitably amplified ethnological associations between Germanness and Nazism. It was certainly not only outside the two Germanys that people speculated on *die deutsche Krankheit* (the German sickness) of authoritarianism and how its symptomatic aggressions could best be managed. Indeed, many of my interlocutors born after 1945 grew up with a strong sense of the "cultural" character of the Holocaust that became interwoven with the states' strategies of managing public memory. Germanness was no longer narrated in Mann's language as something interior and potential extending from within to without; Germanness was heavy, solid, obdurate, an identity shouldering the immense weight of *die Vergangenheit* (the past).

The psychic crisis that the so-called *Vergangenheitsbelastung* (burden of history) of Germanness created should not be underestimated. This was and remains true especially for younger Germans. It is not only the paralysis of guilt for acts one has not committed but also the fear, as Joachim put it, of "the Hitler within." Once the Holocaust was entrenched in social knowledge as a distinctively, ethnologically "German" event, every German citizen, regardless of age or political disposition, was equivalently, culturally capable of the moral collapse and genocidal behaviors of the Third Reich. Of course, many sought privately or publicly to challenge this ethnologic. It could not be entirely ignored, however, arising as it did in encounters with stereotypes of authoritarian, intolerant Germanness. As one woman told me, "I always was most aware of being German when I traveled. There one constantly faced the stereotypes." The singularity of Germanness, the sense that no other nation bore this burden, only further amplified national identity and inward retreat.

If the division of the nation-state exacerbated the ethnologization of Nazism and its horrors, it also provided a providential opportunity to defer fears of "the Hitler within" via the mediating presence of another Germany. Psychotherapist Hans-Joachim Maaz has written insightfully of how the partition allowed, from the very beginning, the opportunity for the suppression of guilt and self-examination through the constitution of new "external enemies."

> From a psychological viewpoint, this partition, from the very start, was [our] big chance for the suppression of guilt. The joint guilt was divided between the two camps—polarization was established—and the dammed up emotions had their distraction without any "work of mourning." Inner self-examination was successfully avoided, and the old mechanisms of denial and projection had new opportunities and targets. We were able to give up the Jew as a common enemy, at least pro forma—the new external enemies now were called Bolsheviks and Communists on the one side, and capitalists, militarists, revanchists, and Nazis on the other. (1995: 187)

The existence of two Germanys provided a scale by which degrees of Germanness could be measured and calibrated. Positive and negative poles of cultural Germanness were defined on both sides of the Wall, and then ethnotypical traits were apportioned selectively to the East and the West. These traits were always significantly dialectical in their character, assigning a

corrupted formality and habit to the government of the other Germany and
depicting it as acting to pervert the energies, values, and behaviors of the
Volk. In the West, the GDR could become an instantiation of German "authoritarian traditions" that threatened a return of the repressed to any future
German nation-state. Meanwhile, in the East, the FRG represented German
cultural qualities of aggression and intolerance honed by the imperialist
imperative of international capitalism. In both cases, the "truly" forward-
looking Germany faced its mirror image in the backward-looking, externally
mediated (either by capital or by totalitarianism) System of the other Germany. To each Germany, the other represented the national-cultural past
against which its postnational futurity could be measured.

Complicating the work to determine which Germany was "more German" in its political and social profiles was the manifest desire of both German states (and of many German citizens as well) to explore postnational
identifications as a means of distancing themselves from the ethnological
burden of history. The GDR, as Borneman notes, came to identify itself as
part of an international socialist constellation centered on the Soviet Union
and emphasized in much of its public discourse the international kinship
and fraternity among all socialist states and citizens. The FRG likewise
sought to foreground its westernness and Europeanness rather than its Germanness through an unshakable adherence to the liberal-democratic ideals
associated with the western occupation forces.

I had the opportunity, as part of a small group of fellows of the Alexander von Humboldt Foundation, to meet for two hours with Chancellor Helmut Kohl in July 1997. He offered us a well-rehearsed but also strikingly
emotional discussion of the trials of postwar German nation building and
explained his administration's emphasis on the European Union and on European integration as "the only possible solution to German history." I was
struck that only in Germany would one find a head of state so committed to
pursuing a postnational politics. To be sure, Kohl knew he was speaking to
an audience of "westerners" in this context. At other times, especially during those months leading up to German unification, he demonstrated that
he was versatile in a language of national renewal and belonging as well. But
Kohl's proffering of Europe as the only possible alternative for escaping Germany's *Vergangenheitsbelastung* underscores the traction of the ethnology
of terror in Germany. According to some, even to Chancellor Kohl, it was
worth some permanent sacrifice of the nation-state to rid Germanness of its
burden.

The events of 1989–90 provoked an unexpected crisis as dialectical
knowledges of longitudinal distinction lost their geopolitical reference but

persisted in public, institutional, expert, and everyday knowledges of self-hood and alterity. The return of the nation-state in 1990 offered citizens precisely the sense of national wholeness and tradition that had been deferred and refracted through relations to the other Germany for four decades. However, the offer was largely rejected. After a brief period of excitement at the prospect of unity (that also ended, formally, the period of international surveillance, occupation, and compensation for the Third Reich), citizens of both Germanys quickly withdrew again to longitudinal and internationalist identifications.

Over forty years, the other Germany had become, in essence, a "prosthesis" (Derrida 1998) of identification and origin. Although by no means a cure to the burden of national history, it stabilized a benign Germanness by holding a worse Germanness at bay. In waking to the "new world" of unified Germany, citizens reached again for the prosthetics of longitudinal distinction to ease the considerable trauma of transition. For, with the one Deutschland, had come again the one history, the one burden. The quick reversal of sentiment in 1989 from the ecstasy of the collapsing Wall to the, almost guilty, retreat again to East/West difference underlines the ongoing psychic cost of Germanness. A former *Eulenspiegel* satirist told me a joke from the autumn of 1989 that captures this retreat perfectly. "The East German says to the West German, '*Wir sind ein Volk*' [We are one people]. The West German replies, '*Wir auch*' [Us too]." He explained to me that hearing this joke was the moment when he thought to himself, "life is normal again."

Longitudinal distinction in contemporary Germany survives as a means for construing Germanness that shifts the ethnological burden of the past to an eastern or western other. One reads in Werner Kohlhoff's op-ed piece for the *Berliner Zeitung* (1997) how potent a locus longitudinal distinction is for social imagination in contemporary Germany and how its facticity is recursively sedimented through the technical instruments of academic and governmental *Wissenschaft*. Like other axes of social knowledge formation, longitudinalism coordinates and co-elaborates other classificatory schemes in everyday knowing (Butler 1993: 18). So the Ossi's alleged passivity is often gendered feminine, and her categorical lack of civic responsibility is subtly racialized and "species-ized" as the expected characteristic of a not-entirely-human presence.

Although eastern Germans participate in longitudinal distinction as often and as eagerly as western Germans, it is important to note that this is not a balanced reciprocity. Given the domination of western Germans and FRG social institutions over all domains of life in eastern Germany, the FRG side of Cold War mirror imaging has become the inheritance of unified German public culture. Mass media in Germany are virtually exclusively owned and managed by western Germans and continuously project eastern Germany as "the other Germany" within and depict East Germans in variously subtle and overt ways as culturally the "more German Germans" with a propensity to obedience and intolerance and with antidemocratic sympathies. It has not been lost on eastern Germans that such public-cultural representations position them to bear the burdens of Germanness and German history into the future. Many of my eastern interlocutors reported feeling that their alleged "pastness" was precisely correlated to West Germans' unwillingness or inability to honestly engage their own history. At a public event hosted by the *Berliner Zeitung* in May 1997 on the future of the East/West divide in Germany, then Partei des Demokratischen Sozialismus congressional representative Lothar Bisky received thundering applause when he said, "I am looking forward to the day when *the West Germans* have a history too."

Vergangenheitsbelastung and the Politics of Institutional and Professional Transition in the Eastern German Media, 1990–1994

To understand the nuances of dialectical knowledges of easternness and westernness among journalists in eastern Germany, one also needs to look more carefully at how knowledge of the *Vergangenheitsbelastung* of former GDR citizens organized and legitimated institutional and professional transitions in the eastern German media after 1990. I focus my discussion on the politics of "unification" (the sober rationality of this term scarcely conveying the contentious and improvisational character of the actual transition process) in media organizations and among journalists. But many of the general trends outlined below can be recognized in other institutional situations and with other occupational groups in eastern Germany as well (see, comparatively, De Nike 1997; A. Glaeser 2000).[6]

As has been widely observed, the critical decision to unify the two German states according to Article 23 rather than Article 146 of the FRG Basic Law allowed the Kohl administration to rapidly unify the two German

---

6. Given space and thematic considerations, I will not attempt a full description of the complex historical processes involved in the unification of the two German media systems after 1990. This would largely be an exercise in summation since there is already an abundant secondary literature on this history, to which I direct the reader eager for more detailed accounts: Boyer 2000, 2005a; Boyle 1992; Dennis 1993; Dümcke and Vilmar 1996; Humphreys 1994; Mast 1993; Meyn 1994; Reck 1996; Sandford 1995; Schneider 1992; Spielhagen 1993. On media transformations in eastern Europe more generally, see Sparks 1991, 1998; Splichal 1994.

states through an extension of West German economic, legal, political, and social standards to what have become known as the "new federal states" of eastern Germany (Jarausch 1994: 169–76; Maier 1997: 243). Sympathy among eastern voters for Kohl's agenda in 1990 was due to multiple factors, including deep suspicion of the eastern political elite (both mainstream and radical-democratic), a desire to quickly attain the standard of living of western Germans, and an expectation, which Kohl did nothing to disabuse in his speeches, that the unification process would treat eastern citizens as equal partners in the process of national formation. When it later became evident that the western political elite's conception of unification was less an offer of equal partnership than an offer to mentor former GDR citizens in what were taken to be the transparently superior institutions and lifeways of the FRG, critical discourse on the western "colonization" of the East became widespread both publicly and privately in eastern Germany.

In interviews with western German politicians in the autumn of 1996, I heard several variations on the paternalistic dialectical wisdom that East Germans had been stunted in their moral and individual development by a SED System that was uniformly described as dictatorial. To address East German *Vergangenheitsbelastung* and to help them develop an appreciation of the responsibilities and freedoms of democratic citizenship, these politicians explained that East Germans needed a phase of reeducation (*Umerziehung*) to function effectively in the West. Importantly, in the logic of the passive, past-embedded Ossi, East Germans were not described as being capable of this transition themselves. They were too "stamped" (*geprägt*) by the old System to "find their way into their new world." Other politicians preferred to analogize them as being childlike in their good intentions but also in their lack of ability and of self-reflection. East Germans, it was said, were not yet *reif* (mature, ready) to participate in a democratic process that they, through no fault of their own, did not fully fathom. Therefore, it was better if unification was arranged, as a service, on their behalf.

The cunning of the language of the "not yet" deserves remark. Like Cold War "allochronism" (Fabian 1983) more generally, East Germans were depicted on the same time line of evolutionary advancement as West Germans, just some distance behind. The shift in temporality legitimated sweeping judgments about East German character and sweeping plans for re-forming it without conveying the sense that anything was being done beyond restoring them to their proper temporality. It was entirely unclear, of course, what East Germans would have to do specifically to prove that they had entered the same temporality as West Germans. One is reminded of Bourdieu's observation in another context of the "art of *making someone wait*" to guarantee submission to a dominant power (1988: 89). Until that distant day of temporal conjuncture, it was perfectly reasonable that the "adults" in unified Germany, the West Germans, should occupy a leadership role in all domains of unified German society.

Knowledge of East Germans' Systemic habituation and democratic deficiencies organized and justified the process of transition in eastern German print media and electronic broadcasting (television, radio). Institutional transformation in the eastern German media was negotiated and executed without public referenda and largely without the input of rank-and-file media professionals despite the democratic reforms and initiatives that eastern German journalists had themselves undertaken in their media organizations during the autumn of 1989 (Apsel 1996; von Törne 1996; von Törne and Weber 1996: 279). The Kohl administration never seriously entertained any eastern German proposals for "third-way" models of media organization that departed from both GDR and FRG standards (Humphreys 1994: 314; Spielhagen 1993). Instead, beginning in mid-1990, rapid planning began for the transition of the eastern German media to the FRG model of market-capitalist print media and (since the 1980s boom in cable and satellite television), mixed private-public electronic broadcasting.

The new order coalesced from 1990 to 1992 through the sale of former SED-owned newspapers to western publishers via the giant government liquidator, the Treuhand (Jürgs 1997), and through the incorporation of GDR Radio and GDR Television into the West German ARD public-broadcasting network. In most cases, the shift in ownership brought an immediate shift in organizational management to install what were described as "western standards of democratic journalism." One of the first issues that new managers confronted was staffing. GDR media organizations were overstaffed by western standards, in large part owing to the guaranteed right to work in the GDR, and western chief editors repeatedly described to me their shock at arriving to find that they sometimes had three or even six times as many journalists (*Redakteure*) in a given department as they could possibly, profitably employ. Scarcely separable from fears of a poor bottom line in print media were concerns—concerns acutely shared by public-broadcasting czar Rudolf Mühlfenzl—about the lingering presence of "comrades" in newsrooms. Like Gregor's comment about Albert above, new western German managers were exceedingly uncomfortable with the idea that they were allowing "propagandists" to contaminate the fragile new public sphere (*Öffentlichkeit*) of unified Germany.

The specter of mediatic journalism emerged again in the first years of institutional transition as western managers in both print and public broadcasting sought to determine which former GDR journalists were spoiled by too great an excess of GDR history to be allowed to participate in the *Meinungsbildung* (education/formation of opinions) of the eastern German public. The key term was *"belastet"* (burdened). A journalist could be deemed *belastet* by his or her GDR career on several grounds: (1) age—the vast majority of journalists working in the eastern German media over the age of fifty were laid off or sent into early retirement, a de facto guideline that swiftly unemployed an entire generation of former GDR journalists, (2) a vocal lack of enthusiasm for the process of media reform, (3) a contentious relationship with new management, (4) a lack of competitive or independent "spirit," or (5) an unwillingness to commit oneself to learn new skills and techniques.

The rationale for age-based retention decisions was largely justified through negative dialectical characterizations of older GDR journalists as "too deep in the old System" or as having the GDR System "inside their heads." For younger journalists, moreover, one can see how the shading of criteria 2, 3, and 4 placed them in an uncomfortable bind. To follow obediently the directives of the new management could easily result in being classified either as suspiciously "cagey" or as possessing a lack of independent spirit. On the other hand, to voice concerns or criticism in the newsroom could be construed as a lack of conviction in the new "democratic" orientation of the media or even as nostalgia for GDR journalism (see Boyer 2000). The occasionally contradictory criteria by which one could prove oneself *unbelastet* (unburdened) created a highly stressful environment that encouraged some journalists to resign and seek either freelance work or new careers altogether. One man who had been an ADN foreign correspondent retired and started his own business editing technical manuals for cars: "In terms of journalism, let's just say that I didn't want to learn everything all over again." Albert told me, when deeply mired in professional uncertainty in 1997, "I have to say, Dominic, that I don't know how much longer I want to do this. I get sick of being treated like a schoolboy or a beggar."

In many cases, evaluations of *Belastung* were informal, based on the chief editor's interpretation of whose journalistic spirits were not yet entirely formed by the GDR System and were therefore "still capable of change." Other media organizations hired consultants to determine which former GDR journalists should be retained and which should be laid off or sent into early retirement. Evaluations sometimes involved questionnaires to gauge journalists' political sympathies and understandings of the responsibilities of "democratic journalism." Sometimes they involved research into what journalists had written before 1989 to distinguish the "real comrades" from the *Mitläufer* (fellow travelers). Maryellen Boyle describes the vetting process administered by a hired consultant that took place after the conservative Axel Springer Verlag acquired a controlling stake in the former SED regional daily the *Leipziger Volkszeitung:*

> The new Springer consultant informed chief editor Tiedke that he should discontinue covering media politics: "No one is interested in this. Put more information in . . . about the soaps and other TV series." That command ended the only systematic coverage of the unfolding East German broadcasting politics within the east press. Leftist journalists, meaning journalists openly critical of the CDU state or federal government, were released. All the journalists heard that this media analyst had developed a check list—three "red stars and you were out." Then the reform era chief editor Wolfgang Tiedke was fired. The official word was that he wasn't a "newspaper man." One after another the reformers in all the former SED newspapers would receive their walking papers. Many noted that the "Yes men and women" of the SED era remain there, in positions of some authority. (1992: 441–42)

When I interviewed chief editors and assistant chief editors who had been involved in the transition process, most explained that their primary criteria were talent and willingness to adjust to the new System. They did not hesitate, however, to tell me that they also felt entirely justified in removing *die roten Socken* (the true reds, literally "the red socks") from the public sphere. These were ideologists not journalists, they said. Having served a corrupt and criminal regime in the GDR, they had no right to participate in the formation of public opinion for a new Germany.

A few, like Karl G., assistant chief editor at a regional daily in Saxony, lamented to me in 1996 that his newspaper had not gone far enough in the first few years after unification. He expressed concern that it was impossible to guarantee *sauber* (clean) journalism with an overabundance of former East German journalists in place:

> [This] is an enormous newspaper and in many areas we have no competition at all—thus it is we alone who are educating public opinion. Very few of the GDR-era journalists have been let go here. . . . Especially in our local offices where nothing has changed since before 1989. We have journalists out there many of whom have absolutely no idea of journalism or of anything else for that matter. That's a problem for us now. But one thing we have tried to do is to hire more younger East Germans and through internships to bring in more westerners as well, so that now

every local office has one or two West Germans. . . . This was a former
Communist Party paper and all the old journalists had to be party members in order to work here. And it's often not clear how much people
have changed, internally I mean, since that time.

West German managers generally expressed preferences for hiring
younger East Germans (with no journalistic experience in the GDR) and for
hiring qualified West Germans over the retention of former GDR journalists.
The problems with these strategies of labor management, they immediately
noted, were that the former is a very gradual and long-term solution and the
latter is only marginally effective since western Germans, I was told, had little interest in living anywhere in the East besides Berlin and would quickly
abandon their jobs at eastern media organizations when offered comparable positions in the West. So, with some resignation, most agreed that the
reeducation of former GDR journalists was the most pragmatic managerial
policy for the short run. Practices of reeducation varied widely from organization to organization. In many, western managers hired a few journalists
from the West to occupy senior positions and to "teach by example" the
techniques, attitudes, and praxis of "western journalism." These guidelines
and accompanying critical feedback were primary disciplinary techniques.
Other organizations organized seminars on praxis or even paid for younger
journalists to intern at western media organizations to observe how western
journalism operated.

Most of my eastern interlocutors did not speak willingly or often of the
period of reeducation. They glossed over it in professional narratives, occasionally wryly noting its parallels to the disciplinary tactics they had known
in the GDR. "You know, it became clear to us that the West has a System
as well," one man commented. A few journalists offered more critical commentary. Marcus H., a journalist at a Berlin boulevard newspaper, condensed
his recollection of the arrival of the new western German management as
follows:

The West Germans came over here in 1990 with the opinion, let's be honest, that everything that happened in the East during the previous forty
years was idiotic. The people were stupid. The structure was stupid. The
newspaper business was in the hands of a bunch of reds who had absolutely no idea of how to do journalism right. Which later proved itself
to be a joke because some of the regional dailies pretty much carried on
with few changes after 1990 and did very well for themselves and kept all
of their readers, whereas some of these papers like the *Berliner Zeitung*

where West Germans instituted one change after another lost thousands of readers. Anyway, what was happening here was that people were wandering around in ties and collars they didn't feel comfortable in because they didn't even know what the expectations for dress were anymore. And the West Germans were big mouths, knew everything better, and the East German journalists were totally on edge. Everything they wrote, even a ten-line report, was always wrong; they had to rewrite it. It was difficult for people to come to terms with this kind of treatment. Of course, there were many new things to learn and a new and precise kind of boulevard journalism to adapt to. But, frankly, there was very little goodwill demonstrated by the new owners.

I asked him whether it was a kind of student-teacher relationship, and he replied:

Worse than student-teacher, more like the dumb remedial schoolkid to the wise professor. It took a very long time to be accepted as a journalist. Then after this phase of grinding against one another, there eventually came a phase of mutual tolerance. Finally, maybe a year later, things had reached the point where you didn't really know who was who anymore.

My friend Rudi, sitting on his porch one starry Leipzig night, described to me with a smile his experience of being transferred to a western radio broadcaster to learn the new journalism. After having been lectured about how different and formative this experience would be for him, he was shocked to discover how familiar the environment was:

After the *Wende*, I worked for a month at Süddeutsche Rundfunk too and some of the things I witnessed there . . . [*Shakes his head.*] You could say that in the GDR we wanted socialism but at Süddeutsche Rundfunk they had actually achieved it. I found it *very* curious then to hear the way people from the West criticized *us* for being stuck in the past. They had a very socialist attitude. For one thing, the early morning shift was from 4 a.m. to 8:30 a.m., four and a half hours, and *that* was considered *a full working day* for those people.

Interestingly, it was at eastern German public broadcasters like mdr and ORB where layoffs and retirements were not as intense and where former GDR journalists continue to maintain a significant (if subaltern) presence in station management that I heard fewer openly voiced concerns about the *Vergangenheitsbelastung* of GDR journalists. On the other hand, as a residue of the Mühlfenzl era, former GDR journalists working in eastern German public broadcasting have been subjected to much more intensive archival evaluations than journalists working in the print media normally have. Rudi once announced to me over a beer that since 1990 his name had been run through the Gauck organization (see n. 3 above) to check for past complicity with the Stasi no fewer than three times: "I must be the best *gegauckt* journalist in all of Germany!" he declared with mock pride.

In the final analysis, according to the best available labor statistics (see Böckelmann, Mast, and Schneider 1994: 41–47, 127), the size of the journalistic labor market in eastern Germany only dropped from 8,500 to 7,950 full-time positions from 1989 to 1992. But this relatively small decrease masks the large numbers of former GDR journalists who exited the workforce during these three years. At least 1,520 former GDR journalists over the age of fifty-five were sent into early retirement between 1990 and 1992. Meanwhile, at least 1,620 journalistic positions (20.4 percent) were occupied by eastern Germans with no professional experience in the GDR media system, and 1,050 positions (13.2 percent) were taken by West Germans. These figures suggest that no more than slightly over half of the journalists working in the GDR in 1989 (4,810) had full-time employment as journalists three years later. Those former GDR media professionals who did not retire or find jobs in other professions have entered what media researcher Walter Mahle estimates as a pool of between twenty and thirty thousand freelance journalists variously employed across Germany (1993: 102). These statistics illuminate primary trends in the journalistic labor market in eastern Germany that have continued, although more gradually, since the early 1990s.

Fifteen years later, in 2004, it is worth noting that the regional journalisms of eastern and western Germany are largely indistinguishable from one another: there is little substantive difference, for example, in the technical quality, content organization, layouts, or spectrum of editorial opinions to be found in eastern and western German print media and public broadcasters.[7]

---

7. The thematic proportions of content do differ, however, with economic and social problems receiving more coverage, for example, in the eastern media since, as chief editors explained to me, real unemployment rates continue to hover between 20 and 30 percent in some areas of eastern Germany (see also Reissig 1998).

Longitude and the Lesser Professional

My friend Marianne, who was studying journalism at Leipzig when the Wall
came down, wrote me an email in 1997 summarizing her experiences of
professional and institutional transition at several media organizations in
Berlin and eastern Germany after 1990:

> I can only speak for myself and I must tell you that I have had the most
> varied experiences. At the beginning I must say that I was deeply curi-
> ous about the West Germans and even treated them with reverence, al-
> though at the time I was still basically a beginner in the profession. The
> older colleagues from the East definitely had greater misgivings. They
> became fenced off; feelings of inferiority led them to react spitefully to
> new changes. The West Germans, for their part, made it far from easy
> for the older East German colleagues to find their way into the new jour-
> nalistic reality. While younger (according to the West Germans, "histor-
> ically unburdened") people like me were supported and promoted, the
> majority of the extant East German journalists were given the clear im-
> pression that they would not be needed for restarting the East German
> press. They were treated with indifference, with arrogance, indeed with
> animosity—according to the logic: whoever worked in the GDR media
> were servants of *Macht* [power]. In this period of radical change the mood
> at many papers was strained; there was a great deal of uneasiness: Who
> was still in the running? Who would be let go?
>
> After these questions had been more or less decided (1992/93), the
> situation became somewhat calmer. Although for many there was still
> a great deal of uncertainty, because on the heels of the question "Will I
> survive?" came the next concern, "Is my paper going to survive?" One
> found the requisite composure only very rarely among the older East
> German journalists. Only those who had been unofficially honored with
> the title of *Edelfeder* [literally, "noble pens"] could bring their entire en-
> ergy and a positive attitude to work (normally this group included the
> best reporters). They were acknowledged and respected by the western
> bosses and sometimes were even admired by them. As a countermove
> the free-flowing *Meinung* [opinion] and carefully groomed culture of ar-
> gument fostered by the western colleagues was increasingly admired and
> adopted. Over time, a kind of internal balance developed in many papers
> that in most cases persists today. I would roughly sketch the nature of
> the balance as follows: there is a group of "tolerated Ossis," who help
> to keep the technical and editorial enterprises running without hope of

vertical advancement. Then there are the "sponsored Ossis," who the publishers use to show off the *Ostkompetenz* [competence in eastern issues] of their publications and who once in a while even demonstrate this competence. And then there are the many Wessis, who in the final analysis dominate most editorial collectives in varied capacities. The longer this status quo lasts, the more people become accustomed to it. The question of [longitudinal] origin is in all cases much less dramatically discussed and cultivated than it was directly after the *Wende*.

When I worked for *Die Wochenpost* in 1996, it was my impression that the East/West template no longer fit the daily life of journalism anymore when it came to debates about texts and themes. The most important criterion meanwhile had become professionalism and we oriented ourselves thereby to a more eternally valid yardstick. The working atmosphere was much more relaxed than it had been in the early years. The time of mutual suspicions seemed to have passed. Personal sympathies had now become decisive for the relations between colleagues, and I noticed that trust and friendship had developed alongside distance and unapproachability. That's the way it always is when people get to know one another, no?

Marianne, a respected young journalist, one who likely modeled her own category of the "sponsored Ossi," was intimately aware of the status hierarchy that supported the "internal balance" in eastern German media organizations. Yet her narrative also suggested a historical process of transition from longitudinalism to professionalism within these organizations. Indeed, many of the eastern journalists with whom I spoke in 1996 and 1997 reported feeling that relations with their western colleagues and managers had normalized since the early 1990s. Cultural and behavioral differences between the two sides persisted, to be sure, I was told. Most agreed, however, that even these had eroded to the point where it was no longer possible to easily recognize "who was who" on the basis of speech, dress, manner, and so on. Most felt that they were respected as professionals by their western colleagues, and indeed, many (if not all) western managers and colleagues confirmed this impression.

Marianne's feeling of perduring longitudinal dividedness balanced against the "eternally valid yardstick" of professionalism makes perfect sense when one considers how journalistic professionalism in eastern Germany has absorbed dialectical knowledge of easternness into itself by assigning to eastern journalists a particular "regional" subjectivity and expertise that are different and appurtenant to western journalists' "national" subjectivity and expertise. It is a comparable professionalism, a lesser professionalism to be sure, but not the absence of professionalism alluded to in the early days of unification and codified in the initial politics of reeducation and apprenticeship in media organizations.

There is perhaps no better evidence of the normalization of professional difference between eastern and western journalists than a passage in the essential manual of German journalistic practice, *ABC des Journalismus* (ABCs of Journalism), a book one will find in nearly every journalist's office in Germany. The manual states definitively:

> East German journalists differ, as a survey of eastern German media organizations has shown, in their performance capabilities from their West German colleagues (Mast 1993: 71–81). There are deficits in their production of news bulletins, in their research skills, and in their ability to think and act in a competitive fashion. The strengths of East German journalists lie in their superior regional knowledge as well as their familiarity with the people who live there and in a sensitive approach to their public. In opposition to the western journalists, who are said to be lone agents and individualists, eastern journalists are more compromise oriented and integrate themselves more easily into teams. Journalists from the west, however, continue to significantly exceed their East German colleagues in specialized knowledge of functional mechanisms and institutions of a free political and economic system. The growing together [*Zusammenwachsen*] of the two German professional cultures is still a long way off, as clear traces of principles of political affiliation [*Parteilichkeit*] and tractability, residua of their former socialist propaganda work, have been left behind in the professional ranks. Moreover, the demands of the market and of a plural society have not yet been completely internalized [Böckelmann, Mast, and Schneider 1994]. (Mast 1994: 81)

The positive classification of East German journalists in the manual as being more context sensitive, team oriented, and regionally knowledgeable moderates the no less sweeping, but far more professionally injurious, description that they are politically tractable, that they have not yet internalized the "demands . . . of a plural society," and that they are loathe to question authority and to think creatively on their own. West German media scholars Claudia Mast, Klaus Haasis, and Matthias Weigert contrast West German journalists' noticeable superiority in "initiative, pleasure at making contacts, willingness to take responsibility, and wealth of ideas," as well as in "determination, perseverance, and ambition," with the professional inheritance of "GDR journalism that did not allow such professional qualifications to be developed" (in Böckelmann, Mast, and Schneider 1994: 436).

Academic literature on eastern German media reifies the category of the "East German journalist" and defines him or her as a regional specialist and a subaltern member of a journalistic team who can provide an eastern media organization, if not with first-class reporting and editorial skills, then with intimate and important (given the character of his or her audience) knowledge of regional history and regional culture. It is an allochronistic figuration of the eastern journalist as a "not yet" professional who must continuously strive to transcend his or her regional subjectivity in order to achieve competence in journalism for the nation. In this respect, the "East German journalist" conforms to the broader settlement of social knowledge in Germany that buries the excess of history in the eastern region, thus unburdening the future of the unified nation.

Strikingly, the "regionalization" of the East German journalist is widely affirmed by both western and eastern journalists. During interviews, I heard many variations on the proposition that East German journalists' intimate knowledge of their public and West German journalists' critical and managerial know-how made a winning combination. Given the preceding discussions, it is perhaps unsurprising that western German journalists would participate actively in this discourse. But why, one wonders, do eastern German journalists embrace a regional subjectivity when this embrace bars them from being identified as "German journalists" or even just as "journalists"? It is a dilemma reminiscent of Antonio Gramsci's sociological study of the "spontaneous consent" (1971: 12) granted by subaltern to dominant groups or of Frantz Fanon's psychoanalytic autobiography of the Antillean's embrace of "Negro culture" only to realize that this embrace does not steal agency away from the colonizers so much as it further advances the pathology of racism (1967: 123–40).

Of course, not all eastern German journalists accept their regional identity willingly. Some bristled particularly at the idea that their supposed easternness should influence judgments about their professional expertise. Others assert different kinds of expertise, not a lesser professionalism but even a metaprofessionalism, a recognition of the West German System for "what it really was" based on their intimate knowledge of the GDR System. After laughing in my face when I cautiously asked him whether his

experience of GDR journalism made him more appreciative of the professional autonomy of journalism in a market-capitalist society, Jörg K. replied,
shaking his head derisively:

> Yeah, it's an advantage I guess to have experienced both kinds of media,
> but it sounds so pathetic to say, "I have a better appreciation of freedom
> because I lived in the GDR." I would never say something like [*rolling his
> eyes*], "Oh, I do *so* appreciate the freedom we have today, which we never
> had before." I would never say something like that. I don't really believe
> it either. But I would say that we are in general much more sensitive to
> ruptures and especially to stagnation in a System from having lived in
> the GDR. That's it, people who lived in the GDR are much more sensi-
> tized to the weaknesses of a System because we've watched one System
> collapse already. This is an important distinction because instead of be-
> ing more sensitized to freedom and to the positive aspects of the System,
> what we're actually more sensitized to because of our backgrounds is see-
> ing stagnation, lack of creativity, the signs of decay, the negative aspects
> of a System. Thus, I don't think we value the freedom more; rather, my
> inclination is to notice weaknesses of this System. And in my personal
> opinion, in my experience of opportunism and adaptation in the GDR,
> I see just as much opportunism and adaptation in this System today.
> Just like in the GDR. The same journalists who were opportunists back
> then are opportunists now as far as I have seen. It's true. The kind of
> person who would work for *Bild Zeitung*[8] is *exactly* the kind of oppor-
> tunistic assholes we had in the GDR. Oh, maybe they complain about
> the kind of journalism that they're forced to do there, but then they say
> to themselves, "Oh, but I make good money, so that's a reason to stay."
> Opportunism and adaptation are just as marked in this System as they
> were in the GDR, that's my honest evaluation.

But, with these divergences in mind, many former GDR journalists expressed to me a sense of themselves as professionally and personally "eastern" in character, a social fact that they felt legitimated their professional
specification as "regionals." One journalist explained, "I'll never know the
West like they [the West Germans] do—so much of their knowledge came
to them in their mothers' milk." Others spoke of the role of the parental

---

8. *Bild Zeitung* is the largest national daily in Germany. Published by Axel Springer Verlag,
it symbolizes for most German media professionals boulevard journalism and mass culture at its
most obscene (see Walraff 1977).

home (*Elternhaus*) in providing West Germans with an intimate knowledge of western society that they would never be able to internalize. Others explained that the unified German society was not their System. They had not grown up and been stamped (*geprägt*) by it. Therefore, they would always remain somewhat estranged from it, and this fact could not be masked in their journalism.

While it would be tempting to explain eastern German journalists' acknowledgment of their regional character either as a kind of "team front" presented to the inquisitive outsider (Goffman 1959: 77–78) or as evidence of the *habitus* of professional fields so insightfully outlined by Bourdieu (1988: 73–127), the knowledge I am describing is by no means limited to professional and organizational contexts. The broader question is why former GDR citizens tend to either embrace their easternness (see Boyer 2001b) or gesture to the inescapability of their easternness even though this so often forces them, in the politics of identification in unified Germany, to shoulder alone the *Vergangenheitbelastung* of Germanness. To answer this question, let me make two points. (1) As the ironic epigraph to this chapter demonstrates, former GDR citizens face a continuous stream of signals in public culture (many of them licensed as "scientific findings") of their social difference and excess of history. These signals help to cultivate a social knowledge of eastern alterity and deficiency that is expansively "hegemonic" in Gramsci's sense. (2) As dialectical social knowledge locks selfhood into alignment with System, non-Systemic senses of self seem both fragile and transient. Negative dialectical understandings of the *Prägung* of self by System and history help explain why former GDR journalists speak of both the "normality" and the "inescapability" of their easternness. In the next sections of this chapter, I seek to convey a richer sense of how the epistemic moments of (1) and (2) are interleaved in journalists' individual projects of self-knowing both inside and outside organizational contexts.

Brigitte among the Ossis

I met Brigitte and Marianne on the same day in October 1996 in the Berlin office of the weekly paper *Die Wochenpost* (hereafter *DW*). *DW* was once one of the most popular weekly magazines in the GDR, but it had endured a severe loss of circulation since 1989 (from approximately 1.3 million copies/week in 1989 to 105,000/week in 1996).[9] Meanwhile, it had

9. This was not untypical of the precipitous drops in circulation endured by other GDR-era national publications, including *Neues Deutschland* and the German Socialist Youth's *Junge Welt*.

relocated its editorial offices from eastern Berlin to Oranienplatz in the trendy Kreuzberg 36 district of western Berlin. It had also changed its format and profile from a family-oriented weekly paper to a weekly that mixed news, literary journalism, and political commentary and that explicitly defined itself as an "East-West weekly paper," meaning that German-German relations and tensions were forefronted in its coverage. *DW*'s profile was fascinating from the point of view of my own research project, but the paper continued to lose readers, perhaps, as one journalist remarked, because in 1996 East-West relations were no longer of such interest to readers: "They've moved on with their lives."

When I first visited *DW*, it employed a small, mixed staff of eastern and western journalists (although only one of the journalists (*Redakteure*) had been continuously employed by *DW* since before the *Wende*) under a western German chief editor, who had formerly worked at the highly respected *Süddeutsche Zeitung* in Munich. Its offices were modest, even cramped, and I detected anxiety among the staff from my first day there that the steady decline in readers and revenues boded poorly for the future of the paper. Yet no one, including the chief editor so far as I could tell, had foreseen that the publisher would shut the paper down in less than two months, in November 1996.

I came to *DW* to interview Brigitte, who was a friend of a mutual acquaintance who worked at *Der Tagesspiegel*, one of Berlin's three major dailies. Our acquaintance had suggested Brigitte to me as someone who was unusually outspoken about East/West relations in media organizations. Indeed, Brigitte struck me from our first encounter as an uncanny performer of several elements of the stereotypical Wessi profile. She was energetic, stylish, sometimes argumentative, and always a flurry of motion. After a brief tour of the office, she whisked me across Oranienplatz and down the block to an earth-toned café, where we settled in at a corner table encircled by hanging plants and paintings. Hardly pausing to order coffee and light a cigarette, she told me quickly about her youth in West Berlin, her university experiences in the United States, and her arrival back in Berlin just in time for the *Wende* of 1989. She noted that she had already heard from our mutual acquaintance that I was interested in East/West relations in the media and assured me that there was a great deal to be said about these relations. Before launching into an extended series of observations about her eastern colleagues at *DW*, she cast glances to either side of her and leaned, somewhat conspiratorially, across the table: "What you have to understand about these people [East German journalists] is that they are princes who have lost their kingdom. Journalists, like writers in the GDR, were an incredibly privileged class and many of them are upset because they feel these privileges were a legacy that they should have inherited but didn't. It took me about a year here of feeling uncomfortable, and I really wasn't badly received, you know, until I figured this out."

Brigitte had, I sensed, a great deal of sympathy for some of her eastern colleagues. She shared several stories about her efforts to counsel them and build up their self-esteem. She often told me that one of the reasons she wanted to work in the East was to share her professional knowledge with former GDR citizens. Not unlike other western journalists I came to know, she believed strongly that it was the ethical duty of western professionals to donate their time to help educate and ready eastern professionals to participate actively and as equals in unified German society. Yet Brigitte's paternalism had a very sharp edge. Almost as though she could not help herself, her mentoring narratives were peppered with irony, satire, and even caustic criticism. Her stories, for example, of counseling her eastern colleagues almost always seemed to revolve around their timorousness, indecisiveness, and lack of self-confidence. Brigitte would then intervene as the wise, cosmopolitan adviser to help them and, in one example, get up the nerve to travel to the United States. Every story was accompanied by a small theater of gestures. I could not help laughing out loud when she brilliantly mimed her trembling colleagues or when she mimed her own appearance on the scene, her back erect, wagging a finger remonstratively at them.

On one representative occasion, a tale of her role in the further *Bildung* of her eastern colleagues shifted into an excoriation of the communitarian, obedient, tractable character of "the East Germans":

> When I first came to *DW* it was like being sucked into this *community* [*opening her arms and pulling them toward her chest*]. Everyone treated you like you were a relative. You were supposed to all go out to lunch together, to do things at night together. People got together on the weekends, and after a few weeks I just thought, "I don't need this, I have my own family and I want to go back home." . . . And within the community criticism and conflict were definitely suppressed. You know, that's the difference with the West; in the West you and I can be sitting here talking about whatever and we'll do it like so [*pounding her fist into her hand*], no? We can be talking about something as friends and still it'll be conflictual. You'll say something and I'll say, "No, no, it's like this instead." But that wasn't the case in the East. If I wrote something that

the editor didn't like, then instead of calling me in and criticizing me, he'd say, "You know we all really appreciate what you're trying to do and we understand your point but we really feel like now is not the time to publish that."

I sensed that Brigitte felt uncomfortable at the level of intimacy certain of her colleagues expected from her and then genuinely hurt when some of these same colleagues circumvented what she felt was professional collegiality and complained about her and her critical attitude to management. She did not like being positioned as a typical "conflict-mongering Wessi" just because she spoke her mind. And she liked even less not being confronted openly about it. Her image of her eastern colleagues' relationships with one another often took a conspiratorial turn, as though they sought to accomplish through subterfuge and secret alliances what she preferred to approach through public, critical engagement. Many of our conversations focused on the inimical presence of this shadowy eastern "counterpublic" in the office. She saw its communitarianism—from which she was now excluded—as supportive of the worst holdovers from GDR journalism.

The residue of GDR journalism in her eastern colleagues' work at *DW* was a matter of great concern for Brigitte. Her comments on this subject varied widely. On the one hand, there were humorous observations on the asynchronous temporality of her eastern colleagues and how they were either too nervous or too sanguine for the work rhythm of the office:

> So once I was on the bus with a colleague of mine from the East, and here she is visibly trembling because of all the work she has to do [*mimes the trembling, arms wrapping around her torso*]. She's completely at a loss as to what to do, but for me, you know, I know how long everything's going to take. Fifteen minutes here, half an hour there, and it's no big deal. Sure I'll complain about how much work I have to do, but the important thing is that I'm used to it. But for her she was completely paralyzed. That's one extreme and the other is that some of them feel like they can just do things when they get around to them, and there I am standing over them [*mimes pointing to her watch*] saying, "Well, where is that piece?"

On the other hand, Brigitte offered more serious indictments of their professional ethics:

> There are a lot of examples I really can't divulge, so I'll just give you one. I was once in an eastern colleague's office when she got a phone call

regarding an article she was working on about an East German politician. And, I *couldn't believe it*, she was talking with this politician as though they were relatives! In a completely friendly way. If that had been me, I'd have been going, "OK, you say X, but give me facts, numbers, figures to back that up, I want everything!" But with my colleague, there was none of that. She just hung up the phone, and, you know, I couldn't say anything about it because I just happened to be in the room and probably shouldn't have been listening to her conversation as it was, but it's shocking when things like that happen.

At this point I interjected the question whether she saw this as an individual matter or as something that characterized her East German colleagues generally.

In my opinion, I think it's true across the board. It's much more common for them to have these really close, friendly relationships to politicians. Which obviously has its advantages. If someone needs to go up to Rostock to interview a local politician, then the East German is obviously going to have an easier time than the West German. . . . But, for example, the other day I went to hear a Brandenburg politician speak, and at the end all of the East German journalists applauded and I thought, "*Why are you applauding, what's wrong with you?*" For myself, I would never applaud for a politician. It's just not right as a journalist to do that; you have to stay critical. This is another problem for the East Germans: they have trouble maintaining that critical position, and I believe that really very few of them can do it.

At this moment, I sensed deep concern bordering on fear from Brigitte (not unlike Gregor's concerns that I portray in the next chapter) about the *Vergangenheitsbelastung* of eastern journalists, about how they might erode the normative ideal of journalistic objectivity through their intimacy with *Macht*. These ideals were already under assault in the 1990s by the expansion of private, corporate media and ratings-oriented media managerialism in Germany as elsewhere in the world (see Bagdikian 1997; McChesney 1997). With the sense of her colleagues becoming cheerleaders for regional politicians, one can see how deeply unsettling this apparent capitulation of critical journalistic Spirit to external political and/or economic interests would be. For Brigitte as for others, the "East German journalist" was a locus of attention and mediatic anxieties about the future of journalism and the public sphere; East Germans' *Vergangenheitsbelastung* was identified as a

seed of journalistic corruption that might all-too-readily flourish in the increasingly corporatized media. I heard wry remarks from other western and
eastern journalists about how the SED "yes-men" were considered perfect
employees by corporatist managers because they knew how to take orders
and because they were not troubled by journalistic ethics. Typically, such
yes-men were said to populate competitor organizations.

What I would like to emphasize is not that Brigitte indexed and repro-
duced with uncanny precision so many elements of western discourse on
East German *Vergangenheitsbelastung* and professional alterity and deficiency. What I would like to emphasize is to what extent Brigitte's own
sense of professional and personal selfhood was entangled with her image of her East German colleagues. This was, in fact, true of many of my
western interlocutors. The negative dialectical characterization of eastern
colleagues or of the "East German" more generically was everyday epistemic material, a resource always "on hand" for the production of positive
dialectical knowledges of self and creative intellectual ability. My friend
Gregor, for example, did this routinely. A veteran of many start-up print
media projects in the early 1990s, Gregor expressed little respect for older
East German journalists and routinely figured his own sense of himself
as an agentive and savvy investigative reporter by stressing their passivity and cluelessness: "None of [the East German journalists] had a clue
what was going on. They got paid for forty years *not* to tell people what
was going on. They got their hush-money [*Schweigegeld*] and they were
satisfied with that. [The GDR] was a selective System, you know, and it
basically selected the wrong kind of people for what we wanted, people who
were content to look the other way instead of getting out there and doing
something."

In this respect, individuals like Karl G., Gregor, and Brigitte were strikingly blunt in their longitudinalism, in their predication of self on rigorous
distinction from an eastern half-self, half-other. Other western journalists
were more subtle or reticent in their strategies of identification. And still
others, particularly younger journalists working in the East, actively differentiated themselves from what they described as "a Cold War mentality"
of emphasizing East/West difference and deficiency. Jürgen A., for example,
spoke to me of how much he had learned about journalism from his eastern
colleagues: "[M]y colleague T. always tries to find a way to make compli-
cated topics easier for people to read. He's always looking for a way to put
things in such a way that people actually understand the issues. That's really valuable. You can really learn a lot from that as a journalist." Maria R.,

a former chief editor of a GDR-era magazine, identified herself in opposition
to a generic "West German" mentality as well:

> In general, West German journalists belong to that category of "highly
> sensitive" people who lump everything having to do with socialism to-
> gether as unjust. They assume there was nothing of value in the East
> before, but "now I'm here" and everything will suddenly be different.
> They bring that attitude into the newsroom and that's a real problem,
> this behavior by many West German journalists, which shows that they
> are still somehow very afraid of the East German journalists. I don't just
> mean a general fear of contact with East German journalists, but then
> there are also the additional political issues when conservative journal-
> ists from the West come here. They have the attitude that every eastern
> journalist comes from a suspicious background and every one of them
> had better acculturate themselves to the new order. You find this mis-
> sionary approach elsewhere too: that the Reds must be disposed of. Then
> perhaps later they actually meet some eastern journalists and find out
> that they're actually okay, they're solid journalists. But I think I can say
> accurately that most eastern journalists were trained as leftist journal-
> ists at the Karl-Marx University down in Leipzig; their studies had a high
> proportion of Marxist-Leninist theory. How are the western journalists
> going to react to that? Because then you also have the situation where the
> western journalists say, "Well, if I'd lived in the GDR then, I would have
> behaved completely differently; I would have been a resistance fighter!"
> And so the two sides fight with one another, never realizing that civic
> courage is not an abundant quality of humanity under the best of cir-
> cumstances, and perhaps even less so in Germany. When you hear them
> talk this way, you definitely get a sense that people really haven't learned
> much from history.

I feel compelled to add that I more often encountered individuals of
Brigitte's disposition than of Maria R.'s during my field research. At the same
time that the diversity of strategies of knowing self and other among self-
identifying "westerners" complicates any effort to gloss their social knowledge, the continual recourse to a principle of longitudinal difference (e.g.,
even in Maria R.'s critical remarks about Wessi attitudes) means that the
facticity and meaningfulness of East/West difference is rarely challenged. In
this epistemic environment, eastern Germans face extraordinary difficulties
in articulating a selfhood beyond their easternness, one that is "true to their

history" and yet that does not position them as being a "more German" German, a creature of *Belastung*, and a lesser professional.

Marianne In Between

At the end of my first meeting with Brigitte, as we strolled back across Oranienplatz, she seemed somewhat concerned that she had vented too much criticism of her eastern colleagues, that she had given me a skewed sense of their journalistic capabilities: "I want you to understand that I have some colleagues from the East who do not fit this portrait at all," she assured me. Brigitte led me back to the office and promptly introduced me to Marianne, whom she described as one of her "very best colleagues." Several days later, I picked Marianne up on a cool rainy evening and we spent an evening at a chic yet subdued and candlelit café called Osswald in the Prenzlauer Berg district of eastern Berlin. Whereas Brigitte had offered me the informal "*Du*" register as a sign of our fraternity as *Westmenschen*, Marianne offered me "*Du*" on the basis of our common age. We spent most of the evening talking about her experiences at *DW* and more generally about the behind-the-scenes politics of the Berlin and eastern German media both rumored and confirmed.

Marianne's soft-spoken calm and self-possession struck me immediately, as did her intelligence and thoughtful engagement with her work as a journalist. As our friend-in-common Albert has quipped, "When I think of cool, I think of Marianne." Albert and I continue to exchange frequent emails with one another, and Albert often refers to Marianne cryptically and without name as "an extremely self-possessed and capable young East German journalist" or as "a superwoman who has mastered the western System." Marianne meanwhile denies that she has ever been "cool." "We East Germans are *gründlicher* [more thorough, more substantive] than that," she has told me with a wry smile on another occasion.

Marianne began telling me her professional history by explaining that she was still in the Leipzig journalism program when the *Wende* came so she never really had a chance to work as a journalist in the GDR except as an intern. She was glad of that. Her father, as I found out only much later, was formerly the chief editor of a SED regional daily. She has never said much to me about her family, however, other than that they were very loyal to the party (*parteitreu*). I continue to wonder how much her family connection to journalism influenced her own decision to train for journalism in the GDR. She explained only that she had always been interested in *DW*, even before the *Wende*, so she went to work there in the politics department in 1990. To contextualize what working at *DW* was like in those days, she mentioned a book to me written by a former West German intern at *DW* right after the *Wende* (Reck 1996), a book that she said she found to have its strengths and weaknesses. "But one thing he was right about is that *DW* slept through the *Wende.* That it most certainly did. You see, as one of the few papers, along with *Sonntag* and *Die Weltbühne,* which were much smaller papers, that were actually popular with people in the GDR, they felt like they didn't really have to change that much in the *Wende.* So, ironically, the old SED papers and regional dailies actually improved themselves much more quickly than *DW,* which didn't change its editorial leadership until 1991."

In 1991, as its circulation collapsed and *DW* was unable to sustain itself, the western German media corporation Gruner + Jahr (a subsidiary of transnational media giant Bertelsmann AG) purchased the paper and instituted changes in management and format similar to those detailed above. The editorial collective elected internally in March 1990 was dissolved and replaced by a new chief editor, Matthias Greffrath, who had formerly worked at *Die Zeit* in Hamburg. I had the opportunity in 1996 to speak with the eastern German chief editor whom Greffrath had replaced, Brigitte Zimmermann, about this transition at *DW,* and she remained deeply embittered about how Gruner + Jahr had approached the transition process.

> In the GDR, this was really *our* paper. We identified with it and our readers identified with it. But when Gruner + Jahr came [*shaking her head*] it didn't matter to them at all that we had the trust of many of our readers in the East. They were obsessed with this idea that *es muss anders sein* [things have to change], but the question was "how." [Gruner + Jahr] didn't really know, so they did things like change words. What we called the "Kultur" section they changed to "Feuilleton"—you know, things like that. . . . Our page which we called "Ratgeber" they called "Alltag" [*laughs*]. So the paper became ever more foreign, and step-by-step everything did become different for us and for our readers.

Marianne, however, remembered this transition process in generally positive terms. She said that the atmosphere at *DW* when she began in 1990 still seemed "very GDR" to her. I asked her what she meant by that. She explained to me, echoing Brigitte, that the GDR was a consensus society (*Konsenzgesellschaft*) whereas the FRG was a conflict society (*Konfliktgesellschaft*) and that this difference in the character of the Systems produced different kinds of personality types and organizational cultures in the GDR and FRG.

You see, newspapers in the GDR period were typically organized like
"families," where it was expected that you would do all kinds of group
activities with the other journalists. For example, all birthdays were celebrated together; every weekend it was expected that all the journalists
would take trips together; all the holidays were celebrated together and
so on. This had declined by the time I got there, but among the older
colleagues there was a lot of talk of needing to keep traditions alive, to
keep finding time to all go out together. They would keep saying, "We
really have to get together and go and do this or that together," but then
one or another person would have another commitment and so on, and
so the whole thing seemed to fade.

Marianne also liked Greffrath personally, as did many of the other journalists who had worked with him at *DW*. And she liked the journalistic direction of the new *DW*, which was more *grossfeuilletonistisch* as she put
it, more "grand literary journalism," than the family-oriented profile of the
old *DW*.

Marianne, however, was let go, a victim of cost-cutting measures. She
went to work for two years for Ostdeutscher Rundfunk Brandenburg (ORB)
in Babelsberg and Frankfurt/Oder before being hired back in 1996 when
Gruner + Jahr sold *DW* to a Bavarian publisher, who brought in another
chief editor and a concept for the paper that emphasized balanced political
and literary journalism focusing on East/West issues. Marianne explained
that she missed *DW* while she was at ORB; she missed the tensions and
open discussion of East/West themes in editorial meetings. "I found [ORB] a
bit, I don't know, claustrophobic. ORB is really completely composed of East
Germans. I mean there are a few younger Wessis there perhaps, and then the
upper hierarchy around the director is certainly all Wessis, but the middle
hierarchy is pretty much all Ossis. I find it really a bit provincial." Marianne
missed, among other things, the forthrightness and self-confidence of her
West German colleagues, even, she chuckled, the outspokenness of people
like Brigitte. I told her that that surprised me only because this forthrightness often seemed to come hand in hand with certain criticisms of East
Germans.

Some amount of conflict is a good thing though I think. This is really
a generational issue. The West Germans tend to be much more self-
assured and aggressive in defending their points in editorial meetings,
whereas East Germans tend to be more quiet. This is especially true with
the older East Germans, who really take any criticism very personally. If

somebody criticizes something they've written, they take it as an attack
on them personally and on everything they stand for. It's very difficult
for them.

Marianne often describes herself and her generation as uneasily positioned between easternness and westernness. At the café, she told me the
story of a friend who was training to be a teacher and went to study at a
West German university: "Oh how he would complain about the Wessis,
'These Wessis, they're so superficial! Sure they can talk well and they're
self-assured but there's no depth to them!' And then later he got a position
teaching in the East, and now he's complaining constantly about the Ossis, 'These Ossis, they've never changed, they're so narrow and limited!'"
We both laughed and I suggested that maybe it was just human nature to
always think the grass was greener. She nodded, "Yes, it really does have
to do with humanity [*Menschlichkeit*]. When you're alone among all these
strangers [*Fremden*], you wish you were back home and criticize their way
of life." I noted though that it was interesting that her friend had felt equally
estranged among both East Germans and West Germans. "Yes, *that* has to
do with our generation. We were born late enough in the GDR that it was
fairly easy for us to move beyond it. But then we're still not quite there, are
we? I mean, we're not West German."

I was struck by the reflexive certainty of Marianne's final clause. I pressed
her on it because I wanted to understand what it was to feel that one's identity exists on the cusp of the binary formulation of East/West difference in
unified Germany. She paused, reflecting on her sense of betweenness for a
few moments, and then triangulated her knowledge of longitudinal difference through gender:

I'd actually say that the biggest difference since the *Wende* is the difference between East German and West German women. I actually get
along very well with the West German men who have come over here.
But, and maybe this is just because I am a woman, when I look at or
compare East and West German male journalists, I don't really see them
as being that different. But the women I see as being very different. I
feel like it has something to do with what you said earlier that many
West German women have had to give up families for their careers or
that at least they've put their careers ahead of their families. So there's
something missing with them, something that isn't there, I don't know.
[*Pauses, thinking.*] For me, you know, what comes to me will come to
me. I don't have any particular ambition to become department head and

then assistant chief editor and then chief editor, but these West German women really do have this ambition always to achieve something or to prove themselves.

Like Brigitte's relationship to her eastern colleagues, Marianne's sense of self, as both an "easterner" and a female professional, was measured against the grain of longitudinal alterities, particularly against the image of the ambitious western woman who has chosen career over family. But Marianne's negative figurations of the GDR as a closed, limiting System and her many appreciative comments about the West and West Germans suggest a complication of the "standard" parameters of longitudinal identification. This was not uncommon among nominally "eastern" journalists of Marianne's generation. Most sought to codify an identity that belonged to neither the Ossi nor the Wessi. Yet, as exemplified by Marianne's discussion of her betweenness, I was often struck how narratives that began with a trajectory away from easternness never quite reached a noneastern identity except in partial, conditional terms. As narratives of self-identification stalled in corrections like "we're not really West German," they were prone to be bent back into the orbit of a non–"West German" selfhood. In the binary logic of unified German social imagination, non–West German could only signify "East German." Another man recognized the fragility of his efforts to escape being sealed into a category of easternness in the context of his journalistic work: "And how is it that I am an 'East German journalist' when I never really worked in the GDR? Moreover, why should it make any difference if an East German or a West German handles a specific story? And yet these categories of thought [*Denkkategorien*] seem very difficult to remove for some people." Marianne confirmed this for me in another conversation, lamenting that "it is sometimes so difficult to lose this title of 'East German journalist,' even if, for many of us in the younger generation who were scarcely trained in the GDR, it doesn't really make any sense."

Brigitte Not Quite in the East

It was almost two months after the closing of *DW* when I had a chance to speak to Brigitte again, in early 1997. I visited her at her apartment in a trendy section of eastern Berlin's Prenzlauer Berg district. I could not help commenting immediately on her enormous wrist braces, and she quipped that this was a curse of the writer's profession. She had been doing a number of freelance projects on tight time schedules, and these had eventually led to carpal tunnel syndrome. "The most recent one was translating the screenplay for David Lynch's new movie. I am sure I'd be terrified if I ever went to see it!"

Sitting across from her at her kitchen table, warm tea in hand, I asked her to tell me what it felt like to have the paper suddenly disappear.

> It's funny, it took a while to sink in. For two weeks, I kept going to the office every day and working and then suddenly it occurred to me that this really wasn't my office anymore and that the paper was gone and so why was I going in to work. One only incrementally got used to the fact that the paper was gone. Probably the most annoying thing is dealing with other colleagues and friends about it. It's a little embarrassing with everyone calling and asking you how you are and if you've found anything else yet. The other day I met a friend at a lecture and it was so nice, we just talked about what we had heard in the lecture and not at all about *DW* going under, that was just such a relief! Not to pick up the phone and have somebody go, "How are you doing?" "What's going on?" "Have you found anything new yet?"

Brigitte was at once more passionate and more calm than in previous conversations. Although no less fierce in her opinions and humor, her gestures were muted as she sat quietly with her elbows on the table. I asked her whether she felt that the experience of being laid off so suddenly gave her a better appreciation of the anxieties of her eastern colleagues. Glancing under the table, she shrugged and said quietly, "Yes, I think so. It's been difficult for all of us." I took this opportunity to ask her whether she felt that, in the end, she had come to learn something from her eastern colleagues at *DW*. Her reply suggested that her experiences had taught her something about the "how" (if little about the "whether") of educating East Germans:

> My biggest impression is probably how much I overestimated, I mean underestimated, no overestimated the degree to which I'd be able to have productive yet critical relationships with my East German colleagues. There were only a couple of cases where that happened and I really was surprised. I thought I'd have been able to do that much more.

I asked again whether she had learned anything as a journalist.

> Well, from the point of view of the trade, what they used to do in the East was not really any good by western standards. It wasn't really journalism at all. . . . The thing I'll take away from the experience is that you can

never explain things to people too much, you can never explain in too much detail. We forget about things like that in the West. We write with all these assumptions that everyone knows what we're talking about. My experience here made me realize how much of that is a part of our writing. . . . Now, when I read the FAZ [*Frankfurter Allgemeine Zeitung*] business section, it makes me a little angry. I wish they would explain what they are talking about more. I mean, they make all kinds of assumptions there about the kind of economic knowledge people have. I don't know if it's just having been in the East and realizing that things have to be made clearer. But yes, that's something I'll take away from this, that things need to be explained.

Later, at dusk, we walked slowly around her neighborhood, stopping in at a couple of shops to run some errands. Gesturing broadly to the streets around us, I asked Brigitte what she thought of the neighborhood. She answered enthusiastically, "Oh, it's wonderful, I've really enjoyed it here. It's exciting to watch the city transform around you." But then she explained that there were still so many little day-to-day struggles. She missed the simplicity and amenities of life "in the West." I asked her to give me an example.

OK, well, I haven't found a dry cleaner's around here anywhere, so eventually I found a little family-owned place in Pankow, and I thought that I really ought to support this place. So I brought a few things in and they tell me that it's going to be two weeks. "*Two weeks!!*" I said, and then I said that I was hoping to maybe have them done on Monday. And they said, well, just this once they could make an exception and have them ready by Wednesday, and I was still shocked. I mean I've been struck by the complete absence of service here in the East.

Marianne Not Yet in the West

I saw Marianne most recently in the summer of 2002. She is now, contrary to her professed lack of ambition, the chief editor of a small magazine, *DM*, in Berlin. *DM* was a popular periodical in the GDR with a reputation for pseudoerotic content, but, like so many GDR titles, it underwent a number of ownership and profile changes after the *Wende* and now exists on the verge of profitability with a readership mostly in eastern Berlin and eastern Germany.

When I arrived at *DM*'s small storefront office in the Mitte district of Berlin, Marianne poked her head out of her office to greet me and to tell me that she needed a few minutes to finish an email. Her secretary handed me a copy of the most recent issue of *DM*, and one of her other colleagues chatted with me about a relative teaching at Oberlin College. Marianne popped back into the front office for a moment and, pointing to the magazine in my hand, said, "You can see that we've done an overhaul of the magazine to try to bring it, I don't know, more in contact with the real world. We had to change the direction because the whole erotic thing is really a dead end; the market for it hasn't expanded at all." It is a very attractive magazine, and she smiled when I suggested to her that it is the closest thing Berlin has to the *New Yorker*.

A few minutes later, we walked quickly to one of the upscale restaurant-cafés that have become a standard feature of Mitte in the years since the *Wende*. We stopped at a place in the middle of a sunny courtyard, and Marianne whispered that this area was supposed to have become the "Silicon Valley" of Berlin before the dot-com crash of 2001. After sitting down and ordering, I mentioned to Marianne that she looked a bit stressed, and she nodded, telling me about the trials of her new job and life, balancing the care of two young children and the more-than-full-time job of running *DM*.

All in all the conversation was a bit gloomy. Unfortunately, *DM* was in danger of going under as a result of the recent meltdown of the advertising market. Ad revenues were perilously low, she said, and some of the advertisers who remained were making invasive demands about the textual content of the magazine. They had all done market research on the words and emotions associated with their products (see Boyer 2001b; Mazzarella 2003) and they wanted to be certain that the text surrounding their ads was not "dissonant" with their brand image. Marianne told me she resisted these demands on principle but that the constant back-and-forth sapped her energy. She was also struggling with her publisher over the direction of the magazine: the publisher wanted to see it servicing its eastern German audience more intensively, whereas Marianne hoped to build readership in western Berlin through good literary journalism. At the same time, she recognized that it was incredibly difficult to make a magazine appealing to both eastern and western Berliners. "They really do speak different languages; a journalism that would attract one would repel the other," she said with a sigh. So, despite the fact that she found it very important to try to bridge western and eastern reading publics, and to speak especially to the generation of younger eastern Germans who find themselves between easternness and westernness, she was not entirely optimistic that she would be able to manage it in the end.

Marianne brightened up when she mentioned to me that she had been reading Alexander Osang's recent novel *die nachrichten* (the news; 2002).

She recommended it to me with great enthusiasm as offering fabulous insight into the "dilemma of my generation." The novel concerns a young eastern German journalist, Jan Landers, who moves from Berlin to Hamburg to become the only East German newsreader for the venerable pillar of West German television news, ARD's *Die Tagesschau*. Landers is drawn to the West for reasons he does not entirely understand. Yet he is quickly seduced by its luxury and vitality and comes gradually to see the GDR as a dark place (interestingly, several of my eastern interlocutors also articulated this feeling of the "brightness" of the West in opposition to the "darkness" of the East). Landers becomes restless with his life and past in Berlin, including aging parents and an estranged wife and child:

> The longer he worked in the West, the more boring he found the conversations in the East. He increasingly had the feeling of stepping backward every evening when he drove home. The arrogance of the Ostler toward the West seemed to him more baseless than the arrogance of the Westler toward the East. His marriage fell apart. He couldn't listen to Kathrin anymore. She got on his nerves. Every evening she would complain about the western schooling, about unemployed parents, about orientationless children, and about the spread of useless bureaucracy. He felt like he was a schoolboy getting ideology lessons again. She looked at him as if he were a traitor whenever he wore a new shirt. She reacted hysterically when he wanted to subscribe to the [West Berlin daily] *Tagesspiegel*. She hated the West and he couldn't stand wearing those sperm-colored men's summer shoes with their little holes and molded yellow rubber soles anymore. When he got the offer to go to Hamburg, he only thought about it overnight, even though he knew that it meant they would be finished. (2002: 94)

In Hamburg, Landers acquires a national reputation, a beautiful loft, a luxury car, and a magnificent girlfriend, but he never really "arrives" in the West either,[10] remaining painfully aware at every turn of his foreignness (his last name itself suggests this rather bluntly; "*Land*" denotes "country" and "*anders*" denotes "other"). Landers is attracted to his self-assured, cosmopolitan coworkers and stands in a state of ethnological wonder at their habits and values. He wants desperately to possess their sense of ease with

---

10. Marianne and others of her generation often spoke to me of the contingency of their *Ankunft im Westen* (arrival in the West). This is a formulation that Osang's writing has done a great deal to popularize.

their social environment, but he is plagued by the anxiety that he is giving himself away as an "East German" through his missteps, that he is too obviously an outsider trying to imitate a western lifestyle.

At the same time, Landers is aware that his colleagues know his easternness despite the fact that it rarely arises in conversation. He finds it inevitable, for example, that he is steered to sit next to the only other East German at a dinner party. In editorial meetings, his opinion is rarely solicited except in those rare cases when something to do with eastern Germany arises. At one meeting, he daydreams until his chief editor, Grundmann, interpellates him with a question presuming Landers's intimate knowledge of the East:

"In short, we've been mostly losing viewers in the East, Landers, that is, in the five new federal states. I'm not going read the exact numbers out to you again, but it's a big drop as you can see," Grundmann said. His pen gleamed over the pale red line. A deep, constantly falling line. The red East. The western curve was blue like the sea. And it was stable.

"And we were thinking about why that might be. Is it too much Stasi coverage? We did a couple things on Gysi and Wolf and Stolpe. So I thought that your, how should I put it, your, well, former countrymen might have been annoyed by that. That was all I really wanted to know from you, dear Landers."

Who did he think he was anyway? A psychologist of mass consciousness?

And the way he pronounced "former countrymen" made it sound like he was saying "Zonie morons," people who weren't quite capable of thinking clearly, people who simply couldn't get it, people, like him, who napped while their future was being discussed.

"Honestly, I don't feel like I am in the position to give you exhaustive information about the preferences of my former countrymen. There are simply a few too many of them. Former countrymen, I mean. But I can tell you what I think."

"Then get on with it, by all means," said Grundmann.

As he saw how Brahnstein rolled his eyes in boredom before he returned again to examining his fingernails, Landers became a bit angry. For Brahnstein, Chemnitz was farther away than Salt Lake City.

"It doesn't annoy me that we report who was working for the Stasi and who wasn't. What annoys me is that we do so as though we really knew what we were talking about. Most of us or you, I don't know, know nothing at all about the East. I no longer and you never. And it annoys

me how you said "former countrymen" just now. You're never going to
get the curve up that way. Your red curve there." (Osang 2002: 123)

To these words, which Landers instantly wishes he could take back,
Grundmann only shrugs and says, "Aha," and then continues the meeting.
Landers's easternness is invoked to solicit his insight into the mysteries of
East German character. Both Grundmann's and Landers's tarrying with pro-
nouns is significant. Neither is entirely certain where Landers fits in the
we/they indexicality of East/West distinction. Grundmann ultimately set-
tles Landers into the "they" of the East, whereas Landers attempts to for-
mulate his response as a former "they," as someone who once but no longer
belongs to the East, but who also does not belong to the "you" of the West.
Yet, in the end, Landers's effort to squeeze himself into the interstices of a
binary logic of identification, and even his criticism of Grundmann, provoke
no outrage. The message is simply not receivable; to the ear attuned to the
intuitive certainty of East/West difference, it is like white noise. The routine
habits of social knowledge have resisted Landers's tentative intervention,
and it is Landers who, in the end, feels guilty for having spoken.

A few weeks after our lunch, I wrote to ask Marianne whether the years
since unification had done anything to dispel the logic of East/West difference for her. She answered me by email:

> Your question is even more difficult to answer today than when we first
> met. I think that I have become quite westernized [verwestlicht] in my
> way of life. I live a comparatively carefree existence but also one free
> of responsibility, that is, besides my children and my immediate family
> (including also good friends and my own business). Despite this "arrival
> in the West" [Ankunft im Westen], I notice that I still observe public
> life for the most part through an East German filter. My thinking is not
> cosmopolitan; I don't read foreign newspapers or watch CNN or listen
> to the BBC. I think I am very German in my sensibilities. And I'm still
> automatically interested in stories whose actors and scenarios take place
> in the new federal states. Of course, that's also a professional malady,
> since one is constantly keeping one's eye on the competition.

Even now, Marianne is not ambivalent about her relationship to easternness. She notes her western lifestyle in contrast to the deeper "filter"
of her easternness and to her "very German" sensibilities through which
she intellectually engages public life. Marianne struggles, like many of my
eastern interviewees did, not with the fact of her easternness but with the

significance of its facticity. The gravity of the much-discussed *Belastung* of history weighs Marianne down. It keeps her self-knowledge German, just enough so that she doubts she will ever attain the postlongitudinal, postnational future celebrated in the West. But there is also comfort there, comfort in being assured of one's substance, of one's lack of exteriority, and, correspondingly, of one's inwardness (*Innerlichkeit*). Like all identity perhaps, the experience of easternness anchors the possibility of selfhood in the very foreclosure of a nonrelational subjectivity.

Wende: Spirit without System

I have noted how frequently the term "System" appeared in both eastern and western journalists' narratives of self, other, and history. We have heard much of this language above: the opposition of self to System, the *Prägung* of Spirit by System, reflections on the principles by which certain Systems operated, comparative moral valuations of Systems, and so on. In a moment of consternation one day, I asked Albert to tell me what the opposite of System was. He replied, "The opposite of System? It would be easier to explain the opposite of silicon." His analogy was apt; the word "System" conveyed both a sense of integrated totality and a sense of pervasive, constitutive influence from without to within. I often wondered whether it was possible to have selfhood without System. Listening to my interlocutors, I became doubtful since, as we have heard above, self is described as emerging dialectically in the ratio of inner and outer forces, in the striving to create from within to without balanced against the certainty of the power of System to form from without to within.

For my eastern interlocutors, the implication of self in System was equivalent regardless of whether we were speaking of the GDR System, the FRG System, or the System of unified Germany (which was the same as the FRG System for many). They tended to emphasize that although these Systems were not identical, they were equivalently Systemic in their unyielding rationalization of human life to a core principle or dynamic. For example, when I asked magazine journalist Urte V. to comment on whether she felt that western journalism was as "free" as it claimed to be, she offered an analogy between the place of party ideology in the old System and the place of money in the new System:

> Money is the center of things today. Certainly, there are forces in West Germany at work, there are constraints at work. And the pressure is much greater now, the pressure to produce quantity. Everyone knows

that we had a lot of time on our hands in the GDR, too much time certainly, because a certain amount of pressure is positive, but not too much pressure. That affects the quality. My greatest challenge, and existential problem, now is to find ways to maintain the quality of my work. And not to give in to this pressure to do more, more, more, faster, faster, faster. In my opinion it's the quality and not the quantity that counts. Sometimes a single article on a topic can have a greater effect than five others. And for the westerners this is difficult because what they're used to is having a continuous public presence, of always having your name in the media. It's all the same to them whether your name is on top of a good or a mediocre article. And they're always much more used to writing things coldly. I mean treating everything as though it were objective reportage. They write a good introductory sentence, that's how they're trained, and then they go pull something out of the archive and basically rewrite what some other paper has already written. That's the way it has to be because of this enormous time pressure. Now I understand the end product of this process: cynical, melancholy journalists, cynical, melancholy, and smug journalists. Now I understand why they end up that way. Because at some point your strength runs out from working under these conditions; you lose your physical and psychic energy.

The only predictable exception to my eastern interlocutors' sense of the total, inexorable character of System was when they described their personal and professional experiences of the *Wende* of 1989. The *Wende*, I found, was singularly systemless (*systemlos*).

The *Wende* was not the kind of event that can easily be put into words; but the joy my interviewees took from the effort made this topic one of the few where I felt certain that I was not imposing upon them or dredging up painful recollections or provoking politically sensitive judgments.[11] The *Wende* was an event my younger interviewees very much wanted to describe to me so that I might begin to grasp the totality of its significance for them. "Describe" may be a poor choice of words since recollections of the *Wende* routinely tested the limits of language. Many responses to questions such as "What was the *Wende* like?" began with "How can I describe it to you . . . ?" and then trailed off through minutes of searching for apt

---

11. I must qualify this "joy" with the observation that journalists over age sixty at the time I interviewed them did not typically express such feelings. For the most part, they described the *Wende* as both a personal and a social loss.

metaphors and similes, false starts, agitated silences, and sighs. One man simply laughed at me and said, "Herr Boyer, I would be very happy to explain it to you, but the problem is, we're not even certain ourselves what it is that happened to us."

When I began my fieldwork in 1996, I assumed that the *Wende* denoted the period of time between SED General Secretary Honecker's resignation in October 1989 and German unification in October 1990. This was, to an outsider's mind, the period that bounded the most radical political and social transformations in eastern Germany. Only after listening to dozens of *Wende* narratives did I come to understand that the *Wende* referenced less a phase of exterior social, political, and professional transitions than a time of inner potentiality, positive dialectical reaching forth, and vocational redemption. There were no fixed calendrical parameters for the *Wende*; it began as the structures of the GDR System collapsed and ended with the reinstatement of the FRG System. The *Wende* was reported to be both brief and timeless; it was a quality of time, not a quantity of time to be measured and rationalized. It was instead "a gigantic time" and "an extraordinary time" according to my interviewees, a time that like Walter Benjamin's "Messianic cessation of happening" was blasted "out of the homogeneous course of history" (1968: 263).

Journalist Dietmar L. emphasized the "fairy-tale" quality of the *Wende* as the time between Systems:

> To experience the end of a System, there's nothing like it. It was like in fairy tales; there's no way to describe that. You could look out the window and there were demonstrations on the street. And the journalists suddenly discovered that they were creative, that they could do things they hadn't dreamed of before, and likewise that an amazing amount was possible all of a sudden. It was a time when one System had come to an end, and the next one hadn't yet come to take its place. There were no regulations. It was also a time of silliness. But people like me with a bit of foresight knew that it wouldn't last; we knew that the structures would come again. They wouldn't be the same structures as before, of course, but there would be new ones to take their places. The *Wende* was unstructured, and a lack of structure is magnificent for people who write and who work creatively. For a while so much was possible; there was a new feeling on the part of those who write and also on the part of the readers. Journalists were opening their desks and taking out all the ideas that they'd been collecting for all these years and that they had always wanted to write about.

The language of *Wende* was the language of *Bildung*, of creative energy unleashed from its structures and regulations and allowed to form itself, from within to without. Most of my interlocutors prefaced themselves with the difficulty of mnemonically "completing after the fact" (*nachvollziehen*) the nature and events of the *Wende*. There was no simile that could capture the phenomenology of the event, because there was no point of comparison, nothing "like it," as I heard again and again. "It was like going to sleep in one world and awaking in another," one man offered. Most, after a few tries, concluded that there was probably nothing in my own experience to which an American could compare the *Wende*. With watery eyes, Jürgen F. told me of the night of 9 November 1989, when the Berlin Wall was opened:

> In the great country of America where you come from and where so many things happen every day and everything's possible and where people go to realize their dreams, maybe this all seems very parochial. But what happened right here on the night of 9 November to 10 November, *this* one night, well . . . I actually came home early that day, so I saw everything. This night, that *we* experienced, that is something that is truly unique; no one can take that away from us, this night of nights. I'm sorry, I know this doesn't have much to do with journalism, but somehow it's all related. I remember the next morning everyone was asking, "Were you?" "Were *you?*" meaning of course were you on the other side, and then "When did you come back?" Someone said it's not the kind of thing you can write about; that would make it too concrete, too fixed somehow, this one night. I know this has little to do with journalism, but age doesn't matter, whether one is twenty, thirty, sixty years old, no matter. It was a very invigorating time. It was like a break for us, but a break in the positive sense, I mean.

Jürgen F.'s apologetic reiteration that the *Wende* did not "have much to do with journalism" underscored his feeling that the *Wende* transcended the routines and parameters of normal professional life. It was beyond journalism also in the sense that its feeling of boundless, if fleeting, possibility—of intellectual energy, enthusiasm, and utopian visions—could not be "fixed" or made "concrete" through language. The *Wende* was pure excess, Spirit without System. A younger journalist, Thomas K. commented:

> I mean, when I go to work now, I know more or less what to expect, how much work, what will happen, and I know what'll happen the next week, and the week after that as well. Back then—you can't even conceive how

it was back then. Every day was a surprise. For journalists it was a really wonderful time. We already had our own sense of self, and we had a purpose, because people suddenly believed what was in the newspapers. To accompany a process like that, it's just wild. And everything happened so quickly.

Reiner H., a news agency journalist, echoed Thomas K. on the unique sense of creative journalistic agency inspired by the *Wende:*

> It was unbelievable for all journalists. Suddenly there was this unlimited freedom in the press, almost anarchy I would say, and it was shamelessly exploited by the journalists. Suddenly, there were tremendous changes in television, the newspapers, and the news agencies as well. ADN was also an object for protesters, as you can imagine. One slogan was "ADN! Quit napping!" It was a gigantic time, a time when you could do anything; there was a feeling of revolution everywhere. But by the second half of 1990 though, people knew it wouldn't go farther; they realized that with the end of the GDR everything was slowly going to return to normal again. But it was an extraordinary time. . . .
>
> There were no taboos anymore as to what you could write about. You really should read the papers from this time period to see what I mean. There were no more restrictions on issues. You see, the thing was that there were really no owners at that time—the old ones had fled and the new ones hadn't come in yet—and under normal circumstances you have to do what the employers say, but just then we were on our own.

The *Wende* remained, my eastern interlocutors agreed, the most important, defining experience of their lives both personally and professionally. It was both a matter of emancipation from the GDR System and a matter of vocational redemption: before the FRG System established itself in the eastern German media, the *Wende* "proved" that eastern journalists had genuine, creative intellectual powers. In this respect, the experience of *Wende* became a central feature of identity formation that differentiated them from western colleagues. One journalist mused, "One of the advantages of being East German is that we know that *Wenden* are possible. Or, at least, that they're not impossible." By contrast, West Germans were deemed less mature and less capable of recognizing "the weaknesses in their own System" because they had not yet reached that point of contradiction between Spirit and formality-for-itself where true reflection and self-analysis were possible. In Hegelian terms, their owl of Minerva was still grounded. West

Germans were construed as defending the integrity and principles of their "free and democratic media system" with a kind of adolescent conviction that reminded my eastern interlocutors of their own youthful belief in the purity of party journalism before contradictions between the ideals and the actuality of professional practice disenchanted them. Thus, in this one dimension of their history, my eastern interlocutors assured me that it was they, and not the West Germans, who were the more mature and experienced professionals.

I must note that there was something historically unique about the social organization of media production in eastern Germany between the autumn of 1989 and the spring of 1990 that provides some sociological corroboration to the positive dialectical phenomenology of creative agency during the *Wende*. For several months after October 1989, all GDR media organizations were still wholly financed by the SED, and yet the SED exerted virtually no effective political control over media production and, more importantly, had no profit expectations from its press. Thus, until the SED cut free the majority of its party press in April 1990 and, with that, its subsidization, the majority of GDR journalists were being paid to write about whatever the democratically elected chief editor and his or her staff decided was worthy of publication, with no expectation of ideological or market accountability. This was, I should emphasize, an absolutely unprecedented arrangement in the history of the German media (mass circulation, with organizational autonomy, no governmental controls, and no profitability considerations) and probably unknown in the history of mass media more generally. Little wonder then that former GDR media professionals consider the *Wende* period to be the apex of their vocational experience as journalists—there actually was something like a "free press."

Journalists recall suspecting even during the *Wende* that the absence of System could not last. Several described the open horizons of this interlude as a *Narrenfreiheit*, or fool's paradise. Others described it to me as a fertile bed for clever opportunism masquerading as Spirit. All had stories about *Wendehälse* (turn-necks)[12] among their acquaintances, individuals who had not changed internally but who had all too easily been able to change their tune in order to adapt to the new System. The return of System, and with it, social and professional normality, was expected and experienced with what

---

12. The *Wendehälse* is a kind of woodpecker that can turn its head easily in different directions (see A. Glaeser 2000: 247). The aptness of the metaphor results from the bird's tropic capture of ambivalent orientation and from its lexical contiguity with the political and social *Wende* of 1989.

was retrospectively described by many as a sense of composure (*Gelassenheit;* the term has Protestant religious connotations of the pious acceptance of predestined order). After the experience of the *Wende,* however, there seemed less incentive to return to the everyday satisfactions and compromises of professional journalism. In memory, the taste of Spirit without System provided both a sense of inner satisfaction and a certain feeling of restlessness. "Who *really* wanted it to end?" one man mused.

Leaving Journalism

My friend Joachim is one of the many former GDR journalists who never really came to terms with the return of System to journalism. At our first meeting in 1996 at his office, he expressed misgivings about the direction in which management was taking news journalism. He explained to me that there was one philosophy of news journalism "that says that one should always strive to engage the most important issues and another that holds that one should give people the news they are most interested in." Joachim did not demean the latter philosophy, but he made it clear to me that he had little interest in servicing it. In 1999, Joachim quit his job as news director against the wishes of many of his colleagues and decided, after a rocky period of transition, to become a writer instead.

Joachim has never offered me the details surrounding his resignation but he has said that he felt it was time to leave journalism, in part because he felt that he was becoming "narcissistically obsessed" with his work and in part because he did not like the direction in which he saw news journalism headed in Germany. In 1989, Joachim had belonged to the group of democratically elected journalists who had helped to reform GDR Radio. He recalls those days in the *Wende* fondly as a time of great, and largely missed, opportunities to do a kind of journalism that exceeded what had evolved in either the FRG or the GDR System. Before 1989, he had sought to escape the rigors of party journalism by writing radio plays that were aired at such obscene hours of the night that the party had little interest in them. In one, *Der Käseesser* (The Cheese Eater), a man is trapped in a claustrophobic, overheated train compartment with another man, who insists on trying to feed him one kind of cheese after another until his victim loses consciousness. Michael joked to me that Joachim had brilliantly captured one aspect of life in the GDR with that play: "You see, no matter what the party said they were giving you, it was always more cheese, until eventually you just couldn't take it anymore."

One afternoon in June 2002, in the garden of Michael's house in the Berlin suburb of Biesdorf, Joachim explained in more detail his frustrations with contemporary news journalism that had eventually contributed to his desire to find creative and intellectual outlets outside the profession. Michael had invited us over just to catch up, but he pulled me aside just before Joachim arrived to tell me that he thought we should both really try to convince him to come back to journalism. While cutting an enormous custard torte into slices, Michael shook his head and said, "He's really much, much too talented to just be sitting around at home." Shortly thereafter, Joachim strolled into the garden looking rested and sanguine. After a quick coffee with Michael's wife, Karin, the three of us stood near the large stone grill in the garden trying to avoid billowing clouds of smoke while Michael stoked the fire. As Michael readied a large piece of lamb for grilling, he made the mistake of showing us a very kitschy grilling apron and gloves that his daughter had bought for him for his birthday. Joachim insisted that I take a picture of Michael in the apron, "strictly for the purposes of scientific research."

JOACHIM [*sternly*]: Come now, Michael, let Dominic get a picture of you in that beautiful apron.

MICHAEL [*blushing*]: No, no, I don't think so. I don't want him to get any wrong ideas.

JOACHIM [*laughing*]: Really, it looks very smart; put it back on.

MICHAEL [*amused but still blushing*]: Perhaps if he wasn't an ethnologist—you know, he's here to study the German way of life and so forth and he'll spread some funny ideas about German culture when he goes back home.

JOACHIM: Oh, that's ridiculous, I'm sure they have grilling aprons in America too. They love to grill as well. No one will think anything of it.

To change the subject, Michael asked Joachim what he had been doing with himself. Joachim replied, smiling, "As I told Dominic, I am three things: one, an unemployed journalist, which takes a surprising amount of time; two, a sometimes successful investor in the stock market; and, three, a budding writer. So you see I have three jobs which keep me quite busy." We settled in the shade at the garden table to eat the lamb with a generous spread of goat's cheese, white peppers, and yogurt. Together with Karin we discussed the United States after 9/11, my new job, regional politics, school reform in Germany, and their neighbors, who, much to Michael's chagrin, still like to sing GDR songs.

At several points during the afternoon, Michael tried to steer the conversation back to journalism in the hopes of getting Joachim interested in returning to work. But it became clear to both of us that Joachim would not be easily convinced. Joachim spoke with particular bitterness of the accelerated tempo of work that left precious little time for reflection and of the mediating forces of politics and the market that continuously pushed news journalism in the direction of either public-relations work or an information industry. Joachim has often said that he envisioned his work as helping to stimulate people to think through issues rather than trying to persuade them of something or just bombarding them with uncontextualized "facts."

To corroborate Joachim's point, Michael mentioned a recent event in his news department that had reminded him of the GDR and of the extent to which political parties could manipulate journalism in the western system. The campaign for the German chancellorship had been heating up during the summer, and Christlich-Demokratische Union/Christlich-Soziale Union candidate Edmund Stoiber had just assembled his shadow cabinet, to whom he referred as his *Kompetenzteam* (literally, "competence team," with dual neutral and positive connotations to the term just as in English).

MICHAEL: A few days ago in the campaign coverage, Stoiber held a press conference where he mentioned adding someone to his *"Kompetenzteam,"* and without fail all the journalists in the office were suddenly using this term and talking about Stoiber's *"Kompetenzteam"* and who else might be added to it. My reaction was: *"Kompetenzteam!"* Now what's that all about? They really ought to have used the term *"Wahlmannschaft"* [election team], which is more accurate and neutral. But it's characteristic of the problem that a phrase like that is floated by the parties and then suddenly it becomes part of everyday journalistic language.

JOACHIM [*nodding*]: The thing is that half the time the journalists don't even realize they are doing it. They are going about busily doing their business and they hardly even notice how those in power are manipulating them. It really is more of an unconscious process. Because, on the one hand, you have what I see as a general decline in objectivity in journalism, especially in the last, let's say, five to seven years. And then in public radio you have the entire party system that intersects with this and intensifies it. I think the real problem is that there are no longer any forums in which to discuss the praxis. Given the character of the work nowadays, there is precious little time to think or to talk about what it is that you are doing, so it is very hard to step back from the work and to identify where these sorts of political manipulation are taking place. Something needs to change and it has to start, in my opinion, with the news agencies [*Michael murmurs his assent*] because it is the news agencies, the *holy* news agencies, which really dominate news-making nowadays. They have incredible influence over what is transmitted, but you never get the feeling that they are thinking too closely about what it is that they are doing. What I'm sure they *aren't* doing is spending much time on training the younger journalists. This is the other huge problem— that there is no real training for journalists in Germany. . . . In Germany one can't assume any longer that the young colleagues are being trained on the job either.

DOMINIC: Why not?

JOACHIM: Because it's expensive to commit journalists to do this kind of [train-ing] work, mostly.

At this point in the conversation, Karin called Michael into the house momentarily, and Joachim ruminated for a bit, concluding:

In terms of news journalism, there was one event that I took to be a watershed in this process, and that was the death of Princess Diana. How the media handled that, the way it was allowed to dominate (*pauses*) felt to me like a point past which you could never return again. I mean, what is a news bulletin anyway? Is it the same crap you find hawked continuously in the boulevard press? Do people even want that, since they're already getting it from the boulevard? Well, after that it seemed as though any crap that was in the boulevard press was fit for the news, according to the logic that this is what the people want to hear about. But continuously?

Sympathetically, I remarked to Joachim that I had had exactly his re-action to the media coverage in the United States as well. Joachim nodded to me quietly, still troubled. When Michael came back, he asked Joachim bluntly whether he could be persuaded to return to journalism. Shaking his head, Joachim replied curtly, "I don't see it. Anyway, it's time to move on."

✍

About a week later, Joachim invited me to take a steamboat ride with him and Tamara and their daughter around Potsdam. Once on board and seated with cups of warm coffee to ward off the remarkably cold and wet air of the Havelsee, I produced a gift pilfered from Nalepastraße, a ceramic cup

from the abandoned canteen in the security building. With uncanny tim-
ing, a waitress walked by our table at just this moment and commented to
Joachim, "That looks like something from a GDR canteen." "Why it is,"
Joachim replied to her chuckling. "It's like an archaeological relic." As he
turned the cup over in his hands, Joachim began to laugh deeply.

CHAPTER FIVE

Dialectical Knowledges of the Contemporary: Formal and Informal

What Marx showed to be the case in regard to the category of labor holds true for this as well: "how even the most abstract categories, despite their validity—precisely because of their abstractness—for all epochs, are nevertheless, in the specific character of this abstraction, themselves likewise a product of historical relations and possess their full validity only for and within these relations." The theory of communicative action can explain why this is so: the development of society must *itself* give rise to the problem situations that *objectively* afford contemporaries a privileged access to the general structures of the lifeworld. — *Jürgen Habermas, Theorie des kommunikativen Handelns* (trans. T. McCarthy)

The opposite of System?

It would be easier to explain the opposite of silicon.

The Greek word means order.

So the opposite would be DISORDER.

A system, more precisely, is an order that is logically constructed
    according to unified standpoints.

In CHEMISTRY there is a PERIODICAL SYSTEM.

There is a system of government.

In a sense, you are pursuing a "systems analysis."

There are "system errors."

Someone or something can be "INIMICAL TO THE SYSTEM"
    [*systemfeindlich*]. For example, certain so-called civil rights
    activists in the GDR. Others conformed to the system [*waren
    systemkonform*].

GDR journalists, including all those older than 30–32 years old now,
    were *systemkonform.*

The collapse of socialism could have been IMMANENT TO THE
SYSTEM [*systemimmanent*]. The all-powerful status of money in
capitalism is *SYSTEMIMMANENT.*
Sakharov was a critic of the system. I was too in the GDR (whenever I
was drunk).
A hated system is brought down.
WHAT IS THE OPPOSITE OF SYSTEM?
Something, a situation perhaps, can be unsystemic [*systemlos*].
Without system.
In a football match, there may be "no recognizable system."
It operates "without a system." DISORDER prevails.
Thus unsystemically.
Or with DISORDER as its opposite.
— *Albert to the author, via email, 5 December 1997*

In the introduction to this book, I argued that dialectical social knowledge
spans many registers of epistemic expression, that it can be located in
the formal, elite registers of theoretical and philosophical language as well
as in informal and intersubjective processes of producing social knowledge.
This premise in hand, my case studies have traveled widely in their exploration of dialectical knowledge in German intellectual culture, moving from
nineteenth-century dialectical philosophy to the dialectical ideologies of the
NSDAP and SED party-states to the dialecticism present in the memories
and social knowledge of German journalists in the postunification German
media. In this final ethnographic chapter, I would like to revisit and to further elaborate my opening argument through the juxtaposition of two intellectual communities that have produced rich dialectical knowledges of the
contemporary. The first community will likely be better known to the academic audience of this book: German systems theorists, a highly vigorous,
original, and influential group of dialecticians who have moved an analytics
of System to the center of their paradigms of modern sociality and history.
The second community—less well known but no less vigorous and original—is a Berlin *Stammtisch* (regulars' table at a restaurant or bar) of eastern
and western journalists whose lively, open-ended discussions of current affairs, regional politics, and national history provide compelling comparisons
and arresting contrasts to the technical rigor of academic theory.

It becomes clear below that charting the dialectics of Spirit and System is a matter of great interest and considerable passion for both systems
theoreticians and *Stammtisch* members. Both groups likewise display the

phenomenology of expertise outlined in chapter 1, sacralizing epistemic form by cultivating inattention to epistemic context. And yet the two communities' communicative and social conventions vary considerably, creating qualitative differences between the kinds of dialectical knowledge they produce. The professional and institutional character of academic labor accentuates the rational attention and context-insensitivity of its knowledges and evaluates them accordingly. At the *Stammtisch*, meanwhile, the decontextualizing, rationalist tendencies of intellectual exchange are somewhat diminished by its situational expectations for humor, play, argument, and open-ended dialogue. Still, both groups of intellectuals engage in the common project of producing apt and persuasive social knowledge. The modes of dialectical knowing I contrast in this chapter differ more in degree than in kind.

As I compare the contours and nuances of everyday dialecticism to its most formal and authoritative registers, I develop my earlier argument that the dialectic expresses a phenomenological tension in knowing that can be articulated across a range of possible degrees of epistemic formality from the inchoate and poetic to the technical and transcendental. Indeed, as we learned in chapter 2, philosophy and theory often codify in a transcendental idiom social knowledge that has already emerged inchoately with very specific historical and phenomenological reference. In this chapter, we see that this is no less the case for contemporary philosophy and social theory, which translate into ontology a quite mundane social phenomenology of the restriction and compromise of Spirit by the technical forms and relations of social System.

By briefly exploring systems theorists Niklas Luhmann's and Friedrich Kittler's analyses of the ratio between human agency and System we gain insight into an extreme negative dialectical characterization of modern society where human subjectivity is dissolved into a series of interlocking ontogenetic systems, where even human epistemic capacity (the essence of Spirit) is determined to be a phenomenon of System. Then, in Jürgen Habermas's *The Theory of Communicative Action*, we encounter a contemporary dialectical philosophy of history where System is diagnosed, in Weberian fashion, as a phenomenon of modern societal complexification. Yet Habermas also reveals his vision of a new positive dialectical principle "within" human social experience that promises to arrest the empty formality of the contemporary phase of history and to stimulate a new period of social and historical *Bildung*. In all three variants of systems theory, we see how negative dialectical knowledge of modern sociality is rendered ontological or ontohistorical through the analytics of System. At the same time, we note the limits or "remainder" of this formula as the systems theorist imbues "himself"[1] with a special intellectual agency of revelation that is denied other human subjects, rendering the analytic language of System as a vehicle of theoretical Spirit.

Comparatively, at the *Stammtisch*, we find a communicative space saturated with informal dialecticism, where the dialogical and often vulgate character of intellectual practice allows a plurality of epistemic modes, from the sober and rationalistic to the drunken and poetic, to flourish. As with systems theoreticians, negative dialectical knowledge deeply informs the intellectual work of the *Stammtisch*, but it appears less often in reference to questions as abstract as the character of modern sociality (although the arbitration of "German history" and "Germanness" is often fair game). Negative dialectical concerns and anxieties, as well as expressions of positive dialectical assertion, tend to be geared more to the immediate (for this group) problems of negotiating the *Belastung* (burden) of GDR history and the dynamics of contemporary East/West relations. The tension of System and Spirit emerges again and again at the *Stammtisch* as a key axis of social and self knowledge.

Juxtaposing the two cases suggests the wide range of possible modes of dialectical knowing as well as the impact of different situational expectations for epistemic virtuosity upon specific expressions of dialectical knowledge. It is also my hope that the comparison will offer the reader at least a schematic sense of the interactive dynamics of formal and informal dialectical knowledges in intellectual culture, especially where the former grants the latter a sense of intellectual authority while the latter grants the former a sense of intuitive wisdom. Systems theory can thus be viewed as a codification and ontologization of the kinds of negative dialectical intuition one finds saturating other, more informal spaces and practices of intellectual culture like the *Stammtisch*.

As a caveat, I must note that this chapter does not push much beyond a provocative juxtaposition. I do not offer, to be sure, a rigorous comparative analysis of the two intellectual communities. This is, in part, a strategic decision because I want to resist "overtheorizing" the knowledge of the *Stammtisch* and thus subtly acquiescing to the academic expectation of allowing informal modes of knowing to be digested by more formal modes of knowing. By contrast, the method of juxtaposition aptly represents the mundane entanglement of formal and informal dialectical knowledges that

---

1. Much more could be made of the masculinity of systems theory (and of philosophy more generally) than I am able to do here (see Boyer 2005a).

characterizes the everyday life of intellectual culture in Germany and elsewhere. Even were I so inclined, however, I could not pursue a more extended comparative analysis since I lack experiential knowledge of the making of systems theory comparable to that of the *Stammtisch*. Although I am
well aware of the textual artifacts of systems theory and of the subsequent
academic debates they continue to generate, I can offer little specific biographical insight into their academic conditions of production (besides some
general observations about the phenomenology of academic labor offered below). As I have argued elsewhere, a more serious ethnographic engagement
with academic life and its methods of producing knowledge is the pressing
challenge of reflexive anthropology (2003a, 2003b). I hope that the conceptual and anecdotal reflections that I offer below will constitute an adequate
placeholder for, and invitation toward, a richer anthropological engagement
with academic intellectual culture and its theoretical practices (Falcone n.d.;
Thorkelson 2004).

System in Systems Theory

Systems theory, Jürgen Habermas tells us, emerged as a sociological method
to engage the phenomena of social complexification and rationalization that
Max Weber first identified within his historical sociology (Habermas 1984:
143–271). Weber defined a rising tension in modern society as social forms
"detached" from their ethical and normative bases and became increasingly
autonomous and instrumentally oriented. Detachment was not intrinsically
negative for Weber but rather was part of an ontohistorical process of social formalization that, in other eras, had guaranteed the rise of forms of
ethical universality on the basis of religious communality. Yet, with the
further complexification of social life, "the inherent conflict between the
religious postulate and the reality of the world does not diminish but rather
increases. With the increasing systemization and rationalization of communal relationships and of their substantive contents, the external compen-
sations provided by the teachings of theodicy are replaced by the struggles
of particular autonomous spheres of life against the requirements of religion" (1963: 209). Although religion and ethics are never extinguished by
autonomous social spheres according to Weber, he saw them nonetheless at
risk in modern society, as the normative basis of society found itself challenged by an increasingly elaborate mesh of external social forms (summed
up in the figure of the "iron cage") that operated according to their own
extranormative principles.

Unlike Weber's historical sociology of a ratio of forces (religious, ethical, and systemic-rational) tipping *toward System,* contemporary systems theory takes an analytics of System as its point of departure. The term "System" no longer indexes the accelerating societal formalization and mass-cultural degeneration that it did for Weber and his *Gebildeten* contemporaries; it is no longer a danger or horizon of modernization but rather an ontogenetic state in its own right. The analytic presence of System in systems theory suggests a phenomenology of knowledge making wherein the domination and/or mediation of inner creative powers by exterior forces and networks are complete. Much like the recent film *The Matrix,* human "subjectivity" itself is revealed as a cybernetic imaginary created by the interaction of psychical and environmental systems. And yet, unlike *The Matrix,* there is no "Neo," no excess or remainder of human agency in systems theory (beyond, as I discuss below, the systems theorist himself) that continues to contest the machine world even once the terrible truth of the phantasm is revealed. The relationship of self to System is no longer one of within to without, since there is no more "within" in the vision of much systems theory. Human selfhood and agency, including human knowledges of selfhood and agency, are said to be produced as effects of the routine operations of System.

Niklas Luhmann's sociology is perhaps the extreme case of this tendency. Luhmann is truly a theorist for whom, to recall Albert, System is silicon. Luhmann's model of the functional differentiation of modern society centers on systems as operationally closed, self-determining and -reproducing spheres of action. Each system has its own function; and Luhmann's human beings are entities at the convergence of several systems, one biological, another psychical, and finally a diverse ecology of social systems (1995). Among social systems, the mass media, to take a relevant example, form the operational constructivist basis of society's production of its own reality. According to Luhmann, media as System originated through the dissemination of print technology, which allowed the mass mediation of representational forms to decouple from local spheres of oral communication and become a self-sustaining system (see also McLuhan 1962, 1964). Luhmann writes, "Of course, oral communication is still possible as a reaction to things which are printed or broadcast. *But the success of scheduled communication no longer depends on it.* This is how, in the sphere of the mass media, an autopoietic, self-producing system is able to emerge which no longer requires the mediation of interaction among those co-present" (2000: 16).

All systems are, for Luhmann, essentially decoupled spheres of mediation that reproduce themselves according to their own internal logics.

Luhmann's systems are purely negative dialectical, existing formally-for-themselves, exerting coordinating influence over human beings without any place for co-constituting human agency. They are pure "without," pure containment. Since Luhmann specifically defines System in opposition to agency, his sociology deftly polices itself against the intrusion of "outsider" (historicizing) influences, much as Luhmann tells us systems themselves do. In what he terms a "radically constructivist epistemology" (2000: 109), Luhmann's analysis mirrors the work of the mass media system's own operational constructivism. "In the operationally current present the world as it is and the world as it is being observed cannot be distinguished" (11). In other words, we cannot know systems beyond their capacity to produce knowledge of themselves that is available to biologically systemic humans through their psychical systems. Intellectual agency disappears as human beings become functional receivers (and, indeed, thinkers) of messages that are always being systemically preconceived for us. Luhmann's autopoetic epistemology is transhuman in this regard. Spirit is extinguished, at least in theory.

Friedrich Kittler's study of *Aufschreibesysteme* (discourse networks/information systems) in 1800 and 1900 offers a parallel cybernetic analysis of the "data processing" (1990: 370) of intellectual culture. In the afterword Kittler explains, in effect, that his project can be read as *Aufschreibesystem* 2000 digesting the print culture of the nineteenth century in order to discern its computational and informatic systems. "Literary criticism can learn from an information theory that has formalized the current state of technical knowledge, and thus made measurable the performance or limits of information systems. After the destruction of the monopoly of writing, it becomes possible to draw up an account of its functioning" (370). Following McLuhan's dictum that old media become the content of new media, Kittler describes his project as a phenomenon of contemporary computational data processing reading its origins and originating self-awareness in a print culture that has just ceded its monopoly to an electronic culture. Like Luhmann, Kittler's project can be read (or reads itself?) in the direction of transhuman epistemology as human authors functionally mediate the knowledge production of ontogenetic systems. Individual authorship is a functional element of the *Aufschreibesystem* and even the systems theorist would seem to be little more than an apt stylus for System to produce its self-knowledge.

Although both Luhmann and Kittler seem to acknowledge the historicity of System through their analyses of media technology, neither seems to conceive System as a remediable problem of modern sociality. After all, in the logic of the autopoetic System, what difference would it make to support a transcendental illusion of escape? Habermas, by contrast, pursues his systems theory with a divergent dialectics of the contemporary. He rejects the Luhmannian vision of System as ontogenetic state and instead characterizes System as the residue of a particular phase of historical development that may yet be replaced by a future phase of positive dialectical *Bildung* providing that human beings are able to harness the power of "communicative action" to reshape their history.

Charting this remedial dialectics of history is the work of Habermas's opus, *The Theory of Communicative Action*. Habermas sees nothing inevitable in the societal systems (government, markets, bureaucracy, and so on) that have developed around industrial capitalism as the driving force of societal modernization. But neither does he underestimate the threat of what he terms their "internal colonization of the lifeworld [*Lebenswelt*]" by a framework of institutional subsystems, or "steering media," that have decoupled, in Weberian fashion, from their normative and ethical bases. These steering media now operate according to a dominant logic of instrumental rationality, but Habermas argues that there is no intrinsic reason for this operational structure. Habermas imagines that societal media could just as well operate according to other, more normative and ethical bases. In a supremely positive dialectical move, Habermas suggests that the *Bildung* of a more humane and emancipating modernity can yet replace the decoupled, austere systems generated around industrial capitalism. He offers the possibility of cultivating what he terms "communicative rationality" as a new normative medium of modern sociality, one that would naturally combat the dehumanizing character of capitalist modernization were it allowed to crystallize itself in society.

Communicative rationality, according to Habermas, centers on the production and negotiation of "criticizable validity claims" with the purpose of "reaching understanding." The "yes or no" with which any criticizable validity claim can be met ensures, Habermas argues, that communicative rationality cannot be predicated upon nonnormative or self-interested considerations in the long run, but rather only upon intersubjective coordination and normativity (assuming, as Habermas does, that all participants in communication have relatively equivalent agency and rationalist dispositions). For Habermas, the blueprint for this more rational, coordinated mode of sociality has always lain dormant in the logical functions of rational communication. It is a linguistic potentiality inherent in propositional structure that has been "unexploited" apparently for no other reason than that subjects do not fully appreciate "the potential of the binding (or bonding) force of good reasons" (1984: 305).

Given its intrinsic emphasis on reaching reasoned agreement, Habermas argues, the cultivation of communicative rationality into forms of "communicative action" will naturally undermine decoupled systems and their instrumental-rational emphases upon formal organization, bureaucratic proceduralism, and individual autonomy. Concomitantly, it will empower the human lifeworld, that "transcendental site where speaker and hearer meet, where they can reciprocally raise claims that their utterances fit the world (objective, social, or subjective), and where they can criticize and confirm those validity claims, settle their disagreements, and arrive at agreements" (1987: 126). This lifeworld is no place but rather is a reserve of positive dialectical energy and imagination empowering communities to explore their inner normative purposes, to reach collective understandings, and then to extend their coordinated agency into actual societal forms.

How, precisely, communicative rationality can be made actionable remains unclear, however. After so many hundreds of pages of preliminaries in *The Theory of Communicative Action*, one learns surprisingly little about how communicative action may or will actually transform the systems of modern society. Habermas makes only fleeting mention of counterinstitutions that "are intended to dedifferentiate some parts of the formally organized domains of action, remove them from the clutches of the steering media, and return these 'liberated areas' to the action-coordinating mechanism of reaching understanding" (1987: 396). And, as with Luhmann and Kittler, human agency is strikingly evanescent in the framework of Habermas's theory. Yet this apparent elision neatly brings Habermas and his systems theory back within the fold of dialectical philosophy more generally. His unwillingness to predict the forms that the new phase of *Bildung* will assume is consistent with how dialectical philosophy often situates the philosopher with respect to knowledge of the unfolding of history from within to without. The philosopher recognizes the dialectic of history but does not see (as Marx could scarcely glimpse a communist society) the subsequent phase of historical *Gestaltung*. For Habermas, communicative action can, like Hegel's world-spirit, be apprehended only through its historically manifested forms and these can be fully recognized only at a moment of world-historical transition: "The development of society must *itself* give rise to the problem situations that *objectively* afford contemporaries a privileged access to the general structures of the lifeworld. . . . [T]he systemic imperatives of autonomous subsystems penetrate into the lifeworld and, through monetarization and bureaucratization, force an assimilation of communicative actions to formally organized domains of action. . . . It may be that this provocative threat, this challenge that places the symbolic structures of the lifeworld as a whole in question, can account for why they have become accessible to us" (403). Habermas accounts for the historicity of his own philosophical project by arguing that the contemporary phase of societal complexification, with its sluggish, detached, and dehumanizing systematization, produces the symptom of a theory of communicative action at the moment of its positive dialectical reawakening.

On the Spirit of the Theoretician and the Academic Phenomenology of Expertise

The apparent paradox of systems theory as intellectual practice is that the systems theorist locates his intellectual agency in theorizing the totality of System in human life. The situation seems less paradoxical, however, if we consider that, in the social imaginary of systems theory, Spirit is never truly extinguished but rather centered and condensed in the person of the systems theorist. Without ever having to impugn explicitly the intellectual agency of other human beings, the systems theorist positions himself as the singular exception to the rule, the one human being whose epistemic capacities can exceed System enough to produce objective and authoritative knowledge of its totality. Such transcontextual positioning is, of course, by no means limited to systems theoreticians. For example, in contemporary anthropology, it is entirely reminiscent of the kinds of "technical anthropology" inspired by the works of philosophers like Michel Foucault (1979, 1981) and Bruno Latour (1999) that pour great passion and artistry into crafting into ontology negative dialectical knowledge of the "technologies of power" or "entelechies" that mediate or erode human agency. In these cases as well, System becomes both medium and foil for academic Spirit.

Luhmann might counter that systems theory is itself the cybernetic imaginary of a particular phase of Systemic development. But I would argue that systems theorists experience their labor as something more than simple inscription or diagnosis. Indeed, the embrace of System is itself positioned as an act of Spirit and the recognition of transhuman epistemology as a new transcendental, cybernetic *Wissenschaft* (see Luhmann 2000: 109; Kittler 1990: 369–72). The passion and precision of their theoretical writing is the best testament to this. Think, for example, of the exhaustive and artisanal care with which Habermas incrementally reveals to us, over hundreds of pages, the hidden power of communicative rationality. Or consider the similar time and energy Luhmann devotes to outlining the functional interrelationships of his social systems. In both cases, the agency of revelation belongs to the theorist, the one who displays to his audience an inner logic of social experience and its ramifications hitherto unknown to them. Even as medium, the systems theorist has intellectual singularity and sanctity. Yet, somehow, these traces of Spirit are never made to confront reflexively the content of systems theory, which explicitly denies a humanistic sense of human intellectual autonomy and agency. The absence of reflexive concern is neither accidental nor disingenuous, I would argue, but rather an extreme and informative instance of the routinely decontextualized self-understanding of elite knowledge practices, a self-understanding consonant with the "phenomenology of expertise" discussed in chapter 1.

To reiterate that discussion, the phenomenology of expertise may be characterized as a focus of attention and energy on the cultivation of epistemic form that, in turn, renders the appearance of epistemic form as the essence and principal value of knowledge. Its focus of attention, moreover, requires a certain degree of "bracketing" (Husserl 1986) intellectual activity to its environs. This process is never perfectly accomplished, of course; it is habitual and normative rather than absolute. But the intensified focus of attention on and energy into the formal, rational dimensions of knowing, the overriding concern with "knowledge," inevitably genders the world "without" to some degree as an impediment and distraction to intellectual activity. Much as with the early-nineteenth-century ideal of *Wissenschaft*, the phenomenology of expertise casts the context of intellectual reflection into a state of triviality *even when, as in the case of social theory, social context becomes an explicit and expert matter of attention.* This explains how a social theorist can produce brilliant knowledge of social conditions and relations while being always prone to ignore his or her own immediate conditions and relations of knowledge making. Reflexive social science confronts this dilemma continuously.

In turn, the conventions of academic labor and communication tend to reward and to naturalize the condition- and relation-denying attention of the phenomenology of expertise. Academic labor, especially academic humanist labor (as opposed to academic laboratory research, for example), is focused on individual epistemic performance, and this performance is both monitored institutionally and cultivated as a vocational ideal of the disciplined pursuit of "knowledge for-its-own-sake." Whether or not the acquisition of "cultural capital" is a social physics of academic life, all of us feel institutional and professional pressures to be active and productive, to develop "name recognition" (Williams 2001), to focus our activities and attention on individual epistemic achievement and recognition. Much in keeping with Foucault's treatise on modern institutions (1979), one is also struck by how academic humanist institutions are designed to promote solitary, confined, and focused epistemic attention. The physical environment of most university buildings, for example, tends to be organized around individual offices that bracket and insulate the interface of an individual with a computer terminal or printed page. The university hallway and lounge are, to be sure, spaces of conviviality and dialogue, but they are also experienced as spaces of "surveillance," in Foucault's sense of the recognition of abstract principles of social evaluation and judgment. In hallway conversations, guilt is often expressed for lingering in the pleasures of informal communication, and the intention of "getting back to work" is often declared. Context, relation, and transaction are treated as luxuries next to the necessities of independent epistemic engagement and production.

The specialized languages of academic communication likewise contribute greatly to the decontextualizing phenomenology of academic labor. Academic language conforms well to what Mikhail Bakhtin has described as the sociolinguistic norms of "professional language" (1981: 289) more generally. Bakhtin observes that although all communication is context sensitive to some extent, professional language communities cultivate a heavy emphasis on formality and denotationality to produce a sense of epistemic fixity required by their "cultures of expertise." The eliteness of professional language is guaranteed precisely by its denial of attention to the kinds of contextual cues that occupy most speakers. Charles Peirce strongly defended, for precisely this reason, the need "to avoid using words and phrases of vernacular origin as technical terms of philosophy" in his essay "The Ethics of Terminology" (1998: 263–66). The very formality and austerity demanded of language becomes a formality projected upon knowledge, a sense of its fixity and density of referential substance that is construed as an intrinsic quality of knowledge rather than as a social condition of knowing (see Johns 1998: 6–40).

Of course, the formality and austerity of academic knowledge making are easily overstated. All of us know, for example, that personal relationships and nonprofessional networks are as significant as or more significant than competitive markets at every stage in our academic careers. Likewise, much of academic life unfolds outside individual studies in interactional settings like classrooms, faculty meetings, public presentations, sherry hours, dinner parties, and so on. Even ideally sanctified office space is itself continuously subject to invasive "distractions." As I am writing this paragraph, for example, strong morning sunlight dapples my desk. A warm breeze blows from outside, reminding me that I could instead be enjoying the fine weather outside. I can hear the university carillon just beginning to sound in the distance, but it cannot drown out the hum of my computer monitor nor the frenzied buzzing of a fly seeking to escape through my window. I am distracted by hunger and by waiting for a student to arrive who is late. Like the fly, I am somewhat frantic with a sense of stolen time. My leg is beginning to fall asleep but I rattle on trying to get a few more sentences out before my attention is drawn away to other concerns.

Who needs such information to evaluate the artifacts of academic knowledge, you might well ask. That is precisely the point. What seems trivial and intrusive to the "real business" of theoretical work are precisely the nuances of the "outside" of academic labor, including all those forms of knowing and knowledge that seem extraneous to our own practices of knowledge making (see Herzfeld 2001: 72). The denial of the outside—more or less successfully on a moment-to-moment basis to be sure—abets the centering of epistemic formality in attention, producing in the end an expectation and appreciation of intellectual activity as decontextualized in its very character. This is the camera obscura, if you will, of academic humanist labor, the method by which the social and phenomenological conditions that envelope and define a form of activity appear to become the essential attributes of that activity. The academic camera obscura finds its zenith in activities like theory and philosophy whose epistemic attentions are resolutely formal and context denying. In recognition of their "purity" from the residues of contextual attention, theory and philosophy achieve distinction as elite modes of intellectual activity, indeed, of intellectual virtuosity.

In the next sections of the chapter, I will explore dialectical knowing and knowledge in another setting of contemporary intellectual culture. It is a setting where somewhat different expectations for, and conventions of, intellectual virtuosity dominate but where the relationship of Spirit to System is no less a matter of intellectual concern.

Stammtisch: The After Hours of Spirit and System

Gregor, as he often does after the third or fourth round of beers, is holding court, telling us all stories from his early days at *Super Illu*—that lone, vastly successful survivor of the many boulevard papers that the western German media conglomerates rushed to sell the East in the months after the *Wende*. He becomes increasingly animated as his story takes shape, waving his hands in the air, tugging his collar, squinting, and jabbing his index finger to scatter emphasis throughout his monologue. Karl is sitting next to him, alertly interjecting a point now and then: he too is a veteran of *Super Illu*'s early years, a former assistant chief editor of the GDR central news agency (ADN) turned boulevard journalist in the final stages of a long career. They seem an unlikely pair of *Kumpel* (mates),[2] one a thirty-year-old from a wealthy, small-town Bavarian family, with a deftly hyperbolic and sarcastic sense of humor, and the other a gentle, more serious and proud man in his sixties whose working-class manner and values have not been entirely effaced by many years in high-status positions within the GDR media hierarchy.

GREGOR [*to Karl*]: Do you remember that one guy, the guy who was actually crazy and had to be locked up? That was back in 1990 or 1991, I think, and the Wessis were letting anyone be a journalist.

KARL: Back then it was possible for anyone to become a journalist. They would let anyone in without training or anything—

GREGOR [*derisively*]: Yeah, the Wessis loved him because he had no past. He had actually been locked in a madhouse by the Stasi or something like that, if you were to believe his stories. Anyway, he came up with just crazy, crazy ideas, [*to Karl*] do you remember? He was there for I don't know how long, months anyway, and as time went on his stories got crazier and crazier, this stuff about the Stasi. [*Pauses.*] The last one, the clincher, was that he got it into his head that there were canisters of poison gas hidden out in the Baltic Sea and that he was going to find them. So this guy goes out of the office and *he hails a cab* because his driver's license had apparently been confiscated in 1976 *for political reasons*—[*miming a confidential aside*] yeah, only for political reasons I'm sure—and he takes this cab all the way up to Rostock, three hours away. And after a while the driver is looking around and saying, "Can you pay for this?" And the crazy guy says, "Listen, I don't have any money now but I'm with this important paper [*tugs at his collar*], you know, so just fill out a bill and send it to Berlin." So they get up to Rostock, and then the guy drops out of contact. I mean, he doesn't report to the office for three days. And, don't you know, the chief editor is completely calm, his attitude is "no problem." The first we hear of him is when somebody from the taxi company comes by the office three days later and says, "Oh, yes, we took one of your journalists up to Rostock, and by the way that'll be 3,000 marks" because the meter had been running for three days straight. And the chief editor is still ridiculously calm, "No problem," he says. "But could you tell me if you've seen or heard anything about our journalist?" Because he hadn't called in three days. The guy says, yeah, apparently he rented a boat out there and two divers. He didn't have any money for that

2. *Kumpel* is a term derived from mining and the life-or-death fraternity miners shared with one another. Like British mateship, being *Kumpel* is a working-class ethic that presupposes deep emotional loyalty between men.

either but he said [*another collar tug*], "I don't have any money right now but I'm with this very important paper, you know, so just send a bill to Berlin." So eventually the guy shows up back in Berlin at the end of the week, and meanwhile he's rented a car up there because it's occurred to him that that was cheaper than the cab. So the chief editor is like, "OK. Well at least you can show us the car so we know you're telling the truth," but, whoops, seems there was an accident on the way back. Because he didn't have a license he called his son up and his son rushed all the way to Rostock to drive him back, but on the way there was an accident and the car was totaled, and his son is dead or whatever. And the chief editor says, "Well, at least there must be a wreck somewhere between here and Rostock so we can confirm this story . . ." But no. Apparently it was all towed away by the police because there had been a Kalashnikov[3] in the car with them. "A Kalashnikov?" the chief editor asks. "Well, how did that get in there?" Apparently he had bought it from a Russian in Rostock and he wanted to bring it home as a souvenir. He was absolutely crazy this guy, but the West German editors would rather have this guy as a journalist than an East German; they thought he was great. But that's really the problem, you know; they would look at this bunch of East Germans dressed in shabby clothes with no pretensions or whatever, and then they'd see this guy all colorful and flashy who stormed into the job interview saying, "I know everything!" and they'd take him; that's the image they wanted. It wasn't just in journalism but everywhere there were Wessis flooding in.

DOMINIC: What happened to this guy in the end?

GREGOR: They put him back where he came from. He went back into the madhouse. The Wessis were desperate for people to staff these papers, and they couldn't get the kind of people they wanted. Let's look at the breakdown of the Wessis who came over here too. They're either in their twenties, hoping to make a career for themselves, or they're old, you know what I mean, too old to be employable anymore in the West, because they've lost their spirit or whatever. And everyone in between would have had to have been a madman to come over. There are no competent, respectable people in that age range at all. They come over only if they can't find a job in the West. I mean what guy who's thirty-five or forty-five and good at what he does is going to give up his ten or twelve thousand marks a month to come to Cottbus or some other stinkhole in the East and work for half the pay at a local paper [*Heimatzeitung*]? None of them, they're not crazy. So the breakdown of the

---

3. Soviet-era rifle.

Wessi group is always a few of these guys too young to know anything, then a few of these old sausages, and the rest are lunatics. I mean, the people who really couldn't find work in the West if they tried. And not just in journalism, that's the same everywhere, look at the Treuhand, for example, how many competent people did you have over there anyway? You had the young kids, the old folks, and the rest were lunatics. But better an insane West German than an East German. That was the motto back then.

After draining his beer, Gregor wipes his mouth on his sleeve and continues:

When Karl and I were first working together on this new start-up illustrated magazine for the East—it's since gone under, thank God—but when we were there, I was in charge of a local office in Magdeburg and I was desperately trying to recruit four or five good people to work with me there. But I couldn't do it for the life of me. The people were so stuck in their ways I couldn't budge any of them. I looked through all the papers and I went to the people who were working for the old GDR newspapers there, like the *Volksstimme,* and I said, "Listen, I can give you twice what you're making now, five or six thousand. Why don't you come and work for me instead?" But I couldn't get a single one of them to do it. I kept hearing: "Oh no, we'd rather stay here making twenty-five hundred a month or whatever. What you're suggesting sounds dangerous. We like our jobs." I couldn't believe it. I even put ads *in the paper.* I never could have imagined doing that in the West. I was thinking, here I am in a city of two hundred thousand people, why can't I find two or three competent journalists? I wouldn't even have cared if they'd had no training. All these unemployed journalists, and no one calls! So I am sitting around my office one day, getting really desperate, and I decide that no matter who it is, the next person who comes through my door is getting a job. Our phone number is still in the ads every day and finally someone walks through the door. He looks terrible, all disheveled, his hair's messed up and wouldn't you know it?! [*Slams his hand on the table.*] He was a West German! And he asks, "Is there any chance I could get some work here?" and I told him, "You're hired, here's your six thousand a month!" But it was terrible, the guy was awful. He was here in the East because he had gotten kicked out of, like, eight newspapers in the West. He came to work drunk all the time. He drank about twelve schnapps a day, and he was already drunk by about six in the morning. But that's the way it was. I couldn't find anyone else.

Restaurant Sternchen, Berlin

By the end of Gregor's tale of carpetbagger Wessis and timorous Ossis, we are all, Karl, Harold, Walter, Matthias, and myself, convulsing in tearful laughter. Together, we composed the regulars of a weekly *Stammtisch* that convened nearly every Monday night in 1996 and 1997 at a restaurant called Sternchen (Little Star) that is nestled imperviously among the towering high-rise apartment buildings of the Mitte district of former East Berlin. The restaurant has existed for many years, long a favored meeting spot of high-ranking party members who lived in the adjacent buildings. Remodeled in the early 1990s, Sternchen's interior is now dominated by lush configurations of dark wood and red brick. Plastic ivy climbs the walls in several spots. The restaurant is always noisy in the early evenings when we meet but also strangely cozy as the *Stammtisch* fills in a corner booth to create its communicative space. Looking across the other tables, one sees families out for dinner and groups of friends out for a drink after work or watching the football game on the television. A few tables over from our booth, another long-standing *Stammtisch*, this one of GDR sports reporters, meets on the same night of the week.

Our group requires a little biography. Gregor was only twenty-two and going to university in the West when the *Wende* came. He immediately dropped out and headed to Berlin, working on several different short-lived ventures before finally coming to *Super Illu* in 1990. Gregor is the only western regular of the *Stammtisch:* his incisive sarcasm and wit are appreciated by the group, especially when he directs it at other Wessis and their colonialist misadventures in the East. Like Marianne, Gregor often sought to define himself outside East/West duality. He once told me he considered himself, not a Wessi, but a Wossi, a liminal figure who tried to be equally critical and accepting of both the West and the East. Despite misgivings at Gregor's argumentativeness and his tendency to interrupt others, pick fights, and dominate discussions, I believe Gregor was accepted into the *Stammtisch* because the other regulars sensed he made an effort to be bipartisan with his criticism and sarcasm.

Karl is the other dominant personality of the *Stammtisch.* In a sense, it is "his" *Stammtisch.* After twenty-five years, he is the longest-standing member of the group and the one who had initially invited me to come and listen to their exchange of opinions. Karl grew up in a working-class family in Thüringen and came to journalism by working first at a factory newspaper. During a long career in the GDR media, Karl rose through the ranks of the ADN hierarchy to become one of General Secretary Honecker's protocolary journalists, which meant that he traveled with Honecker as part of his international entourage, transcribing speeches and writing reports on the various state events in which Honecker took part. Outside the context of the *Stammtisch,* Karl never discussed his professional history in detail with me other than to say that he was never in a real position of power or authority and that he had simply found his niche in a bad profession and had done his own share of work (*Stück Arbeit*) as honestly as he could. Yet, like Albert, Karl was relatively well known to other former GDR journalists, who were considerably more negative in their evaluations of him. For several, Karl represented the *Wendehals* (turn-neck) incarnate, a characterless opportunist who would thrive in any regime under any conditions and demands.

For my part, I was struck by the dialectical complexity of the memories Karl voiced at the *Stammtisch.* Although he often told us that GDR journalists as a whole were decent men (*anständige Menschen*) who did the best they could to practice their vocation cleanly, he also expressed a deep sense of shame at the party's *Lenkungssystem.* On several occasions Karl described himself as "a creative person," far more creative than the professional compromises of either GDR or FRG journalistic *Systeme* could satisfy. Now, in 1997, he channels much of his time into sideline interests. In the first year that I knew him, Karl built a house for one of his children, developed a game, outlined a novel restaurant concept with Harold and Matthias, and began organizing a business of blind-cleaning franchises.

Karl and Gregor are fond of one another although they clash often and sometimes bitterly, especially when the conversation turns to the herme- neutics of GDR history, which Karl feels Gregor is too immature to un- derstand fairly and which Gregor feels Karl is too historically encumbered (*belastet*) to judge accurately. Gregor often teases Karl about his past and his entanglement in the exteriorities of the GDR power apparatus. But when Karl narrates a story from his former professional life about his convivial interactions with top GDR functionaries, Gregor listens silently and respect- fully with a look that seems to me half-disbelief and half-wonder. Other- wise, on matters of current affairs, Gregor freely interrupts Karl whenever he disagrees with him, which is interpreted by the others perhaps as typical Wessi conflict mongering and disdain for others' opinions, and while Karl patiently, repeatedly pleads, "Could you *please* just let me finish?" Gregor drones on as though never hearing him.

To Karl's left is Harold, a man in his mid- to late forties who had also worked as a journalist at ADN before the *Wende*. Now he does mostly free- lance editing, translation, and writing. Harold is the quietest of the group; he has a calm, deliberate, thoughtful manner and speaks in a soft voice that is rarely audible unless you are sitting next to him. He is prone to sit silently for long stretches of conversation, smoking or cleaning his pipe with prac- ticed care. Harold, like Walter, differentiates his experience of the GDR from that of Karl, who he feels is somewhat too much an apologist for the GDR and its media. There is a good deal of history between the two of them that is never discussed openly in my presence but is often indexed obliquely. For example, whenever Karl asserts, as he often does, that all GDR journalists were "simply playthings in the hands of the power brokers," Harold inter- rupts him and quietly disagrees, "*I* wasn't a plaything, Karl," and then Karl lapses into silence.

Walter, to Harold's left, is Karl's age, wears horn-rimmed glasses with thick lenses that dominate his face, and is a former member of the Bürger- bewegung (civil rights movement) that developed in the GDR just before the *Wende*. He still works part-time for a grassroots organization that supports research on the victims of the GDR state and of Stasi terror. Walter had once been a professional photographer in the GDR but received a *Berufsverbot* for writing a letter addressed to Honecker asking why GDR citizens were not allowed to see their own Stasi files. For several years thereafter he made do in the demimonde of GDR intellectuals who had fallen out of favor with the regime. Unfortunately, because of his advancing age and the politics of the reunified German labor market, he never returned to photography professionally after 1989 and now is still forced to cobble together a living from several different sources: working at a museum, giving lectures, editing a small pamphlet on current affairs. He has been a *Kumpel* of Karl's and Harold's for a long time, but he is very fond of Gregor and his politics: they have in common a righteous disdain for the GDR System and its political legacy, as well as a livid desire to see those who profited from the System's calumny and terror finally brought to justice. This leads Walter into frequent disagreement with Karl, but unlike Karl's relationship with Gregor, the two always argue until they find some point on which they can agree.

Finally, to Walter's left is Matthias, the only regular at the *Stammtisch* without any prior or current journalistic experience. In fact, Matthias, now in his early forties, was formerly one of Honecker's battalion of chefs. Karl and Matthias have already coproduced a cookbook for the GDR nostalgia market with recipes from Honecker's state dinners. Matthias tends to withdraw from the political debates and to turn the conversation toward vacations, restauranting, the minor absurdities of western society, and so on; he is still a chef and restaurant owner.

It is a lively circle, and Gregor, at the end of one evening, tells me how lucky I am to have found such a representative sample of Germany before 1989. Chuckling, he points to everyone putting their jackets on, "Look [*gesturing to Walter*], you've got the civil rights' guy, [*to Karl*] the OM,[4] and then me, the Wessi asshole."

⦿⦿⦿

The *Stammtisch* (literally, "tribal table") is a venerable political and social institution in Central Europe where a group of individuals, usually exclusively men, gather together at the same table at the same local pub on the same night of every week to discuss the relevant issues of the day and to drink a great deal of beer. Traveling in some of Germany's smaller towns, one still finds certain tables in pubs reserved with a "*Stammtisch*" sign on them. Historically, *Stammkneipen* (regulars' pubs) were particularly important sites for *gemütliches Beisammensein* (convivial togetherness) among the working classes. Some also became *Parteilokale* (party pubs) in the late nineteenth century for communist and social democratic movements. They permitted political gatherings and communication relatively insulated

---

4. *Offizieller Mitarbeiter* (official employee of the state). Gregor is playing on the terminology for Stasi informants, who are labeled *IM*, or "unofficial" employees of the state security apparatus. In Gregor's joking, Karl's complicity with the GDR System is a constant theme.

from the state surveillance of print media and public gatherings. In an excellent study of alcohol use in nineteenth-century Hamburg working-class life, Ulrich Wyrwa writes:

> The regulars' and corner pubs were crystallization points for the political education of the workers, sites of their *Meinungsbildung* [education of opinions], and for communication among themselves. These pubs connected the social and political aspects of the workers' struggle and drew this energy into the workers' movement. Especially in times of political oppression, pubs served as communication and distribution centers for working-class organizations. The informal political debates in the pubs then found their public expression in events organized by the workers' movement. (1990: 208; see also Evans 1989; Lidtke 1985: 55–56)

Now by no means limited to lower-class strata, *Stammtische* continue to serve as local forums for the exchange of news and opinion and avid political debates and as informal loci in intellectual culture for the hermeneutics of everyday life (see Karp 1980; Rotenberg 1984; Thornton 1987: 109–10). In this capacity, the open dialogical character of the *Stammtisch* inverts certain formal conventions of the public sphere (*Öffentlichkeit*); around the table, passions and humor are heated, differences of opinion can be fierce, and verbal play is expected and affirmed. For these reasons, some of my journalist friends and academic interlocutors seemed somewhat shocked that I was participating in a *Stammtisch*. They described *Stammtische* as dangerous political spaces where wasted time, bawdy jokes, and beer merged with vulgar political and moral judgments.

The sociolinguistic conventions of a *Stammtisch* are indeed antihierarchical and vulgate. The *Stammtisch* is a place for *Kumpel* (mates) to gather together, and even complete strangers will use the informal "*Du*" with one another. In contrast to public situations where maintaining personal distance is formally observed, at the *Stammtisch* men hug one another, slap each other on the back, and by the end of an evening will call each other "*mein lieber.*" The dynamics of the *Stammtisch* do not exactly correspond to the deeper intimacy of domestic or family space, however. The fraternity of the *Stammtisch* is transient and predicated upon the temporary creation of an informal masculine[5] space where the responsibilities and accountabilities of domestic relationships can be escaped through serious discussion and

---

5. I did attend a *Stammtisch* of former members of the GDR civil rights movement on one occasion that seemed to have at least one female regular.

through joking (Papataxiarchis 1991: 176). In this respect, the *Stammtisch* belongs to a broad category of "private-public" voluntary domains and rituals in German society, as do contemporary *Vereine* (clubs, interests groups) wherein convivial, relatively nonhierarchical relationships are cultivated between individuals sharing common interests or convictions (Eidson 1990).

Like coffeehouses and men's clubs (Festa n.d.) in many parts of the world, the *Stammtisch* is a "political arena, at once actual and expressive" (Herzfeld 1985: 152). It thrives on the negotiation of social knowledge and interpretive meaning, and it demands from its participants a poetic virtuosity with language and analysis no less a matter of genius than the rigor of academic theory. At the Sternchen *Stammtisch*, the group's intellectualism was marked by our consistent focus on the conversation itself and by our relative suspension of contextual attention. Environmental phenomena ranging from the murmur of a television with the soccer game in the distance, to the incessant warbling of British pop music, to the presence of other patrons in the bar were considered extraneous or trivial and never commented upon. The only purpose for leaving the table was to visit the bathroom; as though respecting the desire for a reciprocal lack of intrusion from the outside, our waitress would silently refill beers as soon as the glass was empty without waiting to be asked.

National and regional politics and historical events dominated most of the conversations at which I was present: we debated the contemporary politics of unified Germany and East/West relations exhaustively as well as the Stasi legacy and what should be done about it, former GDR elites and what ought to be done with them, many minor events in German history, the politics of the reunified media, unemployment and economic stagnation, workplace issues, the rebuilding of Berlin, and, for my benefit presumably, America and its relationship to Germany. Domestic themes were generally avoided; in the months I attended the *Stammtisch*, despite the stereotype of "East German warmth," I never learned the name of anyone's wife, nor were spouses or families often raised as topics of discussion.

I, too, was incidental to the primary dynamics of the group in the sense that I occupied a discretionary "honored guest" status as one of Karl's and later Gregor's *Kumpel*. In this identity as a marked outsider, I was by no means allowed to blend into the woodwork. Gregor and Harold in particular were very interested in my field research and about how I was planning to portray East German journalists and their past complicities. Harold and I had a few tense situations when he tried to pin me down on exactly what the thesis of my dissertation would be while I hedged that the only way to avoid caricatures would be to present a full spectrum of opinions. Gregor, who, like Harold, favored a critical representation of the GDR media, would often code-switch into English to provide commentary to me on some debate that was going on at the table, in part to differentiate himself from the rest of the group, solidifying our identification as *Westmenschen* (western people), and in part simply to pique Karl, who did not speak English and who would then be forced to call to Gregor, "Stop speaking English to him! He's supposed to learn German here!" Karl was particularly interested in asking me more about America and about which of his entrepreneurial schemes and literary side-projects might find a market there.

Over time, I cultivated friendly relationships with all of the *Stammtisch* members. I was generally treated as a naïve, if well-meaning, foreigner who needed the complexities of German history and society explained to him lest he fall under the sway of ideologists. Occasionally, however, my Americanness was signaled in reference to provocations about the *blöde Amis* (dumb Yanks) in the spirit of the following exchange:

GREGOR [*jabbing his finger*]: On the topic of dumb Americans—[*aside, to Dominic*] no offense—I have a friend who's up in Rostock right now and he's making a killing offering trips to groups of American tourists from Warnemünde to Rostock for about $50 each. You know, Warnemünde is like one train stop away from Rostock, so the tickets cost him maybe four marks each way, the trains would run anyway, but he takes the Americans down there to Rostock and then [*mimes looking at his watch*] lets them run around a little bit, then they meet back at the train station and he takes them back to Warnemünde. It's a great business. And now he's offering a special deal, from Rostock to Berlin on the train for $400. [*Roars of laughter from the table.*] You know, how much does that cost? Maybe fifty marks or whatever, because none of them know any better.

KARL [*to Dominic*]: You know, you may be missing a great opportunity here. Forget this book and stay and open a tourist office for your American countrymen.

DOMINIC: Sure, I could offer $100 trips to Köpenick.

GREGOR: I've always thought that if you really wanted rake in the money, all you'd have to do is rebuild some of the Wall. There are, what, 180 million Americans over there and the only thing they know about Berlin is the Wall and then they come here, just like my uncle from California, and the first thing he says to me when he meets me here is "Where's the Wall? I can't find the Wall!" It's true, they all want to see the Wall, they've all got pieces of it at home. All you'd have to do is to rebuild a part of it, 300 meters or so, and then charge admission and they'd all come and pay to see it.

HAROLD: And for $1,500 then you could be shot by a real border guard.

GREGOR: Yeah [*laughs*], that's what Berlin ought to do, rebuild some of the Wall as a tourist attraction.

HAROLD [*to Dominic*]: But then half of the Wall is already back in your home now.

DOMINIC: But only in small, colorful pieces.

HAROLD: Yes, that's all the Wall is now, isn't it, a few colorful pieces of art.

DOMINIC [*laughing*]: Maybe one of you should just rebuild a bit of the Wall in your garden and then charge admission. The Americans won't know the difference.

HAROLD [*seriously*]: But, Dominic, what you have to understand is that what the Wall was wasn't just the physical object; it stood for the whole System. You'd have to rebuild the entire System.

DOMINIC: No, I know that, I just meant that for many tourists the Wall is only a few colorful chips of concrete.

HAROLD: That's right, that's what it has become. But what the Wall was wasn't just the Wall, even if you threw in the minefields and the barbed wire and the guard towers. It was more than all of that—it was the whole System in the GDR.

In this exchange, as in so many others, the fluidity of levity and gravity, irony and tragedy, at the *Stammtisch* becomes apparent, as a running joke evolved into emotionally laden reflection upon the GDR System. The conversational shifts from joking to recollection to social analysis, and the rapid shifts of idioms and tropes make the interpretations and opinions cascading around the table difficult to codify as the negotiation of stable, social "knowledge." Yet epistemic order was continuously staked and at stake as we sought to persuade one another of our interpretations of events in the outside world or to ask questions of interest or clarification.

The ratio of serious judgment to serious play fluctuated depending on mood, on theme, and on the contributors to the conversation. Yet, when the *Stammtisch* conversation came to focus on the significance of GDR history, as it invariably did, I found that the discussion quickly became emotionally charged, more highly charged than with reference to any other topic. The arbitration of East German *Vergangenheitsbelastung* immediately captured the attention and emotion of the group, in large part because of the group's rare juxtaposition of self-identifying East Germans and a West German and because of the division among the East Germans between those who stood "against the System" (Walter and Harold) and those who stood "for it" (Karl, even though he vigorously resisted the others' characterization of him in this way). The GDR System, often in comparison to the FRG System, was a constant point of departure and return in our conversations and continuously bent, as noted in chapter 4, seemingly unrelated discourse back into dialectical knowledge of the "burden of German history" and to the particular contribution of the GDR to that burden.

Karl was particularly passionate about how the postunification state had handled GDR history. He often spoke bitterly of a West German predisposition to obliterate any trace of past history that did not conform to the ideological conditions they set for the future. As Karl once noted grimly, "These West Germans can tolerate the imperial past and they can tolerate the next millennium, but nothing in between." Karl complained to me on several occasions both at and away from the *Stammtisch* about the mean-spirited *Siegerjustiz* (victors' justice) of the West Germans whereby they felt it necessary to erase all traces of the GDR, including the positive ones, in order to render their domination of East Germans, their identities, labors, and memories complete.

Karl's complaints clearly irked Gregor, who felt that West Germans, although they had admittedly made some mistakes with the *Treuhand*, had done the best they could in an impossible situation to transpose the East as rapidly as possible to FRG societal, technological, and political standards, a transposition, he asserted, for which the East German people had themselves voted in March 1990. Moreover, Gregor admitted an utter lack of empathy for why anyone would want to maintain legacies from the GDR anyway: for him, it was clearly the second German dictatorship and a dangerous and shameful historical legacy for the newly unified nation-state. The other *Stammtisch* regulars rarely echoed Karl's indignation to the same degree. Most of them felt much more ambivalently about the GDR and were less apt to describe events since 1989 as part of a western conspiracy to erase their identity. But likewise, many of them resisted Gregor's naturalization of the process of imposing FRG standards, suggesting at various points that the West German System had its own shameful legacies (particularly with regard to its normalization of many NSDAP members) and that those calling for the *Aufarbeitung* (working through) of the GDR past had never been subjected to the same scrutiny.

As evidence to support his interpretation of postunification reconstruction efforts, Karl once raised the controversial topic of the stalled renovation of the Palast der Republik, the former GDR state "hall of the people" in the Mitte district of Berlin (Glaeser n.d.). Karl described how, in his opinion, the West Berlin political elites had closed it under the pretense of asbestos removal, anticipating a more favorable political climate for tearing it down along with other monuments of the GDR era:

KARL [*loudly and with certainty*]: It was a clear political decision to close the Palast der Republik. Because of the functions it served during the GDR, because of its history. They [the West Germans] say that there's asbestos in the building and that's why they had to close it to the public. But it's been closed now for five years! So that was obviously just an excuse to keep the building closed. At the same time, the same time mind you, that these reports of asbestos in the Palast der Republik came out they also reported that there was asbestos found in one of the government buildings in the West. Well, they had that building cleaned out and reopened within a couple of months, so obviously there's more to the story here. They probably only assigned a few workers to do the job.

HAROLD: But, Karl, it's not quite as simple as that. What you also must take into account is that they can't reopen it to serve its former purpose as a center for the people that it had during the GDR, and no one's come up with an idea yet for what to do with it.

GREGOR: It's really lived up to its moniker as the Ballast der Republik.

KARL [*waving dismissively at Harold*]: There's no reason why they couldn't find something to do with it if they wanted to. [*To Dominic:*] You must understand that this building is considered something of an architectural marvel worldwide. . . . There's nothing like it anywhere, and during the GDR, experts used to come from around the world to study its construction—

MATTHIAS: The entire building had something like four bowling alleys, fifteen restaurants, bars, everything you can imagine.

KARL: It was a place where families could go and enjoy themselves. It was someplace for the normal people to enjoy themselves. And this is also a building of historical significance—it was in this building in the parliament [*Volkskammer*] where the German reunification was voted into existence!

DOMINIC: Well, they won't tear it down then; they'll probably give it some kind of protected status.

KARL: Probably, yes, but that hasn't happened yet.

MATTHIAS [*grabbing Karl and hugging him*]: It's also remembered for such famous phrases as "*Ich liebe Euch doch alle!*" [*Laughs.*][6]

---

6. The allusion is to a statement allegedly made by ex-Stasi chief Erich Mielke to the GDR *Volkskammer* during the *Wende:* "But I *do* love you all!" Over the ensuing years, Mielke's statement has become a popular metaphor for the SED elite's utter lack of awareness of the depth of popular animosity toward their regime.

KARL: The decision to close the *Palast* was a definitely politically motivated action, don't believe anything else. The West Germans don't want it there, it doesn't fit into their vision of Berlin, so they closed it until the situation progresses to the point that they can tear it down without too much trouble. But this asbestos story is just a ruse; they think people are stupid enough not to see what's going on. I remember one time I was there poking around, and there was a group of politicians from Bonn there at the same time touring the place and they had these little rags covering their mouths. That shows you how foolish these people are, that they play along with this.

GREGOR: Listen, if it was all a political decision then they would have just turned the building over to the *Treuhand* along with every other GDR dinosaur, and it would have been sold to some western firm for about one mark and now it'd be a big hole in the ground. But that didn't happen, did it? So I don't think you can say it was a political decision.

KARL [*trembling with anger*]: It *was* a political decision.

Karl was convinced that the West German powers-that-be (*Machthaber*) in unified Germany were continually plotting to erase the cultural, political, social, and architectural legacies of the GDR in order to harmonize the public culture and built environment of the unified German nation-state with their own System. Karl had lived and worked near a vortex of Systemic power for many decades and said he had an almost instinctive feeling for the matrix of forces and interests that governed the lives of playthings (*Spielzeuge*) like him. He articulated his sense of relentless western Systemic insinuation into the "East German" lifeworld both orally and somatically as he trembled and turned red denying Gregor's claims of a disinterested closing of the *Palast*. Such unrest was less marked with the other regulars. Calmly cleaning his pipe, Harold, for example, once proposed a class idiom for the dissolution of the "East German heritage," explaining that it was simply another instance of the rich occluding the histories, identities, and contributions of the poor. ("Everything I've seen in Germany since 1989 makes me believe that the ostensible difference between West and East has gradually become a difference between rich and poor.")

Gregor, in the exchange above, as in others to which I was witness, took Karl to task for presuming conspiracy in every misadventure instead of simply recognizing the imperfect process of normalization to the standards of a civilized democratic society. Karl asserted on several occasions that he was convinced that no former GDR Politburo member would ever receive a fair trial in the FRG, nor should they even be tried, he continued, since they were government officials of a foreign regime, not war criminals.[7] When Karl once said he felt that the West German judges serving at the trial of Egon Krenz and Günter Schabowski were tied down (*angebunden*) as to what judgment they could possibly render, it was Gregor's turn to register bodily anger: he rose out of his chair in professed shock and dismay that Karl would question the autonomy of the German judicial system ("You're being ridiculous, Karl! To which Karl replied, "Show me a System where the judges aren't *angebunden*!").

For Gregor, even if he, like Habermas, was ambivalent about the perfection of the western System, the relatively greater *Prägung* and perversity of the GDR System was blindingly clear to him. As he voiced on several occasions, these former GDR Politburo members had been complicit in maintaining the shoot-to-kill order for the poor souls trying to escape the country, they had implicitly supported the Stasi, and they therefore were individually accountable, like the Nazi leadership circle, for a System that held its citizens in a state of captivity and terror. Gregor wondered aloud how Germany was supposed to start its reincarnated "wholeness" with a modicum of moral character if such criminals and opportunists (or "dirty assholes" as Gregor more often characterized them) were granted clemency? How Karl could fail to recognize the independent justice of a guilty verdict astonished him, and Gregor said he had to assume then that either Karl was blind to the terrible things that happened during the GDR or he was an apologist for them.

Karl responded that Gregor would never understand how the System worked in the GDR or the pressure that the GDR government was under from the Soviets and that furthermore Gregor was naïve to think that his own government did not include the same kind of corrupt and self-interested people as the GDR had. For Karl, the FRG System was also imperfect, coercive, and dehumanizing, so who were West German politicians, as the stewards of that System, to pass judgment on East German politicians' morality and ethics? Karl argued that Krenz and Schabowski could not be set free

7. During my fieldwork in 1996 and 1997, four surviving GDR Politburo members (Horst Dohlus, Gunther Kleiber, Egon Krenz, and Günter Schabowski) were tried in German courts for culpability for the deaths of GDR citizens shot while trying to cross the border to the FRG. All were eventually found guilty but given limited sentences. The legality of the trials was hotly debated in the German media as well as by the public (see Borneman 1997 on the praxis of retributive justice in postunification Germany). Former GDR citizens were particularly polarized—many thought the Politburo members were criminals and ought to be punished but felt angry that the West Germans had arrogated the right to judge East Germans' history for them.

because they, like all East Germans, still had to be made into scapegoats to bear the common burden of German history and its Systemic failures.

Karl and Gregor's arguments—their exchanges more often than not dominated the *Stammtisch* when the conversation turned toward the GDR and its political legacy (with the rest of us remaining quietly attentive for long stretches)—would often develop this way, falling back quickly from the immediate point of conflict into more durable lines of negative dialectical entrenchment: for Gregor, the GDR was the "second German dictatorship" that had added to the moral and cultural burden upon Germany created by the first German dictatorship and its crimes against humanity. Those culpable for the "East German past" therefore had to be judged and punished in order to move forward with establishing a democratic civilized order in the East and to guarantee the integrity of democratic values in the unified state. Gregor spoke constantly of the need to "work through this [GDR] past" and to assign blame and to punish its historical perpetrators. For Karl, the "East German past" was criminalized precisely so that the West Germans could force the East Germans to exclusively carry the moral burden of collective German history, thereby eliding the need for critical discourse on their own imperfect System.

Just as Karl would often initiate conflict with Gregor by criticizing the western obliteration of positive aspects of GDR history, Gregor would drive Karl to exasperation with what Karl saw as an obsession with the veracity of the Stasi files as a scale of judgment upon which one could weigh the moral purity of every former citizen of the GDR, separating them into traditional categories of accountability: *Opfer* (victims) and *Täter* (perpetrators). Karl, like others of my interlocutors, was more apt to characterize the majority of GDR citizens as *normale Mitläufer* (normal, marginally complicit "fellow travelers"), with a small elite circle in the Politburo responsible for defining the core principles of state ideology and thus bearing the primary burden of moral accountability for the spiritually corrupt and corrupting System that had crystallized around these core principles. Karl recoiled from what he interpreted as Gregor's effort to make "normal people" like him responsible for the GDR System.

During my months at the *Stammtisch,* Gregor declared a personal vendetta against Manfred Stolpe, (now former) minister president of the federal state of Brandenburg (SPD party), an exceedingly popular eastern German politician with a professional background as the consistorial president of the GDR Protestant church and with strongly suspected, yet inconclusively proven, ties to the Stasi. Gregor, clearly frustrated with his own inability to find any conclusive evidence of Stasi connections, characterized Stolpe as the personification of the duplicity and corruption of the GDR. Although Karl also believed Stolpe was lying about his past and said that he would not mind seeing this Janus-faced minion of the SED go either, he was uncomfortable with the self-righteous and credulous tone of Gregor's hunt for Stasi evidence. In the following exchange, Gregor launched into a half-serious drunken tirade about Stolpe that set Karl on edge:

GREGOR [*leaning in, pointing his finger*]: That dirty asshole Stolpe—he's lied and lied and lied. Lied his way right up to the top, pretending he's this great democrat when in the GDR he was a spy and an informer. He was completely an ally of the SED the whole time, and now he plays the role of this great church man and this great democrat. It pisses me off that this guy snaked his way into a legitimate party and then into the government. At least you can say that, for Gysi,[8] he went into the right party for his background, the SED or PDS or whatever; at least he's *that* honest. But Stolpe, it drives me crazy to think I have to live in the same place as that asshole and that liar playing the great democrat when in reality he was completely supporting the GDR regime. I think it's horrible that someone like him could become minister president of somewhere I have to live. [*To Dominic:*] It'd be as if an old KGB man came to the United States and got elected president. [*Everyone laughs.*] I'm not going to stop until I get this bastard [*turns to talk to Walter*].

DOMINIC [*to Karl*]: What did they find in Stolpe's Stasi files anyway?

KARL: Stasi files . . . [*Waves his hand in disdain.*] You're never going to find a file that explains what Stolpe is. Stolpe is a SED man through and through, one who was sent to represent the SED in the church. I have proof of that.

DOMINIC: You mean he was recruited then?

KARL: Yes, he was recruited but by the SED, not by the Stasi. Let me explain something. The SED never left anything to chance. What they did was select certain people very young, when they were in the FDJ cadre and they would groom them to go on and take leading roles in the "opposition" parties or in the church. They were there, you know, to keep an eye on things and just to attempt to steer things in the SED direction or to make sure that at least no one strayed too far. So they'd come to you while you were in the FDJ and say, "You go to the church," or "You go to the farmers' party and make sure that they abide by the party line." And this guy worked for the LDPD but at home he had his SED party book locked away in the safe; this guy went

---

8. Gregor Gysi is a former member of the Bundestag and fraction leader of the Partei des Demokratischen Sozialimus (PDS). Gysi has also been the object of a concerted public campaign of discreditation for inconclusively proven Stasi ties.

to the NDPD[9] but at home he kept his SED party book in the safe. They recruited these young prospects to do this, and so it came to be that the best comrades were often actually in the other parties, to keep an eye on them and to influence their decisions. Even though they already had all the power in the GDR, the SED *never* left anything to chance. But you see, there are no records of this, no files, it has nothing to do with the Stasi, it went higher than them. The SED was the ruling party and the Stasi were subordinate to them. The SED was the authority. Everything was taken care of orally, or with a handshake after a brief discussion, so you're never going to find evidential proof of it. They left no paper trail. I became sure of this with Stolpe when in 1988 there was an article published in *Neues Deutschland*. Stolpe had made some move to speak out against how the regime was handling church affairs, and so of course they ran this article criticizing Stolpe in *ND*. I know for a fact that this article was written by Honecker personally although there was no mention of that, of course. The article said at the very end after criticizing Stolpe for taking a hostile attitude toward the state, the very last line was "Herr Stolpe would do well to remember his experiences in the FDJ," and then I knew immediately for certain what he was, what position he had been given. But that's how the subtle use of the language is, and no [*waving his arm with annoyance at Gregor, who is obliviously talking to Walter*] West German journalist is ever going to be able to understand it; the West German journalist doesn't *want* to understand this, but that's how it actually was. Sometime in the 1950s there was a conversation between Stolpe and Honecker when Honecker was the head of the FDJ, we know that much, but there is no file in the world where it is written down what happened at that meeting. But I'll tell you what probably happened. Honecker said to Stolpe, "We think you're a fine loyal young man, and we need someone like you in the church, to be our man in the church," and that was it. They shook hands and that was it. That was the decisive moment for Stolpe, because once you were in, you were in. Once you were a SED man, then you were a SED man for life. That explains Stolpe to me: he was a consummate SED man. And if you were a powerful SED man already, then of course the Stasi didn't or couldn't have anything to do with you. You went above the Stasi, you went right to the top, you were insulated from the Stasi really. They couldn't touch someone who was a real SED man. But the West Germans [*pointing to Gregor*] keep on with their Stasi files. They keep thinking they're going to find a file

9. The LDPD (Liberal-Demokratische Partei Deutschlands) and NDPD (National-Demokratische Partei Deutschlands) were two of the GDR so-called block parties, opposition parties managed and kept artificially weak by the SED in order to preserve the international image of a multiparty state.

somewhere that proves Stolpe was one of them. He was one of them, but they'll never find that file, and the West Germans simply can't accept that. It's always the Stasi, always the files with them, over and over again, but they don't understand how the System worked. I remember I was in the Central Committee building once in the 1980s, and who did I see coming down the stairs from the Central Committee chamber but Stolpe. He was definitely one of them, but there'll never be concrete proof of that.

DOMINIC: I have noticed this need to find written proof of everything.

KARL: They always want to find it in the documents, yes. [*To Gregor and Walter, who have gradually begun paying attention to our conversation:*] As I was just saying to Dominic here, Stolpe's connection went right to the top in the Central Committee and not to the Stasi; that wasn't necessary. They'll never find any concrete proof of that because there were a few minutes or an hour perhaps when Honecker gave Stolpe the assignment to be the SED man in the church and *that was the decisive factor* for Stolpe. Everything that came afterward [*shakes his head and crosses his arms*] is just nothing by comparison. And this West German here doesn't want to believe that.

GREGOR [*waving his hands in the air*]: OK, I take your point, Karl, but then why don't you come to my defense then in the office when I say we need to do more on Stolpe or whatever and I then get these strange reactions from certain of our colleagues along the lines of "Oh, that fucking Wessi hard-liner is at it again, trying to uncover more Stasi dirt! Why doesn't he just be quiet?!"?

KARL [*shrugging*]: Well, because I don't think you're going to find any evidence—

WALTER [*to Gregor*]: It's because you're coming from blackest Bavaria[10] and trying to work on this issue! [*Laughs.*]

KARL: There's not going to be any proof, I think. There's no written record of this, and you can't just go around writing what you *think* might have happened. The problem is no one will ever know what actually happened—

GREGOR: But I just can't abide such a dirty asshole like Stolpe running around scot-free. I'm not going to rest until I get him.

KARL: Wait, let me just finish—

GREGOR [*laughing, thumping his fist on the table*]: It's war! It's war! It's time to get serious about fighting this asshole!

10. Walter is playing on the heraldry of the German parties. Each political party, as well as constellation of political sympathies, is associated with a color in popular discourse: red for the Sozialdemokratische Partei Deutschlands, pink or red for the PDS, yellow for the Freie Demokratische Partei, green for the Greens, brown for Nazis and Neo-Nazis, and black for the Christlich-Demokratische Union and its Bavarian sister party, the Christlich-Soziale Union. Thus, "from blackest Bavaria" signifies being from the indexical depths of regional opposition as well as from an area associated with "black," or "conservative," politics.

WALTER [*laughing, to Dominic*]: It's war for him now, he's a war correspondent.

DOMINIC: But he's in the war himself.

WALTER: That's right, he's in the war himself, so we need a war correspondent to write about him.

KARL: I can't possibly be party to this kind of coarse journalism. [*Standing up to go to the bathroom, patting Gregor on the back.*] You need facts to write the story and I don't think you'll ever find them.

GREGOR [*still thumping his fist*]: Who needs facts? This is war! [*Laughing.*]

Once Gregor had succeeded in dissipating his frustration into a joke, it was impossible for Karl to get him to acknowledge what he felt was a serious shortcoming of "West German journalism" when it came to locating accountability for the GDR System. Gesturing toward Gregor across the table, Karl was himself able temporarily to localize and anthropomorphize his sense of frustration with the "coarse" and credulous reliance of western journalists on the facticity of Stasi involvement in the absence of a more nuanced, experiential understanding of the political dynamics of the GDR System. Karl attempted on several occasions to educate Gregor that complicity within the GDR System was a far more complex phenomenon than the archive of the Stasi files could articulate, but Gregor did not seem keen to listen to him, instead joking about Karl's apologetics for the "dirty assholes" or reasserting the legitimacy of interpreting the GDR in bipolar terms of accountability. After Karl returned from the bathroom, he tried again, this time with a personal anecdote, to explain to Gregor that being "an informer" did not imply homogeneous practices or sympathies:

KARL: You see, not every informer in the GDR was run by the Stasi. I remember when I was in the FDJ brigade in Thüringen, there was a pastor down there who was very critical of the GDR. I was in one of the leading positions in the local FDJ group, and we were requested, not by the Stasi but by the party, to go down to a church meeting and see what was going on and to come back and report about it. [*Gregor jerks his thumb at Karl and shakes his head at Dominic in disbelief.*] Things like that *could* happen; it was the only time I was asked, thankfully.

GREGOR [*confidentially to Dominic*]: Sure, the *only* time . . .

KARL: So we went down to the meeting. There were four or five of us, and since I had a religious background, I was there singing all the songs, but then the pastor gave his sermon and I was so enthralled by it that I forgot everything about which I was supposed to report when I went back. The point is only that this sort of thing was very common and didn't involve reporting to the Stasi at all.

WALTER: I have a personal story that can confirm that too. In the fifties, my mother was approached by the party. They wanted her to join the GDR Christian Democratic party because of our Christian background and so that she could then keep an eye on them. But because of my father's history, informers were completely loathed and hated in my family, so she flatly refused them. Then later, when the Stasi tried to recruit me, it was the same story, no chance, because of our family past. You see, I was actually born in Düsseldorf but then my family moved to the East after the war and my mother became a SED member in 1948. My father was killed by the Nazis in 1943 because he was denounced by someone for being involved in a communist-led movement to end the war. But my father was no communist at all, the farthest thing from it. He was a monarchist during the Weimar Republic. He just wanted the war to end.

GREGOR [*incredulously to Walter*]: You say you were born in *Düsseldorf?*

WALTER: Yes.

GREGOR: Then why on earth did your family come over here? Were they idiots? You could be driving around in your Mercedes right now as we speak. What a bunch of fools. They had already escaped! Why on earth would they come back? You must have foolishness in your roots there. [*Laughs.*]

WALTER [*earnestly and somewhat taken aback*]: We came because we thought the GDR was the best chance available to fight against fascism.

GREGOR: But then for God's sake why did you stay when you saw how it really was?

WALTER [*seriously*]: I was just a child at the time.

GREGOR: No, no, later, why did you stay?

WALTER [*quietly*]: My mother, relatives, family, then later, my wife, and our family. [*Shrugs; Gregor continues to stare at him in utter disbelief.*]

KARL [*whispering to Dominic*]: That is a very German story, isn't it?

Gregor knew a great deal about GDR history, far more than most of my western interlocutors, but he nevertheless demonstrated a genuine inability to conceptualize life in the GDR as "normal" in any sense. In his disbelieving interrogation of Walter about why anyone would voluntarily remain in the GDR, he indexed a vision of the GDR as so monstrous a penitentiary that no positive sociality in the terms with which he was familiar could have existed within its pure, terrible System. Gregor's playful shouts of "It's war! It's war!" articulated a more serious, sober, and fundamental apprehension of the GDR as a place of total *Prägung*, agglomerating the worst traits of German culture and history. In fairness to the heterogeneity of his disdain, Gregor also privately expressed sympathy to me for the frustration of East Germans with the West German guidance of reunification. On several occasions, he criticized the Wessis who came over to make fast money after the *Wende* as having ruined any potential for future trust between the two sides. The problem was, Gregor maintained, that cleansing postunification society of Stasi informers and similar residue of GDR power was a moral imperative regardless of how painful or poorly administered the process was. The *Bildung* of postunification society depended upon this cleansing. Moreover, Gregor regarded efforts to compare the two German Systems as disingenuous since it was abundantly clear to him that the FRG System was no dictatorship and thus not part of the same "authoritarian tradition" that had produced the GDR and the Third Reich.

Karl, for his part, saw Gregor's compulsive derogation of the GDR System as evidence that West Germans would not or could not understand the immanence of Systems, their perhaps superficially different forms yet commonly inhuman and exterior apparatus of power. He cited Gregor's innocence regarding the way the FRG System really worked, how Gregor's own lack of experience and idealism made it impossible for him to recognize the comprehensive totality of Systemic operations that abandoned "nothing to chance." Karl often seemed to feel sorry for what he perceived as Gregor's naïveté, attributing this to his youth as much as to his "westernness." He sought, paternally, I felt, like a father trying to prepare his son for some unpleasant future encounter, to explain to Gregor the complexities of System and the compromises it eventually exacted from every "creative person." The compromise of Spirit with System, as Karl whispered, was "a very German story" for him. For Karl, Germanness was defined by the same capitulation of Spirit to System that Thomas Mann had categorically denied in his portrait of the "dialectical German." Part of being German and a plaything of power, for Karl, was coming to terms with a Luhmannian vision of System as societal order for-its-own-sake. As his *Kumpel*, Karl tried to prevent Gregor from behaving as a "typical West German" and from participating in the false consciousness and moralizing of the FRG as a "free society."

Gregor expressed a reciprocal paternalism toward Karl as a decent man who was the victim of historical circumstances and a System beyond his agency. Alone together on another occasion at the end of a long night at the *Stammtisch*, Gregor told me that he respected the decisions Karl had made during and since the *Wende:*

GREGOR: Karl was one of the assistant directors of ADN at the end. In 1989, there was the director and three or four assistants and Karl was one of them. He was also the only one of them [*tapping his forehead*] who seemed to have any clue of what was going on and that there were big changes coming. Burda[11] was looking for office space, which was incredibly scarce back then because of state ownership, and Karl said, "Look, we have this huge building and we don't even need all of the space. We used to have one floor just for the party functionaries, and now they're all gone. That's one floor free. We used to have a floor of administrative stuff and they're all gone. We used to have a floor for the Stasi; [*laughing*] now they're all gone. So we have all these rooms free. Why don't you come in and take them over?" So Karl helped Burda to arrange the deal and in turn all he wanted was a job. That was actually very smart of him. He didn't want anything more than that, just a job, and that got him off the sinking ship. That's how he came to work with us. I mean Burda offered him I think 6,000 marks a month, but this was 1990 you've got to understand, before the currency union. There were still East marks floating around back then, and suddenly he's making 6,000 West marks! That must have been a fortune for him. And he's probably still making the same amount that he was back then, but that's fine for what he's doing. I don't think Karl was ever really interested in making a career here in the West; that wasn't what it was about for him. He just wanted a job to cover him for the next ten years or so until he could retire. He must be in his early fifties by now I guess—

DOMINIC: Or older.

GREGOR [*confidentially*]: Yeah, and listen, he's not doing a great job here; he's not the best journalist we have. He's doing a mediocre job, but that's all that he needs to do in his position, and all he really wants anyway is just to do his job quietly and then to be able to retire. And that's to his credit, I think. He never had any ambition to take on a leadership position here, that's not what he wants, and so, for what's expected of him, doing a mediocre job is just fine. I mean, I know a lot of people in similar jobs who are worse than he is. That's why he's made it, I think, because there were a lot of other people from the East whom we took on back then and none of them are here anymore, but Karl made this deal and he stuck to it. I mean, he knows that for thirty years he was something else, and he knows that you can't just start over and pretend like nothing ever happened. I think he's kind of given up on journalism anyway, because he did something completely different for thirty years or whatever and he doesn't really want to try to start over

11. Burda Verlag is the publisher of *Super Illu*.

again in this System. But that's why he's still here, because he hasn't tried
to become powerful; he's just gone about his job. I mean, the guy is building
two houses right now for his kids, he's got all of these other projects, like this
game thing here and lots of others, and that's where he's putting his energy
now. He doesn't really have the energy for journalism anymore. But I can
respect that, given his history. At least he's not trying to lie about it.

By differentiating Karl from the category of lying, opportunistic *Wendehälse* like Stolpe, Gregor emphasized Karl's humanity over his *Prägung*
in a way I found he often did when he was not arguing with Karl over some
point of interpretation of GDR history or postunification politics. Yet Gregor's degradation of Karl's journalistic skills, even in the process of defending his character, reflected a pervasive uneasiness in their relationship—the
need to make the longitudinal other negate the virtues of the self was in
tension with the caricature-dissolving intimacies of friendship. Their arguments often exuded a feeling of strained reciprocal indulgence: Gregor positioned himself as Karl's hierarchical, journalistic, and moral superior who
felt kindness toward the older man, a basically honest former functionary
who would sadly never be able to shake the burden of his past complicity
and who thus remained understandably somewhat embittered. Karl, meanwhile, situated himself as an older, wiser, and more pragmatic partner to his
younger friend, who was a well-meaning idealist for whom life and System
had not yet dispelled the illusion of the existence of pristine categories of
moral accountability, like "victims" and "perpetrators."

The *Mitläufer* and the *Querkopf*

When I returned to Berlin in 2002, I was sorry to hear from Karl that the
Stammtisch had stopped meeting. Karl, having taken early retirement from
Super Illu, had sold his apartment in Berlin and had moved with his family
to a greener suburb. Matthias had also moved away to run a new restaurant
business outside Brandenburg, and Karl and Walter appeared to have suffered
some kind of falling out. Gregor also told me he had not seen Karl in several months and was a bit anxious as to whether Karl would want to speak
with him at all. But, in honor of my return, Karl told me, we would have to
reconvene on a Monday night at Sternchen.

It was a very pleasant evening—both Karl and Gregor were on their best
behavior; the dynamics of conversation were calm and friendly, and disagreement never spilled over into heated conflict. It struck me that Gregor
had become, perhaps in the manner Karl had predicted, less certain of the

gap separating the East and West German Systems than he had been several years beforehand. He was certainly less emotionally invested in GDR history than he had been in 1996 and 1997 and laughed along with some of Karl's favorite stories from the GDR (see Boyer 2001c). There had been other changes in Gregor's life as well; he had separated from his wife, even though they continued to live in the same building, and he seemed to be at odds with some of the senior management at *Super Illu* over his desire to do more investigative reporting. Gregor spoke with particular cynicism about how his reputation as a would-be *Wendeheld* (hero of the *Wende*) in the office had been reinforced by his having been pulled off stories with high-profile eastern public figures like Manfred Stolpe and skater Kati Witt when they complained about his overly critical questions. Karl and I teased Gregor that he must have finally brought about Stolpe's "downfall" since the Brandenburg politician had retired the previous week. Gregor dropped his head and nodded, "That was a good day."

Gregor now seems resigned to the fact that few share his sense of urgency for "working through" the GDR past. He noted to me on several occasions during the summer that the leadership at *Super Illu*, for example, were much more interested in sweeping news of Stasi complicity under the rug in order to appease their mainstream eastern audience than in supporting the kind of investigative journalism that Gregor found so vital to the health of the nation-state. Gregor described as typical of this mentality how *Super Illu* had tried its best to suppress the news that one of its own assistant chief editors was recently revealed to have been a Stasi informer. Instead of firing her outright, Burda Verlag had arranged a comfortable "advisory" position for her.

KARL: It's clear that she knew what she was doing, and what they were doing with her?

GREGOR: Oh yeah, the Stasi were giving her tips on how to improve her skills. [*Laughs.*] A little more of this, not so much of that. You should really take a look at the file. It's quite fascinating—how they were giving her feedback on her performance.

KARL: You know, if she hadn't become so nasty, if she hadn't come to treat her fellow East German colleagues so nastily, then I would feel badly for what happened to her. Because, you know, I brought her to *Super Illu*. I knew her from ADN and she could write good stories. She was unemployed at home then, and I told her she should really come to *SI*. Then later she went to *Bild*—

GREGOR: And if she'd stayed at *Bild* she could have kept this quiet for another thirty years, because no one in the West gives a shit about the Stasi anyway.

KARL: What I don't understand is why they gave her this advisory position, anyway.

GREGOR: You know, basically so she could stay an assistant chief editor at *Super Illu* without it looking that way.

KARL [*thoughtfully*]: So it was inconsequential to them, inconsequential, very interesting . . .

GREGOR: They really didn't care that much about the Stasi file, I think.

DOMINIC: So did she ever stand up and explain herself to her colleagues?

GREGOR: Yeah, at the Wednesday meeting. I wasn't there of course. But she got up and apologized to everyone about having worked for the Stasi and—which isn't even the point, you know. No one has to apologize for having worked for the Stasi anyway. I think it's clear that people worked with them in a variety of circumstances and for a variety of reasons. The point is that she was on the leadership track, and in three or four years she might have been chief editor of *Super Illu* and then she would have been out in the public sphere [*Öffentlichkeit*], hobnobbing, at the annual awards show or wherever, with all the politicians, you know. You can imagine her standing between Kohl and Biedenkopf, and that's the problem. That she would be out in the public, representing the magazine, the figurehead, and then were all this to have come out then, it would have been really disastrous. Alone, the Stasi activity is neither here nor there. They called themselves the "sword and shield of the party," and I think that a lot of people saw it as a civic duty to give information when called upon.

KARL [*nodding enthusiastically*]: No one knew what *IM* were in the GDR, for example. I had regular relations with Stasi men as part of my job, but I had a professional, distanced relationship with them though. On a couple of occasions they tried to call on me to do something else; like once they approached me to help them get some information about a woman they were interested in. But I always turned them down because it seemed suspicious to me. And I think they couldn't put too much pressure on me because of my time at the *Parteihochschule*;[12] I was *Nomenklaturkader*, you see. And there was a taboo in the GDR that protected the leadership cadre from the Stasi.

DOMINIC: So the decision to fire her was [chief editor] Wolff's call? He didn't have to discuss it with the publisher?

GREGOR: No, it was Wolff.

12. Especially promising young SED members who were being groomed for elite positions in the party were invited to the *Parteihochschule* (party institute) in Berlin for special seminars on the theory and praxis of socialism and socialist leadership. Other invitees have confirmed Karl's understanding that, upon graduating the *Hochschule*, one became explicitly, in the eyes of the party leadership, a member of the *Nomenklaturkader* (party leadership cadre).

DOMINIC: I still don't understand why, if they fired her, they then felt like they had to give her this advisory position. Were they afraid of a lawsuit?

GREGOR: No, no, listen, you've got to see that basically they didn't care about the *IM* activity. What they cared about was the public-relations damage, the damage to the "image" of the magazine. No one in the West cares about this at all. It's only in the East that they care and then they only care about it at the level of the leadership. If she had been smart and had stayed at *Bild* she wouldn't have had any problems at all. *Kein Schwein interessiert sich dafür. Kein Schwein.* [No one cares about this at all. *No one.*]

As one of those who continued to care, Gregor felt himself estranged from the mainstream politics of history in both the East and the West. On both sides, Gregor felt, people were too eager to reestablish normality without having worked through the burden of the past. One night he took me with him to a *Stammtisch* in the Prenzlauer Berg district composed of former GDR civil rights activists. Gregor clearly admired and identified with these individuals for their guerrilla warfare against the state in the last years of the GDR and for their continuing efforts to bring those who profited from the GDR System to justice. As we sat across the table from Roland Jahn, a well-known journalist at *Sender Freies Berlin* whose forced expatriation from the GDR became highly publicized in the West, Gregor whispered to me:

Roland there was involved since the early 1980s organizing demonstrations and so forth and was eventually jailed by the Stasi for subversion of the state. And in jail they tried to make him sign a paper saying he wanted to leave the GDR voluntarily, but he wouldn't do it. They asked him why and he told his interrogator, "Because someday I want to be able to tell your children about what you are doing to me here." After six months, Amnesty International had gotten wind of what had happened to him, so they let him out and he went right back to organizing demos. Then, in the summer of 1983, they burst through his door at six in the morning and shackled him, threw him into one of the trains bound for West Berlin, shackled him to the side of the car, and then in a few minutes he was forcibly expatriated into the West.

It was not until this evening in 2002 that I realized the depth of Gregor's personal investment in the GDR past. Later that night, we stood in Gregor's bare kitchen looking out the back window of his apartment toward the cemetery behind St. Marienkirche. He pointed out the gravestones scarred with bullets from the Nazis' defense of Berlin against the Soviet army in 1945. Gregor turned to me with unusual gravity and said, picking up our prior conversation about Jahn and his friends, "I mean, think about what they did without any hope at that time that the System was on its last legs. You and I have to ask ourselves what we would have done under those conditions. Would *you* have been interrogated like Roland day after day for six months and refused to sign that form? I can imagine saying to myself, there are other nice places to live too [*laughs*]. Why should I sit here and wrangle with this corrupt old communist day after day? Los Angeles is nice too [*laughs*]. I could earn some money, enjoy the sun. I don't know. But what's certain is what these people did. *That's indisputable.*"

For Gregor, the gravity of the question was unavoidable; he had perhaps asked it of himself many times. Who would he have been in the GDR? Would he have been Roland Jahn or Karl? What, moreover, would I have done? Without hope, would we have asserted Spirit to confront the merciless, self-affirming power of System or would we have simply adopted the more common route of marginal complicity, seeking agency and locating selfhood in small acts of self-assertion or state subversion? Could either of us have avoided embracing the identity of the cog or screw?

In his own effort to resist what he construed as mainstream indifference to the weight of East German history, Gregor was seeking a kind of redemption for acts he had never committed but for which, given the postwar ethnologization of Nazism, he was still transitively accountable. Gregor desired certainty in his knowledge of his character, a certain answer to his and others' interrogation of Germanness. Which kind of German was he, the *Mitläufer* or the *Querkopf?*[13] The creature of System or of Spirit? At this moment, it seemed not only a German question to me but also a human question. I replied to him that, for his part at least, I couldn't imagine a situation where he wouldn't be stirring up some kind of trouble. With a shrug, Gregor smiled.

13. A *Querkopf* (literally, "diagonal mind") is a person who is said to think against the grain.

CONCLUSION

God knows, as we have already said, what a soul is anyway. There can be no doubt whatsoever that the burning desire to obey only the call of one's soul leaves infinite scope for action, a true state of anarchy, and there are cases of chemically pure souls actually committing crimes. But the minute a soul has morals, religion, philosophy, a well-grounded middle-class education, ideals in the spheres of duty and beauty, it has been equipped with a system of rules, conditions and directives that it must obey before it can think of being a respectable soul, and its heat, like that of a blast furnace, is directed into orderly rectangles of sand. All that remains are only logical problems of interpretation, such as whether an action falls under this or that commandment, and the soul presents the tranquil panorama of a battlefield after the fact, where the dead lie still and one can see at once where a scrap of life still moves or groans. Which is why we cross the bridge as quickly as we can. If a person is plagued by religious doubts, as many are in their youth, he takes to persecuting unbelievers, if troubled by love, he turns it into marriage; and when overcome by some other enthusiasm, he takes refuge from the impossibility of living constantly *in* its fire by beginning to live *for* that fire. That is, he fills the many moments of his day, each of which needs a content and an impetus, not with his ideal state but with the many ways of achieving it by overcoming obstacles and incidents—which guarantees that he will never need to attain it. For only fools, fanatics, and mental cases can stand living at the highest pitch of soul; a sane person must be content with declaring that life would not be worth living without a spark of that mysterious fire. — *Robert Musil, Der Mann ohne Eigenschaften (trans. S. Wilkins)*

In its broadest scope, this book has explored one dimension of human beings' epistemic engagements with their social worlds. I have focused attention on a certain set of spatial and temporal relations in social knowledge—those of internality/externality and potentiality/actuality—and I have argued that their confluence frames the basic intuition of what I have termed "dialecticism." Dialectical knowledge, whether distilled as "the dialectic" in Hegelian philosophy or exercised through tropes in everyday judgment, always signals a tension between an inner poetic capacity and a world of exterior powers and forms. In some situations, awareness privileges the potent "becoming" of the former over the latter (positive dialecticism) and, in others, the powers of constraint and compromise are leveraged by the latter over the former (negative dialecticism). The two modes of dialecticism are always intertwined to some extent in the making of social knowledge: each concerns the relationship between poesis and form, between agency and structure, between "Spirit and System."

My case studies have focused on modern German intellectual culture owing to its rich self-awareness, codification, and expression of dialectical tensions. The studies explore how dialectical tropes and intuitions saturate knowledges (both informal and expert) of social relations (both immediate and abstract) in modern German intellectual culture. In each study, I have investigated a range of sociological and phenomenological reasons why positive and negative tendencies in dialecticism became amplified or dampened in specific social and historical contexts. I have also measured the important lateral effects of dialectical knowledge in Germany in terms of its saturation of social imagination (e.g., of the typical qualities of German culture and German history) and its orientation of social practice (e.g., through the cultural ideologies of the SED and NSDAP states or in the coordinated "reeducation" of East German journalists after 1989). And I have explored the subtle entanglements of dialectical knowing and knowledge in a variety of contexts of intellectual activity ranging from theory and philosophy to ideology and policy to informal practices of identification, analogy, and judgment.

Despite my focus on German intellectuals and their social knowledges, I have resisted characterizing this book as a study of the Germanness of the dialectic despite the fact that many have claimed dialecticism as the essence of German character. There are, as discussed in chapter 2, particular social and historical relations responsible for producing "the dialectical German." Moreover, I highly doubt that any ethnological imagination is entirely free of dialectical figurations of social being and becoming. Likewise, my focus on intellectuals does not imply that I believe dialecticism "belongs" to them either. It is true that I have argued that intellectuals make exemplary case studies in the anthropology of knowledge for the same reason that theory and philosophy, in their epistemic formalism, codify inchoate processes of knowing into readily identifiable, heuristically valuable forms. But I hope that I have adequately conveyed to the reader my sense that dialecticism is also something simply human. I mean this not in the abstract sense of a "universal feature" of human life but rather in the sense of signaling certain mundane epistemic capacities and settlements of knowledge of which human beings other than those whom I have studied are also capable.

With this overview in mind, I conclude *Spirit and System* with a reflexive application of its attentions, methods, and arguments. This book has been concerned from its first pages with the historicity and phenomenology of epistemic forms, so it seems only fair to focus its final pages on the social phenomenology and historicity of its own enterprise. In a sense, this conclusion can be read as a reflexive exploration of reflexivity.

The Dialectic Within

We might begin with a reflexive confession of this author's own investment in, and entanglement with, dialectical knowledge. This entanglement began with my first contact with dialectical theory as an undergraduate at Brown University's Center for Modern Culture and Media. It was a remarkable intellectual community; both teachers and students engaged theory with great passion, reverence, and certainty as to its radical transformative possibilities for the outside world. Reading Marx and then Walter Benjamin, I felt what Musil terms the "mysterious fire" of Spirit, and I was quickly, entirely seduced by the thrill and promise of intellectual agency. In the grasp of critical dialectical theory, I felt myself able to exceed my considerable adolescent awkwardness and empowered to dismiss the "empty" bourgeois forms and routines that surrounded me, privileged me, and yet that seemed so artificially exterior to me.

Within a few years, however, my sense of intellectual agency had become less ecstatic and more tempered. I began to be unsettled by the radical claims of the avant-gardes and even found them estranging and pretentious. No longer quite sharing their passion, I encountered their exhibitions of Spirit as formal and exterior, as signs of investment in a prestige economy of "high theory" that integrated an elitist community of experts. Bourdieu would not be at all surprised to know that this was also the moment when I began to consider graduate school and an academic career. In Musil's terms, the blast furnace of Spirit was coming to be directed "into orderly rectangles of sand." The professionalizing crucible of graduate school further channeled my attention and energy into an academic, disciplinary economy of knowledge. Yet it also provided fresh bursts of Spirit in the form of contact with unfamiliar theoretical languages and with ethnographic knowledge and in the conviviality and intellectual energy of a new community of insiders. But these encounters were, phenomenologically speaking, quite distinct from my earlier ones. Musil captures so beautifully the refuge of living for Spirit rather than in Spirit. All-encompassing theoretical passion was finally replaced by Spirit in installments, by the comforts and predictable excitements of intellectual routines.

As Alexander Osang and my friend Karl testified, the cunning of System is its incrementalism. Indeed, one could say that, in such moments, the trope of System captures and condenses principally a sense of the incremental channeling of the open horizons of intellectual youth into the more specialized interests and attentions of intellectual maturity. This confession of dialectical "becoming" is therefore also a confession of professionalism, of increasing investment in a social economy of expert knowledge making. My field research concerned professionals in a state of transition, precisely as I was in a state of transition into professionalism. If dialectical tropes and idioms were at play in many of the intellectual engagements of my field research, they were crafted and codified as "dialectical knowledge" as I later sat at home or in my office with the dual tasks of writing a book and planning a career. In the end, I have managed to recognize and to articulate my own dialecticism only in the mirror of the "dialectical German." They have co-evoked one another. I cannot deny that my anthropology of dialectical social knowledge could be read as the culmination of this process, a codification and distillation of certain features of knowing with the expectations of a professional academic economy of knowledge in mind.

On my last research trip to Berlin in 2002, Albert, always a sharper observer of my intellectual development than I, pointed to me and said to Marianne, "You can see how he is gaining a professional identity now. He now describes himself as an anthropologist and makes jokes that begin with, 'As an anthropologist . . .' He never used to do that before." This seems to answer Gregor's question as to where my dialectical allegiances lie.

The Social Phenomenology of Crisis
among Academic Humanists Revisited

My dialecticism also signals something more than personal idiosyncrasy. There is, I would argue, a broader dialectical phenomenology that has contributed to this book's reflexive ambitions and anthropology of dialectical knowledge. One clue to this connection, already noted in chapter 1, is that the work of reflexive social science has long been allied to negative dialectical knowledge in intellectual culture. Mannheim's relational sociology, for example, reacted directly to pervasive negative dialectical knowledge of a plague of mass culture afflicting modern society. Through the method of the sociology of knowledge, Mannheim sought to assert some sense of analytic containment and epistemic certainty over what he regarded as a collapsing (Enlightenment) regime of objectivist truth claims. Mannheim's intervention, one could say, was a positive dialectical project aimed at displacing or alleviating the anxieties associated with the abundance and heterogeneity of his intellectual culture that so many of Mannheim's academic contemporaries simply excoriated as the decline of *Wissenschaft* and *Kultur*. The therapy of reflexive, contextual knowledge helped to calm the mediatic nightmares associated with being an artisanal academic humanist faced with a vast and increasingly unknowable cosmos of epistemic activity.

There are many similarities between Mannheim's moment in academic humanism and our own, similarities that extend to our reflexive responses. In chapter 2, I outlined three factors influencing the amplification of negative dialectical knowledge in German academic humanism of the late nineteenth and early twentieth centuries: (1) the sense of a general loss of prestige and political influence on the part of nonnoble *Gebildeten*, (2) the increasing professionalization and compartmentalization of intellectual culture, and (3), most immediate to the humanists, their sense of a loss of prestige and influence within universities relative to the advancement of so-called big science (*Großwissenschaft*). None of these contextual considerations had disappeared from intellectual culture or from the social phenomenology of academic humanists at the other end of the twentieth century. Professionalism and compartmentalization in intellectual culture, as Durkheim long ago predicted (1984: 298–301), continue. New technical and scientific specializations have proliferated, often garnering public attention and recognition far in excess of the knowledge works of humanists. None of us has failed to witness the spectacular fantasies of social and natural revolution that continue to flourish around new modes of electronic mediation (Castells 1996; Graham 2000) and biotechnology (Helmreich 1998; Rabinow 1996, 1999). Feeling a bit perhaps like the Silesian weavers of the next millennium, many of us academic humanists reacted defensively or ironically in the 1990s to the celebration of "knowledge economies" that seemed collectively utterly disinterested in our epistemic contributions. And we greeted the burst pretensions of the "New Economy" (Ross 2000; Terranova 2000) with a certain *Schadenfreude*. But even now, in the immediate wake of the Internet stock crash of 2001 and, of course, in the thrall of the post-9/11 security regime, the complexly compartmentalized and heterogeneously abundant intellectual culture in which American academic humanism finds itself embedded has not fundamentally altered.

Under these circumstances, it should not surprise us that contemporary American humanists (like the German academic mandarins of the early twentieth century) frequently transpose their own phenomenological sense of marginalization and decline to the fates of abstract entities like "culture" and "nation" and "knowledge." Regardless of nominally left- or right-wing political disposition among humanists, a negative dialectical language of pending crisis and social decline is widespread in academic culture. Many of us recall the scandalously overbilled "culture wars" of the 1980s and subsequent academic debates over literary canons that declared stakes like the future of Western civilization or American pluralism. More recently, we have produced and listened to narratives on the "crisis of the university" and its implications for citizenship and culture globally (see Z. Bauman 1997; Derrickson 2003; Martin 1998; Nelson 1997; Readings 1996; Slaughter and Leslie 1997).

Informing these narratives and debates is a general sense of unease, unrest, and distrust about the future of higher education in the United States and especially about the place of academic humanism within this future. In my experience, such concerns pervade hallway conversations, faculty meetings, efforts to interpret the actions and motives of university administrations, and so on. Sometimes, individuals are singled out as mediatic agents of pernicious exterior forces. At other times, threats remain shadowy and abstract. I have noted, for example, that "big science" remains a locus of negative dialectical attention and suspicion for humanists.[1] One anecdote should suffice: my employer, Cornell University, recently announced both a $600 million Life Sciences Initiative and a $2 million Social Sciences Initiative. Despite the fact that most of the $600 million was due to be raised in new capital campaigns, the staggering scale of the difference in proposed funding was taken as evidence by many of my colleagues of

---

1. Research universities do generally devote larger portions of their budgets to financing capital-intensive scientific research than to social-scientific and humanistic research (e.g., see Clotfelter 1996: 88–89, 152–54). But this is not to say that academic humanists are poorly compensated or that their most privileged representatives are not very privileged indeed. Overall, salary and support levels between the academic divisions are strikingly comparable in statistical terms, a fact that does little to assuage common wisdom among humanists (and likely among others as well) that they are not receiving their fair share of resources.

the shifting loyalties of Cornell's administration (itself a locus of Systemic agency according to many nonadministrators). Criticism, resignation, and irony were legion among humanists when informally discussing the new initiatives. The language of "initiatives" itself was singled out by many as quintessentially Systemic and estranging, a sign of the increasing "managerial mind-set" of the university and of the neoliberalization of American society more broadly (see Derrickson 2003; Martin 1998; Nelson 1997; Slaughter and Leslie 1997).

Negative dialecticism dominates much of the communicative space and social intuitions of contemporary academic humanism (itself a negative dialectical statement if ever there was one!). To be sure, positive dialecticism is richly represented in our intellectual activity as well. But I have been impressed by how many conversational threads lead in the direction of concerns about the compromise of intellectual Spirit by the Systemic forces of institutional routine, professional expectation, bureaucracy, capital, and so on. Sometimes these threads lead to sober rhetoric of the "crisis" we are facing, and sometimes they are laughed off as business as usual. But, in all cases, negative dialectical knowledge suggests our awareness of the contingency and limited efficacy of our own knowledge practices. For example, one of the reasons academic managerialism is much on our minds and popular administrative discourse on "innovation" and "initiatives" seems so estranging is our recognition that we do not have anything radically "new" to contribute to human knowledge. Academic humanists are not, for example, likely to produce technical innovations like PCR (Rabinow 1996) that have extended human agency over genetic identification and modification. Our struggle has rather been to persuade other strata of society of the significance of what we already know and to critically and analytically interpret transformations in the world. We can answer discourse on innovation only through withdrawal or by "innovating" at the level of language, through the production of new jargons and subspecializations, or by "taking initiative" at the level of performance, through the relentless demonstration of intellectual activity via publication or the organization of countless symposia, seminars, workshops, and so on.

The practice of such answers has, in turn, helped to amplify the sense of paralyzing demands from the outside to which our intellectual lives are beholden. Colleagues at Cornell and elsewhere have frequently shared with me their negative dialectical knowledge of accelerating, dehumanizing expectations for productivity and performance. "It used to be that only one book was required for tenure; now at some places it is two." "No one has the time to read anymore." "The pressure to demonstrate activity is crippling." Indeed, common patterns of academic identification and alterization duly follow the criteria of productivity and performance. Our Ossis and Wessis, our phantasmic creatures of form, are the "deadwood" academics, who are said to have lost their productive spirits, and the "trendy careerists," who are said to be beings of motion and appearance rather than of substance (see LaCapra 1998). Whether or not increasing expectations for production are as general and ineluctable as they are perceived, their intuition contributes generously to a negative dialectical apprehension of the increasing indenture of intellectual Spirit to the exterior demands of academic System.

Responding to the "Crisis" of Epistemic Abundance

These observations are admittedly anecdotal and incomplete. Yet they speak to a negative dialectical sensibility in contemporary academic culture that I doubt is entirely foreign to the reader of this book. This sensibility interleaves knowledge of intellectual constraint and compromise even in narratives of intellectual agency and redemption. The recent academic carnival surrounding tales of a "postmodern condition" or crisis in knowledge (Baudrillard 1983; Harvey 1989; Jameson 1984; Lyotard 1984) captures this dialectical entanglement precisely. A book like Jean-François Lyotard's *The Postmodern Condition* offers a heart-pounding celebration of intellectual agency compromised by a disquieted reverence for the decaying "master narratives" of modernity. In portraits of a "postmodern" or "postindustrial" society (Bell 1973), academic humanists have depicted wondrous new opportunities for intellectual expression that are nevertheless always suffused with anxious reminders of the vulnerability and contingency of our knowledge works. Senses of the *Bildung* and *Prägung* of intellectual activity are compressed, elating in one moment and eliciting dread in the next.

Spirit and System is a child of this time. It reacts obliquely, as other recent projects in reflexivity have as well, to shifts in intellectual culture since the 1970s such as a proliferation of electronic mediation that has made the multiplicity of knowledge increasingly immediate for us and such as the diversification of technical knowledges and expertise that have often served as the proximate indices of our pluralized "postmodern condition." In this moment of great epistemic abundance, "knowledge" itself has come to be codified as a principal force of production in society, and greater "knowledge of knowledge" has been widely recognized as a pressing concern. This acknowledgment has also served as an invitation to reflexive social science. Yet, perhaps daunted by the brilliant complexity of epistemic activity that surrounds us, we humanists have tended to use this invitation as an opportunity to turn reflexive analytical attention back inward upon our own knowledge labors in order, following Mannheim, to achieve a more secure sense of the epistemological foundations of our intellectual activity. In anthropology, for example, we have made great strides toward analyzing our representational practices (Clifford 1988; Clifford and Marcus 1986; Geertz 1988), as well as toward understanding the dialogical constitution of anthropological knowledge (Crapanzano 1980; Dwyer 1982; Tedlock and Mannheim 1995). My anthropology of the dialectic, for the most part, follows this trajectory. Like every other project in the anthropology or sociology of knowledge before it, *Spirit and System* has struggled to close the shutters to the outside world enough to limit the blinding background light, thereby allowing some outlines of epistemic forms and relations to become evident in the foreground.

In the end, however, I too have become concerned about the narrow horizons of this project and about the limits of its reflexive gestures. Despite the variety of methods I have utilized, this book seems as much a performance of the limited attentiveness of the phenomenology of expertise as an analysis of it. The problem is, at least in part, that I have all along engaged "knowledge" solely through expert intellectual practices and attentions. I have, in essence, tried to produce expertise of expertise and then wondered why my "intervention" appears largely to have resulted in the extension of its own premises. Despite the best of intentions, my anthropology of the dialectic, like other inwardly focused reflexivities, could be accused of elaborating precisely the social and epistemic conditions it is reacting against. This is not, I think, a sufficient or satisfactory horizon for reflexivity. With no disrespect to Mannheim, reflexivity—the critical analytical capacity of self-knowing—is too important to restrict to analyses of epistemic context or to epistemic interventions more broadly.

No Crisis: Opening Reflexivity

What might reflexivity look like if its epistemic attentions were turned outward and more fully opened to human experience? The real question to my mind is how to restore the possibility of amplifying positive dialecticism—the sense, ultimately, of creative human agency and possibility. Here, I follow Marx's wisdom that human beings are inherently, heterogeneously self-productive despite the focusing of our productive capacities that is intrinsic to any social division of labor and historical moment. In other words, whatever we might choose to classify as System is always subject to the

intentionality and agency of Spirit providing that one makes critical engagement with System into a life project in its own right.

My own positive dialectical figure of reflexivity is an ethics of intellectual practice that does not resolve itself within the parameters of our professional labors but that, rather, self-consciously seeks to divert our energies
also into extra- and contra-professionalizing activities, perhaps creative, perhaps physical, perhaps political, perhaps pedagogical, perhaps sensual, and
so on. Like all good positive dialecticians, I leave the details to the imagination. Still, I am certain that the heart of an opened reflexivity would involve denaturalizing what I have described here as "the phenomenology of
expertise" by engaging it, not as the physics of intellectual life, but rather
as a continual, urgent reminder to disarticulate ourselves from professional
routines and to extend ourselves intellectually and otherwise. In this respect, reflexivity can be understood foremost as a question of attention and
engagement, attention and engagement that could become ethically thera-
peutic by encouraging modes of knowing and relations to knowledge that
are not functionally consonant with the demands of professionalism and its
economies of expertise.

This is an invitation to ardor and extension rather than to crisis or so-
lace. If we intellectuals, for example, are not solely the cogs, screws, and
styli of System, then we can (and do) exceed our socialization into professional economies of knowledge making and their inevitable investment in
epistemic formalism. Yet, it remains to be said, a life project of exceeding
professionalism, expertise, and the exteriorities and formalities of knowledge cannot be undertaken solely in the language of expertise, at professional
conferences, or on the "battlefield" of the printed page. It is undertaken in
the arms of your children. It is a matter of how and where you invest your
productive energies. At best, the rigor of the former inspires the diversification of the latter. In this spirit, I offer nothing more than a gentle reminder
of what we are capable.

∽

This book began with a theologian, Hegel, who discovered divine order in
the exacting *Wissenschaft* of philosophy; it is fitting to give the final word
to a scientist, Miroslav Holub, who was driven to poetry:

What the Heart Is Like

Officially the heart
is oblong, muscular,
and filled with longing.

But anyone who has painted the heart knows
that it is also

spiked like a star
and sometimes bedraggled
like a stray dog at night
and sometimes powerful
like an archangel's drum.

And sometimes cube-shaped
like a draughtsman's dream
and sometimes gaily round
like a ball in a net.

And sometimes like a thin line
and sometimes like an explosion.

And in it is
only a river,
a weir,
and at most one little fish
by no means golden.

More like a grey
jealous
loach.

It certainly isn't noticeable
at first sight.

Anyone who has painted the heart knows
that first he had to
discard his spectacles,
his mirror,
throw away his fine-point pencil
and carbon paper

and for a long while
walk
outside.

KEY TERMS

ADN Allgemeine Deutsche Nachrichtendienst (GDR central news agency)

Argu Colloquialism for the weekly "argumentation" sessions held at the SED's Department of Agitation when the party line was handed down to the heads of the GDR media

Beamten Civil servants, functionaries

Beamtentum Civil service, officialdom

Berufsverbot Professional ban (utilized in the GDR as a disciplinary technique)

Besitzbürgertum Propertied bourgeoisie (a twentieth-century analytical category utilized to describe the commercial and industrial middle-class strata of nineteenth-century German-speaking Central Europe and to distinguish them from the *Bildungsbürgertum*)

Bildung Formation, cultivation, education, culture, civilization (formation from within to without)

Bildungsbürger. See *Gebildeten*

Bildungsbürgertum Educated bourgeoisie, cultured middle classes, intelligentsia (a twentieth-century analytical category utilized to describe the cultured or educated middle-class strata of nineteenth-century German-speaking Central Europe and to distinguish them from the *Besitzbürgertum*)

FDJ Freie Deutsche Jugend (German Socialist Youth), a feeder organization for the SED

Führerprinzip Leadership principle (NSDAP centralization of authority into the person of Adolf Hitler)

Gebildeten Educated, enlightened individuals (social self-identification of cultured middle classes in eighteenth- and nineteenth century German-speaking Central Europe)

Geist   Spirit, genius, creative genius, creative power, soul (creative,
               formative agency within that extends into the world as *Bildung*)

Gestaltung   Formation (its use in Hegelian philosophy parallels the technical
               definition of *Bildung* offered above)

Gleichschaltung   Coordination (NSDAP agenda to bring all social institutions
               in Germany into alignment with the direction of the NSDAP
               movement)

Innerlichkeit   Inwardness (an attribute of *Geist*)

inoffizielle Mitarbeiter (IM)   Unofficial employees of GDR state security (Stasi),
               informers

Klassenfeind   Class enemy (SED term for western capitalists/imperialists, often
               used to refer to West Germany)

Kultur   Culture, cultivation, spirit (a principle of inner, spiritual, often
               collective unity)

Kulturstaat   Cultural state (according to *Gebildeten*, the ideal social unity that
               would be realized through their control over state administration)

Kulturträger   Culture bearers (the image *Gebildeten* had of themselves as
               bearers of the incipient cultural unity of the *Volk*)

Lenkungssystem   Guidance or control system (a term used to describe the
               system of surveillance and control over the GDR media)

Macht   Power, authority (often counterposed to *Geist* as a principle of
               external power directed inward)

Machthaber   Powers-that-be, power brokers

Massen   The masses (often defined as a kind of "raw material" of the *Volk*, in
               opposition to the spiritual character and power of *Gebildeten*)

Massenkultur   Mass culture (like *System*, often a trope of pervasive, counterfeit
               cultural exteriority that constrains and perverts true *Geist* and
               Kultur)

Meinungsbildner   Educators of opinion (vocational ideal of German journalism)

Mitläufer   Fellow traveler (often implies a sense of routine marginal complicity
               with a *System*)

Mittel   Means, media

NSDAP   Nationalsozialistische Deutsche Arbeiterpartei (National Socialist,
               or Nazi, Party, the governing party of Germany from 1933 to 1945)

Öffentlichkeit   Public sphere, public culture, publicity (usually employed to
               figure a more positive and authentic kind of public culture than that
               represented by *Massenkultur*)

Opfer   Victim (category of accountability commonly employed to describe victims of a *System*)

Ossi   Eastie (quasi-derogatory term for an East German)

Ostler   Easterner

Parteilichkeit   Party affiliation, partiality (invoked as a virtue or vice to describe the alignment of individual *Geist* with a collective political program)

Parteilinie   Party line (a hermeneutic settlement dispersed from above to below in the *Lenkungssystem*)

Prägung   The act or process of stamping, minting, or embossing (formation from without to within)

Querkopf   Literally, "a diagonal mind," someone who thinks against the grain (a category of personal accountability and critical agency that is opposite to the *Mitläufer*)

Redakteur   Editor (journalist with a fixed contract)

Schere im Kopf   Scissors in the head (phrase used by journalists in both the Third Reich and the GDR to describe practices of self-censorship)

SED   Sozialistische Einheitspartei Deutschlands (Socialist Unity Party, the governing party of the GDR from 1949 to 1989)

Stammtisch   Regulars' table at bar or restaurant

Stasi   Colloquial name for the GDR Ministry for State Security

System   System (organic exteriority of form and mediation unified by a central principle or logic)

Täter   Perpetrator (category of accountability typically employed to describe agents of a *System*)

Verein   Club, union, voluntary association

Vergangenheitsbelastung   Burden of history/the past (a sense of the *Prägung* of an individual or collective by history, particularly in reference to the Third Reich or the GDR)

Volk   People (often a figuration, like *Kultur*, of inner spiritual unity realized through collective cultural forms)

Volkslehrer   Educators of the people (like *Kulturträger*, an image *Gebildeten* had of themselves in the nineteenth century in which they construed themselves in a pedagogical, cultivating relationship to the masses)

Weltanschauung   Worldview

Wende   Turn (colloquial expression for the collapse of the SED party-state in autumn 1989)

Wendehals   Turn-neck (pl. *Wendehählse;* colloquial expression in eastern
            Germany after 1989 for an opportunist)

Wessi   Westie (quasi-derogatory term for a West German)

Westler   Westerner

Wissenschaft   Science, knowledge (a disciplined attention to the cultivation of
            knowledge that seeks the universal in the particular)

BIBLIOGRAPHY

Adorno, Theodor. 2003. *Negative Dialectics.* Trans. E. B. Ashton. New York: Continuum.

Althusser, Louis. 1971. *Lenin and Philosophy, and Other Essays.* Trans. B. Brewster. New York: Monthly Review Press.

Anderson, Benedict. 1983. *Imagined Communities: Reflections on the Origin and Spread of Nationalism.* New York: Verso.

Anderson, Margaret Lavinia. 2000. *Practicing Democracy: Elections and Political Culture in Imperial Germany.* Princeton: Princeton University Press.

Applegate, Celia. 1990. *A Nation of Provincials: The German Idea of Heimat.* Berkeley and Los Angeles: University of California Press.

Apsel, Jeannine. 1996. "Vom ost-konservativen DFF zum west-konservativen MDR." In *Kolonialisierung der DDR: Kritische Analysen und Alternativen des Einigungsprozesses,* ed. W. Dümcke and F. Vilmar. Münster: Agenda Verlag.

Arendt, Hannah. 2003. *Responsibility and Judgment.* Ed. J. Kohn. New York: Schocken.

————. 2004. *The Origins of Totalitarianism.* New York: Schocken.

Arnold, Karl-Heinz, and Otfrid Arnold. 1994. "Herrschaft über die Medien: Die Gleichschaltung von Presse, Rundfunk und Fernsehen durch die SED." In *Das Große Haus,* ed. H. Modrow. Berlin: Edition Ost.

Asad, Talal, ed. 1973. *Anthropology and the Colonial Encounter.* Atlantic Highlands, NJ: Humanities Press.

Augustine, Dolores L. 1991. "Arriving in the Upper Class: The Wealthy Business Elite of Wilhelmine Germany." In *The German Bourgeoisie,* ed. D. Blackbourn and R. J. Evans. New York: Routledge.

Bagdikian, Ben H. 1997. *The Media Monopoly.* Boston: Beacon Press.

Bakhtin, M. M. 1981. *The Dialogic Imagination.* Trans. C. Emerson and M. Holquist. Austin: University of Texas Press.

Bathrick, David. 1995. *The Powers of Speech: The Politics of Culture in the GDR.* Lincoln: University of Nebraska Press.

Baudrillard, Jean. 1983. *Simulations*. Trans. P. Foss, P. Patton, and P. Beitchman. New York: Semiotext(e).

Bauman, Richard, and Charles L. Briggs. 2000. "Language Philosophy as Language Ideology: John Locke and Johann Gottfried Herder." In *Regimes of Language: Ideologies, Politics, and Identities*, ed. P. V. Kroskrity. Santa Fe: School of American Research Press.

Bauman, Zygmunt. 1987. *Legislators and Interpreters: On Modernity, Postmodernity, and Intellectuals*. Ithaca: Cornell University Press.

———. 1997. "The Present Crisis of the Universities." In *The Idea of the University*, ed. J. Brzezinski and L. Nowak. Atlanta: Rodopi.

Behar, Ruth. 1996. *The Vulnerable Observer: Anthropology That Breaks Your Heart*. Boston: Beacon Press.

Bell, Daniel. 1973. *The Coming of Post-industrial Society: A Venture in Social Forecasting*. New York: Basic Books.

Benda, Julien. 1969. *The Treason of the Intellectuals*. Trans. R. Aldington. New York: W. W. Norton.

Benjamin, Walter. 1968. *Illuminations*. Trans. H. Zohn. New York: Schocken.

Berdahl, Daphne. 1999. *Where the World Ended: Re-unification and Identity in the German Borderland*. Berkeley and Los Angeles: University of California Press.

Blackall, Eric. 1978. *The Emergence of German as a Literary Language, 1700–1775*. Ithaca: Cornell University Press.

Blackbourn, David. 1991. "The German Bourgeoisie: An Introduction." In *The German Bourgeoisie*, ed. D. Blackbourn and R. J. Evans. New York: Routledge.

———. 1998. *The Long Nineteenth Century: A History of Germany, 1780–1918*. Oxford: Oxford University Press.

Blackbourn, David, and Geoff Eley. 1984. *The Peculiarities of German History: Bourgeois Society and Politics in Nineteenth-Century Germany*. Oxford: Oxford University Press.

Blaum, Verena. 1985. *Ideologie und Fachkompetenz: Das journalistische Berufsbild in der DDR*. Cologne: Verlag Wissenschaft und Politik.

Böckelmann, Frank, Claudia Mast, and Beate Schneider, eds. 1994. *Journalismus in den neuen Ländern: Ein Berufsstand zwischen Aufbruch und Abwicklung*. Konstanz: Universitätsverlag Konstanz.

Bödeker, Hans Erich. 1992. "Die "Gebildeten Stände" im Späten 18. und Frühen 19. Jahrhundert: Zugehörigkeit und Abgrenzungen; Mentalitäten und Handlungspotentiale." In *Bildungsbürgertum im 19. Jahrhundert*, vol. 4, ed. J. Kocka. Stuttgart: Klett-Cotta.

Bohrmann, Hans, ed. 1984. *NS-Presseanweisungen der Vorkriegszeit*. Vol. 1. Munich: K. G. Saur Verlag KG.

Borneman, John. 1992. *Belonging in the Two Berlins: Kin, State, Nation*. Cambridge, UK: Cambridge University Press.

———. 1997. *Settling Accounts: Violence, Justice, and Accountability in Postsocialist Europe*. Princeton: Princeton University Press.

Bos, Ellen. 1993. *Leserbriefe in Tageszeitungen der DDR: Zur "Massenverbundenheit" der Presse, 1949–1989.* Opladen: Westdeutscher Verlag.

Bourdieu, Pierre. 1977. *Outline of a Theory of Practice.* Trans. R. Nice. Cambridge, UK: Cambridge University Press.

———. 1984. *Distinction: A Social Critique of the Judgement of Taste.* Trans. R. Nice. Cambridge, MA: Harvard University Press.

———. 1988. *Homo Academicus.* Trans. P. Collier. Stanford: Stanford University Press.

———. 1991a. *Language and Symbolic Power.* Ed. J. B. Thompson. Trans. G. Raymond and M. Adamson. Cambridge, MA: Harvard University Press.

———. 1991b. *The Political Ontology of Martin Heidegger.* Trans. P. Collier. Stanford: Stanford University Press.

Bourdieu, Pierre, and Loïc J. D. Wacquant, eds. 1992. *An Invitation to Reflexive Sociology.* Chicago: University of Chicago Press.

Boyarin, Jonathan, ed. 1993. *The Ethnography of Reading.* Berkeley and Los Angeles: University of California Press.

Boyer, Dominic. 2000. "On the Sedimentation and Accreditation of Social Knowledges of Difference: Mass Media, Journalism and the Reproduction of East/West Alterities in Unified Germany." *Cultural Anthropology* 15(4): 459–91.

———. 2001a. "Foucault in the Bush: The Social Life of Post-structuralist Theory in East Berlin's Prenzlauer Berg." *Ethnos* 66(2): 207–36.

———. 2001b. "Media Markets, Mediating Labors, and the Branding of East German Culture at 'Super Illu.'" *Social Text* 68 (Fall): 9–33.

———. 2001c. "Yellow Sand of Berlin." *Ethnography* 2(3): 421–39.

———. 2003a. "Censorship as a Vocation: The Rituals, Institutions and Cultural Logic of Media Control in the German Democratic Republic." *Comparative Studies in Society and History* 45(3): 511–45.

———. 2003b. "The Medium of Foucault in Anthropology." *Minnesota Review* 58–60: 265–72.

———. 2005a. "The Corporeality of Expertise." *Ethnos* 70(2): 243–66.

———. 2005b. "Visiting Knowledge in Anthropology." *Ethnos* 70(2): 141–8.

Boyer, Dominic, and Claudio Lomnitz. 2005. "Intellectuals and Nationalism: Anthropological Engagements." *Annual Review of Anthropology* 34: 105–20.

Boyle, Maryellen. 1992. "Capturing Journalism: Press and Politics in East Germany, 1945–1991." PhD diss., University of California, San Diego.

Bramsted, Ernest K. 1964. *Aristocracy and the Middle-Classes in Germany: Social Types in German literature, 1830–1900.* Chicago: University of Chicago Press.

Breckman, Warren. 1999. *Marx, the Young Hegelians, and the Origins of Radical Social Theory.* Cambridge, UK: Cambridge University Press.

Brenneis, Don. 1994. "Discourse and Discipline at the National Research Council: A Bureaucratic *Bildungsroman.*" *Cultural Anthropology* 9 (1): 23–36.

Breuilly, John. 1992. "The National Idea in Modern German History." In *The State of Germany: The National Idea in the Making, Unmaking and Remaking of a Modern National State*, ed. J. Breuilly. New York: Longman.

Broszat, Martin. 1966. *German National Socialism, 1919–1945*. Trans. K. Rosenbaum and I. P. Boehm. Santa Barbara, CA: Clio Press.

———. 1981. *The Hitler State: The Foundation and Development of the Internal Structure of the Third Reich*. Trans. J. W. Hilden. New York: Longman.

Bruford, W. H. 1962. *Culture and Society in Classical Weimar, 1775–1806*. Cambridge, UK: Cambridge University Press.

———. 1965. *Germany in the Eighteenth Century: The Social Background of the Literary Revival*. Cambridge, UK: Cambridge University Press.

———. 1975. *The German Tradition of Self-Cultivation: "Bildung" from Humboldt to Thomas Mann*. Cambridge, UK: Cambridge University Press.

Brunöhler, Kurt. 1933. *Die Redakteure der mittleren und größeren Zeitungen im heutigen Reichsgebiet von 1800 bis 1848*. PhD diss., Universität Leipzig. Leipzig: Gutenberg-Druckerei.

Buchsteiner, Jochen. 1997. "Wir bedanken uns für dieses Gespräch." *Die Zeit*, 11 July, p. 2.

Budzislawski, Hermann. 1966. *Sozialistische Journalistik: Eine wissenschaftliche Einführung*. Leipzig: VEB Bibliographisches Institut.

Bürger, Ulrich. 1990. *Das sagen wir natürlich so nicht! Donnerstags-Argus bei Herrn Geggel*. Berlin: Dietz Verlag.

Burke, Kenneth. 1969. *A Rhetoric of Motives*. Berkeley and Los Angeles: University of California Press.

Busch, Alexander. 1959. *Die Geschichte des Privatdozenten: Eine soziologische Studie zur großbetrieblichen Entwicklung der deutschen Universitäten*. Stuttgart: Ferdinand Enke Verlag.

Butler, Judith. 1993. *Bodies That Matter*. New York: Routledge.

Castells, Manuel. 1996. *The Information Age: Economy, Society, and Culture*. Vol. 1, *Rise of the Network Society*. London: Blackwell.

Chartier, Roger. 1987. *The Cultural Uses of Print in Early Modern France*. Trans. L. G. Cochrane. Princeton: Princeton University Press.

———. 1991. *The Cultural Origins of the French Revolution*. Trans. L. G. Cochrane. Durham, NC: Duke University Press.

Clifford, James. 1988. *The Predicament of Culture: Twentieth-Century Ethnography, Literature, and Art*. Cambridge, MA: Harvard University Press.

Clifford, James, and George E. Marcus, eds. 1986. *Writing Culture: The Poetics and Politics of Ethnography*. Berkeley and Los Angeles: University of California Press.

Clotfelter, Charles T. 1996. *Buying the Best: Cost Escalation in Elite Higher Education*. Princeton: Princeton University Press.

Collins, Randall. 1998. *The Sociology of Philosophies: A Global Theory of Intellectual Change*. Cambridge, MA: Belknap Press.

Comaroff, Jean. 1985. *Body of Power, Spirit of Resistance: The Culture and History of a South African People*. Chicago: University of Chicago Press.

Confino, Alon. 1997. *The Nation as Local Metaphor: Württemberg, Imperial Germany, and National Memory, 1871–1918*. Chapel Hill: University of North Carolina Press.

Conze, Werner, and Jürgen Kocka, eds. 1985. *Bildungsbürgertum im 19. Jahrhundert*. Vol. 1. Stuttgart: Klett-Cotta.

Coser, Lewis. 1965. *Men of Ideas: A Sociologist's View*. New York: Free Press.

Craig, Gordon. 1978. *Germany, 1866–1945*. Oxford: Oxford University Press.

Crapanzano, Vincent. 1980. *Tuhami: Portrait of a Moroccan*. Chicago: University of Chicago Press.

Crick, Malcolm. 1982. "Anthropology of Knowledge." *Annual Review of Anthropology* 11:287–313.

Csordas, Thomas J. 1994. *The Sacred Self: A Cultural Phenomenology of Charismatic Healing*. Berkeley and Los Angeles: University of California Press.

Daniel, E. Valentine. 1984. *Fluid Signs: Being a Person the Tamil Way*. Berkeley and Los Angeles: University of California Press.

Deák, István. 1992. *Beyond Nationalism: A Social and Political History of the Habsburg Officer Corps, 1848–1918*. New York: Oxford University Press.

de Certeau, Michel. 1984. *The Practice of Everyday Life*. Trans. S. Rendall. Berkeley and Los Angeles: University of California Press.

De Nike, Howard J. 1997. *German Unification and the Jurists of East Germany: An Anthropology of Law, Nation and History*. Mönchengladbach: Forum Verlag Godesberg.

Dennis, Mike. 1993. *Social and Economic Modernization in Eastern Germany from Honecker to Kohl*. New York: St. Martin's Press.

Derrickson, Teresa, ed. 2003. "Information University: Rise of the Education Management Organization." Special issue, *Works and Days* 21 (41/42).

Derrida, Jacques. 1998. *Monolingualism of the Other; or, The Prosthesis of Origin*. Trans. P. Mensah. Stanford: Stanford University Press.

Dieckmann, Friedrich. 2003. *Was ist deutsch? Eine Nationalerkundung*. Frankfurt am Main: Suhrkamp.

Dimic, Zoran. 2003. "The Problem of Education in Fichte's Philosophy." *Facta Universitatis* (Philosophy, Sociology, and Psychology Series) 2 (10): 777–88.

Djilas, Milovan. 1957. *The New Class: An Analysis of the Communist System*. New York: Harcourt Brace and Co.

Dornfeld, Barry. 1998. *Producing Public Television, Producing Public Culture*. Princeton: Princeton University Press.

Drescher, Angela, ed. 1991. *Dokumentation zu Christa Wolf, "Nachdenken über Christa T."* Hamburg: Luchterhand.

Dümcke, Wolfgang, and Fritz Vilmar, eds. 1996. *Kolonialisierung der DDR: Kritische Analysen und Alternativen des Einigungsprozesses*. Münster: Agenda Verlag.

Dumont, Louis. 1994. *German Ideology: From France to Germany and Back*. Chicago: University of Chicago Press.

Dundes, Alan. 1984. *Life Is Like a Chicken Coop Ladder: A Portrait of German Culture through Folklore*. New York: Columbia University Press.

Durkheim, Emile. 1984. *The Division of Labor in Society*. Trans. W. D. Halls. New York: Free Press.

———. 1995. *The Elementary Forms of Religious Life*. Trans. K. Fields. New York: Free Press.

Dwyer, Kevin. 1982. *Moroccan Dialogues: Anthropology in Question*. Baltimore: Johns Hopkins University Press.

Eidson, John R. 1990. "German Club Life as a Local Cultural System." *Comparative Studies in Society and History* 32 (2): 357–82.

Elias, Norbert. 1994. *The Civilizing Process*. Vol. 1, *The History of Manners*. Trans. E. Jephcott. Oxford: Blackwell.

———. 1996. *The Germans: Power Struggles and the Development of Habitus in the Nineteenth and Twentieth Centuries*. Trans. E. Dunning and S. Mennell. New York: Columbia University Press.

Engelsing, Rolf. 1966. *Massenpublikum und Journalistentum im 19. Jahrhundert in Nordwestdeutschland*. Berlin: Duncker und Humblot.

Evans, Richard J., ed. 1989. *Kneipengespräche im Kaiserreich: Stimmungsberichte der Hamburger Polizei, 1892–1914*. Hamburg: Rowohlt Taschenbuch Verlag.

Fabian, Johannes. 1983. *Time and the Other: How Anthropology Makes Its Object*. New York: Columbia University Press.

Fabiani, Jean-Louis. 1988. *Les Philosophes de la République*. Paris: Minuit.

Falcone, Jessica. n.d. "The *Hau* of Theory." Unpublished MS.

Fanon, Frantz. 1967. *Black Skin, White Masks*. Trans. C. L. Markmann. New York: Grove Press.

Fehrenbach, Elisabeth. 1994. *Adel und Bürgertum in deutschen Vormärz*. Munich: Stiftung Historisches Kolleg.

Feierman, Steven. 1990. *Peasant Intellectuals: Anthropology and History in Tanzania*. Madison: University of Wisconsin Press.

Feld, Steven. 1982. *Sound and Sentiment: Birds, Weeping, Poetics, and Song in Kaluli Expression*. Philadelphia: University of Pennsylvania Press.

Fernandez, James W. 1982. *Bwiti: An Ethnography of the Religious Imagination in Africa*. Princeton: Princeton University Press.

———. 1986. *Persuasions and Performances: The Play of Tropes in Culture*. Bloomington: Indiana University Press.

———, ed. 1991. *Beyond Metaphor: The Theory of Tropes in Anthropology*. Stanford: Stanford University Press.

Festa, Paul. n.d. "Mahjong Agonistics in Taiwan: Fate, Mimesis, and the Martial Imaginary." Unpublished MS.

Fichte, Johann Gottlieb. 1873. "The Nature of the Scholar." In *Johann Gottlieb Fichte's Popular Works*. Trans. W. Smith. London: Trübner und Co.

————. 1956. "Deduzierter Plan einer in Berlin zu errichtenden höheren Lehranstalt." In *Die Idee der deutschen Universität*, ed. E. Anrich. Darmstadt: Hermann Gentner.

————. 1988a. "Concerning the Difference between the Spirit and the Letter within Philosophy." In *Fichte: Early Philosophical Writings*, trans. and ed. D. Breazeale. Ithaca: Cornell University Press.

————. 1988b. "Some Lectures concerning the Scholar's Vocation." In *Fichte: Early Philosophical Writings*, trans. and ed. D. Breazeale. Ithaca: Cornell University Press.

Föllmer, Moritz. 2002. *Die Verteidigung der bürgerlichen Nation: Industrielle und hohe Beamte in Deutschland und Frankreich*. Göttingen: Vandenhoeck und Ruprecht.

Foucault, Michel. 1979. *Discipline and Punish: The Birth of the Prison*. Trans. A. Sheridan. New York: Vintage.

————. 1981. *The History of Sexuality*. Vol. 1, *An Introduction*. New York: Vintage.

Frei, Norbert. 1993. *National Socialist Rule in Germany: The Führer State, 1933–1945*. Oxford: Blackwell.

Frei, Norbert, and Johannes Schmitz. 1989. *Journalismus im Dritten Reich*. Munich: C. H. Beck.

Freytag, Gustav. 1897. *Die Journalisten*. New York: American Book Co.

Friedrich, Paul. 1986. *The Language Parallax: Linguistic Relativism and Poetic Indeterminacy*. Austin: University of Texas Press.

————. 1991. "Polytropy." In *Beyond Metaphor: The Theory of Tropes in Anthropology*, ed. J. W. Fernandez. Stanford: Stanford University Press.

————. 1996. "The Culture in Poetry and the Poetry in Culture." In *Culture/Contexture: Explorations in Anthropology and Literary Studies*, ed. E. V. Daniel and J. Peck. Berkeley and Los Angeles: University of California Press.

Frisby, David. 1992. *The Alienated Mind: The Sociology of Knowledge in Germany, 1918–1933*. New York: Routledge.

Frykman, Jonas, and Orvar Löfgren. 1987. *Culture Builders: A Historical Anthropology of Middle-Class Life*. New Brunswick, NJ: Rutgers University Press.

Gal, Susan. 1991. "Bartók's Funeral: Representations of Europe in Hungarian Political Rhetoric." *American Ethnologist* 18:440–58.

————. 1998. "Multiplicity and Contention among Language Ideologies: A Comment." In *Language Ideologies*, ed. B. Schieffelin, K. Woolard, and P. V. Kroskrity. Oxford: Oxford University Press.

Gal, Susan, and Judith T. Irvine. 1995. "The Boundaries of Languages and Disciplines: How Ideologies Construct Difference." *Social Research* 62:967–1001.

Gaus, Günter. 1983. *Wo Deutschland liegt: Eine Ortsbestimmung*. Hamburg: Hoffmann und Campe.

Gay, Peter. 1968. *Weimar Culture: The Outsider as Insider*. New York: Harper and Row.

————. 1978. *Freud, Jews, and Other Germans: Masters and Victims in Modernist Culture.* New York: Oxford University Press.

Geertz, Clifford. 1988. *Works and Lives: The Anthropologist as Author.* Stanford: Stanford University Press.

Gella, Aleksander, ed. 1976. *The Intelligentsia and the Intellectuals: Theory, Method, and Case Study.* Beverly Hills, CA: Sage Publications.

Geserick, Rolf. 1989. *40 Jahre Presse, Rundfunk und Kommunikationspolitik in der DDR.*Munich: Minerva-Publ.

Geyer, Michael. 1990. "The Past as Future: The German Officer Corps as Profession." In *German Professions, 1800–1950,* ed. G. Cocks and K. Jarausch. Oxford: Oxford University Press.

Giesen, Bernhard. 1998. *Intellectuals and the Nation: Collective Identity in a German Axial Age.* Trans. N. Levis and A. Weisz. Cambridge, UK: Cambridge University Press.

Gilman, Sander L. 2003. *Jewish Frontiers: Essays on Bodies, Histories, and Identities.* New York: Palgrave.

Glaeser, Andreas. 2000. *Divided in Unity: Identity, Germany, and the Berlin Police.* Chicago: University of Chicago Press.

————. n.d. "The Meaning of Buildings: Berlin's Palace of the Republic, for Example." Unpublished MS.

Glaeser, Hermann. 1993. *Bildungsbürgertum und Nationalismus: Politik und Kultur im Wilhelminischen Deutschland.* Munich: Deutscher Taschenbuch Verlag.

Goethe, Johann W. 2002. *The Sorrows of Young Werther.* Ed. N. H. Dole. Trans. T. Carlyle and R. D. Boylan. Mineola, NY: Dover Publications.

Goffman, Erving. 1959. *The Presentation of Self in Everyday Life.* New York: Anchor.

————. 1961. *Asylums: Essays on the Social Situation of Mental Patients and Other Inmates.* New York: Doubleday.

Gorky, Maxim. 1934. "Soviet Literature." In *Problems of Soviet Literature,* ed. H. G. Scott. New York: International Publishers.

Gouldner, Alvin. 1979. *The Future of Intellectuals and the Rise of the New Class.* New York: Seabury Press.

Graham, Philip. 2000. "Hypercapitalism: A Political Economy of Informational Idealism." *New Media and Society* 2 (2): 131–56.

Gramsci, Antonio. 1971. *Selections from the Prison Notebooks.* Trans. and ed. Q. Hoare and G. Nowell Smith. New York: International Publishers.

Gusterson, Hugh. 1996. *Nuclear Rites: A Weapons Laboratory at the End of the Cold War.* Berkeley and Los Angeles: University of California Press.

Habermas, Jürgen. 1984. *The Theory of Communicative Action.* Vol. 1, *Reason and the Rationalization of Society.* Trans. T. McCarthy. Boston: Beacon Press.

————. 1987. *The Theory of Communicative Action.* Vol. 2, *Lifeworld and System, a Critique of Functionalist Reason.* Trans. T. McCarthy. Boston: Beacon Press.

———. 1991. *The Structural Transformation of the Public Sphere: An Inquiry into a Category of Bourgeois Society.* Trans. T. Burger. Cambridge, MA: MIT Press.

Hahn, H.-J. 1998. *Education and Society in Germany.* New York: Berg.

Hale, Oron J. 1964. *The Captive Press in the Third Reich.* Princeton: Princeton University Press.

Hanks, William F. 1996. *Language and Communicative Practices.* Boulder: Westview Press.

Hannerz, Ulf. 1998. "Other Transnationals: Perspectives Gained from Studying Sideways." *Paideuma* 44:109–23.

———. 2003. *Foreign News: Exploring the World of Foreign Correspondents.* Chicago: University of Chicago Press.

Haraszti, Miklós. 1987. *The Velvet Prison: Artists under State Socialism.* Trans. K. Landesmann, S. Landesmann, and S. Wasserman. New York: Basic Books.

Hart, James Morgan. 1874. *German Universities.* New York: G. P. Putnam.

Harvey, David. 1989. *The Condition of Postmodernity: An Enquiry into the Origins of Cultural Change.* Cambridge, MA: Blackwell.

Hegel, Georg W. F. 1953. *Reason in History.* Trans. R. Hartman. New York: Macmillan.

———. 1986. *Vorlesungen über die Philosophie der Geschichte.* Werke 12. Frankfurt am Main: Suhrkamp Taschenbuch Verlag.

———. 1991. *Elements of the Philosophy of Right.* Trans. H. B. Nisbet. Cambridge, UK: Cambridge University Press.

———. 1997. "Berliner Antrittsrede (1818)." In *Berliner Schriften (1818–1831),* ed. W. Jaeschke. Hamburg: Felix Meiner Verlag.

Helmreich, Stefan. 1998. *Silicon Second Nature: Culturing Artificial Life in a Digital World.* Berkeley and Los Angeles: University of California Press.

Herder, Johann Gottfried von. 2002. *Philosophical Writings.* Trans. and ed. M. N. Forster. Cambridge, UK: Cambridge University Press.

Herf, Jeffrey. 1997. *Divided Memory: The Nazi Past in the Two Germanys.* Cambridge, MA: Harvard University Press.

Herzfeld, Michael. 1985. *The Poetics of Manhood: Contest and Identity in a Cretan Mountain Village.* Princeton: Princeton University Press.

———. 1987. *Anthropology through the Looking-Glass: Critical Ethnography in the Margins of Europe.* Cambridge, UK: Cambridge University Press.

———. 1997a. *Cultural Intimacy: Social Poetics in the Nation-State.* New York: Routledge.

———. 1997b. *Portrait of a Greek Imagination: An Ethnographic Biography of Andreas Nenedakis.* Chicago: University of Chicago Press.

———. 2001. "Irony and Power: Toward a Politics of Mockery in Greece." In *Irony in Action: Anthropology, Practice, and the Moral Imagination,* ed. J. W. Fernandez. Chicago: University of Chicago Press.

———. 2004. *The Body Impolitic: Artisans and Artifice in the Global Hierarchy of Value.* Chicago: University of Chicago Press.

Heym, Stefan. 1993. "Je voller der Mund, desto leerer die Sprüche." In *So durften wir glauben zu kämpfen . . . Erfahrungen mit DDR-Medien*, ed. E. Spielhagen. Berlin: VISTAS Verlag.

Hobsbawm, Eric, and Terence Ranger, eds. 1983. *The Invention of Tradition.* Cambridge, UK: Cambridge University Press.

Hoffmann, Stefan-Ludwig. 2000. *Die Politik der Geselligkeit: Freimaurerlogen in der deutschen Bürgergesellschaft, 1840–1918.* Göttingen: Vandenhoeck und Ruprecht.

————. 2003. "Democracy and Associations in the Long Nineteenth Century: Toward a Transnational Perspective." *Journal of Modern History* 75 (June): 269–99.

Hofmann, Robert. 1993. *Geschichte der deutschen Parteien: Von der Kaiserzeit bis zur Gegenwart.* Munich: Piper.

Hohendahl, Peter Uwe. 1989. *Building a National Literature: The Case of Germany, 1830–1870.* Trans. R. B. Franciscono. Ithaca: Cornell University Press.

Holmes, Douglas R. 2000. *Integral Europe: Fast-Capitalism, Multiculturalism, Neofascism.* Princeton: Princeton University Press.

Holmes, Douglas R., and George E. Marcus. 2005. "Cultures of Expertise and the Management of Globalization: Toward the Re-functioning of Ethnography." In *Global Assemblages: Technology, Politics and Ethics as Anthropological Problems,* ed. A. Ong and S. J. Collier. London: Blackwell.

Holquist, Michael. 1994. "Corrupt Originals: The Paradox of Censorship." *PMLA* 109 (January): 14–25.

Holub, Miroslav. 1990. *Poems Before and After.* Trans. I. Milner, J. Milner, E. Osers, and G. Theiner. Newcastle upon Tyne, UK: Bloodaxe Books.

Holzweissig, Gunter. 1983. *Massenmedien in der DDR.* Berlin: Verlag Gebr. Holzapfel.

————. 1997. *Zensur ohne Zensor: Die SED-Informationsdiktatur.* Bonn: Bouvier.

Horkheimer, Max, and Theodor Adorno. 1994. *Dialectic of Enlightenment.* Trans. J. Cumming. New York: Continuum.

Humphreys, Peter J. 1994. *Media and Media Policy in Germany: The Press and Broadcasting since 1945.* Providence, RI: Berg.

Husserl, Edmund. 1986. *Die Idee der Phänomenologie: Fünf Vorlesungen.* Ed. P. Janssen. Hamburg: F. Meiner.

Hymes, Dell, ed. 1969. *Reinventing Anthropology.* New York: Vintage.

Innis, Harold A. 1950. *Empire and Communications.* Oxford: Clarendon Press.

Irvine, Judith T. 1992. "Ideologies of Honorific Language." *Pragmatics* 2 (3): 251–62.

Jackson, Michael. 1989. *Paths toward a Clearing: Radical Empiricism and Ethnographic Inquiry.* Indianapolis: University of Indiana Press.

————, ed. 1996. *Things as They Are: New Directions in Phenomenological Anthropology.* Indianapolis: University of Indiana Press.

Jacoby, Russell. 1987. *The Last Intellectuals: American Culture in the Age of Academe.* New York: Basic Books.

Jakobson, Roman. 1960. "Linguistics and Poetics." In *Style in Language,* ed. T. A. Sebeok. Cambridge, MA: MIT Press.

Jakobson, Roman, and Morris Halle. 1956. *Fundamentals of Language.* The Hague: Mouton.

Jameson, Frederic. 1984. "Postmodernism: On the Cultural Logic of Late Capitalism." *New Left Review* 146:55–92.

Jarausch, Konrad H. 1982. *Students, Society, and Politics in Imperial Germany: The Rise of Academic Illiberalism.* Princeton: Princeton University Press.

———. 1990. *The Unfree Professions: German Lawyers, Teachers and Engineers, 1900–1950.* New York: Oxford University Press.

———. 1994. *The Rush to German Unity.* New York: Oxford University Press.

John, Michael. 1991. "Between Estate and Profession: Lawyers and the Development of the Legal Profession in Nineteenth-Century Germany." In *The German Bourgeoisie,* ed. D. Blackbourn and R. J. Evans. New York: Routledge.

Johns, Adrian. 1998. *The Nature of the Book: Print and Knowledge in the Making.* Chicago: University of Chicago Press.

Jones, Sydney J. 2002. *Hitler in Vienna, 1907–1913: Clues to the Future.* New York: Cooper Square Press.

Journalistisches Handbuch der Deutschen Demokratischen Republik. 1960. Leipzig: VEB Verlag für Buch- und Bibliothekwesen.

Jürgs, Michael. 1997. *Die Treuhändler: Wie Helden und Halunken die DDR verkauften.* Munich: List Verlag.

Kaelble, Helmut. 1988. "Französisches und deutsches Bürgertum, 1870–1914." In *Bürgertum im 19. Jahrhundert,* vol. 1, ed. J. Kocka. Munich: Deutscher Taschenbuch Verlag.

Kant, Immanuel. 1798. *Der Streit der Facultäten.* Königsberg: Friedrich Nicolovius.

Kapferer, Bruce. 1997. *The Feast of the Sorcerer: Practices of Consciousness and Power.* Chicago: University of Chicago Press.

Karp, Ivan. 1980. "Beer Drinking and Social Experience in an African Society: An Essay in Formal Sociology." In *Explorations in African Systems of Thought,* ed. I. Karp and C. S. Bird. Bloomington: Indiana University Press.

Kaudelka-Hanisch, Karin. 1993. *Preußische Kommerzienräte in der Provinz Westfalen und im Regierungsbezirk Düsseldorf (1810–1918).* Münster: Ardey.

Kershaw, Ian. 2000. *The Nazi Dictatorship: Problems and Perspectives of Interpretation.* 4th ed. London: Arnold.

Keyserlingk, Robert H. 1977. *Media Manipulation: A Study of the Press and Bismarck in Imperial Germany.* Montreal: Renouf Publishing.

Kittler, Friedrich A. 1990. *Discourse Networks, 1800/1900.* Trans. M. Metteer with C. Cullens. Stanford: Stanford University Press.

Klein, Manfred. 1993. "In Verantwortung für den DDR-Hörfunk——Versuche und

Versagen." In *So durften wir glauben zu kämpfen . . . Erfahrungen mit DDR-Medien*, ed. E. Spielhagen. Berlin: VISTAS Verlag.

Klötzer, Sylvia. 1996. "Öffentlichkeit in der DDR? Die soziale Wirklichkeit im *Eulenspiegel.*" *Aus Politik und Zeitgeschichte* 46:28–37.

Klump, Brigitte. 1978. *Das rote Kloster: Eine deutsche Erziehung*. Hamburg: Hoffman und Campe.

Kocka, Jürgen. 1988. "Bürgertum und bürgerliche Gesellschaft im 19. Jahrhundert: Europäische Entwicklungen und deutsche Eigenarten." In *Bürgertum im 19. Jahrhundert*, vol. 1, ed. J. Kocka. Munich: Deutscher Taschenbuch Verlag.

Kohl, Marianne. 1936. "Die Nationalzeitung der Deutschen, 1784–1830." PhD diss., Ruprecht-Karls-Universität zu Heidelberg.

Kohlhoff, Werner. 1997. "Der Ossi, das bekannte Wesen." *Berliner Zeitung*, 21 April, p. 2.

Konrád, George, and Ivan Szelényi. 1979. *The Intellectuals on the Road to Class Power: A Sociological Study of the Role of the Intelligentsia in Socialism*. Trans. A. Arato and R. F. Allen. New York: Harcourt Brace Jovanovich.

Koselleck, Reinhart. 1990. "Einleitung: Zur anthropologischen und semantischen Struktur der Bildung." In *Bildungsbürgertum im 19. Jahrhundert*, vol. 2, ed. R. Koselleck. Stuttgart: Klett-Cotta.

Koszyk, Kurt. 1966. *Deutsche Presse im 19. Jahrhundert*. Berlin: Colloquium Verlag.

———. 1972. *Deutsche Presse, 1914–1945*. Berlin: Colloquium Verlag.

Kroskrity, Paul V., ed. 2000. *Regimes of Language: Ideologies, Polities, and Identities*. Santa Fe, NM: School of American Research Press.

LaCapra, Dominick. 1998. "The University in Ruins?" *Critical Inquiry* 25 (Autumn): 32–55.

Lakoff, George, and Mark Johnson. 1980. *Metaphors We Live By*. Chicago: University of Chicago Press.

Latour, Bruno. 1999. *Pandora's Hope: Essays on the Reality of Science Studies*. Cambridge: Harvard University Press.

Lenin, Vladimir I. 1961. "Where to Begin." Trans. J. Fineberg and G. Hanna. In *Lenin: Collected Works*, vol. 5. London: Lawrence and Wishart.

———. 1962. "Party Organisation and Party Literature." Trans. A. Rothstein. In *Lenin: Collected Works*, vol. 10. London: Lawrence and Wishart.

Lévi-Strauss, Claude. 1966. *The Savage Mind*. Chicago: University of Chicago Press.

———. 1981. *The Naked Man*. Trans. J. Weightman and D. Weightman. New York: Harper and Row.

Lévy-Bruhl, Lucien. 1996. *How Natives Think*. Trans. L. Clare. New York: Washington Square Press.

Lidtke, Vernon L. 1985. *The Alternative Culture: Socialist Labor in Imperial Germany*. New York: Oxford University Press.

Lindemann, Margot. 1969. *Deutsche Press bis 1815*. Berlin: Colloquium Verlag.

Lomnitz, Claudio. 1992. *Exits from the Labyrinth: Culture and Ideology in the*

Mexican National Space. Berkeley and Los Angeles: University of California Press.

⸻. 2001. *Deep Mexico, Silent Mexico: An Anthropology of Nationalism.* Minneapolis: University of Minnesota Press.

Luhmann, Niklas. 1995. *Social Systems.* Ed. T. Lenoir and H. U. Gumbrecht. Trans. J. Bednarz Jr. Stanford: Stanford University Press.

⸻. 2000. *The Reality of Mass Media.* Trans. K. Cross. Stanford: Stanford University Press. ˙

Lukács, Georg. 1971. *History and Class Consciousness: Studies in Marxist Dialectics.* Trans. R. Livingstone. Cambridge, MA: MIT Press.

Lyotard, Jean-François. 1984. *The Postmodern Condition: A Report on Knowledge.* Trans. G. Bennington and B. Massumi. Minneapolis: University of Minnesota Press.

Maaz, Hans-Joachim. 1995. *Behind the Wall: The Inner Life of Communist Germany.* Trans. M. B. Dembo. New York: W. W. Norton.

Mah, Harold E. 1986. "Karl Marx in Love: The Enlightenment, Romanticism and Hegelian Theory in the Young Marx." *History of European Ideas* 7:489–507.

⸻. 1994. "The Epistemology of the Sentence: Language, Civility, and Identity in France and Germany, Diderot to Nietzsche." *Representations* 47:64–84.

Mahle, Walter A., ed. 1993. *Journalisten in Deutschland: Nationale und internationale Vergleiche und Perspektiven.* Munich: Verlag Ölschläger.

Maier, Charles S. 1997. *Dissolution: The Crisis of Communism and the End of East Germany.* Princeton: Princeton University Press.

Malinowski, Bronislaw. 1954. *Magic, Science, and Religion.* Garden City, NJ: Doubleday.

Mann, Thomas. 1984. *Von Deutscher Republik.* Frankfurt am Main: S. Fischer Verlag.

Mannheim, Karl. 1936. *Ideology and Utopia: An Introduction to the Sociology of Knowledge.* Trans. L. Wirth and E. Shils. New York: Harcourt, Brace and Co.

⸻. 1993. "The Problem of a Sociology of Knowledge." In *From Karl Mannheim,* ed. K. H. Wolff. New Brunswick, NJ: Transaction Publishers.

Marcus, George E. 2001. "The Predicament of Irony and the Paranoid Style in Fin-de-Siècle Rationality." In *Irony in Action: Anthropology, Practice, and the Moral Imagination,* ed. J. W. Fernandez and M. T. Huber. Chicago: University of Chicago Press.

Marcus, George E., and Michael Fischer. 1986. *Anthropology as Cultural Critique: An Experimental Moment in the Human Sciences.* Chicago: University of Chicago Press.

Martens, Erika. 1972. *Zum Beispiel Das Reich: Zur Phänomenologie der Presse im totalitären Regime.* Cologne: Verlag Wissenschaft und Politik.

Martin, Randy, ed. 1998. *Chalk Lines: The Politics of Work in the Managed University.* Durham, NC: Duke University Press.

Marx, Karl. 1967a. "Critique of Hegel's Dialectic and Philosophy in General." In *Writings of the Young Marx on Philosophy and Society.* Trans. and ed. L. D. Easton and K. H. Goddat. Garden City, NJ: Doubleday.

————. 1967b. "Free Human Production." In *Writings of the Young Marx on Philosophy and Society,* trans. and ed. L. D. Easton and K. H. Goddat. Garden City, NJ: Doubleday.

————. 1971. *Frühe Schriften.* Vol. 1, ed. H.-J. Lieber and P. Furth. Darmstadt: Wissenschaftliche Buchgesellschaft.

Marx, Karl, and Friedrich Engels. 1978. *The Marx-Engels Reader.* Ed. R. C. Tucker. New York: Norton.

Mast, Claudia. 1993. "Medien und Journalismus im Umbruch: Erfahrungen von Medienunternehmen in den neuen Bundesländern." In *Journalisten in Deutschland: Nationale und internationale Vergleiche und Perspektiven,* ed. W. A. Mahle. Munich: Verlag Ölschläger.

————, ed. 1994. *ABC des Journalismus: Ein Leitfaden für die Redaktionsarbeit.* Munich: Verlag Ölschläger.

Maurer, Bill. 2002. "Anthropological and Accounting Knowledge in Islamic Banking and Finance: Rethinking Critical Accounts." *Journal of the Royal Anthropological Institute* 8 (4): 645–67.

Mazzarella, William. 2003. *Shoveling Smoke: Advertising and Globalization in India.* Durham, NC: Duke University Press.

Mbembe, Achille. 1992. "The Banality of Power and the Aesthetics of Vulgarity in the Postcolony." *Public Culture* 4 (2): 1–30.

McChesney, Robert W. 1997. *Corporate Media and the Threat to Democracy.* New York: Seven Stories Press.

McClelland, Charles E. 1980. *State, Society and University in Germany, 1700–1914.* Cambridge, UK: Cambridge University Press.

————. 1982. "The Wise Man's Burden: The Role of Academicians in Imperial German Culture." In *Essays on Culture and Society in Imperial Germany,* ed. G. Stark and B. Lackner. College Station: Texas A&M Press.

————. 1991. *The German Experience of Professionalization: Modern Learned Professions and Their Organizations from the Early Nineteenth Century to the Hitler Era.* Cambridge, UK: Cambridge University Press.

McLuhan, Marshall. 1962. *The Gutenberg Galaxy: The Making of Typographic Man.* Toronto: University of Toronto Press.

————. 1964. *Understanding Media: The Extensions of Man.* Cambridge, MA: MIT Press.

Merleau-Ponty, Maurice. 1962. *Phenomenology of Perception.* Trans. C. Smith. London: Routledge.

Meyn, Hermann. 1994. *Massenmedien in der Bundesrepublik Deutschland.* Berlin: Edition Colloquium.

Minholz, Michael, and Uwe Stirnberg. 1995. *Der Allgemeine Deutsche Nachrichtendienst (ADN): Gute Nachrichten für die SED.* Munich: K. G. Saur.

Miyazaki, Hiro. 2004. *The Method of Hope*. Stanford: Stanford University Press.

Modrow, Hans, ed. 1994. *Das Große Haus: Insider berichten aus dem ZK der SED*. Berlin: Edition Ost.

Moritz, Karl Philipp. 1784. *Ideal einer vollkommenen Zeitung*. Berlin.

Mosse, George L. 1964. *The Crisis of German Ideology: Intellectual Origins of the Third Reich*. New York: Howard Fertig.

———. 1966. *Nazi Culture: Intellectual, Cultural, and Social Life in the Third Reich*. New York: Schocken Books.

Musil, Robert. 1995. *The Man without Qualities*. Trans. S. Wilkins. New York: Alfred A. Knopf.

Nader, Laura. 1969. "Up the Anthropologist—Perspectives Gained from Studying Up." In *Reinventing Anthropology*, ed. D. Hymes. New York: Pantheon.

Nelson, Cary, ed. 1997. *Will Teach for Food: Academic Labor in Crisis*. Minneapolis: University of Minnesota Press.

Nettl, J. P. 1969. "Ideas, Intellectuals, and Structures of Dissent." In *On Intellectuals: Theoretical Studies and Case Studies*, ed. P. Rieff. Garden City, NJ: Doubleday.

Newborn, Jud. 1994. " 'Work Makes Free': The Hidden Cultural Meaning of the Holocaust." PhD diss., University of Chicago.

Nietzsche, Friedrich. 1966. *Beyond Good and Evil: Prelude to a Philosophy of the Future*. Trans. W. Kaufmann. New York: Random House.

———. 1980. *On the Advantage and Disadvantage of History for Life*. Trans. P. Preuss. Indianapolis: Hackett Publishing.

Nipperdey, Thomas. 1983. *Deutsche Geschichte, 1800–1866: Bürgerwelt und starker Staat*. Munich: Verlag C. H. Beck.

Ortner, Sherry. 1973. "On Key Symbols." *American Anthropologist* 75 (6): 1338–46.

Osang, Alexander. 1996. "Ich mache irgendwie weiter." In *Genosse Journalist*, ed. W. Steul. Mainz: Verlag Donata Kinzelbach.

———. 2002. *die nachrichten*. Frankfurt am Main: Fischer Taschenbuch Verlag.

Papataxiarchis, Evthymios. 1991. "Friends of the Heart: Male Commensal Solidarity, Gender, and Kinship in Aegean Greece." In *Contested Identities: Gender and Kinship in Modern Greece*, ed. P. Loizos and E. Papataxiarchis. Princeton: Princeton University Press.

Parsons, Talcott. 1969. " 'The Intellectual': A Social Role Category." In *On Intellectuals*, ed. P. Rieff. Garden City, NJ: Doubleday.

Peirce, Charles S. 1998. "The Ethics of Terminology." In *The Essential Peirce: Selected Philosophical Writings, 1893–1913*, vol. 2, ed. Peirce Edition Project. Bloomington: Indiana University Press.

Pesmen, Dale. 2000. *Russia and Soul: An Exploration*. Ithaca: Cornell University Press.

Poerschke, Hans, et al. 1983. *Theoretischen Grundfragen des sozialistischen Journalismus*. Leipzig: Karl-Marx-Universität Sektion Journalistik.

Posner, Richard. 2002. *Public Intellectuals: A Study of Decline.* Cambridge: Harvard University Press.

Postone, Moishe. 1980. "Antisemitism and National Socialism: Notes on the German Reaction to the Holocaust." *New German Critique* 19:117–36.

———. 1996. *Time, Labor, and Social Domination: A Reinterpretation of Marx's Critical Theory.* Cambridge, UK: Cambridge University Press.

Quinn, Naomi. 1991. "The Cultural Basis of Metaphor." In *Beyond Metaphor: The Theory of Tropes in Anthropology,* ed. J. W. Fernandez. Stanford: Stanford University Press.

Rabinow, Paul. 1996. *Making PCR: A Story of Biotechnology.* Chicago: University of Chicago Press.

———. 1999. *French DNA: Trouble in Purgatory.* Chicago: University of Chicago Press.

Radin, Paul. 1927. *Primitive Man as Philosopher.* New York: D. Appleton and Co.

Readings, Bill. 1996. *The University in Ruins.* Cambridge, MA: Harvard University Press.

Reck, Roland. 1996. *Wasserträger des Regimes: Rolle und Selbstverständnis von DDR- Journalisten vor und nach der Wende 1989/90.* Münster: Lit Verlag.

Reed-Danahay, Deborah E., ed. 1997. *Auto/Ethnography: Rewriting the Self and the Social.* New York: Berg.

Reissig, Rolf. 1998. "Der ostdeutsche Transformationsprozeß: Trends, Stimmungslagen, Einstellungen, Wahrnehmungsmuster." Unpublished MS.

Requate, Jörg. 1995. *Journalismus als Beruf: Entstehung und Entwicklung des Journalistenberufs im 19. Jahrhundert Deutschland im internationalen Vergleich.* Göttingen: Vandenhoeck und Ruprecht.

Retallack, James. 1993. "From Pariah to Professional? The Journalist in German Society and Politics, from the Late Enlightenment to the Rise of Hitler." *German Studies Review* 16:175–223.

Richards, I. A. 1950. *The Philosophy of Rhetoric.* New York: Oxford University Press.

Richert, Ernst. 1958. *Macht ohne Mandat: Der Staatsapparat in der sowjetischen Besatzungszone Deutschlands.* Cologne: Westdeutscher Verlag.

Richert, Ernst, Carola Stern, and Peter Dietrich. 1958. *Agitation und Propaganda: Das System der Publizistischen Massenführung in der Sowjetzone.* Berlin: Verlag Franz Vahten.

Ricoeur, Paul. 1977. *The Rule of Metaphor: Multi-disciplinary Studies of the Creation of Meaning in Language.* Trans. R. Czerny. Toronto: University of Toronto Press.

Ries, Nancy. 1997. *Russian Talk: Culture and Conversation during Perestroika.* Ithaca: Cornell University Press.

Ringer, Fritz K. 1969. *The Decline of the German Mandarins: The German Academic Community, 1890–1933.* Cambridge, MA: Harvard University Press.

————. 2000. *Toward a Social History of Knowledge: Collected Essays.* New York: Berghahn.

Robbins, Bruce. 1993. *Secular Vocations: Intellectuals, Professionalism, Culture.* New York: Verso.

Röhr, Karl-Heinz. 1968. *Zeitungsinformation und Bildschirm: Die sozialistische Presse unter den Bedingungen des Fernsehens.* Leipzig: VEB Bibliographisches Institut.

Ross, Andrew. 2000. "The Mental Labor Problem." *Social Text* 18 (2): 1–31.

Rotenberg, Robert. 1984. "Viennese Wine Gardens and Their Magic." *East European Quarterly* 18 (4): 447–60.

Roth, Ralf. 1996. "Von Wilhelm Meister zu Hans Castorp: Der Bildungsgedanke und das bürgerliche Assoziationswesen im 18. und 19. Jahrhundert," In *Bürgerkultur im 19. Jahrhundert: Bildung, Kunst und Lebenswelt,* ed. D. Hein and A. Schulz. Munich: Verlag C. H. Beck.

Sabean, David Warren. 1984. *Power in the Blood: Popular Culture and Village Discourse in Early Modern Germany.* Cambridge, UK: Cambridge University Press.

Sahlins, Marshall D. 1996. "The Sadness of Sweetness: The Native Anthropology of Western Cosmology." *Current Anthropology* 37:395–415.

Said, Edward W. 1994. *Representations of the Intellectual: The 1993 Reith Lectures.* London: Vintage.

Sandford, John. 1995. "The German Media." In *The New Germany: Social, Political, and Cultural Challenges of Unification,* ed. D. Lewis and J. McKenzie. Exeter, UK: University of Exeter Press.

Sänger, Fritz. 1978. *Verborgene Fäden: Erinnerungen und Bemerkungen eines Journalisten.* Bonn: Verlag Neue Gesellschaft.

Sangren, P. Steven. 2003. "Reflexivity Genuine and Spurious." Paper presented at American Anthropological Association meetings, Chicago, IL.

Santiago-Irizarry, Vilma. 2001. *Medicalizing Ethnicity: The Construction of Latino Identity in a Psychiatric Setting.* Ithaca: Cornell University Press.

Saussure, Ferdinand de. 1966. *Course in General Linguistics.* New York: McGraw-Hill.

Schabowski, Günter. 1991. *Der Absturz.* Berlin: Rowohlt Verlag.

Scharf, Wilfried. 1985. *Das Bild der Bundesrepublik Deutschland in den Massenmedien der DDR.* Frankfurt am Main: Peter Lang.

Scheler, Max. 1926. *Die Wissensformen und die Gesellschaft.* Leipzig: Der Neuegeist Verlag.

Schelling, F. W. J. 1956. "Vorlesungen über die Methode des akademischen Studiums." In *Die Idee der deutschen Universität,* ed. E. Anrich. Darmstadt: Hermann Gentner.

Schenda, Rolf. 1970. *Volk ohne Buch: Studien zur Sozialgeschichte der populären Lesestoffe, 1770–1910.* Frankfurt am Main: Vittorio Klostermann.

Schieffelin, Bambi B., Kathryn A. Woolard, and Paul V. Kroskrity, eds. 1998. *Language Ideologies: Practice and Theory.* Oxford: Oxford University Press.

Schleiermacher, Friedrich. 1956. "Gelegentliche Gedanken über Universitäten im deutschen Sinn." In *Die Idee der deutschen Universität,* ed. E. Anrich. Darmstadt: Hermann Gentner.

Schneider, Beate. 1992. "Die ostdeutsche Tagespresse—eine (traurige) Bilanz." *Media Perspektiven* 2:428–41.

Scholte, Bob. 1974. "Toward a Reflexive and Critical Anthropology." In *Reinventing Anthropology,* ed. D. Hymes. New York: Vintage.

Schorske, Carl. 1955. *German Social Democracy, 1905–1917: The Development of the Great Schism.* New York: Russell and Russell.

Schulze, Heinz. 1931. *Die Presse im Urteil Bismarcks.* PhD diss., Universität Leipzig. Leipzig: C. Schulze und Co.

Schutz, Alfred. 1967. *The Phenomenology of the Social World.* Trans. G. Walsh and F. Lehnert. Evanston, IL: Northwestern University Press.

Sheehan, James. 1981. "What Is German History? Reflections on the Role of the Nation in German History and Historiography." *Journal of Modern History* 53 (March): 1–23.

———. 1989. *German History, 1770–1866.* New York: Oxford University Press.

———. 1992. "State and Nationality in the Napoleonic Period." In *The State of Germany: The National Idea in the Making, Unmaking and Remaking of a Modern National State,* ed. J. Breuilly. New York: Longman.

Shils, Edward. 1972. *The Intellectuals and the Powers, and Other Essays.* Chicago: University of Chicago Press.

Shryock, Andrew, ed. 2004. *Off Stage/On Display: Intimacy and Ethnography in the Age of Public Culture.* Stanford: Stanford University Press.

Siegel, James T. 2001. "*Kiblat* and the Mediatic Jew." In *Religion and Media,* ed. H. de Vries and S. Weber. Stanford: Stanford University Press.

Silverstein, Michael. 1976. "Shifters, Linguistic Categories, and Cultural Description." In *Meaning in Anthropology,* ed. K. Basso and H. Selby. Albuquerque: University of New Mexico Press.

———. 1979. "Language Structure and Linguistic Ideology." In *The Elements: A Parasession on Linguistic Units and Levels,* ed. R. Clyne, W. Hanks, and C. Hofbauer. Chicago: Chicago Linguistics Society.

———. 1985. "Language and the Culture of Gender: At the Intersection of Structure, Usage, and Ideology." In *Semiotic Mediation,* ed. E. Mertz and R. Parmentier. Orlando, FL: Academic Press.

———. 2000. "Whorfianism and the Linguistic Imagination of Nationality." In *Regimes of Language: Ideologies, Politics, and Identities,* ed. P. V. Kroskrity. Santa Fe, NM: School of American Research Press.

Simmel, Georg. 1900. *Philosophie des Geldes.* Leipzig: Duncker und Humblot.

Simon, Günter. 1990. *Tisch Zeiten: Aus den Notizen eines Chefredkateurs 1981 bis 1989.* Berlin: Verlag Tribüne.

Simpson, David. 2002. *Situatedness; or, Why We Keep Saying Where We're Coming From*. Durham, NC: Duke University Press.

Slaughter, Sheila, and Larry L. Leslie. 1997. *Academic Capitalism: Politics, Policies, and the Entrepreneurial University*. Baltimore: Johns Hopkins University Press.

Sobania, Michael. 1996. "Vereinsleben: Regeln und Formen bürgerlicher Assoziationen im 19. Jahrhundert." In *Bürgerkultur im 19. Jahrhundert: Bildung, Kunst und Lebenswelt*, ed. D. Hein and A. Schulz. Munich: Verlag C. H. Beck.

Sparks, Colin. 1991. "From State to Market: What Eastern Europe Inherits from the West." *Media Development* 38 (3): 11–15.

———. 1998. *Communism, Capitalism and the Media*. London: Sage.

Sperber, Jonathan. 1997. *The Kaiser's Voters: Electors and Elections in Imperial Germany*. Cambridge, UK: Cambridge University Press.

Spielhagen, Edith, ed. 1993. *So durften wir glauben zu kämpfen . . . Erfahrungen mit DDR-Medien*. Berlin: VISTAS Verlag.

Splichal, Slavko. 1994. *Media beyond Socialism: Theory and Practice in East-Central Europe*. Boulder, CO: Westview Press.

Stahl, Ernest. 1934. *Die religiöse und die Humanitätsphilosophische Bildungsidee und die Enstehung des deutschen Bildungsromans im 18. Jahrhundert*. Bern: P. Haupt.

Stark, Gary D. 1981. *Entrepreneurs of Ideology: Neoconservative Publishers in Germany, 1890–1933*. Chapel Hill: University of North Carolina Press.

Stecher, Martin. 1914. *Die Erziehungsbestrebungen der deutschen moralischen Wochenschriften: Ein Beitrag zur Geschichte der Pädagogik des 18. Jahrhunderts*. PhD diss., Universität Leipzig. Langensalza: Beyer und Söhne.

Steul, Willi, ed. 1996. *Genosse Journalist*. Mainz: Verlag Donata Kinzelbach.

Stocking, George W., ed. 1974. *A Franz Boas Reader: The Shaping of American Anthropology, 1883–1911*. Chicago: University of Chicago Press.

Stoller, Paul. 1989a. *Fusion of the Worlds: An Ethnography of Possession among the Songhay of Niger*. Chicago: University of Chicago Press.

———. 1989b. *The Taste of Ethnographic Things: The Senses in Anthropology*. Philadelphia: University of Pennsylvania Press.

———. 1997. *Sensuous Scholarship*. Philadelphia: University of Pennsylvania Press.

Strathern, Marilyn, ed. 2000. *Audit Cultures: Anthropological Studies in Accountability, Ethics and the Academy*. London: Routledge.

Suny, Ronald Grigor, and Michael D. Kennedy, eds. 1999. *Intellectuals and the Articulation of the Nation*. Ann Arbor: University of Michigan Press.

Szelényi, Ivan. 1982. "The Intelligentsia in the Class Structure of State-Socialist Societies." In *Marxist Inquiries*, ed. M. Burawoy and T. Skocpol. Chicago: University of Chicago Press.

Taylor, Lucien. 1997. "Mediating Martinique: The 'Paradoxical Trajectory' of Raphael Confiant." In *Cultural Producers in Perilous States: Editing Events, Documenting Change*, ed. G. E. Marcus. Chicago: University of Chicago Press.

Tedlock, Dennis, and Bruce Mannheim, eds. 1995. *The Dialogic Emergence of Culture*. Urbana: University of Illinois Press.

Terranova, Tiziana. 2000. "Free Labor: Producing Culture for the Digital Economy." *Social Text* 18 (2): 33–58.

Thorkelson, Eli. 2004. "The Silent Social Order of the Theory Classroom." Honors thesis, Department of Anthropology, Cornell University.

Thornton, Mary Anna. 1987. "*Sekt* versus *Schnapps* in an Austrian Village." In *Constructive Drinking: Perspectives on Drink from Anthropology*, ed. M. Douglas. New York: Cambridge University Press.

Toews, John Edward. 1980. *Hegelianism: The Path toward Dialectical Humanism, 1805–1841*. Cambridge, UK: Cambridge University Press.

Tönnies, Ferdinand. 1887. *Gemeinschaft und Gesellschaft: Abhandlung des Communismus und des Socialismus als empirischer Culturformen*. Leipzig: Fues.

Tuchman, Gaye. 1978. *Making News: A Study in the Construction of Reality*. New York: The Free Press.

Turner, Terence S. 1991. " 'We Are Parrots,' 'Twins Are Birds': Play of Tropes as Operational Structure." In *Beyond Metaphor: The Theory of Tropes in Anthropology*, ed. J. W. Fernandez. Stanford: Stanford University Press.

Turner, Victor. 1967. *The Forest of Symbols: Aspects of Ndembu Ritual*. Ithaca: Cornell University Press.

Tylor, Edward B. 1958. *Religion in Primitive Culture*. New York: Harper and Row.

Ulrich, Andreas, and Jörg Wagner, eds. 1993. *DT 64: Das Buch zum Jugendradio, 1964–1993*. Leipzig: Thom Verlag.

Verdery, Katherine. 1991. *National Ideology under Socialism*. Berkeley and Los Angeles: University of California Press.

Die Verfassung der Deutschen Demokratischen Republik. 1950. Berlin: Amt für Information der Regierung der DDR.

von Hallberg, Robert, ed. 1996. *Literary Intellectuals and the Dissolution of the State: Professionalism and Conformity in the GDR*. Trans. K. Northcott. Chicago: University of Chicago Press.

von Harnack, Ernst. 1942. *The Practice of Public Administration*. Ed. J. Schneider. Trans. E. Fraenkel. Chicago: Public Administration Research Fund of the University of Chicago.

von Humboldt, Wilhelm. 1956. "Über die innere und außere Organisation der höheren wissenschaftlichen Anstalten in Berlin." In *Die Idee der deutschen Universität*, ed. E. Anrich. Darmstadt: Hermann Gentner.

von Polenz, Peter. 1994. *Deutsche Sprachgeschichte vom Spätmittelalter bis zur Gegenwart*. Vol. 2, *17. und 18. Jahrhundert*. Berlin: Walter de Gruyter.

von Törne, Lars. 1996. "Mühlfenzl, oder Eine westdeutsche Medienpolitik nach Gutsherrenart." In *Kolonialisierung der DDR: Kritische Analysen und Alternativen des Einigungsprozesses*, ed. W. Dümcke and F. Vilmar. Münster: Agenda Verlag.

von Törne, Lars, and Patrick Weber. 1996. "Zeitungslandschaft Ost: Monopolistische Medienkonzentration oder pluralistischer Pressemarkt?" In *Kolonialisierung der DDR: Kritische Analysen und Alternativen des Einigungsprozesses*, ed. W. Dümcke and F. Vilmar. Münster: Agenda Verlag.

von Treitschke, Heinrich. 1915. *Germany, France, Russia, and Islam.* New York: G. P. Putnam.

Wacquant, Loïc. 2003. *Body and Soul: Notebooks of an Apprentice Boxer.* New York: Oxford University Press.

Wagner, Reinhard, ed. 1994. *DDR Witze.* Berlin: Dietz.

———, ed. 1996. *DDR Witze. Teil 2.* Berlin: Dietz.

Walker, Mack. 1971. *German Home Towns: Community, State, and General Estate, 1648–1817.* Ithaca: Cornell University Press.

Walraff, Günter. 1977. *Der Aufmacher: Der Mann, der bei Bild Hans Esser war.* Cologne: Verlag Kiepenhauer und Witsch.

Walser-Smith, Helmut. 1995. *German Nationalism and Religious Conflict: Culture, Ideology, Politics, 1870–1914.* Princeton: Princeton University Press.

Warren, Kay B. 1998. *Indigenous Movements and Their Critics: Pan-Maya Activism in Guatemala.* Princeton: Princeton University Press.

Weber, Max. 1926. *Politik als Beruf.* Munich: Duncker und Humblot.

———. 1958. *The Protestant Ethic and the Spirit of Capitalism.* Trans. T. Parsons. New York: Charles Scribner's Sons.

———. 1963. *The Sociology of Religion.* Trans. E. Fischoff. Boston: Beacon Press.

Wehler, Hans-Ulrich. 1987. *Deutsche Gesellschaftsgeschichte.* Vol. 1, *Vom Feudalismus des alten Reichs bis zur defensiven Modernisierung der Reformära, 1700–1815.* Munich: Verlag C. H. Beck.

———. 1989. *Deutsche Gesellschaftsgeschichte.* Vol. 2, *Von der Reformära bis zur industriellen und politischen "Deutschen Doppelrevolution," 1815–1845/9.* Munich: Verlag C. H. Beck.

———. 1995. *Deutsche Gesellschaftsgeschichte.* Vol. 3, *Von der "Deutschen Doppelrevolution" bis zum Beginn des Ersten Weltkrieges, 1849–1914.* Munich: Verlag C. H. Beck.

Weindling, Paul. 1991. "Bourgeois Values, Doctors, and the State: The Professionalization of Medicine in Germany, 1848–1933." In *The German Bourgeoisie*, ed. D. Blackbourn and R. J. Evans. New York: Routledge.

Williams, Jeffrey J. 2001. "Name Recognition." *Minnesota Review* 52–54:185–208.

Wilson, Monica. 1957. *Rituals of Kinship among the Nyakyusa.* London: Oxford University Press.

Wolff, Larry. 1994. *Inventing Eastern Europe: The Map of Civilization in the Mind of the Enlightenment.* Stanford: Stanford University Press.

Woolard, Kathryn A. 1998. "Introduction: Language Ideology as a Field of Inquiry." In *Language Ideologies*, ed. B. Schieffelin, K. Woolard, and P. V. Kroskrity. Oxford: Oxford University Press.

Wulf, Joseph. 1966. *Theater und Film im Dritten Reich: Eine Dokumentation.* Schleswig: Rowohlt Verlag.

Wuthnow, Robert. 1989. *Communities of Discourse: Ideology and Social Structure in the Reformation, the Enlightenment, and European Socialism.* Cambridge, MA: Harvard University Press.

Wyrwa, Ulrich. 1990. *Branntewein und "echtes Bier": Die Trinkkultur der Hamburger Arbeiter im 19. Jahrhundert.* Hamburg: Junius.

Young, Katharine. 1997. *Presence in the Flesh: The Body in Medicine.* Cambridge, MA: Harvard University Press.

Zammito, John H. 2002. *Kant, Herder, and the Birth of Anthropology.* Chicago: University of Chicago Press.

Zima, Peter V. 1975. "Der Mythos der Monosemie: Parteilichkeit und künstlerischer Standpunkt." In *Literaturwissenschaft und Sozialwissenschaften 6: Einführung in Theorie, Geschichte und Funktion der DDR-Literatur,* ed. H.-J. Schmitt. Stuttgart: J. B. Metzler.

Zimmermann, Brigitte, and Hans-Dieter Schütt, eds. 1992. *ohnMacht: DDR-Funktionäre sagen aus.* Berlin: Verlag Neues Leben.

Ziolkowski, Theodore. 1990. *German Romanticism and Its Institutions.* Princeton: Princeton University Press.

Žižek, Slavoj. 1993. *Tarrying with the Negative: Kant, Hegel, and the Critique of Ideology.* Durham, NC: Duke University Press.

Zola, Emile. 1998. *The Dreyfus Affair: J'accuse, and Other Writings.* Ed. Alain Pages. Trans. E. Levieux. New Haven: Yale University Press.

Zöller, Hugo. 1925. *Als Jurnalist und Forscher in Deutschlands großer Kolonialzeit.* Leipzig: Koehler und Amelang.

INDEX

ABC des Journalismus, 198
actuality, 10–11, 12, 50, 70, 75, 76, 116, 124, 146, 224. *See also* dialectical social knowledge; potentiality
ADN. *See* Allgemeiner Deutscher Nachrichtendienst
Adorno, Theodor, 86, 99–101
Agitation Division, 132–35, 142–44, 146–47
Aktuelle Kamera, 132, 139–40
alienation, 78–80
Allgemeiner Deutscher Nachrichtendienst (ADN), 128–29, 130–31, 171, 242, 247, 248
Althusser, Louis, 20–21
Anderson, Benedict, 33
Anderson, Margaret, 84
anthropology
  of dialectical social knowledge, 10–13, 274–75, 279
  of knowledge, 13–15, 28, 34, 42, 273–80
  phenomenology and, 36
  theory used in, 15–16
  trope theory and, 36–41
anti-Semitism
  in the GDR, 127n.4
  in the nineteenth century, 89, 94–96
  in the Third Reich, 109–14 passim
ARD (FRG public broadcasting corporation), 2, 162, 190, 216
Arendt, Hannah, 10, 97, 105n.2, 106
Argu, 133–35
Augustine, Dolores, 88–89

Bakhtin, Mikhail, 241
Baumann, Zygmunt, 43

Beamten, 51, 52, 53, 67, 69–70, 74, 83, 92, 93, 97
becoming. *See* potentiality
Benjamin, Walter, 221, 273
Berlin
  media in (*see* GDR Radio, complex in Nalepastraße; *Wochenpost, Die*)
  University of (*see under* universities)
Berliner Abendblätter, 74
Berliner Zeitung, 187, 188
Berlin Wall, 163, 187, 222, 252–53
Berufsverbot, 130n.5, 135–36, 248
Besitzbürgertum, 63n.2
  associational life of, 68
  dialectical social knowledge and, 64
  relationship to *Bildungsbürgertum,* 64–70
  rising social status of, 88–89
Biermann, Wolf, 5, 5n.1
Bildung, 12–13
  defined, 52, 54
  of East German journalists, 203
  ennoblement, as sign of, 66–67
  GDR journalism and, 158
  Gebildeten and, 54, 69–70, 83
  Germanness and, 59
  in Habermas's systems theory, 237–38
  institutionalization of, 69
  in intellectual activity, 278
  interiority and, 58–59
  in Marx's theory, 78, 80
  Nazism and, 110
  negative dialectical knowledge and, 58
  nobility and, 66
  positive dialectical knowledge and, 58

Bildung (*continued*)
  SED and, 124, 146–47
  socialist journalism and, 158
  through universities, 71–75
  as a trope, 58–59
  of the *Volk*, 104, 124, 158
  and the *Wende*, 222
Bildungsbürger. See *Gebildeten*
Bildungsbürgertum, 46–98
  Besitzbürgertum and, 64–70
  communicative practices of, 59–60, 63–64
  decline in status of, 88–90
  defined, 52–55
  demographics of, 63n.2
  and dialectical social knowledge, 64
  and Germanness, 55–64
  imagination of Deutschland, 63–64, 81
  and interiority, 47–52, 55–59
  and the masses, 59
  as a national collectivity, 60
  and nationalism, 49–50
  negative dialectical knowledge and, 55, 80–90
  NSDAP and, 97–98
  post-Hegelian critics of modernization, 77–78, 90–91
  social identity of, 54, 55, 59–60
  social phenomenology of, 70
  the state and, 50, 67, 82, 83, 96, 101–4, 106–10, 114, 118–20
  translocality of, 63–64
  and tropes of self-identification, 55–60
  See also *Gebildeten*
Bisky, Lothar, 188
Bismarck, Otto von, 83–84, 94, 96, 110–11
Blackbourn, David, 16, 49, 62–63, 65
Blecha, Kurt, 146
Bödeker, Hans Erich, 58–59
Bornemann, John, 184, 186
Bos, Ellen, 125
Bourdieu, Pierre, 42, 178, 189, 201, 273
  Homo Academicus, 30–31
  sociology of knowledge, 30–31
bourgeoisie
  in German-speaking Central Europe, 62–63
  Hitler's animosity toward, 107
  ideology and, 24–26
  rationalism and, 25–26
  social identity of, 65
  See also *Besitzbürgertum; Bildungs-bürgertum; Gebildeten; Großbürgertum*

Boyle, Maryellen, 191
Bramsted, Ernest, 60–61
Broszat, Martin, 105–6
Bruford, W.H., 65
Brunöhler, Kurt, 93
Budzislawski, Hermann, 121, 122
Burda Verlag, 265n.11, 267
burden of history. See *Vergangenheitsbelas-tung*
Burte, Hermann, 108

camera obscura, 22, 44, 242
capitalism
  alienation in, 78–80
  Marx's critique of, 79–80
  modernization as driving force of, 237
  SED and, 117–19, 127, 146
  Western journalism and, 158
  See also dialectical social knowledge
censorship
  in the GDR, 132, 137–144, 146–47
  Geist and, 146–47
  in the Third Reich, 114–16
Central Committee, 132–33, 136, 143. See also Agitation Division; German Democratic Republic; SED
class, Marxian theory of, 25–30, 36, 53. See also Marx, Karl: critique of ideology
class consciousness, 25
class enemy, 124, 126–27, 138, 142, 146, 158, 168
collective mentality, 6n.3
communicative action, 237–39
communicative practices
  of *Bildungsbürgertum*, 59–60, 63–64
  in the GDR, 120–47
  of intellectuals, 32
  in the Third Reich, 108–17
  trope theory and, 36–41
  See also language
consciousness
  class, 25
  collective: in the GDR, 102, 147; in the Third Reich, 101, 102, 109, 111
  national, 33
  the *Volk*'s self-, 109, 137, 150
Conze, Werner, 52
Cornell University, 276–77
Craig, Gordon, 83
Crick, Malcolm, 13–14
cultural capital, 30–31, 31n, 44

cultural elite. See *Bildungsbürgertum*;
Gebildeten
cultural redemption, 101–3, 137
culture, 14, 38. *See also* intellectual culture;
Kultur
culture bearers, 57, 61, 70, 72, 85

Deutsche Bühne, Die (Hitler), 107–8
Deutschland
    Bildungsbürgertum's imagination of, 63–64,
        71–75, 81, 85
    Hegel and, 75
    perceived threats to, 97–98, 103–10
    postwar, 117
    See also *Bildungsbürgertum*, social identity
        of; Germanness
dialectical social knowledge
    in academic intellectual culture, 273–80
    anthropology of, 10–13, 274–75, 279
    Besitzbürgertum and, 64–70
    Bildungsbürgertum and, 64
    class consciousness and, 25
    defined, 10–13
    of easternness, 166–67, 183, 188–89,
        197–201, 211–12, 215
    epistemic form, 44–45
    in German intellectual culture, 42–43
    Germanness and, 47–52, 55–60, 185–88
    Hitler and, 108, 110
    intersubjectivity and, 179
    journalism and: in the GDR, 143–45, 147,
        150–59; in the Third Reich, 115–17; in
        unified Germany, 158–59
    Marxian sociology of knowledge and,
        33–34
    the media and, 102–3, 147–50, 235–41
    modes of, 12
    Nalepastraße and, 178–79
    nationalism and, 48–51, 55–60
    negative: academic intellectual culture
        and, 275–78; amplification of, 80–90;
        Bildung and, 58; *Bildungsbürgertum*
        and, 55, 80–90; censorship in the GDR
        and, 147; in *Dialectic of Enlightenment*,
        100–101; GDR journalists and, 150–59;
        Geist and, 78; in German intellectual
        culture, 90–96, 101, 275; in Marx's
        theory, 78, 80; of nineteenth-century
        journalists, 91–96; SED and, 121, 127;
        of technical anthropology, 239 (*see also*
        longitudinalism)

    NSDAP and, 101–4
    the Ossi and, 183
    phenomenology and, 35–36, 42, 179, 274
    positive: in academic intellectual culture,
        277; *Bildung* and, 58; censorship in
        the GDR and, 147; in contemporary
        intellectual culture, 275, 277; dampening
        of, 80–90; in *Dialectic of Enlightenment*,
        100–101; GDR journalists and, 150–59,
        219–25; *Gebildeten* and, 50, 54–55, 70, 77;
        in German intellectual culture, 50, 54–55,
        70, 77, 101, 275, 279–81; of Germanness,
        47–48, 70, 101, 102–3, 137, 254–58,
        263–64, 269–70; in Marx's theory, 78–80;
        reflexivity and, 279–80; SED and, 118,
        122, 125, 137; of *Volk*, 118–20; of the
        Wende, 219–25
    processes of formation, 13
    reflexivity and, 274–75, 278–80
    SED and, 101–4
    selfhood and, 12, 179, 201, 206–7, 219
    spatiality in, 10–11
    temporality in, 10–11
    trope theory and, 38–41
    the Wessi and, 183
dialecticism. *See* dialectical social knowledge;
    Hegel, Georg W. F., and dialectic
Dialectic of Enlightenment (Horkheimer and
    Adorno), 99–101
Dirks, Walter, 116
division of labor, 21–23, 25, 44, 125, 279
Dohlus, Horst, 257n.7
Dumont, Louis, 58
Durkheim, Emile, 96, 275

easternness
    dialectical social knowledge of, 166–67, 183,
        188, 197–201, 211–12, 215
    East German journalists' self-perception of,
        199–201, 207–8, 217, 218–19
    and gender, 211–12
    Germanness and, 218–19
    See also longitudinalism; Ossi; Wessi
East German journalists
    allochronization of, 199
    cog metaphor and, 7
    and dialectical social knowledge, 181–83,
        210–12, 201–8, 217–19, 266
    evaluations of past selves, 3, 150–59
    and GDR Radio complex, 169–76
    as intellectuals, 33

East German journalists (*continued*)
  as lesser professionals, 198–201, 208
  longitudinalism and, 181–83, 201–8, 210–12,
    217–19, 266
  older, 3, 157, 191, 206, 220n.11
  postunification media and, 3, 151–52, 158,
    163, 165–66
  reeducation of, 2, 190–95, 198, 203, 213–14
  as regionals, 197–201
  self-perceptions of easternness, 199–201,
    207–8, 217, 218–19
  Spirit compromised by *Macht*, 205–6
  at the *Stammtisch*, 246–70
  System and, 7–8, 153–59, 191, 199–200, 209,
    219–25, 253–70 passim
  in unified Germany, 158–59, 225–28
  use of tropes, 153, 157, 219–25, 253
  and *Vergangenheitsbelastung*, 191–95,
    204–8, 219
  views on the GDR, 209–10
  views on other journalists, 160–66
  and the *Wende*, 157, 220–25
  and West German journalists, 2, 151–52,
    165, 167, 192–93, 197–219, 223–24,
    242–70
  West Germans' suspicions about, 190–93
  younger, 2, 157, 191, 193, 211–12, 216
*Economic and Philosophic Manuscripts of
  1844* (Marx and Engels), 78
Eichmann, Adolf, 10
Eley, Geoff, 89
Elias, Norbert, 48, 57, 104
Engels, Friedrich
  *Economic and Philosophic Manuscripts of
    1844*, 78
  The German Ideology, 21–23, 80
Engelsing, Rolf, 92, 93, 94
Enlightenment, 100
ennoblement, 66–67, 89
Entfremdung. *See* alienation
Eucken, Rudolf, 85
Eulenspiegel, 141–43
exteriority, 6, 10, 11–13, 39–40, 42, 47–59
  passim, 64, 70, 75–90 passim, 101–4
  passim, 109, 115, 119, 126, 129, 149, 157,
  179, 219, 221, 235, 248, 264, 273, 276, 278,
  280. *See also* dialectical social knowledge,
  negative; *Macht*; System

Fanon, Frantz, 199
Federal Republic of Germany (FRG)

dialectical social knowledge of, 186
and eastern Germany after 1989, 187–88,
  189
and Europe, 186
and the GDR, 126, 184–86, 187 (*see also*
  class enemy)
media in, 124, 126, 128, 130, 138, 146, 162,
  167, 190
SED and, 126–27, 138, 146
as System, 7, 181, 186, 199, 209, 221, 223,
  225, 253–70 passim
Fehrenbach, Elisabeth, 68
Fernandez, James W., 20, 36–38, 40–41
Fichte, Johann Gottlieb, 54–55, 56, 71–75, 77,
  98
Foucault, Michel, 239, 241
Frankfurter Zeitung, 113
Frankfurt School, 101
Frei, Norbert, 105, 109, 114
Freie Deutsche Jugend (FDJ), 5n.2, 142
Freud, Sigmund, 4, 6
Freytag, Gustav, 92
FRG. *See* Federal Republic of Germany
Friedrich, Paul, 36, 38, 41, 44
Friedrich Wilhelm III (king), 68, 71
Führerprinzip, 111–12, 114, 129, 130
functionalism, 25, 27, 31, 34

Gauck, Joachim, 164n.3
Gauck agency, 164n.3, 195
Gaus, Günter, 149
GDR. *See* German Democratic Republic
GDR Radio, 2, 161–68 passim
  complex in Nalepastraße, 161–62, 168–76,
    178–79
  dissolution of after the *Wende*, 162, 163,
    190, 225
Gebildeten
  as *Beamten*, 67
  and *Bildung*, 54, 69–70, 83
  conservatism of, 83, 88, 89
  as culture bearers, 57, 61, 70, 72, 85, 86
  defined, 52
  ennoblement of, 66
  and Germanness, 68–70
  and *Großbürgertum*, 88–89
  heterogeneity of, 53–54
  Hitler as, 106–7
  journalists as, 93, 93n.7, 96, 117
  knowledge practices of, 54–55, 84–85
  liminality of, 68, 70, 82

and *Massenkultur,* 51, 85–86, 87, 90–91,
    99–101
and modernization of German society,
    68–70
and nationalism, 57, 60–64, 74–75, 97
and negative dialectical knowledge, 50–52,
    77–78
and nobility, 64–70, 82–83
and NSDAP, 97–98, 107, 110, 114
political radicalization of, 96–98
and politics, 84, 87–89, 97–98
and positive dialectical knowledge, 50,
    54–55, 70, 77
and SED, 124
social specialization of, 82, 84–85
in state administration, 53, 67, 81–83, 87–88
tropes of self-identification, 47–52, 55–60
and university reform, 70–75, 81
in *Vereine,* 67
and *Wissenschaft,* 54–55, 70–75, 84, 96
See also *Bildungsbürgertum*
Geertz, Clifford, 37
Geggel, Heinz, 143
Geist
    censorship and, 146–47
    defined, 55–56
    Germanness and, 60
    in Hegel's philosophy of history, 11, 76–77
    interiority and, 55–56
    journalism as perversion of, 92
    journalists' sense of: in the GDR, 124, 125,
        144–45, 153, 157–58, 165; in the Third
        Reich, 116
    as a lexical totem, 39, 60
    negative dialectical knowledge and, 78
    as a trope, 36, 39, 47, 55–56, 219–25
    Wissenschaft and, 54
    See also Spirit
gender, 187, 211–12
German Democratic Republic (GDR), 117–59
    anti-Semitism in, 127n.4
    censorship in, 132, 137–144, 146–47
    collapse of (see *Wende*)
    collective consciousness in, 102, 147
    communicative practices in, 120–47
    cultural policy in, 118–20
    East German journalists' views on, 209–10
    founding of, 117–18
    and the FRG, 126, 184–86, 187
    intellectuals in, 134, 146–47, 151, 248
    journalistic education in, 123–27, 150–52

the masses in, 120–25 passim, 129, 138, 141,
    146
media in, 101–4; citizens' negative attitude
    toward, 147–50, 153; control of, 117,
    119, 127–47; intimacy of party with,
    148–49; journalists' memories of, 150–59;
    representation of the GDR in, 149 (see
    also journalism, in the GDR; journalists,
    in the GDR; School of Journalism)
official language of, 3, 134, 137–41, 146–50
the press in, 121–23, 125–26, 128, 137, 148,
    224
Press Office, 132, 146
professional legacies of, 199
SED hegemony over, 117–18
and Soviet Union, 117, 122, 186
System in, 143–45, 150–59, 181–83, 186,
    189–90, 191, 199, 209, 212, 253–70 passim
    (see also *Wende*)
See also journalism, in the GDR; SED
German Ideology, The (Marx and Engels),
    21–23, 80
Germanness, 32, 39
    and *Bildung,* 59
    and *Bildungsbürgertum,* 55–64, 68–70
    and cultural redemption, 101, 102–3, 137
    dialectical imagination of, 47–52, 185–88
    and easternness, 218–19
    in the 18th century, 61–62
    Geist and, 60
    Hegel's sense of, 76n.3
    interiority and, 55–56
    inwardness and, 47–52, 84, 91, 101, 219
    Kultur and, 56n.1
    language and, 59–60, 64, 67–68, 74
    longitudinalism and, 181, 183–88
    negative dialectical knowledge of, 264 (see
        also *Vergangenheitsbelastung*)
    positive dialectical knowledge of, 47–48,
        70, 101, 102–3, 137, 254–58, 263–64,
        269–70
    social identity and, 32, 39, 48–52, 55–64,
        70–75, 80–90, 91–98, 180, 185–88
    in the Third Reich, 180
    translocal imagination of, 60–64
    tropes of, 49, 55–60, 68, 184–89, 191–95,
        204–8, 216–19, 256–58, 264, 269–
        70
    Vergangenheitsbelastung and, 184–89,
        191–95, 204–8, 216–219, 256–58, 264,
        269–70

Germans
East: allochronization of, 189–90; and
  GDR past, 166–67; reeducation of, 189;
  as regionals, 180; stamped by System,
  189–90; and *Vergangenheitsbelastung*,
  188, 253; views on West Germans, 178,
  264 (*see also* Wessi)
West: dialectical knowledge of East
  Germans, 189; domination over East
  Germany, 187–88, 189, 254–57, 264; and
  GDR past, 166–67; as nationals, 180;
  suspicions of former GDR journalists,
  190–93; views on East Germans, 167, 178,
  188, 189–90 (*see also* Ossi; reeducation);
  and *Vergangenheitsbelastung*, 184–88
German-speaking Central Europe
  bourgeoisie in, 62–63
  fragmentation of, 61–62, 64
  intellectuals in, 63
  political culture after 1848, 83
  universities in, 71
Germany
  during the Cold War (*see* Federal Republic of
    Germany; German Democratic Republic)
  in the nineteenth century, 47–96
  Third Reich, 104–17
  after the *Wende*, 151–52, 158–59, 160–229,
    242–70
  Weimar Republic, 96–98
Geserick, Rolf, 138
Gestaltung, 77, 145, 153, 238
Gewohnheit (habit), 76–77, 154, 157, 168, 182,
  186
Giesen, Bernhard, 31–33, 56, 61, 70
Glaeser, Andreas, 37
Gleichschaltung, 108–10
Goebbels, Josef, 109, 111, 112–14, 130
Goethe, Johann W.
  as *Gebildeter*, 53, 65
  Sorrows of Young Werther, 47
Goffman, Erving, 116
Gorky, Maxim, 138
Gramsci, Antonio, 24–25, 29, 44, 199
Greffrath, Matthias, 209–10
Großbürgertum (haute bourgeoisie)
  conciliation with nobility, 88–89
  defined, 88–89
  and *Gebildeten*, 88–89
Großwissenschaft (big science), 87, 275
Grundrisse (Marx), 22–23
Gruner + Jahr, 209–10

Haasis, Klaus, 198
Habermas, Jürgen, 8, 232, 234, 237–39
habit, 76–77, 154, 157, 168, 182, 186
Handbook of GDR Journalism, 125, 126–27,
  139
Hardenburg, Karl von, 69
Hart, James Morgan, 85n.5
Hegel, Georg W. F.
  critics of, 77–78
  and dialectic, 11, 75–78, 153
  influence on Marx, 23, 78
  philosophy of history, 11, 76–78, 145, 238
  Philosophy of Right, 77
  sense of Germanness, 76n.3
  at the University of Berlin, 75
  See also Young Hegelians
hegemony, 24, 27, 117–18
Herder, Johann Gottfried von, 57–58, 67
Herf, Jeffrey, 127n.4
hermeneutic power, 129–32. *See also* German
  Democratic Republic, media in; SED
Herrmann, Joachim, 130–31, 133, 135
Herzfeld, Michael, 15, 40, 41, 44
Heydrich, Reinhard, 107
Heym, Stefan, 139–41
historicism, 26–29
history
  burden of, 9–10, 184–89, 191–95, 219,
    253–54
  excess of, 165, 190, 191–5, 198–20
  philosophy of, 11, 76–80, 90–91
Hitler, Adolf, 7–8, 9, 48
  animosity toward intellectuals, 107
  Bildung's importance to, 110
  control over mass media, 108–17
  Führerprinzip and, 111–12, 114, 129, 130
  hatred of mass culture, 110
  as intellectual, 106–7
  Mein Kampf, 109–10
  as model of the "genuine artist," 107–8, 113
  nationalism of, 106, 109–10
  and NSDAP, 104–6, 109–10
  passion for *Kultur*, 107
  and the press, 111–13
  on the radio, 112
  rise to power, 104–5
  use of dialecticism, 108, 110
  and the *Volk*, 109, 111
Holub, Miroslav, 280
Holzweissig, Gunter, 130
Homo Academicus (Bourdieu), 30–31

Honecker, Erich, 124, 128, 130–32, 133, 135, 221, 247–49 passim (see also SED, party line; SED, Politburo)
Horkheimer, Max, 86, 99–101
Humboldt, Wilhelm von, 71, 73–75, 77
Husserl, Edmund, 35

ideation. See intellectuals; knowledge
ideology
    Althusser's theory of, 20–21
    language and, 59–60, 64, 67, 74, 134, 137–41, 146–50
    Marx's critique of, 20–24
    under Nazism, 101–12
    under state socialism, 101–4, 117–27, 132–41, 146–47, 183–87
    See also knowledge
Ideology and Utopia (Mannheim), 27
Innerlichkeit. See interiority; inwardness
inoffizielle Mitarbeiter (IM), 175n.5, 249n.4. See also Stasi
intellectual culture
    academic, 240–42, 273–80
    diversity of, 33
    formal and informal knowledge in, 231–34
    German, 16; dialectical social knowledge in, 42–43; negative dialectical knowledge in, 90–96, 101, 275; positive dialectical knowledge in, 77, 101
    politics in, 30–31, 42
    positive dialectical knowledge and contemporary, 275, 277, 280
    stratification of, 26–28, 275
intellectuals
    communicative rituals of, 32
    defined, 43–44
    East German journalists as, 33
    in the GDR, 134, 146–47, 151, 248
    German: and Hegel's philosophy of history, 76–77; journalists as, 91–96; professionalism and, 53, 84–85; self-identification of, 47–52
    in German-speaking Central Europe, 63
    Hitler's animosity toward, 107
    and knowledge, 43–45
    and legitimacy, 33
    in Marx's critique of ideology, 23
    and national consciousness, 33
    organic, 24–25
    and professionalism, 30–31, 44, 273–74, 280
    as social actors, 24, 27, 29–33, 36, 43–45

social phenomenology of, 30
    as specialists in generalization, 32
    in the Third Reich, 107, 112, 114
    traditional, 24–25
interiority, 10–11, 47–52, 55–59, 103, 104, 105n.2, 109–10, 111, 118–20, 132, 137, 141. See also dialectical social knowledge; exteriority
intersubjectivity
    dialectical knowledge and, 179
    nationalism and, 31–33
    in trope theory, 36–41
    See also communicative practices; intellectual culture; selfhood
inwardness, 47–52, 57, 84, 91, 101, 219. See also dialectical social knowledge; Germanness; interiority; Spirit

Jahn, Roland, 269–70
Jews
    as embodiment of antinational forces, 94–95
    journalism and, 94–95, 95n.8, 111
    See also anti-Semitism
journalism
    in the GDR, 2, 102–3; Bildung and, 158; contrast with bourgeois journalism, 138–39; dialectical social knowledge and, 143–45, 147, 150–59; institutionalized satire in, 141–43; language ideology in, 137–41, 146–47; Lenkungssystem and, 127–29, 135, 144, 247; party line and, 129–32, 133–34, 147; perceived legacy of, 204–6; principles of socialist journalism, 120–27, 133; reception by citizens, 147–50, 153; School of, 123–27, 150–52; and SED, 102–3, 120–27; and System, 143, 153–59; and the Wende, 157
    in the nineteenth century: Jewishness and, 94–95, 95n.8, 111; negative views on, 92–96; as a profession, 84, 93–94; as Wissenschaft, 94
    in the Third Reich, 102–3, 108–17
    in unified Germany, 191–95, 225–28; ABC des Journalismus, 198; labor market, 195; professionalism in, 197–98; residue of GDR journalism in, 204–6
    See also journalists
journalists
    in the GDR, 2; and Agitation Division, 132–36, 142–44, 146; and Argu, 133–35; and Berufsverbot, 130n.5, 135–36, 248;

journalists (*continued*)
 and cog metaphor, 122; at GDR Radio,
  161–62; and *Geist*, 124, 125, 144–45,
  153, 157–58, 165; "growing into" party
  journalism, 153–57; model of socialist
  journalism, 122–23; motivations for
  career, 152–53; as mouthpieces of
  the *Volk*, 120–21; negative dialectical
  knowledge, 150–59; and party line,
  130–32, 133–34; political errors, 135–36;
  positive dialectical knowledge, 150–59,
  219–25; protocolary, 247; relationship
  to language, 138–39; and satire, 142–43;
  and SED, 120–27; and System, 3, 120–45,
  150–59, 178–81, 199–201, 219–25, 256–58,
  262–64; training of, 123–27, 150–52;
  typical career of, 150–52; and the *Wende*,
  219–25; and West German journalists, 127
 and gender, 211–12
 as intellectuals, 45, 91–96
 in the Third Reich, 113–17; beholden to the
  state, 109; and censorship, 114–16; and
  Geist, 116; sense of self as *Gebildeten*,
  117
 in the Wilhelmine period: *Gebildeten* and,
  93, 96; and the masses, 94; negative
  dialectical knowledge, 91–96; self-
  understanding as *Gebildeten*, 93, 93n.7
 See also East German journalists; journalism; West German journalists
Journalists, The (Freytag), 92–93
Junge Welt, 133, 201n.9

Kaelble, Helmut, 89
Kant, Immanuel, 72
Karlsbad Decrees, 81–82
Kittler, Friedrich, 232, 238
Klassenfeind. See class enemy
Kleiber, Gunther, 257n.7
Klein, Manfred, 172–73
knowledge
 academic, 240–42, 273–80
 anthropology of, 13–15, 28, 34, 42, 273–80
 defined, 14
 formal, 32, 44–45, 54, 137, 232–33, 234–42,
  274–79 (*see also* phenomenology, of
  expertise)
 Gebildeten and, 54–55, 84–85
 informal, 161–81, 233, 242–70
 intellectuals and, 43–45
 perceived crisis in, 91, 278–79

psychoanalysis and, 36n.2
reflexive, 274–75, 278–80
social formation of, 24, 28, 45; phenomenology and, 42–43; praxis-oriented approach,
 29–31, 32; sociolinguistic approach,
 31–33, 41–42
of subjective experience, 35–36
theoretical, contribution of to anthropology,
 15–16
and *Wissenschaft*, 72, 120, 123, 124, 126,
 129, 133, 139, 146, 148
See also dialectical social knowledge;
 sociology of knowledge
Kocka, Jürgen, 52, 70
Kohl, Helmut, 162, 163, 186, 188–89, 190
Kohlhoff, Werner, 187
Koselleck, Reinhart, 52
Krenz, Egon, 257
Krüger, Gerhard, 110
Kultur
 defined, 56
 Gebildeten as guardians of, 57, 86
 Hitler's passion for, 107
 interiority and, 56–58
 as a lexical totem, 60
 national identity and, 56n.1, 57, 68, 77, 82,
  97–98
 NSDAP and, 97–98, 114
 SED and, 97–98, 118–19, 125–26, 128, 150
 as a social binding force, 68
 the state and, 82, 108–17, 118–47
 as a trope, 36, 56–58
 Vereine and, 68, 82
 the *Volk* in the GDR and, 118–19, 141
Kulturstaat, 73, 77, 81–82
 NSDAP and, 106
 SED and, 98, 117–20
Kulturträger. See culture bearers

Langguth, Dieter, 134
language
 academic, 241–42, 277
 European, 137–38
 in the GDR, 3, 134, 137–41, 146–50
 and Germanness, 59–60, 64, 67–68, 74 (*see
  also* SED, language ideology of)
 models of nation and, 64, 67, 74
 phenomenology of, 36–40, 241–42
 at the *Stammtisch*, 250–52
 Wissenschaft and, 74
 See also censorship; tropes; trope theory

Latour, Bruno, 239
Lausitzer Rundschau, 148
Leipziger Volkszeitung, 192
Lenin, Vladimir I., 3, 117, 122
Lenkungssystem (guidance system), 127–29,
  135, 144, 247
lexical totem, 39
  Geist as, 39, 60
  Kultur as, 60
  System as, 157–58
liminality, 68, 70, 82
longitudinalism (East/West distinction)
  in divided Germany, 184–86
  East German journalists and, 181–83, 201–8,
    210–12, 217–19, 266
  gender and, 211–12
  Germanness and, 181, 183–88
  as principle of social identity, 181, 183
  in unified Germany, 186–88, 197
  West German journalists and, 206–7, 210,
    217–19, 266
  and *Wissenschaft*, 187
Luhmann, Niklas, 8, 232, 235–37, 238
Lukács, Georg, 24–25, 29
Lyotard, Jean-François, 278

Maaz, Hans-Joachim, 185
Macht, 56, 78, 116, 205. See also dialectical
  social knowledge, negative; *Prägung*
Machthaber, 256
Mah, Harold, 56–57
Mann, Thomas, 46–48, 84, 100–101, 113
Mannheim, Karl, 279
  free-floating intelligentsia, 26–27, 30, 32,
    54
  Ideology and Utopia, 27
  sociology of knowledge, 26–29, 32, 33, 42,
    275
Marx, Karl, 273, 279
  Bildung and, 78, 80
  critique of capitalism, 79–80
  critique of ideology, 20–24
  *Economic and Philosophic Manuscripts of
    1844*, 78
  The German Ideology, 21–23, 80
  Grundrisse, 22–23
  negative dialectical knowledge and, 78–80
  positive dialectical knowledge and, 78, 80
  practice theory and, 44
  reformulation of Hegelian dialectic, 78–80
Massen. See masses

Massenkultur
  defined, 85
  Gebildeten and, 51, 85–86, 87, 90–91,
    99–101
  Hitler's hatred of, 110
  NSDAP's disdain for, 97–98, 103, 110
  as opposite of *Wissenschaft*, 86
  SED's disdain for, 96–98, 103, 119, 122, 125,
    128, 132, 137, 138, 149
  as System, 97
masses
  in the GDR, 120–25 passim, 129, 138, 141,
    146
  in the nineteenth-century, 59, 62, 94
  in the Third Reich, 109, 111
mass media
  as extension of the state, 111
  NSDAP control over, 102–3, 108–17
  SED's disdain for, 96–98, 103, 119, 122, 125,
    128, 132, 137, 138, 149
  as System, 235
  in unified Germany, 162, 188
Mast, Claudia, 198
Matrix, The, 11, 235
Mbembe, Achille, 141n.10
McClelland, Charles, 53, 66
mdr (radio station), 4, 162
media
  democratic, 2, 190–229
  dialectical social knowledge and, 102–3,
    147–50, 235–41
  in the FRG, 124, 126, 128, 130, 138, 146,
    162, 167, 190
  in the GDR, 101–4, 117, 119, 127–59 (*see
    also* journalism, in the GDR; journalists,
    in the GDR; School of Journalism)
  institutional transformation of East
    German, 190–229
  mass (*see* mass media)
  Nazi techniques of control, 112–13
  NSDAP and, 103, 109–10
  SED and, 103
  in systems theory, 235–37
  in unified Germany, 3, 151–52, 158, 163,
    165–66, 190–229
  during the *Wende*, 224
Mein Kampf (Hitler), 109
Meinungsbildner, 94
mental labor. See division of labor; intellectuals
metaphor, 36–37. See also trope theory

metonymy, 36–37. *See also* trope theory
Mielke, Erich, 255n.6
Mitläufer, 191, 258, 270
Mittag, Gunter, 143
modernization
  Gebildeten's role in, 68–70
  Habermas's analysis of, 237–39
  Nazi animosity toward, 109
  nineteenth-century German society and, 59
  nobility's role in, 68–69
  post-Hegelian critics of, 77–78, 83, 90
  the *Volk* as collective force of, 97
Mommsen, Theodor, 87
Moritz, Karl Philipp, 94
Mühlfenzl, Rudolf, 162, 190, 195
Müller, Adam, 74
Musil, Robert, 271, 273–74

nachrichten, die (Osang), 215–18
Nalepastraße. *See* GDR Radio: complex in Nalepastraße
Napoleonic occupaption, 71–75 passim
nationalism, 48
  and anti-Semitism, 95
  Bildungsbürgertum and, 49–50, 57, 60–64, 74–75, 97
  and dialectical social knowledge, 48–51, 55–60
  Hitler and, 106, 109–10
  and intersubjectivity, 31–33
  and *Kultur*, 57
  and language, 64
  lexical totems of, 55–60
  NSDAP and, 109–10
  universities and, 70–75
  and *Wissenschaft*, 70–75
Neues Deutschland, 122, 130–31, 136, 143, 201n.9
neurosis, 6
Newborn, Jud, 96
Nietzsche, Friedrich, 47, 58, 110
  negative dialecticism of, 90–91
1989. See *Wende*
Nipperdey, Thomas, 67, 69–70
nobility
  and *Bildung*, 66
  control of state administration, 69, 83
  demographics of, 63n.2
  and *Gebildeten*, 64–70, 82–83
  and *Großbürgertum*, 88–89

and modernization of German society, 68–69
  in *Vereine*, 68
Norddeutsche Allgemeine Zeitung, 96
NSDAP (Nationalsozialistische Deutsche Arbeiterpartei), 8
  compared to SED, 103–4, 106
  control over the mass media, 102–3, 108–17
  and dialectical social knowledge, 101–4
  disdain for mass culture, 97–98, 103, 110
  and *Gebildeten*, 97–98, 107, 110, 114
  Gleichschaltung of political and public culture, 108–10
  Hitler and, 104–6, 109–10
  ideology, 101–12
  journalists and, 113–17
  and *Kultur*, 97–98, 114
  and *Kulturstaat*, 106
  and the media, 103, 109–10
  as a movement, 106
  and nationalism, 109–10
  organization of, 105–6
  preference for radio, 112
  and the press, 111–14
  use of tropes, 118
  universities and, 110
  the *Volk* and, 104, 105n.2, 109–10, 111

objectification, 78–79
Öffentlichkeit, 67
Opfer, 258
ORB (radio station), 162, 210
Origins of Totalitarianism (Arendt), 105n.2
Ortner, Sherry, 38
Osang, Alexander, 155–57, 215–18, 274
Ossi, 180, 187, 189, 246, 278
  as creature of System, 181–83
  defined, 181–82
  and dialectical social knowledge, 183
  playing the, 163, 166–67
  See also Germans, East

Palast der Republik, 254–56
Parteilichkeit, 123
Parteilinie, 111. *See also* SED, party line
Peirce, Charles S., 241
Pesmen, Dale, 60
phenomenology, 12
  anthropology and, 36
  dialectical social knowledge and, 35–36, 42, 179, 274

of expertise, 25, 43–44, 54, 232, 240, 279, 280 (*see also* intellectuals; knowledge, formal)
of language, 36–40, 241–42
Marxian sociology of knowledge and, 35–36
psychoanalysis and, 36n.2
trope theory and, 38–43
of the *Wende*, 222
philosophy
dialectical, 11, 20–24, 75–80, 90–91, 99–101, 234–39
Großwissenschaft and, 87
of history, 11, 76–78, 90–91, 145, 238
Wissenschaft and, 72
See also knowledge, formal
Philosophy of Right (Hegel), 77
poesis, 30, 31, 41, 100. *See also* potentiality; Spirit
Politburo. *See* SED: Politburo
Postmodern Condition, The (Lyotard), 278
Postone, Moishe, 95
potentiality, 10–11, 12, 76, 221. *See also* actuality; dialectical social knowledge
practice theory, 29–33, 44
Prägung, 12–13, 80, 101, 104, 183, 189, 201, 219, 264, 278. *See also* Spirit; System
press
freedom of the, 224
in the GDR, 121–23, 125–26, 128, 137, 148, 224
in the nineteenth century, 94–96, 236
in the Third Reich, 111–14
Primitive Man as Philosopher (Radin), 15
proletariat, 79, 97
Protestantism, 55
Prussia, 57, 69, 71, 77, 83
psychoanalytic theory, 36n.2

Querkopf, 270

Radin, Paul, 15, 32
radio
East German, 162
in the GDR, 128, 132, 137, 148
Hitler on, 112
Nazi preference for, 112
in the Weimar period, 112
Redakteur, 93nn. 6–7, 190, 202. *See also* journalists

reeducation
of East German journalists, 2, 190–95, 198, 203, 213–14
of East Germans, 189
reflexivity, 274–75, 278–80
Revolution of 1848, 83
Richter, Ildephons, 112
Ringer, Fritz, 27, 60, 82–83, 89
Röhr, Karl-Heinz, 138

Schablinski, Rudolf, 131
Schabowski, Günter, 141, 257
Scharf, Wilfried, 126
Scheler, Max, 28, 29
Schelling, Friedrich, 54, 72, 74
Schere im Kopf, 116
Schieferdecker, Joachim, 114
Schleiermacher, Friedrich, 67, 71–75
School of Journalism, 123–27, 150–52. *See also* journalism, in the GDR; journalists, in the GDR
Schütt, Hans-Dieter, 133
Schutz, Alfred, 35–36
Schwarze Kanal, Der, 128
Scott, Sir Walter, 65
SED (Sozialistische Einheitspartei Deutschlands)
and *Bildung*, 124, 146–47
and capitalism, 117–19, 127, 146
and censorship, 132, 137–44, 146–47
compared to NSDAP, 103–4
cultural policy, 118–20
and cultural redemption, 137
dialectical social knowledge and, 101–4
disdain for mass culture, 96–98, 103, 119, 122, 125, 128, 132, 137, 138, 149
founding of, 117
and *Gebildeten* ideal, 124
hegemony over the GDR, 117–18
and institutionalization of satire, 141–43
journalism and (*see* journalism, in the GDR; journalists, in the GDR)
and *Kultur*, 97–98, 118–19, 125–26, 128, 150
and *Kulturstaat*, 98, 117, 119
language ideology of, 134, 137–41, 149
and mass media, 102–3, 121
negative dialectical knowledge and, 121, 127
newspaper (see *Neues Deutschland*)
party discipline, 129n.5
party line, 129–32, 133–34, 135, 147

SED (Sozialistische Einheitspartei Deutschlands) (*continued*)
Politburo, 118, 129–30, 132, 141–43, 148–49,
256–58
positive dialectical knowledge and, 118,
122, 125, 137
and the press, 121–23, 125–26, 128, 132, 137,
224
propaganda (*see* Agitation Division)
and radio, 128, 132
taboo system, 133–34, 137, 143
and television, 128, 132, 147, 148
use of tropes, 118, 122, 125, 127
the *Volk* and, 117–21, 124–25, 127–132
passim, 137, 139, 141, 150, 158
and the *Wende*, 224, 255n.6
and the West, 124
and West German media, 124, 126, 128, 130,
138, 146
and West Germany, 126–27, 138, 146
and *Wissenschaft*, 120, 123, 124, 126, 129,
132, 139, 146, 148
See also German Democratic Republic
selfhood
dialectical social knowledge and, 12, 179,
201, 206–7, 219
intersubjectivity and, 35–36, 38, 219
in systems theory, 235
SFB (radio station), 162, 165, 167
Sheehan, James, 60–62, 66
Siegel, James, 95
Silex, Karl, 116
Simon, Günter, 124
Smith, Adam, 23
social identity
of *Bildungsbürgertum*, 54, 55, 59–60
of the bourgeoisie, 65
in divided Germany, 180
Germanness and, 32, 39, 48–52, 55–64,
70–75, 80–90, 91–98, 180, 185–88
longitudinalism as principle of, 181, 183
socialism, 117–47
Socialist Unity Party. *See* SED
social theory, 19–45. *See also* practice
theory; psychoanalytic theory; sociolinguistic theory; systems theory; trope
theory
sociolinguistic theory, 31–33, 137–41, 241
sociology of knowledge, 42, 279
Bourdieu's, 30–31
Mannheim's, 26–29, 32, 33, 42, 275

Marxian, 23–34, 42
phenomenological dilemma of, 35–36
Sorrows of Young Werther (Goethe), 47
Soviet Union, 117, 122, 186
spatiality, 10–11, 272. *See also* dialectical
social knowledge
Spiegel, Der, 155
Spirit
in academic intellectual culture, 273–80
in academic knowledge, 240–42, 273–80
actualization of, 11, 76, 132
compromised by System, 76–77, 79–80,
90–91, 100–101, 145, 157–58, 165, 205–6,
264, 277–78
defined, 12
reflexivity and, 280
without System, 219–25
in systems theory, 236, 239–40
as a trope, 36, 39, 47, 55–56, 219–25
and the *Wende*, 219–25
West German journalists and, 223, 243–45,
263–64, 269–70
See also dialectical social knowledge; *Geist*;
Prägung
Stammtisch
defined, 231, 249–51
East and West German journalists at a,
246–70
history of, 249–50
language at, 250–52
the phenomenology of expertise and, 232
Stasi, 136n.8, 164n.3, 175n.5, 248, 257–64,
267–68
state administration
Gebildeten in, 53, 67, 81–83, 87–88
nobility's control over, 69, 83
university education and, 66–67, 73
See also *Beamten*
Stein, Heinrich von, 69, 77
Stoiber, Edmund, 227
Stolpe, Manfred, 258–61, 266, 267
stratification
bureaucratic, 129
intellectual, 26–28, 275
social, 26–27
See also division of labor
Streit der Fakultäten, Der (Kant), 72
students
and nationalism, 63, 73–75
translocality of Central European, 63
subjectivity, 6, 40. *See also* selfhood

Super Illu, 242, 246, 266–68
System
  in academic intellectual culture, 274–80
  as compromising Spirit, 76–77, 79–80,
    90–91, 100–101, 145, 157–58, 165, 205–6,
    264, 277–78
  defined, 12
  East German journalists and, 7–8, 153–59,
    191, 199–200, 209, 219–25, 253–70 passim
  East Germans imprinted by, 189–90
  in the FRG, 7, 181, 186, 199, 209, 225,
    253–70 passim
  in the GDR, 143–45, 150–59, 181–83, 186,
    189–90, 191, 199, 209, 212, 253–70 passim
    (see also *Wende*)
  GDR journalists and, 3, 120–45, 150–
    59, 178–81, 199–201, 219–25, 256–58,
    262–64
  historicity of, 236–39
  as a lexical totem, 157–58
  Massenkultur as, 97
  mass media as, 235–36
  nineteenth-century journalists as anthropo-
    morphs of, 92–96
  as an ontogenetic state, 236–37
  Ossi as creature of, 181–83
  reflexivity and, 279–80
  in systems theory, 234–39
  as a trope, 7–10, 12, 36, 39–40, 47, 90,
    157–58, 274
  unified Germany as, 158–59, 192, 193, 227
  the *Wende* and, 219–25
  Wessi as creature of, 183
  West German journalists and, 223–24, 264
  See also dialectical social knowledge;
    Prägung
systems theory, 8, 232–40

Täter, 258
television in the GDR, 128, 132, 147, 148
temporality, 10–11, 272. *See also* dialectical
  social knowledge
Theory of Communicative Action, The
  (Habermas), 232, 237–39
Third Reich, 48, 99–117
  censorship in, 114–16
  communicative practices in, 108–17
  cultural production in, 114
  Germanness in, 180
  intellectuals in, 107, 112, 114
  journalism in, 102–3, 108–17

journalists in, 109, 113–17
  the masses in, 109, 111
  partition of Germany as price for, 180
  propaganda in, 114–15
  See also *Vergangenheitsbelastung*
Treitschke, Heinrich von, 86, 96
tropes
  anthropological approaches to, 37–41
  anti-Semitic, 95
  culture and, 38
  dialectical: *Bildung* as, 58–59; *Geist* as,
    36, 39, 47, 55–56, 219–25; *Kultur* as, 36,
    56–58; System as, 7–10, 12, 36, 39–40, 47,
    90, 157–58, 274
  of distancing, 149
  of exteriority, 90, 224, 277–78 (see also
    Macht; System)
  formalist approach to, 37
  of Germanness, 49, 55–60, 68
  of interiority, 55–59 (see also *Bildung, Geist,
    Kultur, Volk*)
  NSDAP's use of, 118
  SED use of, 118, 120–22, 125, 127
  of self-identity: *Bildungsbürgertum* and,
    55–60; *Gebildeten* and, 47–52, 55–60
  the social and, 41
  types of, 36–38
trope theory, 33, 35–38, 41
  anthropology and, 36–41
  communicative practices and, 36–41
  dialectical social knowledge and, 38–41
  intersubjectivity and, 36–41
  phenomenology and, 38–42
  poetics, 40
Turner, Terry, 37, 38
Turner, Victor, 38

Ulbricht, Walter, 130
Umerziehung. See reeducation
unification, German. See *Wende*
United States, 2
  academic intellectual culture in, 273–74,
    276–78
  collective accountability and, 9
  system in, 40
universities
  Berlin, University of: Fichte as rector of,
    74–75; founding, 71–75, 81; Marx as a
    student at, 78
  and *Beamten*, 67, 73
  and *Bildung*, 71–75

universities (*continued*)
   enrollments at, 82, 86
   in German-speaking Central Europe, 71
   Göttingen, University of, 71
   Halle, University of, 71
   institutional transformation of, 86–88,
      274–78
   as institutions of nation building, 71–75
   Jena, University of, 50, 56, 74
   Karlsbad Decrees and, 81–82
   Nazi view of, 110
   philosophical faculty in, 71–72, 75
   reform of, 70–75
   and the state, 71–74, 81–83
   and *Wissenschaft*, 70–75, 81, 85
   See also intellectual culture, academic

Vereine, 32
   in contemporary German society, 251
   defined, 67
   Kultur and, 68, 82
   social composition of, 67–68
   as spaces of conviviality, 67–68
Vergangenheitsbelastung, 9–10, 184–89,
      191–95, 204–8, 216–19, 253, 256–58, 264,
      269–70
Vergegenständlichung (objectification), 78–79
Volk
   Beamten and, 70
   Bildung of, 104, 124, 158
   as collective force of modernization, 97–98
   consciousness in Nazi ideology, 109
   consciousness in SED ideology, 137, 150
   dialectical political radicalism and, 96–98
   education at universities, 72–73
   GDR journalists as mouthpieces of, 120–21
   Gebildeten and, 70, 72–73
   Hitler's vision of, 109, 111
   interiority and, 103, 104, 105n.2, 109–10,
      111, 117–20, 132, 137
   and *Kultur* in the GDR, 118–19, 141
   and mass culture, 103
   NSDAP and, 104, 105n.2, 109–10, 111
   positive dialectical knowledge and, 118–20
   SED and, 117–21, 124–25, 127–32 passim,
      137, 139, 141, 150, 158
   socialist journalism's *Bildung* of, 124, 137,
      158
Völkischer Beobachter, 114
Volkslehrer, 73, 75, 120, 124, 152
Vossische Zeitung, 94

Walker, Mack, 63
Weber, Max, 26, 35, 80, 90–91, 93, 234–35
Wehler, Hans–Ulrich, 59
Weigert, Matthias, 198
Weimar Republic, 7, 27, 97
Weltanschauung, 26, 112
Wende, 4, 186, 188–89
   Bildung and, 222
   East German journalists and, 157, 220–25
   freedom of the press during, 224
   phenomenology of, 222
   positive dialectical knowledge and, 219–25
   SED and, 224, 255n.6
   transformation of the East German media,
      162, 163, 190–229
Wendehälse, 224, 247, 266
Wessi, 180, 202, 204, 246–48 passim, 264, 278
   as creature of System, 183
   defined, 182–83
   dialectical social knowledge and, 183
   See also Germans, West
westernness, dialectical social knowledge
      of, 167, 183–88, 211, 215, 264. *See also*
      easternness; longitudinalism; Ossi; Wessi
West German journalists
   dialectical sense of selfhood of, 206–7
   discussion of GDR, West Germany, and
      their Systems, 253–70 passim
   East German journalists and, 2, 151–52, 165,
      167, 192–93, 197–219, 223–24, 242–70 (*see*
      also East German journalists, reeducation
      of)
   and longitudinalism, 206–7, 210, 217–19,
      266
   as nationals, 197–201
   perceived superiority of, 198–99, 203
   and Spirit, 223, 243–45
   at the *Stammtisch*, 246–70
   and System, 223–24, 262
West German media, and SED, 126, 128, 130
Wissenschaft
   defined, 54
   Gebildeten and, 54–55, 70–75, 84, 96
   Geist and, 54
   journalism as, 94
   knowledge and, 72, 120, 123, 124, 126, 129,
      133, 139, 146, 148
   language and, 74
   longitudinalism and, 187
   nationalism and, 70–75
   as opposite of *Massenkultur*, 86

perceptions of crisis in, 27, 85–88, 275
phenomenology of expertise and, 54
philosophy and, 72
SED and, 120, 123, 124, 126, 129, 133, 139,
    146, 148
systems theory and, 239
universities and, 70–75, 81, 85
Witt, Kati, 267
Wochenpost, Die, 201–3, 212–13
Wolf, Friedrich August, 71
Wolff, Larry, 183

Woolard, Kathryn, 137–38
Wörl, Leo, 94
Wuthnow, Robert, 83
Wyrwa, Ulrich, 250

Young Hegelians, 21–22, 23

Zimmermann, Brigitte, 209–10
Ziolkowski, Theodore, 53, 54, 71–72, 74–75
zwischen den Zeilen (between the lines), 116